YALE WESTERN AMERICANA SERIES

Dear Brother

Letters of William Clark
to Jonathan Clark

Edited and with an introduction by
JAMES J. HOLMBERG

Foreword by
JAMES P. RONDA

Published in association with
THE FILSON HISTORICAL SOCIETY

YALE UNIVERSITY PRESS / NEW HAVEN & LONDON

Designed by Mary Valencia.
Set in Cochin type by The Composing Room of Michigan, Inc.,
Grand Rapids, Michigan.
Printed in the United States of America by Vail-Ballou Press,
Binghamton, New York.

Library of Congress Cataloging-in-Publication Data

Clark, William, 1770-1838.
Dear Brother : letters of William Clark to Jonathan Clark / edited and with an
introduction by James J. Holmberg ; foreword by James P. Ronda.
p.   cm. — (Yale Western Americana series)
Includes bibliographical references and index.
ISBN 0-300-09010-2 (cloth : alk. paper)
ISBN 0-300-10106-6 (pbk. : alk. paper)
1. Clark, William, 1770–1838—Correspondence.   2. Explorers—West
(U.S.)—Correspondence.   3. Lewis and Clark Expedition (1804–1806).
4. West (U.S.)—Description and travel.   5. West (U.S.)—Discovery and exploration.
6. Lewis, Meriwether, 1774–1809.   7. York, ca. 1775–ca. 1815.
I. Clark, Jonathan, 1750–1811.   II. Holmberg, James J. (James John), 1958–.
III. Title.   IV. Series.
F592.7.C56   2002
917.804'2—dc21   2001055902

A catalogue record for this book is available from the British Library.

The paper in this book meets the guidelines for permanence and durability of the Committee
on Production Guidelines for Book Longevity of the Council on Library Resources.

10 9 8 7 6

Frontispiece: Portrait of William Clark by Joseph H. Bush, ca. 1817. Courtesy of
The Filson Historical Society.

For those who write the letters
and those who save them

Contents

Contents

Letters

CHAPTER 1. 1792–1802

William Clark, Fort Steuben, Falls of the Ohio, to Jonathan Clark, 2 September 1792. Autograph Letter Signed, 4pp.

Clark, Baltimore, Maryland, to Clark, 4 October 1798. ALS, 1p.

Clark, Mulberry Hill [near Louisville], to Clark, 13 August 1801. ALS, 2pp.

Clark, Louisville, Kentucky, to Clark, 13 October 1801. ALS, 1p.

Clark, Redstone Landing, to Clark, 4 February 1802. ALS, 2pp.

Clark, Mulberry Hill, to Clark, 2 March 1802. ALS, $3\frac{1}{2}$pp.

Clark, Louisville, to Clark, 5 April 1802. ALS, $1\frac{1}{2}$pp.

CHAPTER 2. 1803–1807

Clark, Opposite the mouth of the Missouri River, to Clark, 16 December 1803. ALS, 6pp.

Clark, St. Louis, Louisiana Territory, to Clark, 25 February 1804. ALS, 3pp.

Clark, Mouth of the Missouri, to Clark, 3 May 1804. ALS, $1\frac{1}{2}$pp.

Clark, Fort Mandan, to Clark, April 1805. ALS, $3\frac{1}{2}$pp.

Clark, St. Louis, to Clark, 23 September 1806. ALS, 8pp.

Clark, St. Louis, to Clark, 24 September 1806. ALS, 1p.

Clark, Washington, D.C., to Clark, 22 January 1807. ALS, $3\frac{1}{4}$pp.

Clark, Big Bone Lick, Kentucky, to Clark, 9 September 1807. ALS, 2pp.

CHAPTER 3. 1808–1809

Clark, Near the mouth of the Tradewater River, to Clark, 6 and 7 June 1808. ALS, $1\frac{1}{4}$pp.

Clark, St. Louis, to Clark, 2 July 1808. ALS, $1\frac{1}{4}$pp.

Clark, St. Louis, to Clark, 21 July 1808. ALS, $1\frac{1}{2}$pp.

Clark, St. Louis, to Clark, 22 August 1808. ALS, $1\frac{1}{2}$pp.

Clark, St. Louis, to Clark, 1 October 1808. ALS, 1p.

Clark, St. Louis, to Clark, 5 October 1808. ALS, 4pp.

Clark, St. Louis, to Clark, 9 November 1808. ALS, $2\frac{1}{2}$pp.

Clark, St. Louis, to Clark, 22 and 24 November 1808. ALS, $7\frac{1}{2}$pp.

Clark, St. Louis, to Clark, 10 December 1808. ALS, $3\frac{1}{2}$pp.

Clark, St. Louis, to Clark, 17 December 1808. ALS, 2pp.

Clark, St. Louis, to Clark, 2 January 1809. ALS, 2pp.

Clark, St. Louis, to Clark, 21 January 1809. ALS, 2pp.

Clark, St. Louis, to Clark, ca. 1 March 1809. ALS, $1\frac{1}{2}$pp.

Clark, St. Louis, to Clark, 28 May 1809. ALS, $2\frac{1}{2}$pp.

Clark, St. Louis, to Clark, 22 July 1809. ALS, $1\frac{1}{4}$pp.

CHAPTER 4. 1809–1810

Clark, St. Louis, to Clark, 26 August 1809. ALS, $2\frac{1}{2}$pp.

Clark, St. Louis, to Clark, 16 September 1809. ALS, 1p.

Clark, Mr. Shannon's, Shelby County, Kentucky, to Clark, 28 October 1809. ALS, $2\frac{1}{2}$pp.

Clark, Lexington, Kentucky, to Clark, 30 October 1809. ALS, 1p.

Clark, Bean Station, Tennessee, to Clark, 8 November 1809. ALS, $1\frac{1}{4}$pp.

Clark, Colonel Hancock's, Fincastle, Virginia, to Clark, 26 November 1809. ALS, 2pp.

Clark, Washington, D.C., to Clark, 12 January 1810. ALS, 2pp.

Clark, Fincastle, to Clark, 8 March 1810. ALS, 2pp.

CHAPTER 5. 1810–1811

Clark, Opposite Kaskaskia, Illinois, to Clark, 3 July 1810. ALS, $3\frac{1}{4}$pp.

Clark, St. Louis, to Clark, 16 July 1810. ALS, 2pp.

Clark, St. Louis, to Clark, 14 December 1810. AL, $2\frac{1}{4}$pp.

Clark, St. Louis, to Clark, 31 January 1811. ALS, 1¼pp.

Clark, St. Louis, to Clark, ca. 1 March 1811. ALS, 1p.

Clark, St. Louis, to Clark, 17 August 1811. ALS, 1½pp.

Clark, St. Louis, to Clark, 30 August 1811. ALS, 2pp.

Clark, St. Louis, to Clark, 14 September 1811. ALS, 1½pp.

APPENDIX. 1795–1811

Clark, Greenville, Ohio, to Fanny Clark O'Fallon, 9 May 1795. ALS, 3pp.

Clark, Greenville, to O'Fallon, 1 June 1795. ALS, 3pp.

Clark, Greenville, to O'Fallon, 1 July 1795. ALS, 1½pp.

Clark, St. Louis, to John H. Clark, 15 and 16 December 1808. ALS, 1½pp.

Clark, St. Louis, to Edmund Clark, 27 January 1809. ALS, 1p.

Clark, St. Louis, to Edmund Clark, 15 April 1809. ALS, 3pp.

Clark, St. Louis, to Edmund Clark, 3 September 1810. ALS, 1½pp.

Clark, St. Louis, to John H. Clark, 27 October 1810. ALS, 1½pp.

Clark, St. Louis, to Edmund and John H. Clark, 1 March 1811. ALS, 1p.
with one page autograph list.

Foreword

In William Clark's time it was common to write down the last words of a dying friend or relative. Many believed such words might contain special wisdom or even a glimpse of life after death. So it was that on 20 August 1804, as Sgt. Charles Floyd lay dying, Capt. William Clark paid careful attention to those last words. Knowing he had not long to live, Floyd whispered to Clark, "I want you to write me a letter." And Clark dutifully set down Floyd's words in his own official expedition journal. Floyd's plea for a letter reveals something fundamental about American life nearly two centuries ago. This was an age that placed great emphasis on letter writing. Handwritten letters—whether private or public—were visible signs of social standing, literacy, and personal authority. Sending or receiving a letter was an occasion, an event filled with special meaning. Thomas Jefferson said as much when he implored his friend John Page to write more often, insisting that "you cannot concieve the satisfaction it would give me to have a letter from you." For families on the American frontier, exchanging letters was a way to maintain the ties that bound them to distant friends and cherished places. Little wonder that Floyd asked Clark to remember him with a letter.

In that letter-writing age, before various kinds of electric communication and mass-circulation newspapers, letters carried information about everything from family news and local gossip to national affairs and international diplomacy. Modern readers encountering the important letters in *Dear Brother: Letters of William Clark to Jonathan Clark* may be confused by what seems at first glance a jumble of thoughts and ideas—the personal rubbing shoulders with the commercial, the intimate alongside the public. But we should read and appreciate what William Clark modestly called "this hasty Scraul" for what the letters meant at the time. Like their contemporaries, the Clarks and others in this web of words thought of letters as pieces of an ongoing conversation. Lively conversations, especially between brothers and close friends with common interests and concerns, rarely move in straight lines. Talk is like a river, filled with meanders, twists, and unexpected turns. Imagining Jonathan or some other friend in the room with him, William let his letters flow like any good river of talk. It is our privilege to eavesdrop on at least one part of that hearty conversation.

The distinguished essayist Logan Pearsall Smith once observed that every letter of any value should contain three essential parts. The first of those is gossip. While we might define "gossip" as private talk bordering on the malicious, the word has always had a wider use. Gossip is the daily chatter between friends. It is talk often intimate and personally revealing. William Clark was no gossip-monger, but his letters are filled with gossipy talk about himself, his friends, and his family. A significant part of that gossip centered on his own marital possibilities and the courtships of others in his 9 May 1795 letter to his sister Fanny Clark O'Fallon. It captures Clark's sense of himself as an eligible bachelor. As he explained, he was "very Solecetious" about "the wellfar of the *Ladees* of your Nabouring hood." Bemoaning the fact that his military obligations kept him away from the company of one particular young woman, Clark complained that his courtship ventures had been "baffled by the Calls of Duty." The gossip in his letters—and especially the search for a suitable wife—make plain Clark's understanding of himself as part of a wider family circle. That circle's future depended in large part on his own marriage to someone of appropriate social and economic standing.

William Clark's correspondence fully embodies Pearsall Smith's second characteristic of a good letter—personal news. From his earliest letters, William appreciated the fact that he not only represented the Clark family in the West but was also the eyes and ears for those at home. In a most unusual way, he explored and reported on the frontier east of the Mississippi for his family; he would do the same for the West beyond the Mississippi in the service of his country. William's letters are replete with family news, details about business ventures, and observations on his sometimes-troubled relations with his African American slaves. So we catch glimpses of William Clark as father, businessman, and slaveholder. Nowhere does he more fully reveal himself as a man of his time than in those passages about York and other African Americans who dared think of themselves not as property but as human beings. Any future evaluation of William Clark must portray him not only as explorer and Indian agent but also as slave master with whip in hand. It is to editor James Holmberg's great credit that he has paid special attention to this aspect of the William Clark letters.

Most often we read correspondence from the past hoping to find what Pearsall Smith suggests is the third part of a memorable letter. This is the writer's "generalizations on the universe or the particular part in which you happen to live." William Clark did not presume to comment on the entire universe, but his letters are full of thoughts about the world around him. As both cartographer and letter writer, he had a remarkably sure sense of place. Readers drawn to *Dear Brother* will perhaps be most attracted by those portions that reveal William as politician, Indian agent, and explorer. Here Clark displays his sharp eye and keen ear as he notes the dramatic changes sweeping the trans-Mississippi West. Despite his obvious devotion to family and friends, Clark knew that he was what the nineteenth century called a "public man." He had both a life and a career; his letters report on both. That career took William from the Ohio Country to the most distant outpost of the republic on the edge of the Pacific. These letters allow us to plot not only the curve of one man's career but that of a westering nation. Reading over William's shoulder we follow the westward course of empire.

In 1748, twenty-two years before William's birth, the English man of letters Robert Dodsley wrote a chapter in his *The Preceptor: Containing a General Course of Education* outlining the marks of a sound letter. There is no evidence that William ever read or even encountered Dodsley's book but had he read the letter-writing chapter he would have come upon this telling line. "The truth is," explained Dodsley, "a fine Letter does not consist in saying fine things, but in expressing ordinary ones in an uncommon manner." It is not just William's spelling that is by our standards uncommon. Rather, it is that he expresses both the ordinary and the extraordinary events of a crowded life in a most uncommon manner.

James P. Ronda

Acknowledgments

In any undertaking such as this there are many people to thank. Without their help and support completing such a project would be impossible. First and foremost, I want to thank the six donors of the William Clark letters: James W. Stites, Jr., Ellen Stites Thurber, Dr. Temple Bodley Stites, William F. Stites, George Rogers Clark Stuart, and William A. Stuart, Jr. Their generosity and historical awareness in donating these letters to The Filson Historical Society have assured their preservation and availability to the research community and made this project possible. Thanks also go to Filson board member John S. Speed and former Filson director James R. Bentley for their important assistance in the acquisition process.

The Filson's commitment to publishing the letters also made this book possible. Both financial support and staff time were given toward seeing that the William Clark letters were edited and published. Without that support the project never would have been completed. My thanks are extended to the Filson's Board of Directors and executive director Mark V. Wetherington. Former board president Michael Harreld and current president Thomas Noland have provided special encouragement. Former board members Philip Ardery and Ronald R. Van Stockum were early supporters of the project and remained interested throughout it. My staff in Special Collections was unfailingly supportive and bore without complaint the added responsibilities that my absences working on the letters created for them. My thanks to Rebecca S. Rice, Michael R. Veach, Craig M. Heuser, and Shirley Harmon, as well as former staff member James Trace Kirkwood. Ms. Rice also provided welcome assistance regarding the illustrations. Mark Wetherington and Nelson L. Dawson provided helpful suggestions. Dr. Dawson's painstaking proofing of the manuscript is much appreciated and prevented many William Clark-type spelling and grammatical errors. Pen Bogert of the library staff provided very useful information over the course of the project.

Other institutions also supplied resources and helpful staff. My thanks to Dennis Northcott, John T. Furlong, Martha Clevenger, Duane Snedekker, Ellen Thomasson, and other staff of the Missouri Historical Society; Tom Gruenenfelder of the St. Louis deed office; the staff of the St. Louis Circuit Court–Probate Division; the staff of the State Historical Society of Missouri; James Prichard, Timothy Tingle, and the staff of the Kentucky Department for Libraries and Archives; John Kleber and Joseph Roberts of *The Encyclopedia of Louisville* project; Chet Orloff and John Mead of the Oregon Historical Society; Bruce Kirby of the Library of Congress; Karen Stevens of Independence National Historical Park–Library; and Douglas Clanin, Susan Sutton, and especially Paul Brockman of the Indiana Historical Society. Special thanks to David Morgan of the Jefferson County (Ky.) Office for Historic Preservation and Archives. A number of individuals provided assistance. My thanks to Mimi and Darold Jackson, Kenneth Carstens, Samuel W. Thomas, Ernest Ellison, R. Ted Steinbock, and John J. Holmberg. I am particularly indebted to Mimi Jackson for the information on the possible fate of William Clark papers and artifacts left at Minoma.

Funding is a necessary part of any undertaking like this. The Lewis and Clark Trail Heritage Foundation provided three grants in support of the project. Thomas Industries Inc., through the efforts of William P. Sherman, also donated funds to help support it. A descendant of Jonathan Clark, who wishes to remain anonymous, provided generous support. The Filson and I thank all of them for their important financial assistance.

My thanks to James P. Ronda for writing the Foreword. Professor

Ronda's writings on Lewis and Clark, like the work of so many others I used, made my own work much easier. My thanks to them and all those Lewis and Clark enthusiasts over the years who expressed interest in the letters and thereby helped provide the encouragement to doggedly "proceed on" with the project.

Many thanks are due to the three research assistants who worked with me on the letters: Patricia Lister, James Trace Kirkwood, and Craig M. Heuser. Pat Lister did a great deal of preliminary research concerning the amplification notes. Trace Kirkwood replaced Mrs. Lister and uncomplainingly looked up what I am sure seemed like inconsequential and unnecessary information. Upon Mr. Kirkwood's departure Craig Heuser stepped into this important position and was an excellent assistant. I am sure all three questioned my persistence in trying to track down information for some of the notes, but they complied with a smile and often returned with answers to the myriad questions that I was determined to try to answer. Mr. Heuser deserves additional thanks for his perseverance and good work in proofreading the original Clark letters and their transcriptions with me for accuracy—misspellings and all. Many an error would have gone undetected without this assistance. Without their important help, and the commitment by the Filson to have them assist me, this project would be far from being finished.

My thanks would not be complete without acknowledging the good people at Yale University Press. My editor Mary Pasti and copyeditor Kay Scheuer have my heartfelt gratitude for their work and interest in this project. Mary Valencia, Joyce Ippolito, Keith Condon, Paul Royster, Leslie Nelson Bond, Alexander O. Trotter, and Lara Heimert were also important in seeing the project through the publication process. I would also like to thank Otto Bohlmann, formerly of the Press, who was the acquiring editor. It has been a pleasure to work with them.

I no doubt have neglected to mention others who helped with this project, and to them I extend my thanks. Whether it was providing information, answering a question, or simply uttering an encouraging word, they all helped move this project toward fruition.

Last, but most definitely not least, I want to thank my wife Ruthe and children Elise, Aaron, and Emily for their support and patience. William Clark and his letters have been a part of our lives for ten years. Over the last few years, as the editing accelerated, it took me away from them in body and mind to varying degrees. For their support and uncomplaining sacrifice I thank them.

Editorial Note

In preparing this book for publication, I have used generally accepted current editorial practice in editing the letters. That practice basically is to edit the document as lightly as possible, leaving it in its original form, misspelled words and all, making changes only for the sake of clarity and understanding. Some editors delete portions of documents deemed unimportant or in the interest of space. Others, like myself, do not. All provide notes or annotations in varying degrees of thoroughness to identify and comment on the people, places, subjects, and events mentioned. That has been done here.

In order for the serious and casual reader of these letters to fully appreciate William Clark and his life and times, as well as his creative way with the English language, I have not only made as few changes as possible, but in some instances have forgone certain editorial practices in order to give the reader the clearest sense of the original letters. William Clark had few equals in his approach to spelling and capitalization. No less a Lewis and Clark scholar than Donald Jackson wrote that he "retired in confusion" from his attempts to find some standard for them.

The letter *s* was a particular favorite with Clark. No matter where a word beginning with it might occur in a sentence, it almost invariably received a capital *S*, of varying size. Clark also had a penchant for using lower-case letters as capitals, or simply making them as large as you would a capital letter. This is especially true for proper names. The reverse of this tendency is his frequent use of large lower-case letters to begin words that would not be capitalized. The rule I settled on, as unfaithful to Clark's intentions as it may be, was to consider a lower-case letter, even if larger than midline and used to start a proper name, a small letter. Consequently, many proper names often begin with lower-case letters. I made a few exceptions to this rule when Clark used such a large lower-case letter for a word that should have been capitalized that I believed a capital was indeed intended. A complication to this theory was determining which form of letter was intended when upper- and lower-case letters are similar in appearance. In such cases the size of the letter was generally used as a guide. If it exceeded midline height by very much, I assumed a capital to be intended. The letter *c* is one of the prime examples in this Clarkian grammar. The size of Clark's *c*'s varies widely. *M*'s were also particular favorites in this regard. Clark adds a twist here, however, by using both a capital *M* and a large small *m* (often of varying size) interchangeably for proper names. Whether he intended the latter as a capital is uncertain. Determining what he intended regarding these and other letters and applying a consistent rule were next to impossible. I, like others, have only been able to guess at his intent.

Countless historians and readers have been amazed and frustrated by William Clark's spelling. His scatter-gun approach to spelling can be attributed to either carelessness, ignorance, or a theory that by spelling the word various ways he would hit on the correct form at least once. All three probably figure to some degree. His creative letter combinations in spelling "Sioux" and "potato" are two examples often cited. But this even extended sometimes to basic words and names. He knew how to spell his brother Edmund's name, and almost always spells it correctly. Yet in one glaring departure he spells "Edmund" three different ways in one letter! Just as Jackson, Gary Moulton, Robert Betts, and others have thrown up their hands in surrender I must do the same. I have given William Clark the benefit of the doubt if I was unsure how he meant to spell a word and if the form of a letter is ambiguous. This particularly is true for vowels. It often was difficult to determine if Clark meant what looks like an *o* to be an *a* or an *i* to be an *e*, and vice versa. Similarly, *t*'s have been crossed and *i*'s dotted if it appears that those are the letters he intended. He also had a tendency to "trail off" on words in the closing of his letters, with the result that they look incomplete or illegible. In such cases the obviously intended word(s) or abbreviation has been inserted.

Clark's reputation for creative spelling and grammatical shortcomings is deserved, but it must be remembered that such failings were common during his day. Phonetic spelling was common then—as it still is today—and resulted in many misspelled but understandable words. Also, Mr. Webster's book and its descendants had not yet become the standard references they later would; thus spelling had not reached the codified form it took on later in the nineteenth century. Therefore, to William Clark's talents as a pioneering cartographer, geographer, ethnographer, astronomer, and other roles must be added that of orthographer—of the free-spirit, flexible school.

A few words utterly defeated me in trying to determine what William Clark intended. In such cases a conjectural word has been supplied in brackets with a question mark. This also is true for words unreadable due to paper loss. If I knew the word Clark meant to spell, but it is so far off the mark that its meaning might not be obvious, or possibly confusing to the reader, I supplied the correct spelling in brackets. Brackets also have been used to enclose necessary comments by me in the body of the text and indicate the condition of paper that has affected text. For example, where a word is lost due to a seal tear, I have inserted "[word loss due to seal tear]" or other appropriate explanation at that place in the letter. Clark sometimes later inserted a word or words he had neglected to include. In reading the letter over he would use a caret to indicate where the added word(s) belonged. I have retained that insertion mark and added a bracketed caret to indicate where his insertion ends. Where he crossed out a word or words I have retained that appearance by using the strikethrough feature. Only in the few instances where a section of a letter was crossed out have I not used the strikethrough, but rather have included a note explaining what was marked out. Sometimes he used slashes in place of parentheses. To simplify the transcription, I have not followed Clark's practice of repeating the last word of one page as the first word on the next. This was a common practice, and he intentionally did it. It reveals nothing about his thought processes or idiosyncrasies. Another concession to readability was to lower the raised abbreviations then commonly used.

Punctuation is another area fraught with interpretive danger and frustration. William Clark did not believe in frequent use of periods. Most of his sentences end with a comma, a horizontal slash, or nothing at all. I have generally maintained his punctuation, or lack thereof, making changes only where confusion would otherwise result. The basic change is the addition of extra space to separate sentences. Where dots appeared resembling periods but clearly in the wrong places, I have considered them pen resting places and deleted them.

Clark was as creative in his use of paragraphs as he was with the other areas of English style. He used paragraphs, but not consistently. He also had a tendency to begin a new paragraph simply by skipping space and perhaps dropping down slightly from the preceding portion of that line. If I believed that he intended to start a new paragraph, then I did so. This decision, as with all the editorial decisions, was made in order to present the letters as closely in style as possible to the way William Clark wrote them.

Regarding annotation I have followed the style used by editors Donald Jackson in his monumental accomplishment *Letters of the Lewis and Clark Expedition* and Gary Moulton in his superb *Journals of the Lewis & Clark Expedition*—placing the notes immediately following each letter and day's entry, rather than at the bottom of the page or the back of the book. This practice allows for most convenient access to the annotations accompanying the letters.

Significant effort was made to identify all persons, places, and events mentioned and to discuss and analyze statements, facts, and subjects, especially those of a contradictory, vague, unknown, or confusing nature. I saw this as an opportunity to provide information on people and events that may have slipped through the historical nets, as I am fond of saying, or that the reader may not be familiar with. I quickly discovered in doing research for the notes that information on many of the people who interacted with William Clark was often sparse, widely scattered, and contradictory—if not plain wrong. Therefore, it took a considerable effort to gather the facts necessary to provide the reader and researcher with as correct a sketch or analysis as possible. Basic information about persons and events has been included in the hope that it will be helpful to other researchers. In addition, their connection to Clark is noted if possible. Consequently, some of the notes tend to be rather lengthy. This is especially true for annotations of an explanatory or analytical nature regarding, for example, the expedition, expedition personnel, and the death of Meriwether Lewis. Special effort was made to compile information about the

Clark family's African American slaves mentioned. Some of the people and places identified undoubtedly will be familiar to the reader, but they are included as basic educational information for those who may find it useful. This extends to defining or identifying words of an archaic or unusual nature. A number of words Clark used, common in his day, sent me scurrying to a good dictionary.

Editorial symbols used:

[ ] Brackets enclose a word or words, editorial mark, or comment supplied by the editor.

[?] Brackets enclosing a question mark indicate a conjectural reading of a word or phrase.

^ A caret indicates an insertion by Clark. A bracketed caret, [^], indicates either the end of the insertion or sometimes the start of an above-line insertion which he did not so mark.

~~the~~ Words crossed out by Clark appear in that format using the strikethrough feature.

William Clark Chronology

1 August 1770	Born in Caroline County, Virginia.
November 1784– March 1785	Clark family moves to Jefferson County, Kentucky. Winters at Redstone Landing, Pennsylvania. Settles on their plantation named Mulberry Hill.
August 1789	Accompanies John Hardin's expedition against the White River Indian towns.
May–June 1791	Accompanies Charles Scott's expedition against the Wabash River and Eel River Indian towns as a cadet.
7 March 1792	Appointed a second lieutenant in the United States Army. Travels to Virginia and back to Kentucky. Serves on recruiting duty.
June 1793	Travels to Chickasaw Bluffs, Tennessee (present Memphis), on a mission to the Chickasaw Indians.
August 1794	Participates in the Battle of Fallen Timbers.

September–November 1795	Travels to New Madrid, Missouri, on a mission to Spanish officials.
1 July 1796	Resigns from the army. A first lieutenant at the time. Returns home to Mulberry Hill.
August–October 1797	Visits Kaskaskia, Cahokia, and St. Louis on business.
March–December 1798	Visits New Orleans and Baltimore on business trip lasting almost ten months and covering approximately 4,000 miles.
24 December 1798	Mother Ann Rogers Clark dies at Mulberry Hill.
29 July 1799	Father John Clark dies at Mulberry Hill. Clark inherits Mulberry Hill and a number of slaves, including York.
28 May 1800	Commissioned captain of cavalry in the Kentucky militia.
1801	Travels to Virginia and District of Columbia.
January–February 1802	Moves the majority of brother Jonathan Clark's slaves to Kentucky from Virginia.
Ca. March 1803	With brother George Rogers Clark moves across the Ohio River to property they own at Point of Rocks (later Clark's Point) in Clarksville, Indiana. Sells Mulberry Hill to Jonathan and his mill to brother Edmund Clark later that year.
18 July 1803	Accepts an invitation from his friend Meriwether Lewis to join him as co-commander of an expedition to the Pacific. Begins recruiting men for the trip.
14 October 1803	Meriwether Lewis arrives at Louisville and meets Clark, thus physically forming the partnership of Lewis and Clark. Over the succeeding days the nucleus of the Corps of Discovery is enlisted and the boats piloted through the Falls of the Ohio to Clarksville.
26 October 1803	Lewis and Clark and the nucleus of the Corps of Discovery set out from Clarksville at the Falls of the Ohio on their epic journey to the Pacific Ocean.

1803–1806	On the Lewis and Clark Expedition.
23 September 1806	Corps of Discovery arrives in St. Louis on its return from the expedition.
5 November 1806	Lewis and Clark and a party of expedition veterans and two delegations of Indians arrive at the Falls of the Ohio.
1807	In Virginia and Washington, D.C. Becomes engaged to Judith (Julia) Hancock of Fincastle, Virginia. Returns to the Louisville area and to St. Louis.
March 1807	Appointed chief Indian agent and brigadier general of militia for Louisiana Territory.
September 1807	Conducts a fossil dig at Big Bone Lick, Kentucky, for Thomas Jefferson.
Ca. 5 January 1808	Marries Julia Hancock in Fincastle, Virginia.
June 1808	Moves from Louisville and Clarksville to St. Louis.
August– September 1808	Leads party to Fire Prairie to build Fort Osage.
10 January 1809	Birth of son Meriwether Lewis Clark.
September– November 1809	Travels east for a family visit and on business.
11 October 1809	Meriwether Lewis commits suicide at Grinder's Stand, Tennessee, on the Natchez Trace.
28 October 1809	Learns of the possible death of Meriwether Lewis.
29 October 1809	Receives confirmation of Lewis's death.
July 1810	Returns to St. Louis.
Ca. 10 September 1811	Birth of son William Preston Clark.
25 November 1811	Jonathan Clark dies in his sleep at his home, Trough Spring.
1812–1814	Participates in the War of 1812 in the Mississippi Valley.

1813	Appointed governor of Missouri Territory and ex officio superintendent of Indian affairs.
1814	Leads expedition to Prairie du Chien and builds Fort Shelby.
1 January 1814	Birth of daughter Mary Margaret Clark.
6 May 1816	Birth of son George Rogers Hancock Clark.
Ca. 6 July 1818	Birth of son John Julius Clark.
27 June 1820	Julia Clark dies at her father's estate, Fotheringay, in Montgomery County, Virginia.
1820	Defeated for the governorship of the state of Missouri.
15 October 1821	Daughter Mary Margaret Clark dies in Jefferson County, Kentucky.
28 November 1821	Marries Harriet Kennerly Radford.
1822–1838	Appointed superintendent of Indian affairs by Congress. Oversees Indian affairs for tribes along the Missouri and Mississippi Rivers.
1824–1825	Surveyor general for Illinois, Missouri, and Arkansas.
29 February 1824	Birth of son Jefferson Kearny Clark.
9 September 1826	Birth of son Edmund Clark.
12 August 1827	Son Edmund Clark dies in St. Louis.
1827	Founds Paducah, Kentucky.
5 September 1831	Son John Julius Clark dies in St. Louis.
25 December 1831	Wife Harriet Clark dies in St. Louis.
1 September 1838	William Clark dies in St. Louis. Buried on nephew John O'Fallon's estate and later moved to Bellefontaine Cemetery.

Introduction

"I Write to You without Reserve"

Almost half a century after the death of Louisville attorney and historian Temple Bodley, his six grandchildren set about the task of selling a family house. Their grandmother and uncle had moved there in 1941 following the death of Bodley the previous year. With them went a collection of family papers dating back to Bodley's great-grandfather, Jonathan Clark.

In October 1988 his six grandchildren convened to examine the contents of the house before its sale. In the attic they found two trunks containing family papers. Among the neatly bundled stacks of letters was one bundle in particular that caught the heirs' attention. Still folded just as Jonathan Clark had filed them almost two hundred years earlier was a group of letters labeled "Old Clark Letters Chiefly Gen. Wm. Clarks." Recognizing the letters' importance, the family promptly placed them in a safety-deposit box.

Shortly thereafter I learned of the letters, and in February 1989 I examined them for the first time. What I saw—and touched—that day was electrifying. Before me were forty-seven letters written by William Clark from 1792 to 1811. The information contained in them was enlightening, clarifying, and even disputatious in nature. They truly provided a window to William Clark the man and his world.

Five letters were written during the epic Lewis and Clark Expedition and three in late 1809 during the days and weeks after Clark learned of the death of his partner in discovery, Meriwether Lewis. A number of the letters discussed Clark's slave York—the first African American to cross the United States from coast to coast—and his fate following the expedition. In my hands were letters written from Camp Dubois, Fort Mandan, St. Louis, Washington, D.C., and other places. Here were letters written about the establishment of the Corps of Discovery's first winter camp in December 1803; before setting out into the "extencv and unexplored" country west of Fort Mandan in April 1805; during Clark's 1807 fossil dig for Thomas Jefferson at Big Bone Lick, Kentucky. Here also were letters relating the sad details of the rift between Clark and York after the expedition and transmitting details Clark learned of Meriwether Lewis's last days. His comments answered questions that had bedeviled historians for almost two hundred years. They provided details concerning events and people for which only generalities had heretofore been known.

The William Clark letters reflect the era in which he lived, imparting to us information not only on his contemporaries and times but also on Clark himself. They report on specific events and people in history, some famous, some not. They are microcosmic mirrorings of major events and trends in American history. Society, exploration, territorial administration, western migration, slavery, economics, family, travel, and more are addressed in these letters.

In October 1990 the Jonathan Clark Papers–Temple Bodley Collection, as the forty-seven letters and other material with them had been entitled, was presented to The Filson Historical Society, in Louisville. It is one of the Filson's most important collections. Work on transcribing the letters and editing them for publication began soon afterward. In the summer of 1998, as the editing of the letters was nearing an end, the rest of the family papers from those attic trunks were given to the Filson. Among the voluminous correspondence covering the period from the 1770s to the Civil War were found four more William Clark letters and two powers of attorney, including one filed in Louisville on 26 October 1803, the day the expedition set out from the Falls of the Ohio. One of the letters was of significant historical importance. It was the 28 October 1809 letter Clark wrote to brother Jonathan the day he learned of the possible death of his good friend Lewis. His anguished words "I fear O!

Louisville attorney and historian Temple Bodley, Jonathan Clark's great-grandson; the William Clark letters descended to him. Courtesy of The Filson Historical Society

I fear the waight of his mind has over come him," still evoke emotion to-day. A typescript of this important letter had been made in the early twentieth century, but the whereabouts of the original had been unknown.

A total of fifty-five William Clark letters are published in this volume. Fifty-one are in the Jonathan Clark Papers–Temple Bodley Collection: forty-five written to Jonathan, three to their brother Edmund, two to his nephew John Hite Clark, and one to Edmund and John jointly. To this group have been added four additional William Clark letters already in the Filson's collection. One is his famous 23 September 1806 letter to Jonathan announcing the successful return of the expedition. Given its importance, and because it is actually one of the letters in this amazing series of letters to Jonathan, it was deemed a logical addition. The other three letters were written in 1795 to their sister Fanny Clark O'Fallon and provide good information about the young William Clark. These four letters had descended in another branch of the family and have been in the Filson's collection for many years.

These letters are important not only for the information they impart about events and people around him, but also for the insight they provide on William Clark himself. Before their discovery, letters to siblings and a nephew provided glimpses of the personal William Clark. Unfortunately, there was no lengthy run of his letters to someone close enough to him to allow a good understanding of the man himself. Known letters to friends and associates generally maintained a formality common to correspondence of that time.

These letters written to Jonathan Clark over a nineteen-year period change that. They provide the most detailed perspective yet of what the real William Clark—the man himself—was like. They allow the reader to see beneath the persona of famous explorer and territorial administrator and are a vital source for any biography or study of him. The letters are written in such a personal and informative style that sometimes it seems almost as if you are peeking over Clark's shoulder at the people and scenes he describes. Whether he is writing in a mood of happiness, worry, frustration, or as detached reporter, he chronicles his life and times in an engaging and often enthralling manner. Clark's somewhat inconsistent, and certainly creative, manner of spelling helps rather than hinders in bringing his life and world alive for today's readers.

William Clark was molded by his family and his times. He was born and grew up on the family plantation in Caroline County, Virginia. He received a good education as well as practical outdoor experience, including surveying and cartography. He was a child during the American Revolution, and some of his earliest memories undoubtedly were of his five older brothers—all officers in Virginia units—fighting for their fledgling nation's independence. Two brothers made the ultimate sacrifice for their country. The concepts of duty, honor, and country were instilled in the young William through his family's example.

In November 1784 his parents, John and Ann Clark, moved to Kentucky. With them went William and the three youngest Clark daughters. After wintering at Redstone Landing near Pittsburgh, the Clarks reached their new home outside Louisville in March 1785. Christened Mulberry Hill, the family plantation would be William's home for the next eighteen years. Here on the Kentucky frontier, where adventure and danger were a constant, William Clark grew to maturity. In addition to surveying, traveling, honing his frontier skills, and working on the farm, Clark served in the militia and participated in campaigns against Indian tribes north of the Ohio River. Given his family background, the red-haired six-footer seemed predestined for a military career. In March 1792 he joined the regular army as a lieutenant of infantry.

For the next four years Clark gained valuable experience leading men, planning military activities, traveling through wilderness, and negotiating with Native Americans. A veteran of the Battle of Fallen Timbers and diplomatic missions to the Chickasaw Indians and Spanish, Clark was well respected and well liked, but he grew increasingly dissatisfied with army life. Its adventure and romance were offset by its tedium, frustration, hardships, and slow promotions. He was needed at home to help operate Mulberry Hill and to assist his brother George Rogers Clark with his tangled legal and financial affairs. This, together with a bout of ill health and a desire to seek his fortune in the mercantile trade, resulted in Clark's resignation from the army in July 1796. The experience and contacts he had gained over the previous four years, however, would serve Clark well seven years later when his friend Meriwether Lewis invited him to join him as co-commander on an expedition to the Pacific Ocean.

What the famous partnership of Lewis and Clark and the Corps of Discovery accomplished by traveling to the Pacific Ocean and back has entered the annals of exploration and to this day is one of the most recognized achievements in American history. From July 1803, when William Clark accepted Lewis's invitation to join him, until early 1807, when the captains reported on the expedition to Thomas Jefferson in Washington, much of Clark's effort and energy were focused on the expedition. Lewis and Clark were hailed as heroes and great explorers; accolades and rewards were heaped upon them. Clark was appointed brigadier general of the Louisiana Territory militia and chief Indian agent for the territory. In June 1808 he and his bride Julia Hancock settled in St. Louis. Clark had known Julia before the expedition and seriously courted her following its return. She was immediately embraced by his family, and she was particularly close to some of his nieces and Jonathan's wife Sarah, whom she called her "Kentucky mother."

From 1808 until his death in 1838, William Clark was a major figure in the nation's western affairs. He was a booster for his new home and identified his success with its growth and prosperity. He invested in land, pursued business opportunities, and touted the advantages of settling in St. Louis and the new territory. Clark served as Indian agent and later as Indian superintendent until his death, seeking to balance the white demand for land—Indian land—with what he perceived was best for the native inhabitants. Native Americans placed great trust and confidence in the "Red Headed chief's" efforts on their behalf. Clark did what he could to balance what often were conflicting goals, and ran afoul of settlers who cared nothing for Indian rights and wanted the Indians out of the way.

Before and during the War of 1812, Clark organized frontier defense. War of 1812 hero and future president William Henry Harrison had great confidence in his old comrade-in-arms, stating he would rather have William Clark at his side in the type of war in which they were engaged than any other man in the United States and that Missouri could feel secure in being protected by his military talents. In 1814 Clark led an expedition up the Mississippi River to build Fort Shelby at Prairie du Chien. The campaign initially was successful, but the expiration of the militia's enlistments forced him to return to St. Louis, and the British later captured the fort.

In 1813 President James Madison appointed William Clark governor of Missouri Territory. He remained governor until 1820 when, viewed as part of the St. Louis elite, out of step with the needs of the common settlers, and too friendly toward Native Americans, he lost the election for Missouri's first state governor. This defeat coincided with a tragic time in his life. In June 1820 his wife Julia died in Virginia. Clark had earlier traveled with her to Virginia and did not actively campaign for the governorship, not only owing to this family crisis, but also because he mistakenly thought his record should stand on its own merits and that cam-

The house in Louisville's Highlands neighborhood where the William Clark letters were discovered in 1988. Courtesy of The Filson Historical Society

paigning was unseemly. He continued to be active in Indian affairs, served in 1824 and 1825 as surveyor general of Missouri, Illinois, and Arkansas, and pursued personal business interests. His home in St. Louis and his country estate, Minoma, were centers for Indian diplomacy and St. Louis society.

Explorer, soldier, Indian official, and governor, William Clark enjoyed a long and successful career. His personal life was full and touched by tragedy. Twice a widower, he also endured the deaths of three of his seven children. To these personal losses were added the deaths of close siblings such as Jonathan, George, and Edmund. His nephew John O'Fallon believed him to be an indulgent parent who sometimes allowed the Clark "pride" to affect his judgment. A good education was important to Clark, and just as he had supported his local schools and the education of his nephews, he tried to assure a quality education for his children. O'Fallon observed that in his later years Uncle William began to fail both physically and mentally. The end came on 1 September 1838 at his son Meriwether Lewis Clark's home in St. Louis. He was buried on John O'Fallon's country estate and in 1860 was reinterred in Bellefontaine Cemetery.

The importance of family to William Clark is reflected in his letters to those loved ones from whom he was separated. Even after his marriage and the arrival of his own children, he took great interest and delight in his nieces, nephews, and other kin and supported their endeavors to the best of his ability. He would have liked nothing more than to have had the whole family together, but sadly resigned himself to the reality that that was never likely to happen. Since that was not to be, then writing newsy, heartfelt letters was the next best thing. He was a faithful correspondent, and when he did not receive letters from his Kentucky relations he worried that he had displeased them or that they had forgotten him and Julia. The more regular the contact, he believed, the stronger the bonds of kinship and affection would remain and less likely the chance of a breakdown in that important family connection. Thus the steady stream of letters to Jonathan and other family members, reporting on personal and general news.

Jonathan Clark was twenty years older than William and was held in great esteem and affection by his youngest brother. Not only was he a true big brother to William, but after their father's death he could be considered something of a father figure also. Jonathan was the oldest of the ten Clark siblings, and he was looked to by all the Clarks for advice. Like brothers George and William, he reflected his Scottish heritage. His son George Washington Clark reported that no portrait was ever painted of his father, but he described him as tall and raw-boned, perhaps a bit over six feet tall, with reddish or sandy hair, mixed with gray in his later years. He recalled that his father and William were the same size and had the same color hair. Jonathan was born on 12 August 1750 (1 August by the Julian or old-style calendar, the same date as William's birth by the Gregorian or new-style calendar, and apparently the date he continued to use to celebrate his birthday) in Albemarle County, Virginia. He grew up in Caroline County where John and Ann Clark had moved in the mid-1750s. He received a good education, served as deputy clerk of Spotsylvania County, Virginia, and in 1772 moved to Woodstock, in present Shenandoah County, where he was deputy clerk for three years of what was then Dunmore County. He was a prominent resident of the county and counted Gen. Peter Muhlenburg among his friends.

The Clarks were patriots from the gathering of the first storm clouds with Great Britain. In 1775 and 1776 Jonathan served as a delegate to two Virginia Revolutionary conventions that met to discuss a formal call for independence. Commissioned a captain in the Eighth Virginia Infantry Regiment of the Continental Line in early 1776, he rose to the rank of lieutenant colonel, participating in some of the major battles of the war: Brandywine, Germantown, and Monmouth. Some historians credit him with the plan of attack on Paulus Hook in 1779. On 12 May 1780 Jonathan became a prisoner of war when Benjamin Lincoln surrendered the American army at Charleston, South Carolina, to the British. He was paroled in the spring of 1781 and sat out the rest of the war. He was one of the founding members of the Society of the Cincinnati.

Jonathan Clark's postwar years were filled with business and family affairs. On 13 February 1782 he married Sarah Hite of Frederick County, Virginia. They settled on a plantation in southeastern Spotsylvania County just over the county line from his parents' home in Caroline County. There Jonathan farmed, served as a magistrate, and enjoyed the life of a prosperous and respected country gentleman. He and Sarah had seven children, six of whom lived to maturity. In 1793 he was commissioned major general of Virginia militia.

Compared to brothers George and William, Jonathan was a latecomer to Kentucky but no stranger to it. He had visited Kentucky in late 1783 and into 1784 regarding land affairs and to help prepare his parents' home. He visited again in 1796. Jonathan and his family left their Virginia home on 26 May 1802 for their new home in Jefferson County, Kentucky. Just as Jonathan had done for William and their parents almost twenty years before, William moved his brother's slaves and some household goods to Kentucky for him earlier in 1802. Jonathan and his family arrived in Louisville on 6 July and reached Trough Spring, as his estate was christened, the following day. Trough Spring was just to the east of William's Mulberry Hill plantation, which he had inherited from his father in 1799. When brother Edmund also moved to Jefferson County in 1802, all the surviving Clark siblings and their families were living in the same neighborhood for the first time in almost thirty years.

Jonathan enjoyed the life of a country gentleman and farmer until his sudden death nine years later. Just as he had been in Virginia, he was a prominent and respected member of the community. His diary, kept for over forty years (1770–1811), records that life. He traveled frequently in Jefferson County and across the Ohio River to Clark County, Indiana Territory, covering something of a circuit among his family, friends, and associates. Jonathan already knew many of the neighborhood's inhabitants from their previous residence in Virginia, service together in the army, or his earlier visits to Kentucky. This, together with the network of associates established by his family and friends, apparently made for an easy transition to his new home. Other than one trip back to Virginia in 1807 and a few trips in Kentucky, Jonathan stayed in the Louisville area during his nine years in Kentucky. He died at Trough Spring on 25 November 1811 and was buried in the family cemetery at Mulberry Hill. In 1868 he and other Clarks were reinterred in Cave Hill Cemetery.

Jonathan Clark's surviving papers chronicle his life and indicate how well liked and respected he was. William Clark's own letters to Jonathan reflect this. The first letter in this collection, addressed to "Honorable Sir," indicates the level of respect and formality between William and Jonathan during the beginning of William's career. By the mid-1790s, perhaps believing himself to be more his brother's peer, and as a regular correspondence between them blossomed, William's salutation had become "Dear Brother," and remained so throughout the rest of their correspondence. Growing up, William was able to enjoy his brother's company only when Jonathan returned home for occasional visits. Their greatest opportunity to get to know each other was after Jonathan returned from the Revolutionary War in 1781. When Jonathan settled in Spotsylvania County in 1782, the brothers had two years to deepen their relationship before William moved to Kentucky, and part of that time Jonathan was in Kentucky preparing the elder Clarks' new homesite. It would not be until 1802, when Jonathan moved to Kentucky and they were again neighbors, that the brothers would once more see each other on a regular basis. In the intervening years only infrequent visits by William to Spotsylvania County or a 1796 visit by Jonathan to Mulberry Hill would bring them together. But despite these limitations of time and opportunity, the brothers bonded. Whether it was because of the twenty-year difference in their ages or despite it, the connection between William and Jonathan strengthened. They embraced their respective fraternal roles, which did indeed take on characteristics of a father-son relationship after the death of John Clark. Born on the same date twenty years apart, and apparently strongly resembling each other, the two brothers seemed to indeed be connected. Their letters and occasional visits kept them in touch during the 1790s and into the early 1800s. After Jonathan moved to Jefferson County, they visited regularly, even after William moved across the Ohio to Clarksville in early 1803.

Just as William's move west to Kentucky had separated the brothers in 1784, another westward move severed physical ties in 1803. And, just as they had been able to reunite in 1802, William and Jonathan reunited after William's return from the Lewis and Clark Expedition in 1806 and when he visited the Louisville area thereafter. William was the embodiment of western migration. From moving to the Kentucky frontier in the 1780s, to being one of the leaders of the American surge across the Mississippi River in the early years of the nineteenth century, William Clark was part of the tide of American settlement sweeping westward across the continent. In June 1808, however, when William moved to St. Louis, both brothers realized their lives and relationship had changed. This was especially true for William. Now, except for perhaps an annual visit, the brothers knew they must maintain their relationship through letters.

William Clark had obvious love and respect for Jonathan. It is because of this bond, this strong feeling between the brothers, that we have this extraordinary cache of letters. What William reported on, revealed to, and opined about to Jonathan was often unique in his correspondence, repeated to no one else. Jonathan's views and opinions meant a great deal to William. In order to benefit from his advice, and to maintain their personal connection, he provided Jonathan with as full an understanding of his situation as possible, confident that his wise and practical brother would give him sound guidance. He states his intention to do so in his letters. Not long after settling in St. Louis he wrote, "I wish you to be possessed of the knowledge of all our intentions, views, & prospects, & receive your advice & oppinion." His desire to keep his brother fully informed concerning his activities and news—significant as well as sometimes trivial—is a boon to readers today in learning about William Clark's contemporaries, their times, and about Clark himself.

The sometimes seemingly mundane events described in the letters provide us with excellent vignettes of the hardships of travel; tormenting mosquitoes; Clark's son getting a bath, learning to talk, and marching about town beating his drum; his house; the misery of suffering from a cold; Julia's homesickness; the festival air of a public hanging; and a man in love (who "desirves not only pity but the applaus of his friend[s]"). To these are added more significant subjects of national interest, such as military affairs in 1792; the Lewis and Clark Expedition; the Burr Conspir-

The trunk of Bodley family papers in which the Clark letters were stored. Four more Clark letters were found in the trunk after this photo was taken. Courtesy of The Filson Historical Society

acy; fossil excavations at Big Bone Lick; George Rogers Clark; the building of Fort Osage; the economics of St. Louis and the West; the official expedition history; Corps of Discovery member George Shannon; Indian affairs; dueling; difficulties with his slaves, including expedition veteran York; and the death of his good friend and partner in discovery Meriwether Lewis.

These last two subjects are dealt with in some detail in William's letters. Both men occupied significant places in his life, and he kept Jonathan apprised of both of them and his relationships with them. The lives of both York and Lewis were in part tragic. York, as a slave, suffered from the cruelties and restrictions of that institution; how it affected decent slaveholders also is revealed in the letters. Slavery was an abhorrent institution. The human tragedies caused by it are countless. Slaves, although often well liked and highly valued by their owners, were generally looked upon as property first and persons second. Their feelings and desires often were not taken into consideration. Many times the basis for a decision regarding them—sometimes no matter how close the owner-slave relationship—was economic or financial. William Clark was the product of a slaveholding family and a slaveholding society. He was influenced by this society, and his attitudes and beliefs regarding African Americans and slavery were molded by it, shaping the way in which he perceived and treated his own slaves. What William writes about his enslaved African Americans does not reflect well on him by today's standards and beliefs. But he cannot be judged by modern standards and beliefs. He was the product of a different time and a different culture. Although he worried that Jonathan would think he had become a "severe master," he believed he tried to be a good and fair one. He was capable of enlightened beliefs and recognized the loathsome and inhumane aspects of slavery, but like many others of his day he resigned himself to it. He did emancipate some of his slaves, including York; but he also saw no escape from the system. He owned slaves until his death and helped perpetuate the "peculiar institution" by leaving enslaved African Americans to his children in his will.

William Clark's reporting to Jonathan of news he learns about Meriwether Lewis's death provides previously unknown details concerning not only Lewis's death but William's reaction to it. From his worried confession on 26 August 1809 about Lewis's mental state to his exasperated lament months later about Lewis's failure to write the official history of the expedition, Clark relays information and his feelings concerning Lewis's tragic end that he does in no other known source.

These letters help to tell the story of America and a famous American. We rejoice that they have survived the vagaries of time and fate and exist today to impart their information to present and future generations. William Clark did indeed "feel no restraint in stile or grammar" in writing to his brother Jonathan. He was as good as his word when he wrote him that "I wish you to See & know all." He wrote "without reserve" about himself and the people and events of his world. It is these letters, written to his beloved "Dear Brother," that provide a window through which the real William Clark and his contemporaries and times can be seen.

1

"The Sport of Fortune"

Prologue to Exploration, 1792–1802

It can be said that William Clark was in preparation for his historic trek to the Pacific for most of his pre-expedition life. A childhood on the Clark family plantation in Virginia, a good education by the standards of the day, growing to manhood on the Kentucky frontier, and the life of a Kentucky farmer, together with his brothers' military exploits, his own military experience, and extensive travel concerning military and civilian affairs, were all excellent preparation for the Lewis and Clark Expedition.

The seven letters in this chapter, written prior to 1803 and the beginning of the expedition, illustrate Clark's life as a soldier and civilian and how well qualified he was to help lead the Corps of Discovery. When William Clark joined the United States Army in March 1792 he was following what must have seemed like a natural calling. His five older brothers had all served as officers in the Revolutionary War. Jonathan and George Rogers had attained the rank of general in the Virginia militia, and brothers John and Richard had made the ultimate sacrifice in their young nation's service. George's star had declined by 1792, when the first letter in this collection was written, but not before it had reached its zenith in the war in the West. He had become the Conqueror of the Northwest, the Hannibal of the West. The famous exploits of his idolized older brother together with the solid service of Jonathan, Edmund, and John as officers in the Virginia Continental Line set a high standard for William to follow.

Always concerned that he pass on as much news—and upon occasion gossip—as possible, William Clark strived to write an informative letter. Consequently, he wrote not only frequently but often at length. The result? Informative, newsy letters not only for those who read them some two hundred years ago but for those who read them today. In September 1792 Clark had been in the army only six months but already had traveled east to Virginia and back west again. His recruiting duties kept him on the move and put him in contact with a variety of people and news. This is evident in his 1792 letter, as is the social network of which he was the beneficiary because he was a Clark. The Clarks were a well-respected family in Virginia who could count Thomas Jefferson, Patrick Henry, and George Mason among their friends. Their military and civilian contacts established in Virginia extended to Kentucky when they settled there. William enjoyed access to the highest levels of society, government, and the military because of the family's status and connections. That position, earned over several generations, provided an extensive network that he benefited from and in turn benefited. His family name and who he was himself foretold success for the educated, cultured, and ambitious young Kentuckian. William Clark was very aware of his place in society and was determined to assume that place. He was happy not only to enjoy the benefits but to shoulder the responsibilities of that position.

After four years in the military, the appeal of the soldier's life waned for Clark. Anthony Wayne's campaign against the Northwestern Indians had ended successfully, and peace reigned on the frontier. The excitement of battle was replaced with the tedium of garrison life. Promotion would be slow. Clark suffered from bouts of ill health. His aging father John Clark needed help running the family plantation. William hoped to enter lucrative commercial trade. He despaired of ever rising to a degree of fame and fortune in the army and believed that commerce might provide them. Did family expectations influence him? Perhaps. Success in both military and business pursuits had been achieved by Clarks, Clark relatives, and Clark associates. The letters William wrote to Jonathan demonstrate his desire to achieve and assume his place—what he believed was his proper place—in the world. The financial success he sought would elude him, but the fame and respect would not. Extensive travel on legal and commercial matters provided excellent experience. This, added to his military experience, made William Clark eminently qualified to lead an expedition into the wilderness. His financial fortunes had declined by mid-1803 to the point that he may have welcomed an opportunity to set those matters aside and undertake a new venture, a venture of momentous scale.

Not fond of dwelling on his failures, Clark provides a clue to his distasteful situation in one of his letters. His dedication and commitment to his brother George had cost him dearly. William and other family members had struggled with George's tangled and daunting financial and legal difficulties for years. Virginia's penurious and ungrateful refusal to honor many of George's Revolutionary and Indian Wars debts incurred in prosecuting campaigns against the commonwealth's enemies had ruined him. Creditors and lawsuits were a regular part of George's life. William traveled thousands of miles and impoverished himself in assisting his brother. His 1798 letter was written well into a 4,000-mile trip made in pursuit of business and to help George. Trips had also been made to Washington and Richmond in the east and Vincennes and St. Louis in the west toward these same ends. Once brothers Jonathan and Edmund settled near Mulberry Hill, William probably thought things would be all right. He had moved Jonathan's slaves from Virginia to Kentucky early in 1802 and supervised the building of Jonathan's house to prepare the way for his esteemed brother's move to Kentucky. But it was not to be. Limited success had been achieved in business and in helping George, with the result of pushing William to the brink of financial ruin. Consequently, William and George moved across the Ohio to land they owned in Clarksville, Indiana Territory, in early 1803, hoping for a reversal of their financial fortunes. William sold his plantation to Jonathan and his mill to Edmund. Settling in on his farm at Point of Rocks overlooking the Falls of the Ohio in the summer of 1803, ready to pursue opportunities in order to recoup his fortunes, he received an unexpected invitation from an old army friend to accompany him on a "western tour," an invitation that changed William Clark's life and supplanted thoughts of business and legal affairs for the next four years.

Sketch of Fort Steuben, built across the Ohio from Louisville as part of the area's defenses. William Clark's 1792 letter was written there. Courtesy of the Northwest Territory Collection, Indiana Historical Society

~

Fort Stuben[1] Falls Ohio[2] Septr. 2d. 1792

Honbl. Sir

       I receved your offectionate lettor of the 18th. of June by Captain Rogors,[3] wherein you exprest a desire of Knowing ∧my[∧] particular Situation. I arived here Safe after a Tegious journey of near two months. ⎯ I am ordered to recruit my part of the Company in this State, and have already Inlisted ten men,[4] I expect to Start in a fiew days to Lexington[5] to Compleat my quota of men. ⎯ I am not yet informed perticularly who will Comd. the Rifle Regt. it is Supposed Colo. Dark[6] will. ⎯ Genl. Wilkinson[7] Comds. the Troops of this department at present, our Number of Regulars, do not exceed 1000 offective men ⎯. when we Shall be of Strength Sufficient to take the field, I can't determin; as Recruiting Service go on So Sloly, I fear it will be next, Fall before we Shall have men Sufficnt to Carry out a Suckcessfull ~~army~~ ∧Campain[∧] ⎯ I fear that the 5000 men that are to be rose will not be Seckcessfull, as the Inds. are imbodering [embodying], in different quarters to oppose us. we are informed that the Momis Indians that defeated our army, last fall with 500 warrurs, have Sent runs. [runners] to invite all the Lake Indians to Join them,[8] we are likewise informed that the Creek nation had declar'd war, and are daly on the Frontiers of the Combarland Settlements[9] Killing ∧men[∧] and Stealing horses ⎯⎯. Congress has ordered a Treaty with all the Northern Indians, to be held at St. Vinceence,[10] this month, ⎯ about five hd. warreers have arrived there for the purpose I Sups. of Treating, tho we have not receved any answr. from them ∧by messengers Sent to invite them to a Treaty[∧] our messengers being all Kill'd by them at their arrival in their Towns[11] ⎯ Genl. Putnam[12] one of our Briga: Genls., also an Indian Agent passed this about Eight days ago ~~on his way to St. Vinceence~~, on his way to the Treaty   I fear this Treaty will be of no advantage 'us, as the Indians Say they will Treat untill they can get their prisoners from ~~from~~ the White people, those prisoners are goin on to be given up at this Treaty[13] ⎯ This will give you an Idea of the Situation of Indian afs. in this Quarter ⎯

    I Shall afr. [refer] you to Capt. Rogers for the Police [policies or politics] of Kentucky, as I Kno verry little of them at present.

    my Bro: George[14] talks of going to Virga. this Fall; he has Collected Some certifects respecting claims on the State of Virginia, which he will

Send by an early oppertenity — our Friends in Kentuky are well, Capt. Hite[15] is Mard. to Miss Erickson[16] from Merreland — you will pleas to Give my most respectable compliments to Sister Clark & chidren.[17] Tell Sister Clark, I Shall think my Self honor'd if I am mentioned at her daughters Christning as a Sponsir.[18] you will please to favour me with a lettor when you can make it conveniant, if you will address yoer lettors to Capt. Tanekill[19] at Pittsburgh[20] they will come to me Safe. — I Shall not lose an oppertunity but will at every one, wright to you, my situation, and the State of the army in this department and I reman with the Sincearest offection and Due rspect your oft. Bro:

William Clark

NB

I in close you a plat of your 2000 acres Survey that one coast [cost] was left out, and the Entreys of all your other Tracts, they are Said to be all good Entres except the one that calls for the Lead mine, I can find no man that Knows where this mine is, if you think proper, I will have it withdrawn and Enterd. on the NW. Side of the Ohio[21] —

W C.

1. Fort Steuben was located on the north bank of the Ohio River about one-half mile above the Falls of the Ohio at present Jeffersonville, Indiana. It was constructed in 1786 and first named Fort Finney, for its founder and first commander Maj. Robert Finney, but was later renamed for Revolutionary War hero Baron Friedrich Wilhelm von Steuben. Sources state that it was a strong, defensible fort built of blockhouses and pickets about ninety yards from the bank of the river. It was garrisoned by regular army troops until sometime in 1793. A diagram and sketches of the fort are in the Northwest Territory Collection, Indiana Historical Society. (*The Encyclopedia of Louisville* [hereafter cited as *EL*], 312; Baird, 1:138–41; *History of the Ohio Falls Cities and Their Counties* [hereafter cited as *HOFC*], 2:453.)

2. The Falls of the Ohio were the only major obstacle to navigation on that waterway. It was for that reason that the area on the south side of the Falls had already been identified as a good site for a town by the early 1770s, and that George Rogers Clark established what became Louisville there in 1778. The Falls actually were a series of rapids that included very small falls with an overall drop of some twenty-six feet over approximately two miles. The Falls area is the largest exposed Devon-

ian coral reef in the world. In periods of high to moderate water the Falls could be run, usually by pilots familiar with them. In periods of low water and as large steamboats increasingly were used on the river, goods had to be portaged around the Falls, where they were transferred to another boat or reloaded on the same boat once that craft had carefully been navigated through the rapids. During Louisville's early years inhabitants and visitors sometimes referred to their locale as being the "Falls of the Ohio," "Falls of Ohio," "Rapids of the Ohio," or even "Falls Ohio," as Clark does here, instead of stating the town, usually Louisville. Six towns eventually were established at the Falls, three on each side of the Ohio: Louisville, Portland, and Shippingport on the Kentucky side, and Jeffersonville, Clarksville, and New Albany on the Indiana side. (Verhoeff, 68–69; *HOFC*, 1:41–42; *EL*, 279–80; Yater (1), 1.)

3. Captain John Rogers (1757–1794) was a native of Caroline County, Virginia, and one of the sons of Clark's uncle George Rogers (1721–1802). He was appointed a second lieutenant in the 4th Virginia Infantry Regiment in 1776 and served as a captain in George Rogers Clark's Illinois Regiment from 1778 to 1782. He commanded the detail that escorted Henry Hamilton and other British prisoners from Vincennes to Williamsburg, Virginia, in 1779. Rogers lived in Kentucky and Virginia, apparently never settling for long in one place, traveling frequently. He never married, and died at the Eagle Tavern in Richmond, Virginia. (Gwathmey, 675; Thruston, 24; Edmund Rogers Miscellaneous Papers, The Filson Historical Society [hereafter cited as TFHS], Louisville, Kentucky.)

4. William Clark had been commissioned a lieutenant in the United States Army in March 1792 and at this time was on recruiting duty. He had been in Virginia two months before and had only recently reached the frontier and begun his assignment. Regular army as well as militia companies were being raised throughout Kentucky to fight Indians. Recruitment often went slowly, and there was friction between the regular army and state militias owing to different opinions and objectives and the two disastrous defeats the regular army had suffered, under Josiah Harmar in 1790 and Arthur St. Clair in 1791, at the hands of confederated Northwestern tribes under the leadership of Little Turtle. (Jonathan Clark to William Clark, 18 June 1792, William Clark Papers–E.G. Voorhis Memorial Collection [hereafter cited WCP-VMC], Missouri Historical Society, St. Louis, Missouri.)

5. Lexington, Kentucky, was founded in 1779 by Robert Patterson, and named in honor of the American victory over the British in April 1775 at Lexington, Massachusetts. Patterson had been in the area with a small party of surveyors in the spring of 1775 when they received word of that

battle, and he had vowed to return to the area someday and establish a town named for that victory. Lexington was one of Kentucky's leading towns from its earliest days and earned the nickname the "Athens of the West." Even though Clark wrote the letter from Fort Steuben in Indiana Territory, he is referring to Kentucky when he writes "this State." (Staples, 7–20; Wooley, 3–29.)

6. William Darke (1736–1801) was at that time a lieutenant colonel in the Kentucky militia. He was a colonel in the Continental Line from Berkeley County, Virginia, during the Revolution, and retired from the regular army after the war. He came out of retirement, however, and commanded one wing of the army at St. Clair's defeat in November 1791, was promoted to the rank of general, and led a brigade of Virginia militia in 1794 during the Whiskey Rebellion. A native of Philadelphia, he died in Jefferson County, Virginia. Jonathan and Darke had known each other since at least 1776, when they both served as captains in the 8th Virginia. In addition, Darke and John Clark, Jr., were both captured at Germantown, 4 October 1777, and remained prisoners until exchanged in the fall of 1780. (Gwathmey, 207; Bodley (1), 1:473n; *William and Mary College Quarterly*, 22:70.)

7. James Wilkinson (1757–1825) was a career military officer, businessman, entrepreneur, schemer, and one of the great rascals in American history. A native of Maryland, he studied medicine in Philadelphia and served as an officer in the Revolution. He schemed against George Washington as a member of the Conway Cabal but escaped punishment. Wilkinson moved to Kentucky in 1783, quickly became one of its leaders, and continued his scheming; not only was he on the payroll of Spain, but he also was involved in the Burr Conspiracy. He continued in positions of prominence in the army and government until he retired in 1814. He helped to ruin the reputation of George Rogers Clark, though one assumes that William Clark was unaware of his role here. Clark was one of those army officers who initially supported Wilkinson rather than his superior, General Anthony Wayne, who seemed too slow and cautious in the face of the army's desire to revenge the defeats suffered at Indian hands in 1790 and 1791 under Harmar and St. Clair. Later, however, Clark and most of the others became believers in Wayne and his tactics. One cannot help but believe that if Clark had known about Wilkinson's part in his brother George's downfall, and certainly if he had known of his treachery with the Spanish, he would have loathed him. At the writing of this letter Wilkinson had recently been named commander of western military affairs and had just led an expedition against the Eel River Indian towns (in present northeastern Indiana).

(*Dictionary of American Biography* [hereafter cited as *DAB*], 20:222–26; Jackson (1), 2:686–87n; Jackson (2), 153–54.)

8. Clark may be referring to either the Miami Indian tribe or several tribes (including the Miami) who lived along the Maumee River in northwestern Ohio and northeastern Indiana. The Lake Indians included such tribes as the Miami, Shawnee, Ojibway, Delaware, Pottawatomie, Ottawa, and Wyandot, many of which traditionally had been allied with the French against the British and Americans and later with the British against the Americans. Little Turtle (1752–1812) of the Miami and Blue Jacket (ca. 1754–1810) of the Shawnee were the primary chiefs of this loose confederacy. Under their leadership the confederacy achieved its greatest success in 1790 and 1791 with the defeat of two American forces composed of regular U.S. Army troops and militia, mainly Kentucky militia, in Ohio. The close of the War of 1812 brought large-scale hostilities to an end, and the Miami, Shawnee, and other Lake tribes gradually drifted westward until eventually the majority of the tribes were officially settled in eastern Kansas and then Indian Territory (present eastern Oklahoma). (Wheeler-Voegelin, 66–68; Lamar, 671, 729; Atwater, 133–40.)

9. Creek and Cherokee war parties were actively raiding white settlements in southern Kentucky and in Tennessee along the Cumberland River during this period. The Cherokee lived mainly in northern Georgia and eastern Tennessee, the Creek to the south and west of the Cherokee in Georgia and Alabama. Both were large and formidable tribes. Over years of contact with Euro-Americans, both had adopted a number of their customs, as had the Seminole, Choctaw, and Chickasaw, also of the southeastern United States. These nations collectively became known as the Five Civilized Tribes. Periodic conflict with whites led to decreasing Indian territory and power. By the end of the 1830s the majority had been removed to Indian Territory. (Lamar, 377–79; Crutchfield, 101–4.)

10. Vincennes, Indiana. An early French settlement in southwestern Indiana along the Wabash River established in 1731, it was often referred to as St. Vincent or Post St. Vincent. Prior to 1736 it also was called Au Post and Post Ouabache in addition to Post St. Vincent before inhabitants and officials settled on variations of the latter. Vincennes had been the scene of George Rogers Clark's victory over the British and their Indian allies in 1779. It was one of the major towns in the Northwest Territory at this time and served as the capital of Indiana Territory from its establishment in 1800 until 1813, when Corydon was named the capital. It was often used as the site of Indian negotiations.

The Northern Indians comprised many of the same tribes referred to as Lake tribes, but also included tribes in Indiana, Illinois, and farther north, such as the Winnebago, Chippewa, and others. (Cauthorn, 11–45, 79–109.)

11. The Indians did indeed kill peace emissaries dispatched to them by federal authorities during this period. The most celebrated case was the murder of Gen. John Hardin of Kentucky by a party of Delaware Indians in the Ohio country in September 1792. James Wilkinson requested Hardin to undertake the peace mission, and although the latter thought it very possible he would be killed, he accepted. Hardin's death would have particularly affected Clark. The families knew each other, and William had served under Hardin in a 1789 militia campaign against the White River Indian towns. In May 1792 both were at Fort Washington. When Clark set out for a trip to Kentucky, Hardin gave him $200 to carry to his wife in Nelson County. (*The Kentucky Encyclopedia* [hereafter cited as *KE*], 403; Fenley Family Miscellaneous Papers, TFHS; John Hardin to Jane Hardin, 10 May 1792, 19 May 1792, John Hardin Miscellaneous Papers, TFHS.)

12. Rufus Putnam (1738–1824), born in Sutton, Massachusetts, served as chief engineer of the army during the Revolution and was made a brigadier general in 1783. He was appointed one of the judges for the Northwest Territory in 1790 and is often considered the founder of the state of Ohio, having established the first permanent white settlement in what became Ohio at Marietta on the Ohio River in 1788. (*DAB*, 15:284–85; *Collier's Encyclopedia*, 19:538; Campbell, 29–33.)

13. Indians were held as prisoners by whites, but it was much more common for whites to be held captive by Indians, often being adopted into the tribe. Indian captives primarily were taken to be used as ransom for white captives. One of the more tragic consequences of many peace treaties was the requirement that the Indians return white captives, people who had often been taken as children and remembered nothing of their white families or lives. Many an Indian family was separated, and many a white Indian returned to white society having had no desire to be so rescued. The treaty mentioned by Clark was not signed until 1795 (the Treaty of Greenville) as a result of the Battle of Fallen Timbers.

14. George Rogers Clark (1752–1818) was born in Albemarle County, Virginia, the second son and child of John and Ann Rogers Clark. He received a good education, learned surveying, participated in frontier wars against the Indians, and was active in Kentucky affairs by 1775. He rose to the rank of general in the Virginia militia during the Revolutionary War and earned several sobriquets, including the "Hannibal

of the West," as leader of the campaign that seized the Northwest Territory for the United States. Debts incurred in prosecuting the war that Virginia refused to honor led to his financial ruin and contributed to his political decline. He also slid into alcoholism during this period. One of the reasons that William Clark resigned from the army in 1796 was to help George with his financial and legal troubles. In 1809 George's right leg was severely burned and had to be amputated. Afterward he lived with his sister Lucy and brother-in-law William Croghan at their home, Locust Grove, east of Louisville. Clark's reference to George as "my" rather than "our" brother seems strange by current usage, but apparently use of the singular possessive instead of the more correct plural was rather common during that time. (*DAB*, 4:127–30; *EL*, 197–98; see English, James, Bakeless (1), and Bodley (2) for some of the biographies of Clark.)

15. Abraham Hite, Jr. (1755–1832), was a native of present Hardy County, Virginia (then part of Hampshire County), the son of Col. Abraham Hite (1729–1790), and nephew of Col. Isaac Hite (1717–1795), Jonathan Clark's father-in-law. He served with Jonathan as a lieutenant and captain during the Revolution in the 12th and 8th Virginia, and was captured along with Jonathan and Edmund Clark and the rest of the army at Charleston, South Carolina, on 12 May 1780. He had been in Kentucky before the war, and settled there in Jefferson County by 1785, farming and taking an active part in civic and political affairs. (Sallee, 37–39; Heitman (1), 292.)

16. Elizabeth Eareckson (or Erickson) (1763–1822) married Abraham Hite, Jr., in Jefferson County, Kentucky, on 21 July 1792. (Sallee, 38; Thruston and Healy, 16.)

17. Clark consistently refers to his sister-in-law Sarah Hite Clark (1760–1818) as "Sister Clark." Her nickname was Sally. The daughter of Isaac and Eleanor Eltinge Hite, she was born in Frederick County, Virginia, on 19 October 1760. A birth date of 11 May 1758 also is listed for her in some sources, but the 1760 date was recorded by her brother Isaac in a family record and is used here. She died in October 1818 in Jefferson County, most likely at her home, Trough Spring. She was buried at Mulberry Hill (as was Jonathan) and reinterred in Cave Hill Cemetery in 1868. She married Jonathan Clark on 13 February 1782. In September 1792 the "chidren" were Eleanor Eltinge (1783–1867), John Hite (1785–1820), Isaac (1787–1868), and Ann (1792–1833). Another child, Mary, had died (1790–1791), and two more were yet to be born, William (1795–1879) and George Washington (1798–1883). (Dorman (1), 27–29; Hopewell L. Rogers Genealogical Index [hereafter cited as Rogers Index], TFHS; Clark family file, TFHS.)

18. In Jonathan's letter of 18 June he had passed along his wife's request that William serve as one of the sponsors for his niece Ann Clark at her christening. She had been born on 19 May 1792. She married James Anderson Pearce (1777–1825) on 30 September 1810, and it was through this line that these letters descended. Jonathan's 18 June letter is the only surviving letter of his to William that I found. Clark makes reference in his letters to receiving letters from Jonathan, sometimes citing specific dates. Where are they? My fear is that they have been destroyed. As fortunate as we are that the letters edited here have survived, we are also unfortunate that it may have been the fate of Jonathan's letters to William, additional letters that William wrote to Jonathan, and a large amount of other important historical material to be destroyed by flames. This belief is based on two things. Rogers Clark Ballard Thruston, a descendant of Fanny Clark, took great pride and interest in his heritage, actively locating and collecting family papers. In 1932 he stated that family papers, including Clark family papers, had perished when his brother Samuel Ballard's house burned in 1906. An even sadder story revolves around William Clark's country estate Minoma outside St. Louis. On the property, convenient for hosting large Indian delegations and useful as a retreat from the city, Clark had a colonial-style farmhouse built, which, by the terms of his will, his son Jefferson Kearny Clark inherited. In 1856 Jefferson K. Clark built an Italianate-style mansion near the old farmhouse. A prominent feature of the new Minoma was a square observation tower. In the tower and other rooms of the house were displayed and stored Clark family collections and papers, among which were reported to be artifacts from the Lewis and Clark Expedition. In 1891 Clark and his wife moved to New York City, apparently taking only some of the material with them. That they retained only some of the material would seem to be verified by what is included in the Clark collection at Missouri Historical. There undoubtedly were more manuscripts and artifacts than the society received, and this is especially true for the papers. What about the material left at Minoma? After Clark sold Minoma, it passed through a succession of owners, gradually falling into disrepair. In the 1930s the elderly woman who owned the house grew tired of all the "junk" on the second floor and hired a young couple in the neighborhood to clean it out. They agreed, and for ten dollars they spent one day throwing trunkfuls of old papers, letters, books, clothes, uniforms, furniture, guns, china, and other things out the windows into the back yard. The next day they returned and burned all the material. In thinking back on what they did some sixty years ago, the couple said they believed that all that old "junk" was actually valuable his-

torical material that the Clarks had left behind. If this story is true, which is very possible, it is likely that not only Jonathan's letters to William went up in flames but also priceless historical papers and artifacts. Included in this may have been Meriwether Lewis's 1809 letter to Clark written at New Madrid and other letters written to Clark concerning the death of his good friend, as well as Lewis and Clark Expedition manuscripts and artifacts. Both fires are explanations for gaps in Clark family papers. Minoma itself died a slow death from neglect. By the 1940s an elderly woman, perhaps the same one who had it cleaned out, was using the mansion as a boardinghouse. By the 1950s it was vacant. Neighborhood children used to play in its dusty, cobweb-shrouded interior. In 1960 it was destroyed to make room for suburban development. If this was indeed the fate of the historically priceless collections left in Minoma, and I believe it is a creditable and very likely possibility, it stands as an abject example of what can happen— and has happened countless times—through neglect and ignorance. (Dorman (1), 29; Clark to Clark, 18 June 1792, WCP-VMC; Mimi Jackson to Holmberg, August 1996 conversation and 24 September 1997 letter; *West End Word* (St. Louis), 15 November 1984.)

19. Either Adamson (or Adam) Tannehill (1750–1817) or his brother Josiah Tannehill (1753–1811), who were, respectively, natives of Frederick County and Montgomery County, Maryland. During the Revolutionary War both served as officers in the Continental Army: Adamson in Maryland regiments, rising to the rank of captain, and Josiah in the 9th and later 7th Virginia, attaining the rank of lieutenant. After the war both settled in Pittsburgh and operated a tavern. Adamson married a woman named Agnes and died in Pittsburgh. Josiah married first Nancy Heath, and second Margaret Wilkins in 1786. He later resided in Lexington, Kentucky, and died in Baton Rouge, Louisiana, in 1811. He is referred to as Captain Tannehill in his wife's 1839 obituary. The question of whether Clark is referring to Josiah or Adamson Tannehill depends on the rank held by the men in 1792. If they had not advanced in rank through militia commissions, Adamson Tannehill would seem to be indicated. In 1812 he would be commissioned brigadier general of Pennsylvania militia. Margaret Tannehill's obituary indicates that Josiah achieved the rank of captain at some point. As rank-conscious as people, especially military people, were, Clark most likely would have referred to the man by his current military title, which rank Adamson definitely had in 1792 and which Josiah might have had by that time. (Heitman (1), 532; Tannehill, 44–46; White, 3:3418.)

20. The area where the Monongahela and Allegheny Rivers converge to

form the Ohio was historically significant before Pittsburgh was founded. It was of strategic military importance and was contended over by the British and French in the French and Indian War. A force of provincial troops under George Washington had begun a fortification there in 1754, but was forced to abandon it by a superior French force. The French named the fortification Fort Duquesne. It was abandoned in November 1758 at the approach of a British army and was renamed Fort Pitt, after the British prime minister William Pitt. The settlement that had grown up outside the fort was named Pittsburgh. Pittsburgh was a major western post and town during its frontier period. It was from Pittsburgh that Meriwether Lewis headed down the Ohio with the keelboat to meet Clark at the Falls of the Ohio. (Work Projects Administration, 295–98.)

21. The northwest side of the Ohio River refers to land in the present state of Ohio. Jonathan Clark was granted one tract of land and purchased a number more in present Ohio. William assisted him with some of this activity. The lead mine mentioned may refer to a tract of land twenty miles up the Kentucky River from the Ohio in present Henry County, Kentucky, at Drennon's Lick or Spring that supposedly contained not only a lead mine, but also a silver mine. Jonathan had been interested in this tract in the latter 1780s and apparently was still trying to ascertain its value—if not the mine's existence—in 1792. The reference may also indicate that Jonathan wanted any tract of land that had a lead mine on it. (Jonathan Clark to George Rogers Clark, 9 March 1787, and John Crittenden to George Rogers Clark, 27 April 1787, George Rogers Clark Papers, Draper Manuscripts [hereafter cited as Draper Mss.], 53J66, 70, State Historical Society of Wisconsin, Madison, Wisconsin.)

∼

Baltimore[1] Octr. 4th 1798

Dear Brother

You Will no doubt be Surprised to here from me at this place I have been here only four days, from New Orleans[2] to which place I went with a Small Adventure of Tobacco[3] — and wate here for a letter on business from Trenton which I expect by to-morrows male,[4] if So then next morning I will Set out to Fredricksburgh[5] in the Stage, and expect to have the pleasure of Seeing you at your house on Tuesday next.

Our friends were well in Kentucky not long since, I heard from them by a merchant in this place — as I expect to See you in a few day Shall not enter into a detale of acurnances but request you to present me most respectably to my friends & c. Yr. obt. [obedient] oft. [affectionate] Brother

Wm Clark

1. Baltimore, Maryland, was one of the major cities and Atlantic seaports of the day. Established in 1729 along both sides of the Patapsco River near the northern end of Chesapeake Bay, it was named in honor of the Baltimore (or Calvert) family, founders of the colony of Maryland. Baltimore was one of the major sources of goods for Kentucky and other western merchants. (Hall, 9–70.)
2. Founded in 1718 by the French, New Orleans was the major port for the Gulf Coast and the important Mississippi River trade for the western United States at that time. Farmers and merchants from Kentucky and other western areas relied on the Ohio and Mississippi Rivers as the means to transport their goods. While under Spanish ownership and control, the port and river would periodically be closed to Americans. The American desire to settle this problem provided the impetus for the Louisiana Purchase. (Fortier, 7–37.)
3. Clark had left Louisville 9 March 1798 with a shipment of tobacco for the New Orleans market. He commanded a little flotilla of at least two boats and maybe more which arrived in New Orleans on 24 April. This was Clark's second trip to the city. His first visit was in 1790. After selling his shipment of tobacco he made a trip back upriver to Natchez with horses to sell to the U.S. Army posted there. He then returned to New Orleans by pirogue, arriving there on 16 July, and the next day sailed on the *Star* for Philadelphia. Because of a yellow fever outbreak in Philadelphia the ship put in instead at New Castle, Delaware, on 24 September. Two days later Clark took the stage to Baltimore. (William Clark Memorandum Book, 1798–1801, Breckenridge Collection, State Historical Society of Missouri, Columbia, Mo.)
4. The letter Clark was expecting arrived on 6 October rather than the expected 5th. He left Baltimore on Monday, 9 October, by the first stage traveling southward. He reached Washington, D.C., that same day; Fredericksburg, Virginia, on 11 October; brother Edmund's on 13 October; and brother Jonathan's on 14 October. Jonathan was "over the ridge" (west of the Blue Ridge in the Shenandoah Valley in the Winchester area) when he arrived but returned home on 24 October. William stayed in the area until 11 November, when he set out for Ken-

tucky. He returned home through Virginia, present West Virginia, and Ohio, and on 24 December arrived at Mulberry Hill, the day his mother died. (William Clark Memorandum Book, 1798–1801; Jonathan Clark Diary, 1770–1811, Jonathan Clark Papers, Clark-Hite Collection [hereafter cited as JCP-CHC], TFHS; Dorman (1), 25.)

5. Fredericksburg, in Spotsylvania County, was the major town in that area of Virginia, an important commercial and social center. Located on the south bank of the Rappahannock River, it was officially established in 1727, although colonists already had been living in the area for some fifty years and a settlement that apparently became Fredericksburg (and may have been called that) had been founded about 1680. It was named for King George II's son Frederick, the Prince of Wales. Its tobacco inspection warehouse served as an additional focal point for the area's farmers. Jonathan lived in the southeast corner of Spotsylvania County and visited the town often. The John Clark family lived in Caroline County, just over the line from Spotsylvania, and William visited the town in his youth. Whenever he returned to the area after the family moved to Kentucky, he generally visited family and friends in the vicinity. (Quinn, 37–53; Goolrick, 17–25.)

∽

Mulberry Hill[1] 13th Augt. 1801 -
Dear Brother
I returned day before yesterday, at Cincinnati[2] I obtained from Judge Symmes[3] a Citation and a Supercedeus [supersedeas] to Stop the execution [regarding a legal case; see note 3] which has been issued about two weeks ago. Mr. Sam Gwathmey[4] set out last evening to Vincennes with the papers_ I did not go Comeby George Town[5] & relyed on my influence with the Judces [judges] to obtain my purpes which luckerly has been effected   I came by J. McDonalds[6] he was not at home, and the Ohio was So low I could not get mill Irons down __ I am fearfull nature intended me for the Sport of fortune, and appearencus appear to justify aprehentions __ I never went from home any time, but before I returned was informed of Some loss or misfortune __ The other day on my return [I] found my mill burnt to ashes and in it all me Leather ₐall the mill wrights Tools[ₐ] most of [the] Tools belonging to the plantation, mill saws [and] Stones intirely distroyed, with Several Hundred

Mulberry Hill, Clark family house near Louisville. The estate was the home of William and George Rogers Clark and York from 1785 to 1803. Courtesy of The Filson Historical Society

bushels of grain[7] ___ This is a verry Serious Stroke to me I do assure you ___ we are at Some loss to guess the cause of the moliscous [malicious] act, or in what manner the fire Could have got on the 3d flore without hands, no fire was near the place for Several days previous___ my wheat & Corn is tolerable good, the froot has declined & droped, except a fiew apples ___ Sinc Seting down to Write this letter the excution of W. Bell[8] was served on my bro: it is put off for the present

I have enquired & find it not necessary to record any thin in the NW Territory except Conveyances ___ Some lands have been Sold for Tax due for last year, and Taxes are due on the lands in that Territory for this year with 6 PCent from august & if not paid by the first monday in november to be Sold, or So much off the beginning Corner as will pay the Tax.

Taxes for 1800 1st rate 85 Cents 2d = 60 Cents & 3d = 25 Cents

Taxes for 1801 1 do 55 ___ 2 = 35 ___ 3d = 17 Cents pr. Hundred acres, Majr. Hites[9] lands is advertised   I expected he had impowered Some person to attend to his lands ___ I Shall mention them to Mr. Booth[10] on his return from the Wilderness. Mr. Clark[11] returned & did not do your business for me on green river[12] he depended on Mr. Booth, I will attend to this business ~~of~~ my Self if Mr. Booth does not go foword Shortly to that Countrey   Our friends are all well except two of my nephews John & Charles[13]

please to present my Compliments to Sister Bro Edmund[14] Miss Ellen[15] & the famly

and beleve me to be yr. oft [affectionate]
Bro W Clark

1. Mulberry Hill was the name of the Clark family home in Jefferson County, Kentucky. Now within the city limits of Louisville, at that time it was about three miles southeast of town on the South Fork of Beargrass Creek. John Clark purchased the 256-acre tract from the heirs of George Meriwether (a relative of Meriwether Lewis) on 29 August 1785. The Clarks already were living on the property, so apparently an agreement had been made prior to the actual sale. Additional land was added to the tract so that it totaled 318 acres. The estate was initially christened Ampthill, possibly in honor of the Chesterfield County, Virginia, home of the same name owned at that time by the Temple family, Clark friends and relatives. At some point, probably within several years, John Clark changed its name. Information indicates it was chris-

tened Mulberry Hill because of the presence of those trees on the Poplar Level, as the area was called. One story states that Clark slaves from Virginia used mulberry logs to build the house under the supervision of Jonathan and George Rogers Clark in 1784 in preparation for the family's move there. The house might originally have been one-story, but by 1799 it was a two-story log cabin measuring forty feet by twenty feet, facing northwestward toward Louisville. The kitchen was a detached one-story log structure. There were also other structures, such as slave cabins and a grist mill. John Clark willed the property to William in 1799, and William deeded part of it (a portion containing the house but not the mill) to Jonathan on 2 May 1803. The house stood until about 1900, when neglect caused it to partially collapse. It, along with its dependencies, was completely razed when the property became part of Camp Zachary Taylor in 1917. Today the site of Mulberry Hill is in George Rogers Clark Park. The family cemetery, where John and Ann Clark are buried, is there, but other family members, such as Jonathan Clark, have been reinterred in Cave Hill Cemetery. Also see note 7. (*EL*, 634–35; Ellison; Jefferson Co., Ky., Deed Books [hereafter cited as JCDB], 1:148–49, 6:431; Draper Mss., 2L22–23; Sale, 333–41; Jefferson Co., Ky., Will Books [hereafter cited as JCWB], 1:86; William Clark 1799 Tax Document, WCP-VMC.)

2. Cincinnati was founded in 1788 by John Filson, Robert Patterson, and Matthias Denham. Filson originally named the future town Losantiville (Latin, Greek, and French words combined for "city opposite the mouth") because it was opposite the mouth of the Licking River. Fort Washington was established adjacent to the small settlement in 1789, and the fort's presence, in addition to the location, allowed the town to thrive. In 1790 it was renamed Cincinnati at the request of the Northwest Territory governor, Arthur St. Clair, in honor of the Society of the Cincinnati, the Revolutionary War officers' organization founded in 1783. (Jonathan and Edmund Clark, Richard Clough Anderson, William Croghan, and other Clark relatives were original members of the society.) Clark visited Cincinnati any number of times, especially while stationed at Fort Washington. Meriwether Lewis stayed in Cincinnati for about one week in late September–early October 1803 while descending the Ohio, and undoubtedly had visited it during his army duty in that area. (Leonard, 1:31–109; Metcalf, 34, 85, 97; Jackson (1), 1:124–31.)

3. John Cleves Symmes (1742–1814) was proprietor of the million-acre tract of land between the Great Miami and Little Miami Rivers known as the Miami Purchase. His colony formed a major area of white settlement in what became the state of Ohio. He was a native of Long Island,

New York, moved to New Jersey in 1770, settled on his Ohio property in 1788, and died in Cincinnati. He was a Revolutionary War veteran, New Jersey legislator and official, and a judge for the Northwest Territory. His daughter Anna married William Henry Harrison. Symmes apparently was the judge in a case before the Northwest Territory courts concerning George Rogers Clark and a claim a Vincennes merchant named Laurent Bazedone had against him dating from the 1780s. William and Jonathan were assisting their brother. (*DAB*, 18:258–59; Short family file, TFHS.)

4. Samuel Gwathmey (ca.1778–1850) was Clark's nephew, son of Owen and Ann Clark Gwathmey. A native of Virginia, he moved to Louisville about 1797, and by 1802 he had settled across the river in Clark County, Indiana Territory. Gwathmey served as a county, state, and federal official, and was instrumental in laying out Jeffersonville, Indiana, in 1802. He served as register of the U.S. land office in Jeffersonville from 1807 to 1829, when he was removed for political reasons. He then moved to Louisville and was involved in business, banking, and insurance. On 17 December 1807 he married Mary Booth, daughter of Sarah Hite Clark's sister Rebecca and her husband William A. Booth. The Gwathmeys and Booths became very interrelated. Three Gwathmey siblings married three Booth siblings. Two other Gwathmey siblings married their Anderson first cousins (not uncommon at that time), children of William's sister Elizabeth Clark and Richard Clough Anderson. In addition, Gwathmey sibling Temple married Ann Meriwether Marks, a Meriwether Lewis relative. Clark and Samuel Gwathmey were about eight years apart in age, and, perhaps for that reason, Clark referred to Gwathmey as a cousin at times, but he was his nephew. (Gwathmey family file, TFHS; Rogers Index.)

5. Georgetown, District of Columbia. Clark had gone to Virginia, the District of Columbia, and Baltimore on business and to visit family. He passed through Georgetown on his way to Washington but apparently took another route on his return trip. The legal matters mentioned refer to George Rogers Clark's suit with Laurent (or Laurence) Bazedone of Vincennes regarding goods ordered seized by Clark in 1786 during a campaign against the Indians. (Correspondence, 1801, WCP-VMC; William Clark Memorandum Book, 1798–1801.)

6. Possibly Dr. John McDonald, who married Sarah Hite Clark's sister Mary (b. 1748), but most likely James McDonald (d. 1810) who lived in Frederick County, Virginia, where the Hites lived. He was in partnership with Charles M. Thruston in a mercantile firm in Louisville (McDonald remaining in Virginia and serving as a buyer of merchandise) in the 1790s. He moved to Jefferson County between 1803 and

1810, living at Fair Hope on Beargrass Creek, a farm purchased from Buckner Thruston. (Jefferson Co., Ky., Court Minute Books [hereafter cited as JCCMB], 9:158–59; JCDB, 6:482–84; Wm. Johnson's admin. v. Wm. Clark, admin., 1800, Jefferson Co., Ky., Chancery Court, case no. 300, Kentucky Department for Libraries and Archives [hereafter cited as KDLA], Frankfort, Ky.)

7. The Ohio River being too low for Clark to ship mill irons downstream was a recurring problem in late summer and early fall. (The low water also presented a particular difficulty for Meriwether Lewis's voyage down the river at this season two years later.) The mill was on the South Fork of Beargrass Creek on the Mulberry Hill tract, and was built by John Clark. It was primarily a gristmill, but given what Clark mentions regarding mill saws, it also must have been used upon occasion as a sawmill. He apparently rebuilt the mill, as indicated by later letters to Jonathan printed here and by newspaper advertisements. On 12 August 1802 William began advertising the mill for sale. On 2 May 1803 he sold his brother Edmund a 111-acre tract that included the mill, the same day he sold brother Jonathan a 232-acre tract containing the house. (I have not determined how the 318-acre Mulberry Hill tract became 343 on being sold, but assume that the discrepancy was explainable at the time.) On 2 September 1803 Edmund Clark contracted with Anthony Arnold to work for him on a sawmill he was erecting on the South Fork of Beargrass. William Clark witnessed the agreement. The 26 June 1815 issue of the *Western Courier* advertised the deceased Edmund Clark's 111-acre tract containing a gristmill and sawmill for sale. In addition to the mill information William gives, he provides interesting agricultural information about his growing corn and wheat and having an orchard. (*The Farmer's Library* (Louisville), 12 August 1802; JCDB, 6:431–34; Edmund Clark Papers, TFHS; *Western Courier* (Louisville), 26 June 1815.)

8. W. Bell has not been identified. He and George Rogers Clark apparently were involved in a legal dispute. There was a William Bell living in Jefferson County at this time, but no evidence was found linking him to George Rogers Clark and a lawsuit.

9. Major Isaac Hite (1758–1836), who was the brother of Jonathan's wife Sarah, lived at Belle Grove near Middletown, Frederick County, Virginia. He had studied at William and Mary and served as an officer in the 8th Virginia Regiment late in the Revolutionary War. His first wife was Nelly Conway Madison (1760–1802), sister of James Madison. His second wife was Ann Tunstall Maury (1752–1851). This reference is probably to land in Ohio for which Hite had not paid the taxes. (Wayland, 14–17; Heitman (1), 292; Hite family file, TFHS.)

10. William Aylett Booth (1754–1820) was a native of Gloucester County, Virginia. He served as a burgess from Frederick County in 1779 and as an officer in the Revolutionary War, during which he rose to the rank of lieutenant colonel, fought at Cowpens, and was wounded at Yorktown. He did not move to Kentucky from Shenandoah County, Virginia, until 1804 but before that date spent much time in Kentucky regarding land business. Sources differ, but he apparently lived in the Louisville area. As stated in note 4 he was married to Sarah Hite Clark's sister Rebecca (1754–1815), and three of their children married three Gwathmey siblings. (Rogers Index; Booth family file, TFHS; Gwathmey family file; Hite family file; Franklin, 24; Stubbs, 250–51.)

11. Probably Marston Green Clark (1771–1846), son of Benjamin Clark (1730–1806), and William's first cousin. He was a native of Lunenburg County, Virginia, who moved west to Vincennes about 1786 and spent most of the rest of his life in Indiana. Active in business, the militia, and government, he served for many years in the Indiana legislature and from 1829 to 1835 as an Indian agent and subagent on the Kansas River. He married Lucy Green Harper in 1802. Sources provided conflicting information (as with many persons). The Marston Clark family bible was used as the source for his birth and marriage dates and the spelling of his middle name. (Clark family file; *Biographical Directory of the Indiana General Assembly* [hereafter cited as *BDIGA*], 1:64–65.)

12. Flowing in a westward-to-northwestward course through south-central and western Kentucky to its confluence with the Ohio, the Green is one of Kentucky's major rivers. Its surrounding country was actively claimed as early as the 1780s, and the land south of the river was reserved for grants to Revolutionary War veterans. Marston Clark was supposed to take care of some land-related business for his cousins in the Green River country but did not.

13. John O'Fallon (1791–1865) and Charles W. Thruston (1796–1865) were both sons of William's sister Frances "Fanny" Clark O'Fallon Thruston Fitzhugh. Both boys, but especially John, were close to their Uncle William. He assisted with their education and served as something of a surrogate father (again especially for John); so much so, that in an 1808 letter to John, William refers to him and his other nephews as his "sons." William's first child was not born until 1809. O'Fallon received a commission in the regular army and served in the War of 1812. Frustrated by the lack of advancement, he resigned in 1818 and settled in St. Louis, where he became a very successful businessman and leading citizen. It was on his farm, named Athlone, that William and other Clarks were first buried. Charles Thruston's original middle name was Mynn, as had been his father's and grandfather's, but he

changed it to William to avoid confusion with a cousin of the same name, choosing William apparently in honor of his Uncle William. His father was killed by one of his slaves at his plantation near Westport, Kentucky, upriver from Louisville, on 8 December 1800. Thruston was a businessman and lawyer in Louisville and served in the state legislature in 1824, 1832, and 1844. He married Mary Eliza Churchill (1804–1842) in 1824. His first cousin, William Clark's eldest child Meriwether Lewis Clark (1809–1881), married Mary Eliza's sister, Abigail Prather Churchill (1817–1852). (Scharf, 1:344–54; Clark family file; Rogers Index; Thruston family file, TFHS; John O'Fallon Papers, TFHS; John O'Fallon Collection, MHS; Todhunter, 2:548–49.)

14. Edmund Clark (1762–1815) was the fourth son of John and Ann Rogers Clark. He served as an ensign in the 6th Virginia, and as a lieutenant in the 8th and 1st Virginia regiments during the Revolution, and, like his brother Jonathan, was taken prisoner at Charleston, South Carolina, on 12 May 1780. There is some confusion about his service in the 6th and 8th Virginia, but he did serve in the 1st from his apparent exchange in 1781 until the end of the war. He again served several years in the army in the late 1790s as a captain in the 7th U.S. Infantry when war with France threatened. He was a merchant and mill owner in several towns in Virginia and moved to Kentucky at about the same time Jonathan did in 1802. Except for a brief residence in western Kentucky on a plantation on the Ohio some five miles below the mouth of Highland Creek (in present Union County, nearly opposite the mouth of the Wabash River) in 1807–1808, he lived in Louisville, where he was a merchant and served as a trustee and clerk of the town. He also lived on the Mulberry Hill tract, where he farmed and operated a gristmill and sawmill. He is credited with preserving Louisville's early records. Like his brother George, he never married. (Dorman (1), 26; Heitman (1), 156; Gwathmey, 153; *EL*, 635; Bodley Family Papers, TFHS; Edmund Clark Papers, TFHS; Jonathan Clark Papers, Draper Mss., 2L16.)

15. Eleanor Eltinge "Nelly" Clark (1783–1867) was the daughter and oldest child of Jonathan and Sarah Hite Clark. She married Benjamin Temple (1776–1838) in 1801. He joined the Methodist church ca. 1817, and served as a lay minister and ordained deacon from about 1826 until his death. He probably belonged to the Episcopal church before joining the Methodist church, but it seems rather doubtful that he was an Episcopal minister, as some sources state. They moved to Kentucky with Jonathan, settling first in Jefferson County and by 1808 near Russellville, Logan County, Kentucky. (Dorman (1), 28; *Western Christian Advocate* (Cincinnati), 4 May 1838.)

~

Louisville[1] the 13th of Octr. 1801

D Brother

   I have Drawn on you in favor of Mr. Peter Benson Ormsby[2] /or Order/ Bills of Exchange to the amount of Two Thousand Dollars / in three numbers, and three ˄four[˄] Bills in each number for 500$ — which Sum I have of him in Cash, and appropriated the Same in dischargeing the first payment of a purchase of 410 acres & 64 perches of Land made of Allen Campbell,[3] for and in your behalf — The one half of the Said purchase money will be discharged at this payment the balence amounting to 1880 & 2/3 Dollars is to be Discharged on the 25th of December 1802 as pr. my Bond.

I am D Bro With great Friendship yrs.
William Clark

1. Founded at the Falls of the Ohio by William's brother George Rogers Clark in 1778, Louisville was chartered in 1780 and officially named (it was already being called Louisville) in honor of King Louis XVI of France in recognition of the Franco-American alliance of 1778. Because of its location, Louisville became of major importance on the Ohio and in the West. At this time it was the largest far western town on the Ohio and a major frontier town. (*EL,* xv–xvi; Yater (1), 1–33.)
2. Peter Benson Ormsby (1766–1830) was a prominent, wealthy Louisville businessman. He was a native of Ireland and moved to Louisville in 1797. His brother Stephen Ormsby (1757–1830) was Kentucky's first federal judge. (Pierce, 1–3; *HOFC,* 1:209.)
3. Allan Campbell (d. 1804) was a native of Ireland and the half brother of John Campbell (ca. 1735–1799), a land speculator and prominent local citizen and state official, who owned much of the land on which Louisville was established. John never married, and Allan, who was considerably younger (still being a minor in 1786 when John wrote his will), inherited much of his land. Allan apparently moved to Louisville in 1800 from the Lexington area, to which John had moved in about 1795. He was a partner in the firm of Lowman, Ormsby and Campbell (the Ormsby being Peter; see note 2), which operated a rope-walk, selling cordage and buying hemp and tar. He may be the Allan Campbell who was commissioned a second lieutenant of cavalry in the 1st Regiment of Jefferson County militia on 5 January 1804. He never married and apparently died in Louisville. He spelled his name Allan, but it often appears

Portrait of General George Rogers Clark by Matthew H. Jouett, ca. 1825.
Painted after a posthumous portrait of Clark by John Wesley Jarvis, ca. 1820,
it depicts the "Hannibal of the West" as he may have appeared in his forties.
Courtesy of The Filson Historical Society

as Allen. Clark bought the 410 acres mentioned the day he wrote this
letter on behalf of Jonathan. The tract was on the South Fork of Beargrass east of Mulberry Hill and made up part of Jonathan's Trough
Spring plantation. A "perch" of land equals a rod, and is measured ei-
ther in linear ($5\frac{1}{2}$ yards or $16\frac{1}{2}$ feet) or square ($30\frac{1}{4}$ square rods) form. An
acre equals 160 square rods or perches. A perch also can refer to

stonework. (*KE*, 154–55; *The Farmers Library*, 4 November 1802; JCDB, 6:59–60; Allan Campbell deed, 17 March 1801, Sullivan-Gates Family Papers, TFHS; Jefferson Co., Ky., Inventory and Settlement Books, [hereafter cited as JCISB], 3:99–102; Campbell's heirs v. Rowan's heirs, Louisville Chancery Court Records, case no. 24514, KDLA.)

~

Redstone Landing[1]

Dear Brother   Wednesday the 4th Feby. 1802

We arrived at this place late last evening all in the most perfect health & Spearts. I had precured a worm [warm] room for the ₐblack[ₐ] people to dry their Cloaths &c. I have purchased a Boat, and laid in all my Stores for the voyage down, the boat will be finished at 12 oClock, and we Shall Set out about two this evening. I have given a high price for a Boat with a view of takin the advantage of the water, now high, but falling fast   the Boat will cost $40 which is 10 higher than I could get one for, by Delaying here a few days — The cost of your people to this place has been much higher than I expected owing to the horrid State of the Road rains & high water which obliged me to feed high & give Whiskey frequently as absolutely necessary The cost 22$ & 25 cents to this place, I have purchased at this place 4 axes 42/–, a pan 9/–, a coat & c. for Gilbert[2] 22/–, a Drawg. Knife 4/–, Tools for Frank[3] 9/–, auger, Bacon @ 6½, a Pott 7/6, Two Bars of Iron at 5½ this pr Pound and Several other Small articles, I mention those articles that you may Know what your people has on hand, ——I have had but little Trouble with the negrows & Should have had none atall had Easter[4] prefured her Husband to Frank, we have had but fiew accedenc on the way not worth relateing, ~~the~~   our rout & Stages were from Majr. Hites they advancd a few miles on Tuesday   on Wednesday to Pue Town 25 miles, next day to the forks of the Roads 20 miles, Friday to the South branch, rained the forepart of the day 17 miles, ~~wednesday~~ [ₐ]Saturday[ₐ] to gwins [possibly Givens] at the foot of the Alleganey 20 miles, The North branch verry high, Sundy. to little Copin 19 miles verry bad road, Monday to the Big Copin 17 miles rains all day bad roads, Tuesday To foot of the Lorrell Hill, at a little Town Called Woodstock a miserable place Cold & Snow all day made 21 miles. I pushd to day to get over the mountain before the Snow got too deep, Wednesday a Cold day the roads verry muddy to this place[5]

— This day is the Coldest I have felt this two winters —— I had like to have forgot to tell you, Mr. T_ ⁶ horse was near dieing the night I left Majr. Hites, we were Obliged to Set up & nerss him the greater part of the night, he is now verry well. If you Should not find it Convenient to Send foward to this place to precure Boats &c. on your way out, Mr. Jacob Bowman⁷ Merchent of this place well do any thing for you in that way by your writing to him. I will write you again fron Louis ville, at which place I hope to receve a letter fron you, giving an account of your Speedy recovery.⁸ My Compliments to Sister Clark Bro: Edmund & the famly   and I am most effectunately Yr. Brother

W Clark

[On address leaf]
Mr. Green will please to
Faward this letter to Chiles's Store.

1. Redstone Landing was also known by the earlier name of Redstone Old Fort. The site was occupied first by an early Indian fortification and then by a colonial stockade before the town was officially founded in 1785. Located on the Monongahela River south of Pittsburgh, Redstone Landing was a major jumping-off point for thousands of settlers moving west down the Ohio River, either going by water to Pittsburgh or traveling overland to Wheeling, due west from Redstone Landing, and embarking on the Ohio there. The Clarks spent the winter of 1784–1785 at Redstone during their move to Kentucky. The town's name was later changed to Brownsville after its founders Thomas and Basil Brown. (Work Projects Administration, 598.)
2. Gilbert was one of Jonathan Clark's slaves. William was moving many of Jonathan's slaves and household effects to Kentucky ahead of the rest of the family. They left Jonathan's place in southeastern Spotsylvania County on 19 January and arrived in Jefferson County on 23 February. The 1803 Jefferson County tax list shows that Jonathan was taxed for thirty-nine slaves, twenty of whom were over the age of sixteen. Therefore, Clark was moving approximately thirty to thirty-five slaves, assuming that Jonathan kept some with him in Virginia until he and his family moved a few months later. The Gilbert mentioned most likely is one of two Gilberts owned by Jonathan at the time of his death. An unsigned bill of sale in the Edmund Clark papers states that Jonathan purchased a Gilbert from Daniel Johnson of Caroline County, Virginia, on 20 January 1802, for £136 and that the said Gilbert had al-

ready been delivered to Jonathan (therefore making it possible for him to be the Gilbert with the party going to Kentucky). In the inventory of Jonathan's estate done in December 1811, two Gilberts—Gilbert the Elder and Gilbert the Younger—are listed. The elder Gilbert was married to Hannah the Elder, and she had two children, Alice (or Alsey) and Maria (or Mariah). It is not known whether Gilbert the Elder was the father of Alice and Maria. Because of its nature, slavery was a matrilineal society, and children generally were associated with their mother rather than their father; the phrase "her children" is much more frequently seen than "their children." Children sometimes were associated with their father also, but much less often. The Gilbert-Hannah family group was allotted to Eleanor Clark Temple as part of her inheritance. If they joined the Temple household they would have been taken to Logan County, Kentucky. Gilbert the Younger was inherited by Isaac Clark, who lived at Mulberry Hill. It is possible that he was a son of the elder Gilbert and Hannah, but no mention is made that he was. The 1811 inventory/appraisal lists him as a "young boy." It does not seem likely that he was the son of William Clark's slaves Ben and Venos (also spelled Venus or Venice, but William spells her name Venos so that has been used). In the genealogical notes of Meriwether Lewis Clark, written in 1853, a Gilbert is listed as a slave of William Clark and the son of Uncle Ben and Aunt Venos, longtime Clark family slaves; yet no Gilbert is listed as part of John Clark's estate in 1799. This Gilbert apparently was born after 1799 and either moved to St. Louis in 1808 with his parents when William moved his household there, or was born there. Did William acquire the young Gilbert from Isaac? Or is the Gilbert that M. Lewis Clark remembers a different Gilbert? It is very unlikely that the elder Gilbert was the son of Ben and Venos. He was definitely an adult with his own family, and the ties to William's Ben and Venos seem questionable. It also is doubtful that Gilbert the Younger was Venos's child given the known facts. If the Gilbert mentioned in this letter is the Gilbert in the 1802 document (and I think it may be), Jonathan may have been trying to reunite him and Hannah before moving to Kentucky. It may also be the case that Gilbert and Hannah married after his 1802 acquisition. The purchase of a coat for him might indicate that he had only recently been acquired and was not fully outfitted for a winter journey. As much information as possible will be provided on the African Americans mentioned. Again, because of the nature of the institution and the paucity of documentary information often resulting, generally very little is known about individual slaves. To further confuse things, the Clarks sometimes owned more than one slave (male and female) with the same name. The Gilberts discussed here are a good example. In addition to them, Jonathan Clark's estate inventory lists two Hannahs, three Bettys, two Franks, and two Easters. (John Clark also owned an Easter, who was left to John and Benjamin O'Fallon and William Clark.) Although the latitude allowed slaves in naming their children varied from owner to owner, it was one privilege often granted them. The use of one name for a second and even third time indicates that slaves were allowed that right and probably shows their attempt to identify family connections. (Edmund Clark Papers; JCISB, 3:3, 12–13; Meriwether Lewis Clark family record [hereafter cited as MLClark], 90, TFHS; Jefferson Co., Ky., Bond and Power of Attorney Books [hereafter cited as JCBPAB], 2:56.)

3. Another of Jonathan's slaves. Frank is listed in Jonathan's 1811 estate inventory/appraisal. He is not listed as being married, but it is possible that he was and that his wife was owned by someone else. Jonathan's widow Sarah received Frank as part of the estate division following Jonathan's death, he having died intestate. No will or estate inventory was found for Sarah Clark after her death in 1818, and nothing was found in the Clark-Hite Collection that would provide more information on Frank. (JCISB, 3:3, 12.)

4. Easter appears on Jonathan's 1811 estate inventory/appraisal. It is believed she is the Easter listed as being blind in one eye. Her husband was a slave of Jonathan Clark's named James, and I assume that he is the husband mentioned by William. In 1811 she had at least four children: Sally, Rocksey, Frank, and Charles. Jonathan's son William inherited this family, as well as the other slave named Easter (possibly Esther) as part of the estate settlement. (JCISB, 3:3, 13.)

5. The general route would have been from Jonathan's in Spotsylvania County, Virginia, northwestward to Middletown (where Isaac Hite lived), Winchester (generally following the present US 17), into present West Virginia to Forks-of-Cacapon, Springfield, the north branch of the Potomac near Cumberland, Maryland (generally following the present West Virginia 127 and 28), to present Brownsville, Pennsylvania (the present US 40). Old maps of the area list some of the landmarks Clark mentions, as do current maps. Between Cumberland and Brownsville he followed part of Braddock's old road, and what would become the National Road. His reference to little Copin and Big Copin apparently refers to Little Crossing and Great Crossing, the latter being the ford across the Youghiogheny River. Jonathan basically followed this same route when he and his immediate family moved to Kentucky later that year. (Map Collection, TFHS; Jonathan Clark Diary, May–July 1802.)

6. Benjamin Temple (see letter of 13 August 1801, note 15).

7. Jacob Bowman (ca. 1763–1847) was a native of Hagerstown, Mary-

land. He settled at Redstone Landing (Brownsville) in 1787 and was one of the principal merchants there until his death. (Draper Mss., 26CC42 and 3Q34.)

8. Jonathan had recorded being unwell much of the time since September 1801. By the time William set off for Kentucky with the slaves on 19 January Jonathan seems to have recovered; at least he does not note being sick in his diary after 2 January. Perhaps he voiced fear of a relapse to William. (Jonathan Clark Diary, September 1801–March 1802.)

~

Mulberry Hill March 2nd 1802

Dear Brother

We arrived at Louisville last tuesday,[1] all in perfect helth and Spirits and found all friends well, my mill as usial brook tho not bad _. Mr. Temples Horse is dead I do assure you it was not from any want of attention or care on my part, but unavoidable cause, he appeared to be in purfect helth untill the monit we landed at gooscreek,[2] all at once he apd. verry Sick, he was taken out of the Boat with great Care and Sent to Majr. Croghans[3] where we attended him untill next morning 8 oClock when he died, his maw was eaten through & contained great numbers of worms, please to explain this to Mr. Temple, as I have not time to write to him _. The tenant has not yet moved off your land, I expect he will in a fiew days [∧]at[∧] which [∧]time[∧] I shall begin your house,[4] bro: George has fixed on a Spot in the Clearing, which is thought greatly preferable to the One at the Spring I mentioned to you near Capt. Sullivans,[5] _. It It is Said here that Mr. Anderson[6] has Swoped his land with ∧ G[∧] Southall[7] for the part adjoining yours _ Southalls is to be out this month. Capt. Hite[8] has given a Connection with an explanation of Mr. J Williams[9] land on Goosecreek which I enclose to you, the land on the North end the part purchased by ∧N.[∧] Long[10] is good land Clear of Dispute as you will See by the Connection and is worth the money you was to give _. J Smith[11] has not filed his bill yet, I Shall go up Shortly & will examine further into the thing —— Col Armstrong[12] has Soled all the rent Corn at Miamis[13] (except what is Old and nearly Spoiled) on Credit What remains is not worth takeing away _ my neighbour and friend Col. Thruston[14] died two days before I got home, he had derected his place to be Sold for a Certain price, which price I am told is high —. Mr. Provines[15] Offers Mr. Robertsons[16] place for 4½$ pr. acre, and If I take 1000 acres for 3 $ pr. acre a Curious method to Sell for 3 or 400 acres he asks 27/– and if 1000 is taken the balance will not amount to more than two dollars. I Shall not purchase this place of Mr. Robertsons untill I hear from you or See you as all the Small tracts about appear to be disposed of I will make a kind of a bargin to prevent the Sale untill I hear from you, ~~in case you~~

I saw old Genl. Nevill & Son[17] they both request you would not pass them, if you wish to get Iron ware of any Kind it is from 50 to 100 pct. lower at Redstone than at this place furniture is lower at pittsburgh than it is here. my neighbour Mr. Moore[18] has Sold his land to a Mr. Williams[19] Bricklayor ~~of~~ in the Town of Louisville for £1000 and I am greatly afraid of a Tenant being fixed there who will not be agreeable. Mr. Merrewither[20] has got an Order of Court to build a mill which will efectually distroy Col. Arther Campbells[21] Seat, this I mention that you may not be led into any error in Case you trade with Campbell, this affare has depreciated this tract greatly.

I have not Seen Col. Anderson[22] Senc my return —. please to inform Bro: Edmund that Genl. Clark do not recollect William Coleman,[23] or know any thing of his Right to Land on Sandy[24] as to the Value of the land ∧ in that quarter [∧] they are as highly prised as any lands on the upper part of the Ohio, — I intend to offer Mr. Short[25] an Exchange, bro Edmunds land on Miamis for his near me in the ponds,[26] if I make the exchange I hope it will be agreeable.

Mr. Tompkins[27] will Commince School in a fiew days I found no deficuelty in raiseing a School, I believe 60 in Stud [instead] of 25 Scholars Could be maid up for him if we would Suffer him to recve them. Genl. Brackinridge[28] has ordered Bills execution posponed untill ~~march~~ [∧]august[∧] to give time for me to Comply Bro G Sold a piece of land and the man promises to pay in Augt. if he does all will be well. I fear he will not.[29]

I Shall Set in to build your house Monday next I have ingaged the ~~Hughing~~ Shingles & joiners work to be done imediately, ∧ also the hewing part [∧] I Shall indeavor to have every comfort in as great fowardness for you as possible at your arrival. If I could Know when you would certainly be along, I would meet you Some place on the river,[30] prey write

Trough Spring, the home of Jonathan Clark near Louisville. Built under the supervision of William Clark in 1802, the house has undergone extensive changes and still stands today. Courtesy of The Filson Historical Society

to me Often __ My Brother George & Sister Thruston[31] joins in Compts.
to you Sister Bro Edmund & the family __

With Great Fridsp.   Yr. Bro
W Clark

1. 23 February 1802, exactly one week prior to the date of this letter.
2. Goose Creek is in northeastern Jefferson County and enters the Ohio at the southern boundary of Juniper Beach near present River Road and Lime Kiln Lane. A road from the mouth of Goose Creek inland served as an important transportation route in this area.
3. Major William Croghan (1752–1822) was William and Jonathan's brother-in-law. He was a native of Ireland, came to America in 1769, served in the British army from 1771 to 1774, and in the 8th and 4th Virginia regiments during the Revolution, rising to the rank of major. He served with several of the Clark brothers in the army and with George Rogers Clark as a surveyor, and was a family friend before marrying their sister Lucy in 1789. He was active in business, land investments, and politics. His home, Locust Grove, which was one of the centers of Louisville area society, still stands today and is preserved as a historic house. It is the only known Lewis and Clark–related structure west of the Appalachians. The explorers visited Locust Grove on 8 November 1806 while in Louisville after their return from the expedition. William Clark was close to the Croghans and of course visited them often. After Jonathan died in 1811, it appears that William tended to stay at Locust Grove when visiting Louisville. While on the expedition he wrote Croghan at least four letters. (Thomas (1), 30–61; *KE,* 242–43; *EL,* 524–25; Jackson (1), 1:164, 178, 195, 230.)
4. Jonathan Clark's home was Trough Spring (not "Springs" as it sometimes appears). Jonathan's diary records that he first occupied the house on 14 July 1802. It still stands today off Dundee Road at the end of Trough Springs Lane, but has undergone extensive changes. The information in these letters and in the Jonathan Clark Papers–Clark-Hite Collection provides details about the building of the house. Trough Spring passed out of the family in 1838. For photographs, see the photogravure section of the Louisville *Herald-Post,* 21 April 1929, and the Louisville *Courier-Journal Magazine,* 13 March 1949. (*Herald-Post,* 21 April 1929; Jefferson Co. Houses–Trough Spring historical file, TFHS.)
5. James Sullivan (1748–1815) was a native of Virginia who had settled in the Pittsburgh area with his brother Daniel (1745–1791) by 1768. He

served as a captain in the 13th Virginia and in George Rogers Clark's Illinois Regiment after moving to Jefferson County, Kentucky, by 1780. He and his brother had reputations as Indian fighters. The Clark and Sullivan families became friends and neighbors. Sullivan established stations along the South Fork of Beargrass Creek and served as a Louisville trustee; at one time he was one of Louisville's major land owners. About 1767 he married Susanna de la Buffington (1748–1794), and they went on to have twelve children, the youngest named George Rogers Clark. Land Sullivan had once owned on the South Fork of Beargrass Creek became the major tract for Jonathan Clark's Trough Spring estate. Several members of the Sullivan family settled in St. Louis, including James. He lived with his son John Campbell Sullivan during his last years and was buried in the Fee Fee Cemetery, St. Ferdinand, Missouri. (JCDB, 1:311, 6:59; Sullivan family file, TFHS; Franklin, 172; Gwathmey, 750.)

6. Mr. Anderson has not been identified. It is believed that he is not Colonel Richard C. Anderson because Clark consistently refers to him by his military title.

7. Probably George Southall, one of the heirs and devisees of James Southall, whose 3,000-acre section of a 6,000-acre tract he shared with Richard Charlton adjoined the Clark estate. (Hammon, 20–23.)

8. Abraham Hite, Jr. See 2 September 1792 letter, note 15.

9. Probably John Williams. A John Williams of Monongalia County, Virginia (now West Virginia), sold 500 acres on Goose Creek in Jefferson County, Kentucky, to Nimrod Long of Shenandoah County, Virginia, on 14 June 1802. (JCDB, 6:356.)

10. Nimrod Long; mentioned in the preceding note.

11. J. Smith has not been identified.

12. John Armstrong (1755–1816) was a native of New Jersey. He served in Pennsylvania regiments during the Revolutionary War, was an exceptional scout, and commanded several forts along the Ohio River, including Fort Finney (later Fort Steuben) at present Jeffersonville, Indiana. In 1790 he made a secret expedition to the Missouri River and later that year was present at Harmar's defeat. He married a Miss Goforth of Columbia, Ohio (now in the Cincinnati metropolitan area), in 1793, settled there, and in 1814 moved to Armstrong's Station, on the Ohio River, in Clark County, Indiana. He served as treasurer of the Northwest Territory, as a judge of the Hamilton County Court, and as a Columbia magistrate. He was an associate and friend of the Clarks and assisted them with their Ohio land business (Jonathan had an operating plantation at Columbia). (*Cincinnati Miscellany*, November

1844, 1:37–41; John Armstrong Papers, Indiana Historical Society, Indianapolis, Ind.; Heitman (1), 74–75.)

13. "Miamis" refers to Jonathan's plantation at Columbia at the confluence of the Ohio and Little Miami Rivers. Columbia was founded 16 November 1789 by Major Benjamin Stites, who had led a party of twenty-five men to the area where they built a blockhouse and laid out a town. At that time Columbia was six miles upstream from Cincinnati, but it was eventually absorbed by the latter. (Atwater, 132.)

14. John Thruston (1761–1802) was a native of Gloucester County, Virginia. He served in both the east and the west during the Revolution, including service as a captain in 1781 in the Illinois Regiment. He migrated to Kentucky with his brothers Charles Mynn (Fanny Clark's second husband) and Buckner in 1788. Buckner settled in Lexington, while John and Charles settled in Jefferson County by 1789. Thruston married his cousin Elizabeth Thruston Whiting in Louisville in 1789, and was elected a town trustee in 1793. He served as lieutenant colonel and commandant of the 1st Regiment of Jefferson County militia. Thruston had been in declining health for some time and died in Louisville (most likely at his plantation) on 19 February (the recorded date). Since Clark says he died two days before he got home, that draws into question whether the party arrived on 23 February, as indicated by the opening line of this letter, or whether he was a couple of days off in his reckoning. It is also possible that the stated death date for Thruston is wrong and that he died on 21 February. (Gwathmey, 772; Franklin, 183; Clift (1), 6.)

15. Probably William Provines (d. 1815), listed as being a native of Bourbon County, Kentucky, who came to Clark County, Indiana, in 1806, although he apparently was in the area, at least on business, prior to that date. Provines was a farmer and miller. He married Mary Buchanan (d. 1847) in 1801, and they had seven children. He died on 9 October 1815. (*HOFC*, 2:533.)

16. Possibly Nathan Robertson and land he owned in Clark County, Indiana. On 1 October 1802 Robertson and his wife Elizabeth sold four tracts of land totaling about 600 acres. A widow, Betsy Robertson (possibly the same Elizabeth Robertson), owned 100 acres on Floyds Fork in eastern Jefferson County. Since Provines seems to be associated more with Indiana than Kentucky, Clark's mention of this property could be construed to indicate that he was contemplating buying Jonathan land in Clark County, Indiana. Given the land already purchased, however, and Jonathan's interest in adding to his main tract, I think it more likely that Provines was acting as Robertson's agent for

land located in the area of the South Fork of Beargrass Creek, although a search of the deed and tax records for that period did not list any property in the area of this acreage. (Clark Co., Ind., Deed Books [hereafter cited as CCDB], 1:268–79; Jefferson Co., Ky., Tax Lists [hereafter cited as JCTL], 1801–3.)

17. Gen. Joseph Neville (1730–1819) was a native of Faquier County, Virginia. He settled near Moorefield, Hampshire County, Virginia (Moorefield is now in Hardy County, West Virginia), where he died. He served as a burgess from Hampshire County in 1773 and 1776 and as a delegate to the Virginia conventions of 1775 and 1776. He also served as an officer in the Hampshire County militia, and rose to the rank of brigadier general of Virginia militia during the Revolutionary War. He married Nancy Brown, and they had ten children. His son Presley (1788–1814) married Lucy Gwathmey, daughter of William's sister Ann Clark Gwathmey, in 1812 in Jefferson County, Kentucky. Joseph Neville's daughter Ann married Louisville merchant Cuthbert Bullitt (formerly of Moorefield), and it was at their home on 6 February 1814 that Presley Neville died (*Western Courier,* 7 February 1814). To further intertwine relations, Ann Clark Gwathmey's daughter Diana Moore Gwathmey married Cuthbert Bullitt's brother Thomas. (Bullitt; Heitman (1), 412; Gwathmey, 581–82; Rogers Index.)

18. Robert Kearney Moore (d. 1807) was a native of Philadelphia. He was associated with several Philadelphians who relocated to Jefferson County, Kentucky, and he may have settled there as early as the 1780s. Like many of the Philadelphians who settled in Louisville, especially the Philadelphia French, he was involved in the mercantile trade. He apparently moved to Clark County, Indiana, and the newly established Jeffersonville after selling his plantation on the South Fork of Beargrass Creek. He had inherited early Louisville resident Michael Lacassagne's (ca. 1750–1797) Indiana estate named Richmond and 600 acres on the Ohio just above Jeffersonville, as well as Lacassagne's Louisville house and lots. He and Lacassagne had been close friends and business partners. (Lacassagne and the Clarks also were good friends.) Moore married Catharine Allen Prince in Clark County in February 1806. They had one child. Although living in Jeffersonville, he apparently died in Louisville. The Moores, Clarks, and Gwathmeys were quite close. Moore was the cousin of early Jefferson County settler James Francis Moore, who in turn was very close to the Joseph and Reubin Field family. Robert advertised his plantation for sale in the 7 December 1801 edition of *The Farmer's Library,* providing a description of it, including the fact that it was only half a mile from "Captain Clark's Mill." On 28 January 1802 Moore sold the plantation to

Evan Williams. Local legend states that Richmond was haunted. It was torn down in 1888. (JCWB, 1:76; JCDB, 6:147; Appleman (2), 16–21; *EL,* 496; Craik, 71; *The Pennsylvania Magazine of History and Biography* (1), 23:126.)

19. Evan Williams (1755–1810) was born in Wales and came to the United States in 1784, landing at Philadelphia. By 1789 he was living in Jefferson County. He married Hannah Dubberley (b. 1775) (some sources state Hannah Phillips), a native of Loudoun County, Virginia. He was indeed a builder, or bricklayer, as Clark describes him. In 1800 he had a contract to build a two-story brick house for Clark's nephew John Gwathmey, and in the very early 1800s he built the county jail and clerk's office. He was also a distiller as early as 1789, and a current brand of bourbon whiskey bears his name. (Samuel Thomas to James Holmberg, 27 October 1996; Fenley-Williams Family Papers, TFHS; *EL,* 943–44.)

20. William Meriwether, Jr. (1757 or 1758–1814), a native of Louisa County, Virginia, moved with his family to Jefferson County, Kentucky, in the 1780s, where they settled on the waters of Beargrass Creek. He married Sarah Oldham (1772–1830) in 1788, and they had twelve children. Information gathered indicates that Meriwether was William Clark's immediate neighbor to the west. (Meriwether, 387–88; JCWB, 1:24.)

21. Arthur Campbell (1743–1811) was born in southwestern Virginia in what was then part of Augusta County. He was raised on the frontier. At the age of fourteen he was captured by Indians; he escaped from the Wyandotts after four years and participated in the British capture of Detroit in 1760. Campbell was active in military and public affairs in Virginia for most of his life. For his service during the French and Indian War he received a 1,000-acre land grant in Jefferson County located along the South Fork of Beargrass Creek near the Clark Mulberry Hill tract. He apparently was not related to John and Allan Campbell. He died in what is now Middlesboro, Kentucky. Negotiations regarding the land mentioned had been going on for almost a year at least. Campbell wrote Jonathan on 2 June 1801 about his "seat," mentioning that William had stopped to see him on his way through Wythe County, Virginia, to Jonathan's house and could give him a full description of Campbell's tract on Beargrass Creek. Campbell wanted to know if Jonathan was going to buy the tract, but even if he did not (and he did not) he advised him to "remove soon to Kentucky" because of its promise. William Meriwether had received a writ to build both a gristmill and a sawmill on the creek pending an inquiry. Campbell, apparently also seeing the danger to the value of his tract, protested the

project and himself filed for authorization to build a gristmill and a sawmill. Meriwether, in turn, protested Campbell's plan to build mills. By late 1803 neither man apparently had built his mills and the matter was still in the courts. (*KE*, 154; Arthur Campbell Papers, TFHS; Draper Mss., 2L57; Cook and Cook, 55–56, 233, 254–58, 276, 334.)

22. Richard Clough Anderson (1750–1826) was Clark's brother-in-law, a native of Hanover County, Virginia. He served in the 5th, 6th, 1st, and 9th Virginia regiments successively during the Revolutionary War, and was captured at Charleston. Jonathan most likely knew him from their service in the army. He moved to Kentucky by 1784, and in 1787 married Elizabeth Clark. In 1789 he established his residence at Soldier's Retreat, about seven miles east of Louisville. Like Locust Grove, it became an important social center. Partly because of the family connection and partly because they did surveying and fought Indians together in the 1780s and 1790s, Clark and Anderson were close. When Clark traveled east from Mulberry Hill or Trough Spring, he usually spent the first night at Soldier's Retreat. The original house was razed in the nineteenth century, but four of the original outbuildings and the family cemetery remain. A fairly accurate replica of the mansion was built on the original house's site in the 1970s. (*DAB*, 1:270–71; *EL*, 36–37; Anderson, 49, 78.)

23. William Coleman could not be identified.

24. Refers to either the Big Sandy or Little Sandy River in eastern Kentucky, probably the former. The Big Sandy forms almost the entire border between Kentucky and West Virginia.

25. Peyton Short (1761–1825), born in Surry County, Virginia, graduated from William and Mary in 1780, and in 1785 removed to Kentucky. In 1789 he was appointed the first collector of the port of Louisville. He settled on his estate, Greenfield, in Woodford County, Kentucky, about 1790 and became a leading citizen, serving in the state senate (1792–1796), and operating successful businesses, at least one in partnership with James Wilkinson in Lexington. His involvement in land speculation caused him severe financial difficulties; he was forced to sell his Lexington area property and eventually relocated to the Hopkinsville area in Christian County, Kentucky. He sometimes is referred to as a major, but no documentation confirming that rank has been found. It probably was achieved in either the Virginia or, more likely, the Kentucky militia. In 1789 he married Maria Symmes (1765–1801), daughter of John Cleves Symmes, and following her death, he married in 1802 Jane Henry Churchill (1768–1808), the widow of Armistead

Churchill of New Jersey. He fathered nine children (five with Maria and four with Jane), including the noted botanist Charles Wilkins Short. His brother William Short (1759–1849) served as Thomas Jefferson's secretary when he was ambassador to France and was also his friend. (Barlow and Powell, 244–45n; Short and Richardson, 111–22.)

26. Because of Louisville's location on a flood plain and the great number of springs, ponds were common in the area. Some were of such size that they could have been considered lakes. The large number of ponds combined with poor drainage to create a perfect breeding area for disease-carrying mosquitoes. The problem was serious enough that Louisville had a reputation as being unhealthy in the late eighteenth and early nineteenth centuries, so much so that it received the unwanted nickname "Graveyard of the West." The ponds were gradually drained and filled (sometimes with Indian mounds), and the health of the area greatly improved. The land Clark refers to may have been property Short owned in what is now the "Old Louisville" and University of Louisville area. (*HOFC*, 1:156–57; Johnston, 1:65–66, 338.)

27. George Tompkins (1780–1846) was born in Caroline County, Virginia, and came to Jefferson County about 1802. He taught school in the Clark neighborhood, perhaps at either the Clark or the Hite plantation. His brother Robert taught Jonathan's children in Virginia. George moved to St. Louis in 1810, established a school there, and apparently taught until June 1814. In 1816 he entered the practice of law in Howard County, Missouri. He served as a state legislator and in 1824 was elected a state supreme court judge, retiring from that office in 1845. He was a member of the Tompkins family who were Clark neighbors in Virginia (and who bought part of John Clark's plantation in 1785 after he moved to Kentucky), and immediately continued that connection with William, and later with Jonathan and Edmund when they moved to Kentucky. Jonathan records visiting Tompkins often in his diary. (Scharf, 2:1469–70; Billon, 118, 129, 270–71; *Louisiana Gazette* (St. Louis), 3 May 1810.)

28. Robert Breckinridge, Jr. (1754–1833), was born in Augusta County, Virginia, and served in the 3rd, 4th, 5th, and 8th Virginia regiments during the Revolutionary War, rising from enlisted man to lieutenant. He was captured at Charleston along with his brother Alexander and remained a prisoner until almost the end of the war. After the war he and his brother moved first to Fayette County and then to Jefferson County, Kentucky. He served as a general in the Kentucky militia and

was prominent in politics, serving in the Virginia House of Delegates, as a member of the Virginia Constitutional Convention (being one of only three Kentucky members to vote for ratification), Kentucky's 1792 constitutional convention, the state legislature, and other positions. He was very active in land matters, surveying and serving as agent for a number of people. His stepmother was the sister of Col. William Preston, the father of Maj. William Preston, William Clark's good friend and brother-in-law. Jonathan knew Breckinridge from their service together during the Revolutionary War. (*EL*, 114–15; Heitman (1), 115 ; Franklin, 27; Johnston, 2:614.)

29. This may be a reference to the final financial blow suffered by Clark in his efforts to help his brother George with his troubled financial affairs. It was shortly after this bill would have come due that he began advertising Mulberry Hill for sale. He was forced to sell his plantation because of debts incurred on George's behalf. (John Thruston's Executor v. William Clark et al. [George Rogers Clark's heirs], Jefferson Co., Ky., Chancery Court Records, case no. 1845, KDLA; *The Farmer's Library*, 12 August 1802.)

30. To travel some distance in order to meet and escort an arriving party was a common practice at the time. If William did meet Jonathan and his family on the Ohio, it probably would have been about one or two days travel upstream from Louisville.

31. Clark sister Frances Eleanor "Fanny" Clark O'Fallon Thruston (1773–1825). Family tradition recalls her being known as the "great black-eyed beauty of Kentucky." She first married James O'Fallon in 1791, but the marriage was unhappy and they separated. He shortly afterward died, and Fanny married second Charles Mynn Thruston, to whom she actually had been engaged before marrying O'Fallon, though a misunderstanding had foiled their initial nuptial plans. She married Thruston in 1796, and then Dennis Fitzhugh in 1805; she was widowed both times. After the deaths of her first and second husbands (but particularly the second) William was quite involved in the conduct of her affairs and the welfare of her children. Family tradition states that she and her four fatherless children lived with William and George, first at Mulberry Hill and then across the river at Clark's Point. William was close to several of his nephews and looked upon them almost as sons. Fanny moved from Louisville to St. Louis ca. April 1825 in order to be under the direct care of her son-in-law, Dr. Bernard G. Farrar, but the illness she had been suffering from did not improve, and she died on 19 June 1825. She is buried in the John O'Fallon family lot in Bellefontaine Cemetery. (Dorman (1), 26;

Thruston family file, TFHS; Charles W. Thruston Papers, Charles W. Thruston Collection, TFHS.)

~

Louis ville 5th Apl. 1802

Dear Brother

   I have this day drawn on you in favor of Mr. Dennis Fitzhugh[1] for three hundred Dollars, which Sum I have rceved of him, and intend to apropriate a part to my use to discharge Some demands of our friend, and the remainder to your use. We expect you out in June I flateer my Self I Shall have a house for you a garden &c. by that time. a late fresh[2] has entirely broken my mill dam, I have been fortunate in Saw'g the greater part of the plank for Your house[3]

eft. yr. Brother

W Clark

PS. I wrote you by post a Short tim past all the accurruncs all is will [well], and we have not heard from you Since I left you WC

[Letter carried by Mr. Fitzhugh]

1. Dennis (or Denis) Fitzhugh (1778–1822) was a native of Caroline County, Virginia. He was living in Lexington, Kentucky, by 1802, and apparently had relocated to Louisville by mid-1805, the year he married William's sister Fanny (see letter dated 2 March 1802, note 31). Before settling in Louisville he may have lived in western Kentucky in Hartford, Ohio County, where he was engaged in the mercantile business. Once settled in Louisville, he continued as a merchant and became associate judge of the circuit court. He was one of many who died of cholera during an 1822 outbreak in the region. He and Fanny had two children: Clark and Lucy Ann. There is some confusion over his place of birth. Sources state that he was a native of King George County, Virginia. However, an April 1807 passport for Orleans Territory states that he was a native of Caroline County, was twenty-nine years old, stood 5'11", had light hair, gray eyes, and a light complexion. He also was a first cousin, once removed, to William and his Clark siblings. (Rogers Index; Dennis Fitzhugh Papers, TFHS.)

2. A "fresh" or "freshet" was a term commonly used at that time for a flood.

3. It is not known whether Clark sawed the planks at his mill. He seems to link the sawing of the planks to his broken mill dam and thus mill. He may have replaced the mill saws destroyed in the summer 1801 mill fire and done some saw work, although the structure apparently operated primarily as a gristmill.

2

"What We Are About"

The Expedition Years, 1803–1807

On 18 July 1803 William Clark accepted Meriwether Lewis's invitation to join him in the "enterprise" that became known as the Lewis and Clark Expedition. The friendship of the two men and Lewis's trust in his former army commander was such that he offered him the position of co-commander, equal "in all respects" to his own position. Clark received the invitation with "much pleasure" and "chearfully" agreed to join his friend in the "dangers, difficulties, and fatigues" such a journey entailed. "This is an undertaking fraited with many dificulties," he wrote in his letter accepting Lewis's invitation, "but My friend I do assure you that no man lives whith whome I would prefur to undertake Such a Trip & c. as Your self." Thus was formed one of the most famous partnerships in history. From early 1803, when planning began for the expedition into the vast west of Louisiana and Oregon, to early 1807, when the captains themselves reported on their journey to Thomas Jefferson in Washington, this momentous undertaking encompassed four years.

The journals the captains and some of their men kept during the expedition have been published and help chronicle this most famous of

United States exploring ventures. William Clark's field notes, discovered in an attic in St. Paul, Minnesota, in 1953, were a major contribution to the expedition's documentary record. Added to the journals and field notes as a documentary source are letters. Letters that Clark wrote to friends, family, and associates were known to exist. Some had survived and were available to historians. Nineteen letters written by him from July 1803 to September 1806 are included in Donald Jackson's *Letters of the Lewis and Clark Expedition.* These letters are tremendously important in their own right to the documentary legacy of the expedition. Some of them indicate that Clark wrote to other people also but these letters had never been located. The passage of time and circumstances had conspired to deprive historians of this potentially important source concerning the expedition. One of the recipients of letters from Clark was believed to be oldest brother Jonathan. Evidence indicated that Clark wrote to him, but no letters were known to have survived. His famous 23 September 1806 letter announcing the successful return of the Corps of Discovery was in The Filson Historical Society's collection, and was printed in Jackson. This letter has been traditionally believed to have been addressed to George Rogers Clark, but Jackson theorized that the recipient may instead have been Jonathan. Whether Jonathan or George, did William Clark write other letters to his family? Four letters to his brother-in-law William Croghan are printed in Jackson. If he wrote to Croghan it would stand to reason that he would have written his brothers, or at the least one brother, in order to pass along expedition happenings. Indeed, a letter to a brother is referenced in William's 2 April 1805 letter to Croghan from Fort Mandan. To that one can be added the 23 September letter to either Jonathan or George.

Where were these expedition-date letters? Where were these potential sources of important expedition information? Well, thirty-five years after that attic in St. Paul brought forth Clark's field notes, an attic in Louisville brought forth the expedition-date letters written to Jonathan. Five of the cache of fifty-one William Clark letters found in that attic date from December 1803 to September 1806. In addition, the 23 September 1806 letter is now verified (by one of these five letters) as being written to Jonathan. Descended in another branch of the Clark family, the 23 September letter definitely belongs with the group of letters published here and therefore has been included. Two other letters in the cache are letters written in 1807 that relate to aspects of the expedition. Therefore, they have been included here with the expedition letters.

These six expedition and two post-expedition letters are significant contributions to the documentary legacy of the Lewis and Clark Expedition. As I noted in the Introduction, Jonathan was an important person to William Clark. He not only wanted to keep Jonathan well informed of his activities and of news, but he believed it to be something of his duty. This was reflected somewhat in the pre-expedition letters, and is reinforced in those letters written from 1808 to 1811 after he relocated to St. Louis.

The letters in this chapter provide additional information about the expedition and post-expedition events. Sometimes substantial information is given, sometimes only enticing mentions of events and people. In some cases the information Clark gives contradicts previously believed facts. From details on the illness he suffered while descending the Ohio in 1803 to collecting mastodon bones for Jefferson at Big Bone Lick in 1807, Clark provides additional pieces to the mosaic that is the Lewis and Clark saga. His time line of events and reporting of newsworthy items themselves are both revealing and contradictory concerning established expedition facts. Clark's reporting on his February visit to St. Louis helps to fill in one of the expedition's "dark" periods, when neither journals or field notes were kept. A heretofore unknown collection of over thirty expedition artifacts he sent back to family and friends in Kentucky is a significant addition to expedition documentation, especially when all save possibly one of the items have been lost. What was sent back to Jefferson and Secretary of War Henry Dearborn in the spring of 1805 in the way of journals and reports? Clark's April 1805 letter would seem to answer this. Exceptions were made to the unmarried man rule for expedition personnel, but it was not known until this same letter came to light that York, one of our nation's most famous—but often overlooked—African Americans, was married at the time he served as an unofficial member of the Corps of Discovery. Clark's 24 September 1806 letter confirms that Jonathan was the recipient of his famous 23 September letter and contains a polite but pointed request to have that letter published. The captains knew that a letter to Clark's family in Louisville would be published and spread the word of the expedition's successful return much more quickly than Lewis's official report to Jefferson in Washington. Heeding the request, Jonathan had the letter published in the Frankfort *Palladium*.

After the expedition Clark and Lewis were celebrated as heroes by an enthusiastic government and public. Their lives were forever changed.

Clark was confronted by situations and decisions for which he felt himself ill prepared. His response was to seek Jonathan's counsel. This desire to discuss important situations and decisions with Jonathan became
standard in his post-expedition letters. Jonathan would be a source of
advice and support for him until his death in November 1811. Whether
penning a request for cash or complaining about their brother George
being drunk, as he does from Big Bone Lick in September 1807, William
Clark increasingly relied on Jonathan as a source of advice and stability
in a life that changed forever with his agreement to accompany Meriwether Lewis to the Pacific.

~

	Opposit the Mouth of Missourie[1]
Dear Brother	December 16th 1803

        I expected to have found in the Kohokia[2] post office a letter
from you, but to my great disapointment did not find a Single letter from
any one of my friends_ I hope the next post will bring me a letter from
you _ I will give you Some account of my Voyage to this place_; a fiew
days after I parted with you on the river bank,[3] I was taken Violent <u>ill</u> by
a Contraction of the muskelur Sistem,[4] this indisposition Continued Several days and was ultimately removed by the exertions & Close attention
of Capt Lewis,[5] after a fiew days of tolerable health, I was again attacked
with a violent Pain in the Sumock & bowels, with great Obstruction in ~~in~~
those parts, which Could not be removed untill I arrived at Kaskaskees[6]
which was Eleven Days, at that place I precured Some <u>Allow</u> which
gave me relief   as I was not in a Situation to make observations dureing
this time can inform you but little that happnd.[7] ~~within that time~~ The men
we expected would meet us at Fort Masac[8] were not thure, which obliged
us to Send an express to Tennessee for those men to percue us to our winter quarters,[9] __,   we Calld for a Detachment of 14 men from that garrison to accompany us as far as Kaskaskees at which place we intended to
ogment our permonant party,[10] at the mouth of the Ohio we delayed five
Days in which time I made a Complete Survey of the place, it is in Lat.
37°~00'~23" N~ the width of the Ohio from the point is 998 yards   the
Course N 30½° E _ The Mississippi is 236 poles Course S 33° E, _ [11] I was
at old fort Jefferson,[12] it is entirely grown up with Trees_ Opposit the
mouth of the Ohio on the west Side of the Mississippi a Small Settlement

is formed of four or five Americans,[13] we met with a great many Sho-
wonee Indians,[14] ~~we~~ ∧ and [∧] traded with them for different kinds of
wild meets, Such as Biar, Vensions, Ducs, Tongues, and Beaver Tales –.
We arrived at Kaskaskees on the 29th & Selected 12 men for our party,[15]
and made Some arrangement for our winters Provisions, dureing this
time I had verry Comfartable quarters with Capt. Stodart,[16] and a Mr.
Wm. Morrison[17] a merchent of that place, – here we was informed that
the Lieut. Govr. of upper Louisiana[18] intended to Stop us (at this place we
let our rout be known)[19] this information made it necessary for one of us
to go on to St. Louis[20] by land without delay – my being too weak to ride
that far [∧]Capt. Lewis[∧] deturmined to proceed on, Shew his Vouchers
and do away any Obstruction, he accordingly Set out by Land, and I by
water ~~from that place~~ on the evening of the 4th instant[21] on the 7th I arrived at Kohokia Landing about 3 miles below St. Louis and three above
a Small town of 40 famlys called <u>vietpuche</u>[22] ∧In our language is enpty
[empty] belly[∧] both in view, on the 8th at night[23] Capt. Lewis met me
from St. Louis and informed me "the Lt. Govr. Objected to our passing
up the Missourus, untill he recves orders from his Govr. at New Orleans.
that he had promised to Send off an express imediately in a Canoe with
the Dispatches & c.["] We deturmined ∧not to go Contrary to the wish of
the Govr. butt[∧] to take up our winter quarters ∧on the Mississippi[∧]
Convenunt to good hunting, and within the bounds of a Contrait [coun-
try?] which extended as high as the Missourus at a Situation where our
party might amuse themselves in hunting Clear of the means of Corruption,[24] Several plaices were recomended, I determined to proceed on &
fix on the Spot best Calculated for our views_ after takeing the Latidude
of Kohokia L. 38° 18′ 56″ we proceeded on[25] under Sales & Cullers to St.
Louis, and passed to a landing opposit the center of the Town the admi-
ration of the people were So great, that hundreds Came to the bank to
view us. at the govrs. I found Several of my old acquaintuncs from Vincennes & Kaskasskees—[26] the Govr. persisted in his Objection to our proceeding more by advice than other wise. Stateing many dificuelties &
[∧]Dangs. [dangers][∧] all of which I understood perfectly _ as being
the means he ment to apply in Case we proceeded this winter. The next
morning I set out leaving Capt Lewis who intended to Kohokia to Send
on Despatches to the Governmt. by the mail. In assending the river I
found no place So well Calculated for our purpose as the one I am now at,
which is imdiately opposit the mouth of the Missourus at the mouth of a
Littl river Called Duboićе or wood river,[27] the ∧mouth[∧] of this river

afords a good harbor for my boats; the lands below the River Duboiće
is Suffecntly high for our <u>huts</u>, and the Countrey around affords good
hunting; innoumerable quantiss. of fowls of everry discription are passing, ∧&[∧] at one mile a large Prariee Commencs, ~~which reaches from~~
[∧]at Kaskassies and passing[∧] Kohokia (which is about 18 miles from
this place) and runs Parrelal with the river, towards the Illinois river,[28] in
this Prarie there is more Grouse or heath hen, than I ever Saw Partred-
gus, in any Countrey I saw this day more than one hundred fly over the
Camp, I began to raise the huts for our winter quarters to day, tomorrow
I shall Send ~~off~~ this[29] by Charles Floyd[30] to Kohokia Post office. Capt.
Lewis I expect here as Soon as he answers the letters he expects by the
next mail.

I received a letter from Sam: Gwathmey Since his return, and am
much Concerned at Mr. Mills's[31] failing to make a payment. I wish him
pushed and if possible ~~those~~ force him to pay the money in time to meet
those demands which I left for Sam to pay out of the money he was to
rceive of Mills. I hope to receive a letter from you the next mail, I would
write to bro: Edmd. but am So busey attending the raising of huts that I
have not as much time, please to present my Compliments to him. also to
Sister Clark & the family sincearly I Shall be glad to here from you at all
times. with Sincear effection I am your

Brother

Wm Clark

1. The Missouri River is of course the major western river that the Corps
   of Discovery would begin ascending in May 1804. They established
   their winter quarters near the mouth of the River Dubois or Wood
   River in Illinois, which at that time was opposite the mouth of the Missouri. The camp was on the south side of the Wood River. Owing to
   shifting of both the Missouri and Mississippi Rivers, the site of the
   camp was believed to have come to be on the west side of the Mississippi in Missouri and north of the mouth of the Missouri River, but recent research has indicated that the camp was farther inland than previously thought and may not have been inundated by the Mississippi.
   Information in this letter and other sources indicates that Camp
   Dubois may have been inland some distance, and perhaps not right at
   Wood River's mouth as generally thought, but a reading of Clark's field
   notes clearly indicates that the camp must have been in sight of the
   Mississippi or certainly no more than a short walk away, since Clark

Portrait of Meriwether Lewis by Charles Willson Peale, 1807. William Clark's letters to Jonathan add significant information about the death of his partner in discovery. Courtesy of the Independence National Historical Park Collection

regularly commented on river observations and traffic. (Sparks, 4–9; Osgood, 3–9.)

2. Though the designation is disputed by Fort Crèvecoeur (near present Peoria), Cahokia is generally acknowledged to be the oldest continuously occupied settlement in present Illinois. Founded in 1699 by French missionaries, it became one of the major French settlements in the Illinois country and the Mississippi Valley. It was captured on 6 July 1778 by an American party commanded by Joseph Bowman at the order of George Rogers Clark during his Illinois Campaign. In 1797 William Clark described the town as "low" with "mean houses" and a population estimated at 200. It apparently grew, or revived, afterward, because in 1803 it reportedly had a population of some 700. Lewis used Cahokia and St. Louis as his temporary bases during the winter of 1803–1804, and it was from there that the party sent and received mail. (Moulton, 2:128; Thomas (2), 291–92; McDermott, 4, 27.)

3. Jonathan traveled with William, Lewis, and the nucleus of the Corps of Discovery in the keelboat from Clarksville to a short way downstream where his son-in-law Benjamin Temple had a farm at the mouth of Little Cane Run on the Kentucky side of the river. The creek no longer empties into the Ohio, but this site would have been near present Lake Dreamland subdivision in the area of River Front Road. Jonathan spent 24 and 26 October with the explorers, but recorded only the barest of facts about those visits. Oh, that he had been a devotee of lengthy descriptive diary entries! Imagine the information he could have recorded for posterity about the early stages of the expedition, its members at that time, and its setting out from the Falls of the Ohio, but we are fortunate to have the information we do. (Jonathan Clark Diary, 24, 26 October 1803; JCDB, 6:400–402.)

4. These illnesses that struck Clark were unidentified before the emergence of this letter. No journal was kept from 18 September to 11 November, and no mention of this illness consequently was recorded. Clark's bout of serious gastrointestinal difficulty, with resultant severe constipation, while sailing down the Ohio and up the Mississippi to Kaskaskia was alluded to only by a reference Lewis made to Clark's being "much indisposed" since 16 November and being given some prairie chicken soup. The "Contraction of the muskelur Sistem" may have been not only severe cramping, but the muscle contractions that sometimes occur in other areas of the body as a result of severe diarrhea and vomiting, which can cause dehydration and a chemical imbalance in the body and muscular system. What Lewis did to help his co-leader recover is unknown but may have involved generous doses of medicine

from their medical chest (something Lewis was fond of administering to himself and others). The probable treatment was generous doses of a strong laxative that Dr. Benjamin Rush had concocted using calomel and jalap. Known as "Rush's pills," they had such an explosive purging effect that they also were known as "Thunderclappers." Rush had recommended using two or three or more to help the bowels work. Lewis took a "doze" (I assume he meant dose rather than dozen) on 14 November 1803, and reported that they "operated extremely well." When Clark suffered a relapse, one would assume that he again was dosed with Rush's pills and any other medicines they had to relieve his malady, but they failed to work. Only after reaching Kaskaskia and being dosed with the purgative aloin, from the aloe plant, did he get relief. Either it was a stronger purgative or it acted differently on his system; at any rate, it attained the desired results. (Moulton, 2:86, 101.)

5. Meriwether Lewis (1774–1809) was a native of Albemarle County, Virginia, a regular army officer, and Jefferson's private secretary prior to his assignment as leader of the expedition. He and Clark balanced each other perfectly on the expedition and formed one of the great partnerships in history. Following the expedition, he was appointed governor of Louisiana Territory (still commonly known by the Spanish designation of Upper Louisiana), an administrative post unsuited to his abilities. He possibly was manic-depressive, and this together with political, personal, and financial troubles, and his failure to produce the promised account of the expedition for publication, contributed to a mental breakdown during which it is generally agreed that he committed suicide. A number of books about Lewis are available, including Stephen Ambrose's *Undaunted Courage.* Lewis will be discussed further in connection with the letters William Clark wrote at the time of his death in the fall of 1809. (Lamar, 663–64.)

6. Kaskaskia is one of the oldest towns in Illinois. Founded in 1703 as a French mission, it soon became one of the major French settlements in the Mississippi Valley and Illinois country. It was captured by George Rogers Clark on 4 July 1778, the first of three British posts taken during his famous Illinois or Northwestern Campaign. Early in its history and into the early nineteenth century it was an important post on the Mississippi. By the 1790s it had declined somewhat (William Clark exaggerated in describing it as a "heap of ruins" in 1797), but it revived a bit as more Americans moved into the area. By 1803 some 500 people reportedly lived there. It was the capital of Illinois Territory, 1809–1818, and the state capital for the first two years of statehood. The original site of the town has been submerged since the late nineteenth century when the Mississippi changed course in that area, taking over the

course of the lower Kaskaskia River. It was from the U.S. Army post at Kaskaskia that a number of men (Clark states twelve later in this letter) were recruited. (Moulton, 2:119n; Thomas (2), 289; Flint, 2–5.)

7. The timetable Clark recounts concerning his illness and the party's movements are somewhat at odds with those recorded in the Eastern Journal (the journal begun by Lewis at Pittsburgh that contains sporadic entries kept by the captains for that first leg of the journey down the Ohio and up the Mississippi). The journal indicates that they reached Kaskaskia on 28 November 1803. Clark writes in this letter that they reached that post on 29 November. It may be that they reached the area of Kaskaskia on the 28th but did not actually enter the town until the following day. Lewis records that Clark suffered from his malady beginning on 16 November. However, by Clark's statements he would not have been struck again until 17 or 18 November. The probable explanation is that either Lewis or Clark made a mistake regarding the dates or length of his illness. Even though Clark writes that his illness prevented him from making observations, he did get around somewhat, making excursions at the mouth of the Ohio and Tower Rock for example. (Moulton, 2:101.)

8. Fort Massac was established in 1757 by the French during the French and Indian War. It was the first fortification on the lower Ohio. It initially was named Fort De l'Ascension, but was renamed for the French minister of the marine Massiac when its poor construction necessitated its being rebuilt in 1759. It was located on a promontory near present Metropolis, Illinois, not very far downstream from the mouth of the Tennessee River, and had a commanding view of the river. In 1763 by the terms of the Treaty of Paris ending the French and Indian (or Seven Years) War, Fort Massiac passed to the British. The French abandoned it in the spring of 1764, and a band of Chickasaw Indians soon burned it. The British anglicized the name to Massac, but did not rebuild or garrison the fort. In 1778, having traveled downstream from the Falls of the Ohio to the fort's ruins, George Rogers Clark and his Illinois Regiment debarked at Fort "Massacre," as he called it, and marched overland (most likely along the old French military road) from there to Kaskaskia. The belief that the fort's name was short for Massacre came from the tradition of there having been a massacre on the site years earlier. Clark and other Americans were wrong in this belief, but they continued to use Massac as the fort's name. In 1794 American troops rebuilt and regarrisoned the old post by order of Anthony Wayne. It was permanently abandoned in 1814 when threats in that area during the War of 1812 were ended. Today the site is preserved as a state park, the first established in Illinois. A good reconstruction of the fort is located

beside the identified site of the original fort. The Corps arrived at Fort Massac on 11 November and left on the 13th. The thriving hamlet of Massac Village was located to the fort's west. By 1802 some ninety French and French-Canadians, along with some Indians, lived there. (Illinois Department of Natural Resources; Moulton, 2:85; Banta, 96–97.)

9. Lewis had arranged for a detachment of soldiers from the post at South West Point, Tennessee, (on the Tennessee River near present Kingston, west of Knoxville), to meet him at Massac. For some reason the soldiers were not there when the Corps arrived. The express Lewis sent to get them was George Drouillard, a civilian who apparently lived in Massac Village and the Cape Girardeau District of Upper Louisiana (he listed the latter as his place of residence in post-expedition records) and who was at Massac. He was of French Canadian–Shawnee extraction and raised on the frontier. Hired as a civilian interpreter for the expedition (the agreement was not finalized until December), he was destined to become one of the most valuable members of the Corps of Discovery. The directions for Drouillard to get the men and pursue the Corps to their winter quarters were necessarily vague because the captains had not yet decided where they would winter. At this time they still had hopes of traveling some distance up the Missouri before establishing their winter quarters. Drouillard and eight men (and two horses) from Tennessee arrived at Camp Dubois on 22 December. Three days later, on Christmas, Drouillard agreed to accompany the expedition—undoubtedly one of the best Christmas presents the captains ever received. (Jackson (1), 1:102–4; Osgood, 8.)

10. It has never been determined exactly how many soldiers from Fort Massac accompanied Lewis and Clark either as temporary escorts or on a permanent basis. Joseph Whitehouse is the only known member of the Corps (excluding Drouillard) who was recruited at Massac. John Newman also was recruited at Massac and originally was a member of the permanent party, but he was court-martialed in the fall of 1804 and returned to St. Louis with the temporary party in April 1805. Five permanent members (Hugh McNeal, Robert Frazer, Silas Goodrich, John B. Thompson, and William Werner), and one initially permanent member later sent back for desertion (Moses Reed) came from unidentified military units. It certainly is probable that more than just two out of the fourteen soldiers from Massac became permanent or temporary members of the expedition. (Jackson (1), 1:370–72; Moulton, 2:510–11, 515–25; Large (1), 8.)

11. The party reached the confluence of the Ohio and Mississippi Rivers

on the evening of 14 November 1803. The next day Clark took the survey readings at the confluence. The readings and distances he cites both correspond to and contradict those that he and Lewis recorded in the Eastern Journal. The compass readings for the course of the Ohio and Mississippi at their confluence are the same, although more readings were recorded in the journal. The distance for the mouth of the Ohio corresponds to that recorded in the journal, but that for the Mississippi varies slightly. Lewis recorded Clark's survey of the Mississippi as 1,435 yards and the point as 1,274 yards. Clark himself seems to break the readings into sections that combined come to 232 poles (1,276 yards). The 236 poles cited in the letter is 1,298 yards. (Moulton, 2:86–88, 91–92.)

12. Fort Jefferson was located on the east bank of the Mississippi River, on the north side of Mayfield Creek in present Ballard County, Kentucky. Established by George Rogers Clark in 1780, it was too isolated and vulnerable to be maintained, and it was abandoned the following year. Chickasaw Indians attacked it twice in July and August, the latter attack being led by a British army officer. William Clark, Lewis, and eight men visited the site of the old fort on 18 November. The captains had been through the region before during their various travels, especially Clark, who had traveled through the area at least three times in the 1790s. In 1795 he drew a map (now in the Library of Congress) showing the area of the confluence of the Mississippi and Ohio Rivers that included Fort Jefferson and Fort Massac. In 1802 Secretary of War Dearborn had requested him to report on the best site for a military post at the mouth of the Ohio, which he did, focusing on Fort Jefferson. (Moulton, 2:93; Jackson (1), 1:7–8; Carstens, 261–70.)

13. Lewis mentions this settlement in his 16 and 18 November journal entries. He describes it as the "upper habitation" on the west side of the Mississippi in the 16 November entry. In his 18 November entry he elaborates, describing the community as "some persons" who were living in huts and trading with the Indians. While not exactly clear, he seems to report that some of their men visited this place and got drunk (which was in violation of orders and an infraction that would be repeated). Clark's 1795 map of the area shows a camp of five or six Spanish guards opposite the mouth of the Ohio. His comment here establishes the number of Americans settled there. (Moulton, 2:87, 89, 93–94.)

14. Bands of Shawnee Indians had begun moving westward from Ohio in the 1780s because of warfare with the Americans, primarily Kentuckians, who made campaigns north of the Ohio River into the Shawnee homeland. Some of George Rogers Clark's expeditions inflicted the

most damage to the Shawnee. There were a number of Shawnee and Delaware villages in the Cape Girardeau region. The Delaware had also drifted west for the same reasons. Both tribes received land grants from the Spanish government but were destined to be dispossessed yet again as Americans settled west of the Mississippi. They drifted south and west into Arkansas, Texas, eastern Kansas, and Indian Territory (present Oklahoma) as Americans surged across the Mississippi in the early nineteenth century. (Moulton, 2:88–90.)

15. As mentioned in note 7, there is some question as to whether the party arrived at Kaskaskia on 28 or 29 November. Clark states it was the 29th in this letter, but the Eastern Journal seems to indicate the 28th. Of much more interest is Clark's statement that twelve men were selected from the Kaskaskia companies of Captains Russell Bissell and Amos Stoddard. Ten members of the party (permanent and temporary) were heretofore known to have come from there, but the possible units of some of the others were unidentified. The known Kaskaskia recruits were John Collins, Patrick Gass, John Ordway, Peter Weiser (or Wiser), Alexander Willard, Richard Windsor, John Boley, Isaac White, John Dame, and Ebenezer Tuttle. Of these men the first six listed became members of the permanent party. Identifying these soldiers, combined with the fourteen from Fort Massac, two of whom were known, and the eight recruits from South West Point, four of whom were known, leaves a number of recruits unnamed. The units of six members of the Corps (five permanent: Hugh McNeal, Robert Frazer, Silas Goodrich, John B. Thompson, and William Werner, and one originally included as permanent but dismissed for desertion: Moses Reed) are unknown. The law of averages would seemingly dictate that one or more of these six came from each of these three posts. The best possibility is Daniel Bissell's company at Massac, since that unit apparently provided the largest detachment of the three posts. Muster rolls for the various companies are incomplete or missing, so it is not possible to establish what company these men came from. It also is possible that some of them were civilians living in the Kaskaskia-Cahokia area and did not transfer from one of the companies to the Corps. Given the captains' plan of recruitment, however, and the enlistment date of the men from the three posts, it seems unlikely that these men were civilians who officially joined the expedition at Camp Dubois. (Jackson (1), 1:370–73; Moulton, 2:510–25; Large (1), 8.)

16. Amos Stoddard (1762–1813) was a native of Connecticut, grew up in Massachusetts, and served in the infantry and artillery in the Revolutionary War. Before returning to the army in 1798 he was an assistant

clerk of the Massachusetts Supreme Court, served as a commissioned officer in the suppression of Shays' Rebellion, practiced law in the Maine district of Massachusetts, served in the Massachusetts legislature, and spent two years in the Massachusetts militia. His experience and abilities earned him an immediate captain's commission. In 1803 he commanded an artillery company and had orders to build a fort at Cahokia. Those orders were canceled, and he was then stationed at Kaskaskia with orders to represent the U.S. government at the ceremony to turn Upper Louisiana over to the United States and to then assume temporary duty as the civil and military commandant of the territory. He acquitted himself well in the six months he served in this post. He served as the agent of Clark and Lewis once they headed up the Missouri. He continued to serve in the west, primarily on the lower Mississippi, and was promoted to major in 1807. He was already a published writer when his *Sketches, Historical and Descriptive, of Louisiana* appeared in 1812. During the War of 1812 he helped to prepare the defenses of Fort Meigs and to defend it when it was besieged by the British and Indians. He was wounded in this action and died of tetanus on 11 May 1813. (*DAB*, 18:51; Jackson (1), 1:103; Heitman (2), 1:928.)

17. William Morrison (1763–1837) was a native of Bucks County, Pennsylvania. He worked in the store of his uncle Guy Bryan in Philadelphia, and about 1795 moved to Kaskaskia, where he established a store in partnership with Bryan. The store prospered and Morrison established stores in Cahokia and St. Louis. He also became a large landowner. Louis Houck described him as the most important merchant in the Mississippi Valley at that time. He was involved in early fur trading efforts and in attempts to establish trade between the Missouri Territory and New Mexico. Morrison was married twice, his second wife being the daughter of Daniel Bissell. Clark and Morrison continued not only a business but a personal relationship after the expedition, including Clark assisting with the educational arrangements for William Morrison, Jr., in Kentucky. (See letter dated 22, 24 November 1808, note 9.) (Jackson (1), 1:144n–45; Billon, 219; Houck, 1:155; JCP-CHC.)

18. Carlos Dehault Delassus (1764–1842) was the lieutenant governor of Upper Louisiana and the ranking official with whom the captains, particularly Lewis, had to deal. Upper Louisiana included the vast majority of the Louisiana Purchase. Its capital was St. Louis. Although the territory was owned again by France after 1800, Louisiana's former Spanish owners continued to administer it, usually with their best interests in mind. (Jackson (1), 1:20n.)

19. William Clark's statement that Delassus intended to stop them and that they let their true objective be known at Kaskaskia clarifies the matter of how far the Corps intended to proceed that season and when they officially let their true objective be known. It was previously believed that when Lewis met with Delassus in St. Louis on 7 December the captains already had decided to winter on the American side of the Mississippi and that Delassus's refusal to allow the party to proceed up the Missouri was expected and did not really alter their plans. Rumors as to the true destination of the expedition were circulating, and the Spanish, ever vigilant and suspicious concerning trespassers in their territories or areas of interest, no doubt suspected that the headwaters of the Missouri and the Pacific, rather than the headwaters of the Mississippi, were the Americans' true goals. Either acting on that suspicion and launching a "preemptive strike" against such plans, or reacting to the news that Lewis and Clark were heading for the Pacific, Delassus decided to refuse them permission to enter Upper Louisiana until he had official clearance from his superiors—ideally until the official transfer of the territory to the United States. No official notification regarding this is known of prior to Delassus's 9 December 1803 letter to his superiors Juan Manuel de Salcedo and the Marqués de Cosa Calvo, reporting on his 7 December meeting with Lewis in which he said he lacked the authority to allow the Americans to go up the Missouri and must get permission to do so. Given what Clark writes here, the likely scenario is that Delassus, learning of Lewis and Clark and their intentions, let it be known that he would refuse to allow them to go up the Missouri until it was officially American territory. Either he had this intention unofficially relayed to the captains, or someone learning of this intention transmitted the news to them. (Jackson (1), 1:142–43; Moulton, 2:128.)

20. St. Louis was founded in 1764 by the Frenchman Pierre Laclede of New Orleans as a fur trading post and originally inhabited by French from New Orleans. French-Canadians and some Spanish also settled there, and it soon became the major settlement and fur trading center in that region. George Rogers Clark and an American force helped defend St. Louis and Cahokia against a British-Indian attack during the American Revolution. As America's tide of settlement moved westward, a small number of U.S. citizens crossed the Mississippi, settling in St. Louis and Louisiana by the early 1800s. Perhaps the most famous was frontiersman Daniel Boone. After the United States acquired Louisiana, the influx of Americans greatly increased, but French cultural influence continued for a number of years and can still be seen today in some areas. (Moulton, 2:130.)

21. It has always been assumed that Lewis traveled to St. Louis to see the proper official about entering Louisiana because he was the primary co-leader of the expedition. Apparently the captains discussed who should go, and it was William Clark's current poor health that decided the matter for them. At least this was the reason in Clark's opinion. Because he was very conscious of titles, rank, and his pride, it also may have been an excuse to his eldest brother and family as to why he did not go. He certainly was capable and had dealt with Spanish officials in the past, more so than Lewis. Clark also indicates that they still intended to start up the Missouri that fall if possible. He contradicts his entry in the Eastern Journal by writing that they left Kaskaskia on the evening of 4 December, instead of 3 December as he recorded it in the journal. He also appears to say that Lewis left Kaskaskia on 3 or 4 December and not the 5th as Lewis stated in a letter to Thomas Jefferson. They both report arriving at Cahokia on 7 December. The only apparent advantage of Lewis's leaving the main party and traveling by horseback to Cahokia would be in getting there sooner and being able to make arrangements for two prominent local residents (John Hay and Nicholas Jarrot) to accompany him to St. Louis the next day. Sources disagree as to whether Lewis met with Delassus on 7 or 8 December; Delassus reported they met on 7 December and Lewis reported the 8th. Given Clark's journal entry for 6 December, it appears that Lewis was one day ahead of them, and therefore Delassus may be correct. Clark and the Corps reached Cahokia in the mid-afternoon of 7 December. If Lewis still had been in Cahokia, he surely would have met with Clark and probably recorded it in the journal. When one compares what Clark writes in this letter with previously known sources, the likely chronology seems to be that Lewis left Kaskaskia one day ahead of the Corps, arrived in Cahokia on 6 December, and went across the river to St. Louis and met with Delassus on 7 December. While Lewis was in St. Louis on the 7th, Clark and the Corps arrived at Cahokia. (Jackson (1), 1:145; Moulton, 2:122, 126.)

22. Clark's French name and translation for the town of Carondelet differ a bit from the accepted ones. Carondelet was in decline at the time and eventually was absorbed by St. Louis. Its unflattering nickname "Vide Poche" means "empty pocket." Whether there is any basis for Clark's translating part of the name as "belly" rather than "pocket" is not known. In the journal he spelled the name "Viele Pauchr" and left a blank for the number of families living there. He apparently had learned more by 16 December and reported some forty families. This would correspond to Houck's estimate of approximately 250 residents of the town at this time if the family average was six members. In the

1811 serialization of his *Sketches of the Territory of Louisiana* in the *Louisiana Gazette,* Henry M. Brackenridge reported that the town was six miles below St. Louis and had 218 inhabitants, possibly indicating it already was in decline by 1811. (Houck, 2:63–64; Moulton, 2:127–28; *Louisiana Gazette* (St. Louis), 21 March 1811.)

23. This information relates to the events and dates discussed in note 21. Clark reports that Lewis returned to Cahokia on the night of 8 December. Lewis states in his 19 December letter to Jefferson that he returned to Cahokia on 9 December and joined Clark, who had just arrived there. If this time line is balanced with Clark's (in this letter and the journal) and Delassus's 9 December letter, it appears that it is Lewis whose dates are wrong, assigned to his activities one day later than they actually occurred. Clark contradicts the departure date from Kaskaskia in this letter and the journal but then brings them into agreement as to when they arrived at Cahokia. Lewis apparently left Kaskaskia on 3 or 4 December, arrived at Cahokia on 6 December, conferred with Delassus in St. Louis on 7 December, and returned to Cahokia on 8 December. The party left Cahokia on 10 December. Something of a gap occurs in the chronology because Clark did not make entries in the journal while they were at Cahokia. (Jackson (1), 1:145–47; Moulton, 2:122–24.)

24. Clark uses quotes to relate what Lewis told him Delassus has said; so I assume he must have been quite sure what Lewis said. It is clear, therefore, that it was only after Delassus refused to allow the Corps to start up the Missouri that the captains gave up their intention of doing so, and instead decided to winter on the American side of the Mississippi near the mouth of the Missouri. They then had to find a suitable site for winter quarters, a place sufficiently far from the "means of Corruption" that St. Louis and Cahokia afforded. Later in the letter Clark returns to Delassus's refusal to permit them to enter Louisiana until it officially was turned over to the United States. Clark visited St. Louis on 11 December. (Jackson (1), 1:142–47.)

25. Unless I have missed an earlier use in the Eastern Journal or expedition letters, this is the first use of what became the signature phrase of the expedition: "we proceeded on." "Proceeded" appears before this in the expedition's writings but not in the combination of "we proceeded on" made so famous by the Corps' journalists. Clark commonly used "proceeded on" (also spelling it "proseeded") as early as 1795. The latitude he gives for Cahokia does not appear in the Eastern Journal. (Thomas (2), 281; Moulton, 2:127–29.)

26. Clark's report of the excitement the appearance of the Corps created in St. Louis and the number of people that came to the landing to see

them testifies to the interest their expedition generated among their soon-to-be fellow Americans. His mention of meeting old acquaintances from Vincennes and Kaskaskia at the governor's is interesting in that it demonstrates the continuity of those living on the frontier and Clark's network of acquaintances. Clark had been in Vincennes, as both a soldier and a civilian. He first visited Kaskaskia on 4 September 1797, stayed in the area until the 8th, when he started for Cahokia and St. Louis, and returned on 13 September, staying until the 30th, primarily because of illness. The length of his stay allowed him to form a number of acquaintances, which proved advantageous for the Corps. (Thomas (2), 290–94.)

27. Clark contradicts the prevailing belief that the site for the Corps' winter camp already had been determined. Earlier in the letter he states that several places had been recommended, but that *he* would "fix on the Spot" best suited for their winter quarters. The mouth of Wood River (or River Dubois or River a Dubois) was one of the sites recommended, but according to Clark it only was after inspecting the site that he decided it was the best location. The contrary evidence to this is Delassus's 9 December letter to Salcedo and Calvo, in which he says that Lewis is going to spend the winter on the Dubois River, and Lewis's 19 December letter to Jefferson stating that when permission to begin ascending the Missouri was denied, he decided to winter at the mouth of the Dubois (if it was as described) or some other suitable area site recommended. On the balance of the various sources, it seems likely that Wood River was the most highly recommended site for a winter camp and the one the captains considered likely, though other sites had been suggested. It was up to Clark, as the commanding officer on the scene, to decide where they would winter. Clark concurred with the recommended Wood River site and established the Corps' winter camp there. As stated in note 1 of this letter, it is generally believed that the site is on the Missouri side of the Mississippi River because of the latter's shift to the east, but a growing school of thought maintains that the camp's site has not been inundated and was farther inland from the mouth of the river than previously believed. Also, reflecting American—or at least his own—pronunciation of Dubois, Clark places an accent over the c in Duboice. (Jackson (1), 1:143, 147; Moulton, 2:130–32; Osgood, 3n; Appleman (1), 287–90; Sparks, 4–9.)

28. The Illinois River flows from northeastern Illinois in a southwesterly direction to its confluence with the Mississippi at present Grafton, Illinois, some twenty-five miles upstream from where the Missouri joins the Mississippi. It was a major route for French-Canadian exploration

of the Illinois country and Mississippi Valley. The earliest French settlements in Illinois date from the seventeenth century and were along
the Illinois River. These posts and missions failed to thrive, and the
French shifted westward along the Mississippi from Cahokia south to
Kaskaskia. (McDermott, 1–5.)

29. Clark again contradicts the known time line of Corps events. In his
field notes he recorded that construction of the cabins or "huts" for
their winter quarters was started on 15 December, rather than the
16th as he states here. In addition, his 16 December field notes entry
records sending Charles Floyd to Cahokia with the mail. He also
states that in this letter but writes he is sending him tomorrow, which
would have been 17 December. Clark is correct concerning the dates
and days of the week in his notes, so it would seem that he misdated
this letter, writing it on 15 rather than 16 December. However, a possible explanation is that he wrote it late at night, after midnight, and
recorded the correct date, but still wrote from the perspective of its being Thursday, 15 December. While it is possible that he misdated the
letter, he does record the correct dates in the field notes, so he knew
what day it was. If he did misdate the letter, this conceivably could affect the dates he gives for other events since leaving the Falls of the
Ohio (see previous notes for this letter). Clark is known to have
stayed up late, sometimes past midnight. Therefore, lacking further
evidence, I am inclined to think that he wrote this letter after midnight
on the night of 15 December; dating it correctly as the 16th, but writing it from the perspective of the 15th. (Osgood, 3.)

30. Charles Floyd (ca. 1782–1804) probably was born at Floyd's Station,
Jefferson County, Kentucky. His father was Robert Floyd, not Charles
Floyd as is sometimes stated. By 1799 the family had moved across the
Ohio to the Clarksville area. In 1801 Floyd was appointed the first
constable of Clarksville Township. That a young man of about nineteen or twenty would be named to such a position testifies to his abilities, and explains why he was appointed a sergeant on the expedition
and why he is described by Lewis as a "young man of much merit." He
was one of the Nine Young Men from Kentucky (a term Clark applied
to them after the expedition to identify the nucleus of the Corps recruited at the Falls of the Ohio). He and the Field brothers, Joseph
and Reubin, were the first three permanent recruits. The journals,
field notes, and letters of the expedition all testify to Floyd's being
highly regarded by the captains and men. He died on 20 August 1804
near present Sioux City, Iowa, of an apparent ruptured appendix, and
is buried there. The account of his grave and monument is a story in itself. Ironically, the monument erected to him (the only member of the

Corps to die on the expedition and thus not actually complete the trek) is the largest for any expedition member, including Lewis and Clark. (Yater (2), 4–6; Holmberg (1), 4–13.)

31. Mr. Mills has not been positively identified. There was no Mills listed in the 1803 Jefferson County, Kentucky, tax list. In the 1804 list a Samuel Mills and a Richard Mills were listed as living on Floyds Fork in eastern Jefferson, but it is not known if either of them is the Mills to which Clark refers. No mention of a Mills is made in the day book in which Jonathan Clark recorded business he transacted for his brother while he was away on the expedition. (JCTL, 1803–1804.)

∼

Dear Brother   St. Louis 25th Feby. 1804

Your letter of the first of January I rceivede the post before the last and Should have written you by the last but I was at that time So un-well that I could not, my health at this time is Somewhat better– thoh. not entirely recovered from the Indisposition which attacted me in as-sending the river– I thought at one time I had entirely recovered, but haveing frequint returns of the disorder I am induced to belevie that time and attention alone will destroy the effects [of] it.[1] The due bill which [∧]has[∧] been prosented to you by Mr. Larrance[2] is yet due if William Sullivan[3] has not Settled it, please to enquire of him, & Cosby[4] if either of them Know any thing of Such a Demand, and examine my Shereff re-ceipts if nomention is made of the debt & c.   Capt. Lewis & my self Came to this place a Short time ago, to ∧ to make the ncessary[∧] arrangements for our rout up the Missoureis, which will be arly in aprill next,[5]–

The Lt. Govr. of this place rcived orders last week from his goverment to Deliver up this Provunce to Capt. Stoddard the Ajunt of the French Republic & Comdt. for the United States to recevee the Coloney for the Said States, he imedeately issued ~~orders~~ a procklemation to notify the Citizens & c. ~~Day before~~ yesterday Capt. Stoddard was ascorted into ~~to~~ town ∧~~ascorted~~[∧] by about 20 Citizens. The Lt. Govr. informed him that he was ready to deliver up the provunce to him at any house, ~~this~~ a great Dinner & porrade took place at the Lt. Govrs. – this morning Capt. Stoddard made a Demand in behalf of the french republice ~~whose~~ and recveed an answer, ∧from the Lt. Govr.[∧] that he would expeDete the delivery ∧& he would fix on a time[∧] as Soon as possible, about the middle of this day Capt. Stoddard the Lt. Govr. and about ten officers Came to my Quarters at Mr. Cada Cheautous–,[6] for Capt. Lewis and my Self to accompany them to examine the fortifications (which is in a retched State)[7] we dined as yesterday with the Lt. Govr. a most Sumpcious Dinner, & a large Compy. a great Deel of formality and parade was displayed_ Capt. S_ has Shewn me all his orders & c. whuch he intends to issue, they are Such as I highly approve of – he will reapt. the Comdts. Calculated for their Situations for his temporary government.[8]

I am pleased to inform you that we are like to make good terms with the [warr?]ing [paper loss due to seal tear] Indians.[9] as it is now late [I will?] [paper loss due to seal tear] Say nothing more at this time, please to excuse me to bro: Edmund for not answering his letter, at this time.

I must request you or bro Edmund to attend Mr. Terrells[10] Sale of lots in Clarksville[11] and purchase Some of them for me next to the river, one of them is in my inclosure I wish as many of them purchased as you may think will be use full to me.

Please to present me Sincearly to Sister John Mr & Ms. Temple & the famely and believ me to possess more than brothery effecton

Wm Clark

1. This of course refers to the gastrointestinal malady that laid Clark low while traveling down the Ohio and up the Mississippi. Clark reported becoming ill again in mid-January and was still unwell when he and Lewis left for St. Louis on 10 February. While in St. Louis he did not keep his field notes. He and Lewis returned separately to Camp Dubois at different times and left again for various reasons.

2. Possibly Benjamin Lawrence (1741–1814) or his son Samuel (1764–1822). They were natives of Howard County, Maryland, and moved with their families to Jefferson County in 1799. Both men lived on Beargrass Creek. Jonathan records visiting a Mr. Laurence in his diary. (Thompson, 125–26; JCTL, 1802–1803; Jonathan Clark Diary, 25 July 1803.)

3. William Sullivan (1769–1804) was the son of Capt. James and Susanna Sullivan. He came to Jefferson County, Kentucky, in 1780 with his parents and siblings, and he was raised on the family plantation on the South Fork of Beargrass Creek, making him a Clark neighbor. He married Jane Boyd, 29 December 1791, in Jefferson County, and died

there in 1804. (A family genealogy states that he married a Jennie Boyd and died in 1809, but primary sources provide the information listed. Jonathan regularly noted births, marriages, and deaths of family and close friends in his diary, and he records the death of a William Sullivan in 1804.) John C. Sullivan was the guardian for his brother's children. Given their closeness in age and location it is very likely that William Clark and Sullivan were acquaintances if not friends. (Sullivan family file, TFHS; Jonathan Clark Diary, 6 November 1804.)

4. Fortunatus Cosby, Sr. (1767–1846), was a native of Louisa County, Virginia, a graduate of William and Mary, and a lawyer, serving as a district attorney in Virginia in 1790–1795. In 1795 he married Mary Ann Fontaine, daughter of Capt. Aaron and Barbara Terrell Fontaine. In 1798 he moved with his wife's family to Jefferson County, Kentucky, and settled on Harrod's Creek. Cosby built a successful law practice, and in 1802 he settled in Louisville, quickly becoming one of its leading citizens. He served in the state legislature during 1802–1803 and 1805–1806, and as a circuit court judge 1810–1816. The Clarks and Cosbys were business associates and part of the same social and extended family circle. Col. John Thruston's widow married Aaron Fontaine and the Cosbys and Fontaines were Harrod's Creek neighbors of Clark sibling Ann and her husband Owen Gwathmey. Jonathan records business he transacted with Cosby and others on William's behalf during his absence on the expedition. (*EL*, 223; Joblin, 66–67; Johnston, 2:376–77; Jonathan Clark Day Book, JCP-CHC, fl. 178, TFHS.)

5. William Clark's estimate of leaving in early April proved to be overly optimistic. The gathering of information and supplies, arranging the Osage delegation to Washington, and other preparations delayed the Corps' departure from Camp Dubois until 14 May.

6. Jean Pierre Chouteau (1758–1849) was a native of New Orleans. He was the son of Pierre Laclede and the half brother of René Auguste Chouteau. He had come to St. Louis the year it was founded and had grown wealthy in the Indian trade, primarily with the Osage. He and his half brother Auguste were the two most powerful and influential men in St. Louis. William Clark knew Pierre (or Peter) from his 1797 visit there, though the Chouteaus' association with the Clarks and American officials dates back to George Rogers Clark and his Illinois Campaign of 1778–1779. Pierre led the Osage delegation that journeyed to Washington that spring of 1804, and he was appointed the Indian agent for the tribe. He was one of the founders of the St. Louis Missouri Fur Company and led the 1809 expedition that returned the

Mandan chief Sheheke (Big White) to his home. Clark's reference to staying with him and his family in his 3 May letter (following this) verifies that the "Cada" Chouteau mentioned here is Pierre. This reference to Pierre by this nickname (meaning second born) is potentially confusing because the *Dictionary of American Biography* identifies his son Pierre (1789–1865) as being known as "Cadet" or "Cada," and says nothing about the elder Pierre also being referred to by that name. This letter establishes that Pierre, Sr., also was known by the nickname, apparently because he was the younger brother of Auguste Chouteau. The younger Pierre apparently was known as "Cadet" because he was a junior. In February 1804 he would have just passed his fifteenth birthday and so was too young to have been involved in the things Clark recounts. (*DAB*, 4:93.)

7. St. Louis was ringed by a series of fortifications that had been allowed to deteriorate over the years. The deterioration apparently had accelerated in the last six years because in his 1797 journal William Clark reported a "small fort, one Bastion & 5 Towrs round guards the Town," with no mention of their being in a state of disrepair (a condition he often noted). This decline in the town's defenses perhaps indicates an increased sense of security among the inhabitants and its thriving state. A plan of St. Louis and its fortifications is included in Victor Collot's atlas accompanying his *A Journey in North America.* It was previously known that Lewis had returned to Camp Dubois by 13 February and had gone back to St. Louis on an unknown date. Clark's mention of touring the "retched" fortifications with Lewis on 25 February places Lewis back in St. Louis by that date. (Thomas (2), 292; Collot, 247–49; Moulton, 2:174.)

8. Stoddard has received high marks for his administration of Upper Louisiana. Realizing the need for a smooth transition from French/Spanish rule to American rule, Jefferson and Stoddard both knew that as many former territorial officials as possible should be retained in their offices. Even after Americans began pouring into the territory, the old residents of French and Spanish extraction, particularly the former, continued to serve in positions of influence and authority. Stoddard's showing Clark his official papers, including those he intended to issue, demonstrates the respect he had for Clark and their good relationship. Clark's pride and pleasure are obvious in the letter. (*DAB*, 18:51.)

9. Lewis and Clark were involved in Indian affairs before setting off up the Missouri. In the winter and early spring of 1804 both captains helped keep peace among area tribes. They even went so far as to travel a distance up the Missouri to stop a war party of Kickapoo Indi-

ans from attacking the Osage. (Jackson (1), 1:167–68; Moulton, 2:174.)

10. Richard Terrell (d. 1802) was in Jefferson County by the mid-1780s. He was from Louisa County, Virginia. His sister Barbara probably was the Barbara Terrell married to Aaron Fontaine. A Richard Terrell (often appearing as Terrill) is listed as serving in the Virginia militia, but no information has been found regarding his service either in the Virginia or Kentucky militias. He apparently rose to the rank of captain, since he is so referred to in newspaper ads. (This would appear to be one of the rare occasions when Clark did not refer to someone by his military or other title.) A Richard Terrell is listed as serving as a Jefferson County judge in 1785 and as a member of the first two statehood conventions in Danville, also in 1785. He lived in the Louisville area and in Lexington in the 1780s, but returned home for extensive periods of time because he is listed in Louisa County records into the mid-1790s. He married Lucy Maria Carr (1768–1803) in Louisa County on 5 October 1792 and is listed as removing to Kentucky. Upon establishing full-time residence in Kentucky, Terrell settled in Lexington. He practiced law and was deeply involved in land matters. About November 1795 he removed to a plantation on the Muddy (north) Fork of Beargrass Creek where he not only raised a variety of livestock but also bred horses. He owned extensive property in the Illinois Grant, including Clarksville lots that Clark mentions. He died suddenly in Lexington, on 3 October 1802, leaving a wife and at least four children. His wife and Fortunatus Cosby served as administrators of his estate. (Harris, 414–15; Chappelear and Hatch, 13–14; Collins, 1:354; Wulfeck, 2:39; Carr-Terrell Papers, University of Virginia; *The Farmer's Library*, 6 May 1802, 4 November 1802; *The Kentucky Gazette* (Lexington), 26 September 1796, 5 October 1802.)

11. Clarksville, Indiana, at the foot of the Falls of the Ohio, was ordered established and laid out by the Virginia legislature in 1783. This was accomplished in 1784. Named in honor of George Rogers Clark, it was the first American town established in Indiana. Men who had served with Clark during the Revolution in his Illinois Regiment received grants in this area called the Illinois or Clark's Grant. The Clarks, particularly George and William, invested heavily in Clarksville lots, and George had received a large grant. It was to Clarksville that the two brothers relocated in early 1803, settling on a farm at Point of Rocks, later called Clark's Point, on the river at the foot of the falls. It was their farm that served as the final staging point for the

Corps of Discovery while it was at the Falls. William Clark actively acquired Clarksville lots (as later letters document) and served as a town trustee. Hopes for the growth and importance of the town were frustrated, especially when a canal on the north side of the Ohio failed to be built, and Jeffersonville to the east and New Albany to the west soon surpassed it. Today nothing remains of the original town, but the site of the Clark farm is included in the George Rogers Clark State Historic Site. (Hening, 11:335–37; Esarey, 203–4; Jonathan Clark Diary, December 1802–May 1803; Jackson (1), 1:7.)

$\sim$

Mouth of Missouri   May 3rd 1804[1]

Dear Sir

This will be handed you by my friend Mr. Peter Choteau an inhabitant of St. Louis, a gentleman deservidly esteemed among the most respectable and influential Citizens of Upper Louisiana. Mr. Choteau's Zeal to Serve & permote the Public welfar has induced him, at the instance of our government to Visit the <u>Osage Nation</u>[2] sence the session of this Countrey to the U States — he has brought with him the Great Chief of that Nation, and many other Chiefs of the first Consideration and respectability among them, and is now on his way to the City of Washington in Charge of those Chiefs, with a view to effect a treaty between the UStates and that Nation.   The promptitude and fidelity with [which] Mr. Choteau has fulfilled the wishes of the government on this ocasion, as also the personal dangers to which he has been exposed in the Course of this trans action, entitle him in an eminent degree to the particular attention & best services, not only of yourself but of his fellow Citizens generally. Besides Mr. Choteau's personal merits and his Claims to the attention of his fellow citizens, he has still a Stronger Claim upon my particular friends, arriseing from the marked politeness and attention displayed by himself, his Lady and family, towards Capt. Lewis and my self dureing our residence in this Countrey. On our Several Visits to St. Louis, in the Course of the Winter and Spring, we have made the house of this gentleman our home.

Any Services therefore which you may have in your power to render Mr. Choteau or those of his party, I must beg leave to Claim.   as I have no acquaintenc in the City of Richmond,[3] must request the favour of you to give Mr. Choteau ~~in that place~~ a letter to Some Respectable Charactors in that place.

Your effect Brother &
Sincere friend
Wm Clark

1. This letter is almost identical to the one Clark wrote on 2 May to William Croghan. Much of it is the same as the letter of introduction that Lewis wrote to William Preston the same day that Clark wrote this letter. Donald Jackson states that the rather ornate prose of the letter reveals Lewis to be the composer and Clark the copier. I would agree with this assessment. One of the captains obviously is using the other's letter as a model, and the phraseology is inconsistent with the straightforward style of William Clark. Clark even goes so far as to adopt the formality of using the salutation "Dear Sir" rather than "Dear Brother." The only real difference between the Clark and Lewis letters is the personal information about Chouteau's hospitality toward the captains while they were in St. Louis. Despite Lewis's letter being dated a day later than the one Clark wrote his brother-in-law Croghan, Lewis is the likely author. In fact, it is likely that more than just these three letters of introduction were written. Not only were they in common use at the time, but the captains would have wanted to smooth the way for Chouteau and the Osage delegation the best they could. Unless Clark just happened to have a draft of Lewis's letter at hand (which is possible), it seems rather unlikely that he would use it as a model for two letters to close family members, but quite likely that he would model after it a number of letters to men he knew along the route the delegation was to take eastward. The original of the Lewis letter to Preston (which Jackson cites the typescript for) is in the Preston Family Papers—Joyes Collection, TFHS. (Jackson (1), 1:178–79.)

2. The Osage Indians were the most formidable Native American nation inhabiting the lower Missouri River valley and the present state of Missouri. They were divided into two bands: the Great and Little Osage. French and Spanish traders had vied for their loyalty—and the lucrative business it would bring—for years. When the United States took control of Upper Louisiana, peaceful relations and treaties that included Osage land cessions were priorities, thus the reason for this trip to Washington. (Lamar, 1114–15.)

3. The route the Chouteau-led Osage delegation followed was roughly

due eastward from St. Louis to Vincennes, Louisville, Frankfort, Lexington, through the Cumberland Gap and then down the Shenandoah Valley to Winchester, and on to Shepherdstown, Maryland, Harpers Ferry, and Frederick to Washington. Having just moved to Kentucky from Spotsylvania County, Virginia, two years earlier, Jonathan had a number of friends in Richmond to whom he could write letters of introduction for Chouteau. It is doubtful that any were needed. Richmond would have been quite a detour from the route the delegation took to Washington, and it most likely did not go there. But the route of the delegation may not have been decided when Clark wrote this letter, and he may also have been erring on the side of caution in having letters written that were not needed. Lewis's letter to Preston was addressed to him at Fincastle, Botetourt County, Virginia. Preston lived there, as well as at estates he owned in Montgomery County and Wythe County, and it was to one of these locations that Lewis's letter was delivered by Chouteau. The 13 July 1804 edition of *Bartgis's Republican Gazette* reported that the Osage party had passed through Frederick (then Fredericktown) on 9 July. It reported that the party consisted of eleven Osage men and two boys, accompanied by Chouteau and four or five other white men. The reporter was, like Jefferson a few days later, impressed by the Osages' tall stature. The delegation arrived in Washington on 11 July and met frequently with the president. On 12 and 16 July, he delivered speeches to them. Jefferson stated in a letter that there were twelve Osage men and two boys, rather than the *Gazette*'s eleven. The principal chiefs were White Hair, Dog Soldier, and Bigtrack. After visiting Washington, they toured Baltimore, Philadelphia, and New York. Sometime during their visit, probably in Washington, the artist Saint-Mémin sketched and painted five portraits of at least four of the Osage. These are the earliest known portraits of Plains Indians. By the fall of 1804 they had returned to Missouri, traveling from Pittsburgh down the Ohio to Fort Massac, overland to Kaskaskia, and on to St. Louis. They apparently were quite puffed up regarding their eastern visit and were the envy of other tribes' chiefs. By the fall of 1805, other delegations from Plains tribes were being sent to Washington. (Preston Family Papers—Joyes Collection, TFHS; Preston Family Papers—Davie Genealogical Collection, fl. 190, TFHS; Jackson (1), 1:198–203; Ewers, 12–19; Wright, 2:3, 26; Ambrose, 332–33.)

~

Fort Mandan[1]   April the   [th] 1805

Dear Brother

From this place we Send back to St. Louis Six Soldiers and Some french hands who accompanied us to this place for the purpose of transporting Provisions; by those men we Sind our Dispatches and the Boat we assended to this place in.[2] one of this party Richard Worvington[3] who acts as a Sergeant and has acquited himself verry will [well] has charge of the Boat and party, will deliver you my letters—— I also Send you by him, a map of the missouri and its waters Compiled from the information of the best informed traverlers Indians & c. A Statistical view of the Indians their Situation Trade & c. & c. a Sketch of the countrey through which the different rivers flow. Some memorandoms ~~of~~ discriptive of the Missouri its waters, productions, natives, Climate, Trade & c. & c. a Summary Statement of the rivers, creeks & c. their width and Distances assending. & my notes in form of a journal and Some other papers. all of which I wish you to keep, and to Show them to those of my friends you think proper_ those papers are in their orginal State and verry incorrect as you will observe in reading thim, I Should by verry glad to have them Copied and Connected,_. I have no other Copy of those notes or papers they are the first Sketches which I made from which copies have been taken with the necessary correction's and Sent to the President of the united States & Secretary at War—— I have also Sent to the president of the US my journal in its original State tho' much fuller and more explicit than those notes I send you, they will be kept by him untill my return. If you think proper to publish a revisial of any Small extracts of those papers prey do So.[4] I have been So much engaged all the latter part of this winter and Still ~~am~~ engaged in the accomplishments of those things necessary for the ~~accomplishment of the~~ entirprize in which I am engaged, that it is intirely out of my power to give you or any of my friends a full detail of accurruncs, _ you will See by the notes what we are about and Collect a more perfect Idea than I could give you in a letter__. I send to you three Boxes containing the following articles[5] viz: 1 <u>Shirt</u> worn by the ∧mandan[6] ~~& the~~[∧] Indian women of this countrey made of the Skins of the Antilope or goat, 1 pr. Chiefs mockersons with white Buffalow Skin tops (a white buffalow Skin Sels in this Countrey for about fifteen horses) 2 pr. of Summer & 1 pr. of winter mockersons Com∧r[∧] [comprised?] all of Buffalow Skin, The Skin &

William Clark's letter to Jonathan from Fort Mandan, April 1805. In it Clark itemized over thirty items from the expedition that he was sending back for the family and provided other information, including the fact that York was married. Courtesy of The Filson Historical Society

horns of an Antelope or goat, Called by the french <u>Cabre</u>_. 1 pr. of Mandan legins of the Antelope Skins,_ The Skins of 2 Burrowing Dogs or barking Squirels one Stuffed.   The Skin of a Brarow, which burrows in the grown 2 white <u>hare</u> Skins, one Stuffed, Common in this Countrey. Some Specimons of the Corn of this Countrey which Shoots near the earth_. Ricara[7] Tobacco Seed, the flowr, leaves & Stems of which they Smoke. Some of the root and plant ₍ₐ₎made use of by th Sious to[ₐ] of a Cure the bite of a <u>mad</u> <u>Dog</u> & rattle Snake, and Said to be certain. a Specimon of the wild Sage made use of as a medison by the Mandans for almost every Complaint.

3 horns of the mountain Ram all Small ~~but~~ one a faun those Animals inhabit <u>Coat noir</u>[8] & Rockey mountains in great numbers, and much prized by the Indians (one for Govr. Harrison)[9] a parchment Case

Dressed and used by the mandans to carry their valueable articles in. a Sample of what the Indians mix with their Tobacco to Smoke ie Red-wood & Sackacomma. 1 Skin of a Red fox, which is Common in this Countrey. a Specimon of Indian artachokes common in the plains and much used by the Indians. 1 Small pot in the Mandan fashion. 1 Spoon of the horn of the mountain Ram, Sent by Jo. Fields[10] to his father. Some mineral which I wish Sent to Dr. Brown.[11] they are dangerous when burnt & pounded as we experiancd. Some Plumb Stones of a Delecious flavour which I send to Sister Clark they are of three kinds.

The abov artecles are all in a large red box, and the following artecles are in two [∧]Small[∧] white boxes i‗e five Buffalow Robes of Different figures, one represents three actions ~~with~~ [∧]between[∧] the Sioux[12] & Mandans near this place, the mandans on horsback and suck∧sess[∧]full. the scalps represented **c o** [the symbol Clark draws looks like a lowercase "c" and "o," with smaller circles drawn on the left, right, and bottom of the o] on the Sious of the robe. one other robe of the Chyenne[13] figures which I Send you. The one marked <u>John Shields</u>[14] is Sent by him to his wife. 2 others York[15] tels me that he has put up in the 3d Box ~~2 Robes~~ for his wife & Ben,[16] as marked _ ꝋ. Those 3 boxes I have requested the Commondant of St. Louis ~~to~~ to Send by Some boat or Safe Conveyance to you.[17] I think it probable he will Send a fiew men for that purpose—

When I Shall have the pleasure of Seeing you again is unecrtain I fear not Sooner than next July twelve months,‗; the Countrey before me is extencv and unexplored, ~~thro~~ — Please to present my Compliments most respectfully to Sister Clark and the familey and belivee me to be your Sincere and effectunate

Brothr

Wm Clark

Capt. Lewis presents his "Compliments to you and Lady"

1. Named in honor of the nearby tribe which was the Corps' "host" for the winter, Fort Mandan was located on the east (or north) bank of the Missouri about six miles below the mouth of the Knife River (entering from the west) and across from the lower Mandan village named Matootonha. The search for a proper site for the Corps' winter quarters began on 28 October, two days after reaching the Mandan villages, and a site was selected on 2 November. Construction began on 3 November and was completed on Christmas Day (although the men had moved in by mid-November because of the increasingly cold, snowy weather). The

fort was "U" shaped with a connecting wall across the open end. It included quarters and storerooms along the "U" walls, and the connecting wall consisted of a palisade with a gate. The fort was abandoned on 7 April 1805 when the Corps continued the expedition up the Missouri and the return party started downriver. While passing the fort in August 1806 on their return, they discovered that a fire, apparently a prairie fire, had destroyed most of the structure. For many years it was believed that the original site of the fort was in the river bottoms and possibly partially covered by the Missouri. A current theory states that the site is completely on land, and an archaeological dig is planned at its believed location. A reconstruction of the fort can be viewed near Washburn, and a marker has been placed in the vicinity of the fort's site at Fort Mandan Historic Site. The date of the letter was left blank, probably indicating that Clark was adding to it or intended to add more to it before dating and sealing it. Since the expedition left Fort Mandan on the afternoon of 7 April the "th" placed to follow the intended date would indicate a date of 4–7 April. However, a review of the journals and other letters indicates 1–3 April as the more probable days during which the letter was written. That is when the captains wrote most of their letters to be sent back with the keelboat. (Appleman (1), 111–24, 337–44; Jackson (1), 1:226–34; Moulton, 3:227n.)

2. The keelboat was sent back downriver in the spring of 1805 because it was deemed too large to go farther upriver. It had been intended from the outset to return from the Corps' winter quarters with the temporary party and the material collected and journals and reports produced. The captains originally planned to send the keelboat back in the fall, but decided to wait until the spring instead. The French engagés, or boatmen, still with the party (some already had been discharged) and U.S. soldiers Richard Warfington, John Newman, Moses Reed, John Boley, John Dame, and either Isaac White or Ebenezer Tuttle made up the main return party. Lewis and Clark state that "6 Soldiers" and "6 Americans" were part of the return party; therefore either White or Tuttle was probably included in this group, and the other had indeed returned the previous summer as has been theorized. The captains are very specific about there being six Americans and six soldiers. It would seem that Warfington, even though acting as commander of the party, would be included in this count. If so, then Tuttle or White must not have been at Fort Mandan. A possibility mentioned by both Moulton and Jackson is that Warfington was not included as one of the six soldiers since he was commanding. Indeed, the captains' entries for 7 April can be interpreted that way. That would still not account, however, for Clark stating that "6 Americans" were with the return party. Surely he would have in-

cluded Warfington in that number. Indeed, in this letter, he includes Warfington as one of the six soldiers. Another possibility is that the six Americans were Warfington, Newman, Boley, Dame, Tuttle, and White, and that Reed, already having been dishonorably discharged, was exiled from the party as an undesirable. Joseph Whitehouse is the only journalist to mention him after October 1804. It is doubtful that the captains would have considered him a soldier, and even more unlikely that they would have trusted him to perform faithful service under Warfington on the trip downriver. At the same time, it seems likely that the captains would have believed it their duty to return him to the military authorities for additional discipline. Perhaps he was under some form of arrest and was considered so inconsequential or was so disdained by Lewis and Clark that they did not bother to include him among the Americans or soldiers. Whitehouse's entry for 7 April seems to support this possibility. He stated that a command under Warfington set off for St. Louis, and had the "deserter Reed" on board. The matter is an interesting mystery that may never be solved. The keelboat left Fort Mandan on 7 April and arrived at St. Charles on 20 May, and at St. Louis on 22 May. A lawyer named William J. Clark, no relation to Captain Clark, was in St. Louis and St. Charles taking depositions regarding a legal case in Kentucky involving the Daniel Boone family. He described the arrival of the keelboat at St. Charles and what he saw when he toured it. The keelboat continued on to Fort Massac regarding official business, but apparently is lost to history after that point. It may have continued up the Ohio to the Falls to deliver the boxes Clark had sent back for family and friends, but that more likely was accomplished by pack horse. A report in Cincinnati's *Western Spy* quoted a 5 June report from Vincennes that one of Lewis and Clark's party had passed through that town a few days ago and provided information on the expedition. This most likely was Warfington, and thus he was indeed traveling overland to Louisville. This is further confirmed by the 18 June 1805 edition of the *Kentucky Gazette*, which reported that one of the men who had returned down the Missouri with dispatches delivered them to Louisville. As for the keelboat, it would have continued in government service until destroyed or sold as surplus. Listings appear in the *Missouri Gazette* for government boats being sold at auction. (Large (1), 7–10; Moulton, 2: 509–29, 3:327; 4:711, 12n; 11:132; Jackson (1), 1:233, 237n, 242–43, 372n; William J. Clark Diary, 20 May 1805, TFHS; *The Western Spy* (Cincinnati), 26 June 1805; *Kentucky Gazette*, 18 June 1805.)

3. Richard Warfington (b. ca. 1777) was from Louisburg, North Carolina. He enlisted in the army in 1799, and became a member of the party from John Campbell's company from South West Point, Tennessee. He was

included as a member of the temporary party from the beginning. Clark's praise of him makes one wonder if the captains wished he were continuing with them to the Pacific but knew they needed him to command the keelboat back downriver to St. Louis. Besides, his enlistment had expired in August 1804, and he had agreed to stay on in order to command the return party. His period of service, in Clark's post-expedition list of men receiving extra pay for the expedition, is listed as 14 May 1804 to 1 June 1805. Whether Warfington actually delivered the papers and "souvenirs" Clark sent to Louisville is not definitely known, but he apparently anticipated his doing so. *The Western Spy* and *Kentucky Gazette* reports mentioned in note 2 support this possibility but, if he did, he was not carried on the Corps' roster for this task, unless he reached Louisville by 1 June. (Jackson (1), 1:364–65, 372, 2:378; Moulton, 2:522–23; *The Western Spy,* 26 June 1805; *Kentucky Gazette,* 18 June 1805.)

4. The questions of what papers were sent back and who received them have been matters of confusion and contention among historians. Osgood discusses and analyzes the issue in the introduction to the printed edition of Clark's field notes that he edited. The matter is also discussed in an article Gary Moulton and I wrote on this group of expedition letters in 1991. In reading and analyzing what Clark writes in this letter (which Osgood did not have the benefit of seeing) and Osgood's conclusions regarding what documents were sent back and to whom, I come to the same conclusion that I did in 1991. It appears, given what Clark writes in this letter, that he was sending Jonathan the complete set of his Field Notes (both the Dubois and River journals), and that Jefferson and Dearborn received neater, more detailed copies of the River Journal and Codexes A, B, and C. In addition, he was sending Jonathan the originals of the map of the Missouri River and its affluents, the statistical view of the Indians, the narrative sketch of the country, the summary statement of Missouri River landmarks, miscellaneous descriptive memoranda, and other undescribed papers. As with the River Journal, the copies made from these documents would have been neater and perhaps would have contained a few more details than the original documents. They are alluded to in a letter Clark wrote William Croghan from Fort Mandan. Jonathan apparently did not see that any part of these documents were published, but he did have parts of them copied for friends, as evidenced in a letter his friend and former Virginia neighbor Joseph Herndon wrote him on 8 June 1806, in which he asks Jonathan to thank his sons John and Isaac for "copying the map and other papers accompanying it" and reports that their friends were very interested in them. It is possible that Clark reclaimed these papers upon his return, but no evidence has been found confirming that. The Field

Notes were found among the papers of Gen. John H. Hammond in the attic of a house in St. Paul, Minnesota, in 1953. Why they were among the papers of this Civil War veteran and Indian superintendent has never been determined. The two most commonly stated theories are that the notes had drifted into the Indian Department files while Clark was superintendent and that Hammond, in cleaning out that office years later, found and kept them; or that Hammond, who married a Louisvillian and spent time in Louisville, was a friend of the Clark family and that Jonathan's descendants, knowing his interest in Indians and western affairs, gave them to him. The latter theory is preferred by the Hammond family, but no one actually knows how they came to be in that St. Paul attic. A legal battle between the family and the federal government over their ownership was resolved in favor of the family, and they were later acquired by Yale University. (Moulton and Holmberg, 397–401; Osgood, xvii–xxxiii; Jackson (1), 1:230; Jonathan Clark Papers–Temple Bodley Collection [hereafter cited as JCP-TBC], TFHS.)

5. These three boxes were only alluded to before the discovery of this letter (in a letter William Clark wrote Amos Stoddard, 1 April 1805). Most of the botanical and animal specimens were also sent to Jefferson and have been listed and noted by Jackson, Moulton, and others. An examination of the lists of items sent back (one by Lewis and one compiled by John Vaughan of the American Philosophical Society where Jefferson forwarded them) reveals a couple of specimens sent by Clark to his family that apparently were not sent to the government. The one botanical specimen is the Indian or Jerusalem artichoke. It would seem that such a widely used item would have been sent back, but perhaps because it was common in the East it was not included. One mineral sample apparently was not included either, or I missed it on the lists. It was described by Clark as a mineral that was dangerous when burned and pounded, but no similar description accompanied the mineralogical specimens sent to Jefferson. The largest number of items not duplicated between the Kentucky and Washington specimens can be grouped together under ethnographic artifacts. It is possible that some of the type of items Clark lists were also sent to the president but not separately described. The captains had some items wrapped up in buffalo robes which Lewis described only as articles of Indian dress. Given other items detailed, it is surprising that collections such as moccasins, leggings, shirts, etc., would not be separately listed. Perhaps these were not sent back. If not, it could be a reflection of the captains' focus on scientific rather than ethnographic specimens. Copious notes and reports were made concerning the Native Americans encountered but perhaps that did not extend to a primary concern with collecting Indian items for

the government. The captains may have thought of them as too common or as things that would soon be viewed in the East anyway when tribal delegations visited Washington. It may have been an oversight, though that seems unlikely. One possibility is that such items were in limited supply and Clark preferred sending them to family and friends rather than to the government. He may have been collecting them for that purpose, while Lewis either chose not to or failed to collect such items for Jefferson. We will probably never know. The ethnographic "souvenirs" that Clark sent back which were not itemized as being sent to the government were a Mandan woman's shirt of antelope skin; four pairs of moccasins, one a chief's with white buffalo skin tops considered rare and very valuable, two summer pair, and one winter pair, all made of buffalo skin; one pair of Mandan leggings of antelope skin; a parchment case used by the Mandan to carry valuables (probably a parfleche); and six buffalo robes, five apparently Mandan-made and one made by Cheyenne. While buffalo robes of both a plain and an illustrated nature were sent to Jefferson, such items (particularly decorated ones) can be considered unique works of art. Therefore, I include the robes sent as not being duplicates of items sent to the government. Of these fifteen items not duplicated in the Jefferson shipment and of the thirty-four total sent, the possible existence of only one is known today. One of the bighorn sheep horns may have been given to Clark's sister Fanny, and descended to her great-grandson Rogers Clark Ballard Thruston, longtime president and benefactor of The Filson Historical Society, who presented it to the Filson in 1929. Another possibility regarding the Filson's horn is that it was one of the four large bighorn horns shipped to Louisville from St. Louis in September 1806 after the expedition's return. Whether it was in the Fort Mandan or St. Louis shipment may never be known, as its size falls somewhere between the "small" ones sent in 1805 and the four "large" ones sent in 1806, but it tends toward the latter size. Many historians consider this horn to be the only verified animal artifact from the expedition (excluding birds). The fate of the other items—in both the 1805 and 1806 shipments—remains a mystery. They undoubtedly were distributed to the Clark family and friends and likely disposed of, misplaced, forgotten, tucked away, and destroyed over succeeding years. William Clark may have retained some (most likely from the 1806 group) for his own collection. It is possible that at least one of the pairs of moccasins made their way east from Kentucky to Spotsylvania County, Virginia. In a letter to Jonathan Clark, Joseph Herndon acknowledged receipt of a pair of moccasins and asked Jonathan to thank William for them. Although the letter is dated 11 January 1808, I think it possible that these were moccasins collected on the expedition and possibly one of the pair sent to Jonathan in April 1805. An earlier Herndon letter, dated 8 June 1806, thanked Jonathan for having two of his sons copy a map and other papers, referring, I believe, to those papers included in that Fort Mandan shipment. A few of the items (i.e., plum stones and wild sage) are not specifically identified but match up with specimens of similar description that may be the same as them and are therefore included as items also sent to Jefferson. The specimen of Arikara tobacco sent to Jefferson still exists today as part of the Lewis and Clark Herbarium in the collection of Philadelphia's Academy of Natural Sciences. (Jackson (1), 1:226–27, 234–42; Moulton, 3:258, 304, 325–27n, 330, 454, 458–59, 464–67, 470–78, 8:418–19; Cutright, 349–92; Moulton and Holmberg, 401–2; JCP-TBC; Wilson, 16.)

6. The Mandan were a sedentary tribe of the upper Missouri. They had migrated into the Missouri Valley from the southeast beginning about A.D. 1200. At the time of Lewis and Clark's visit they had declined greatly in power and number due to the ravages of smallpox. They were friendly to whites, and the Corps spent an enjoyable winter as their neighbor. The journals include much information on the Mandan. One legend about them said they were descendants of the mysterious Welsh Indians, remnants of early Welsh (or possibly other European) settlers. Lewis and Clark were aware of this belief and after some observation and thought concluded they were not. On the return of the Corps, Mandan chief Sheheke, or the Big White, accompanied it downriver and on to Washington. In 1837 the Mandan were devastated by another smallpox epidemic, which left only remnants of this once important Missouri River nation. They joined remnants of the Hidatsa and Arikara nations, who had similarly suffered from Euro-American diseases, especially smallpox. All three tribes were settled on the Fort Berthold Reservation in present North Dakota. James Ronda's book *Lewis and Clark among the Indians* contains an excellent account of relations between the Mandan and the Corps of Discovery. (Lamar, 702–3; Ronda (1), 67–112; see Moulton, vol. 3.)

7. The Arikara were a semi-sedentary tribe that lived along the Missouri River south of the Mandan. They were an offshoot of the Pawnee Indians and had migrated to the area from the southwest. Their culture was similar to the Mandan. They also had been decimated by Euro-American diseases that drastically reduced their population and power. Lewis and Clark enjoyed friendly relations with them, but the death of one of their chiefs who had gone downriver with the keelboat in 1805 while on a visit to the East and provocations by American fur trappers and traders made them hostile by 1807. They periodically impeded travel on

the upper Missouri for some thirty years until a smallpox epidemic broke their strength. The remnants of the tribe lived near Fort Clark in present central North Dakota for some twenty years before settling on the Fort Berthold Reservation with the Mandan and Hidatsa. See Ronda for a detailed account and analysis of the Corps' visit with the Arikara. (Lamar, 40; Ronda (1), 42–66.)

8. Coat Noir is Clark's version of the French "Côte Noir," meaning Black Hills (or Black Mountains). The Black Hills, located in present western South Dakota and into northeastern Wyoming, were not visited by Lewis and Clark. The Black Hills were sacred to the Teton Sioux and would become a major point of contention between them and the U.S. government later in the century. At this time the region called the Black Hills also encompassed the eastern outlying ranges of the Rockies. (Moulton, 3:26n, 48n, 136n.)

9. William Henry Harrison (1773–1841), soldier, politician, and U.S. president, was governor of Indiana Territory at this time. Clark and Harrison had known each other since their service together in the army during Wayne's campaign. Harrison aggressively acquired Indian land, which made him popular with western settlers. He became a national hero with victories at Tippecanoe in 1811 and the Thames in 1813, both of which significantly contributed to his election to the presidency in 1840. In the years since leaving the army, they had remained in contact, and Harrison took both a professional and a personal interest in the expedition. His mansion, Grouseland, in Vincennes may be one of the few extant structures west of the Appalachians that Lewis and Clark visited. Clark most likely would have visited it in his travels, and Lewis might have stopped there if he took the Vincennes route from Louisville to St. Louis in 1808. During the War of 1812 Harrison expressed great confidence in Clark's military abilities, stating he would rather have Clark with him in the kind of war they were engaged in than any other man in the United States. What happened to the bighorn sheep horn intended for him is not known. It is quite possible that when the expedition's express (probably Warfington) passed through Vincennes, it was given to him then. (Lamar, 487–88; *DAB*, 4:143; Jackson (1), 1:135, 227–30, 242–44, 246–48; *The Western Spy*, 26 June 1805.)

10. Joseph Field (ca. 1780–1807) was a native of Virginia, possibly of Culpeper County. His family moved to Jefferson County, Kentucky, when he and brother Reubin (ca. 1781–ca. 1823, possibly 1822 but most likely 1823) were small children. They are both often listed as being born some ten years earlier, but this is not likely. A close examination of the facts known about them and their family and the way in

which they are referred to by the captains indicate they were probably in their early to mid-twenties when recruited for the expedition. It is not known who was older, but Joseph tends to be listed first in family legal documents. Such documents often reflect the ages of the children (oldest to youngest), so I speculate that Joseph was the older by a year or two. They were two of the famous Nine Young Men from Kentucky and received special recognition from Lewis for their distinguished service on the expedition.

Like those of so many members of the expedition, Joseph Field's life is largely a blank slate except for the expedition years. He may have been the first fatality among expedition members following their return. Field family legal documents confirm his death by October 1807. Clark, in his 1820s list of expedition members, lists him as being killed, so he must have met a violent end. James Ronda states that he accompanied the rather mysterious John McClellan (or McClallen, see note 17, this letter) expedition westward in 1807. Perhaps he was killed on this foray into the wilderness. It is known that both Joseph and Reubin Field had remained in or returned to St. Louis because they were there in the spring of 1807. If he did accompany the McClellan expedition Joseph must have been killed while traveling to the Rockies. The party is believed to have wintered in present South Dakota, during which time McClellan recruited additional members. A check of the source for the statement that Field and fellow expedition veteran John B. Thompson were with the McClellan party actually reveals that it is based on speculation. Two expedition veterans were known to be with the group, but their identities are unknown. The McClellan party left for the Bitterroot Mountains in March. If the party broke camp some 1,200 miles up the Missouri and Field was with it, how could he have been in St. Louis that spring to sign the petition concerning land grants to the men who had accompanied Lewis and Clark? Did brother Reubin possibly sign for him? The signatures are similar, but there are some differences. The petition appears to have been signed by each of the petitioners, including John B. Thompson. If Field was on the expedition, he must have been killed no later than July in order for word of his death to reach Kentucky. However, the time frame just does not fit Joseph Field dying on McClellan's expedition. A more likely possibility is that he was killed that spring or summer while ascending the Missouri, in St. Louis, or back home in Kentucky.

One possibility is that he was killed on Pryor's abortive attempt to return Sheheke home. Pryor reports that none of his soldiers were killed in the battle with the Arikara but that four men with Chouteau's boats accompanying him were. Is it possible that Joseph Field, perhaps his brother Reubin, John B. Thompson, and other Lewis and Clark veterans were with Chouteau's party and had not been hired as part of the U.S. force? The American force was heavily supplemented by Chouteau's party. It is known that Corps veteran George Shannon and probably George Gibson were with Pryor's party. Gibson was one of the spring 1807 petitioners. The time frame for Pryor's party to return down the Missouri from the Arikara villages fits. The Field family knew of Joseph's death by 20 October 1807. William Clark, in Louisville at the time, knew of Pryor's defeat by 24 October. The battle was 9 September, and the trip from those villages to St. Louis took about one month. If the party returned to St. Louis in early October, word could have been received in Louisville of Joseph's death by mid-October.

The Field brothers' father was Abraham Field (d. 1822). He was a frontiersman who had been wounded at the Battle of Point Pleasant and moved with his family from Culpeper County to Jefferson County in 1784. He worked as a hunter in the Fish Pools area of southern Jefferson County (present Okolona), and in 1790 bought a farm along Pond Creek in the southwestern part of the county. It was in these two areas that the Field brothers grew up and learned to be woodsmen and hunters. They probably also had experience working for their older brother Ezekial making salt, a useful skill during the Corps' winter stay at Fort Clatsop. Clark undoubtedly knew the Abraham Field family and was interested in recruiting the two brothers early on, as evidenced by their official enlistment date of 1 August 1803. One example of their close association is their common Moore connection. When Abraham Field and his family moved to the Fish Pools, they lived at James Francis Moore's station. Moore's cousin was Robert Kearney Moore, the Clarks' neighbor and good friend on Beargrass Creek. Records prove the two Moores had a close relationship. In addition, James Francis Moore had served under George Rogers Clark and was associated with him in administering Clark's Grant. It certainly is possible that the Field brothers visited Robert Moore's plantation growing up and met Clark there (or elsewhere in Jefferson County) on any number of occasions. It also is possible that Moore may have told William Clark about these two talented young frontiersmen and hunters. In addition, it is likely that the Clarks knew Abraham Field and his family, and the Moore connection simply provided another link. George Rogers Clark and Abraham Field both served in Lord Dunmore's War in 1774. Another connection is that Capt. Reuben Field (apparently the Field brothers' great-uncle) served with Jonathan and other Clarks

and Clark relatives in the 8th and 4th Virginia regiments during the
Revolutionary War. Capt. Field settled in Bourbon County, Kentucky,
after the war, but there is evidence that he also spent time in Jefferson
County. (Yater (2), 2–4; Appleman (2), 5–36; Ronda (2), 10–11; Majors, 569, 572–73, 576, 584–85, 598, 605; Jackson (1), 2:342, 378–79,
432–38; Petition, bx.3, fl. 8, WCP-VMC; Thompson, 133–35.)

11. Dr. Samuel Brown (1769–1830) was a native of Rockbridge County,
Virginia, and educated in Virginia schools, including Liberty Hall
Academy (present Washington and Lee University), which his father,
Rev. John Brown, founded, and at Dickinson College. He studied
medicine in Philadelphia (including a course of study as a personal student of Dr. Benjamin Rush) and in Scotland, receiving his degree in
1794. In 1797 he settled in Lexington, Kentucky, in order to be near his
parents and brothers. Brown's interest in medicine and science was
far-ranging, and he soon became one of the prominent men of his day
in those fields. He was elected a member of the American Philosophical Society in 1800. He was a pioneer in the United States in smallpox
inoculation. He moved to New Orleans in 1806 with his brother
James and in 1808 settled on a plantation near Natchez following his
marriage. After his wife's death, he resettled on a plantation near
Huntsville, Alabama. From 1819 to 1825 he taught in the medical department of Transylvania University in Lexington but traveled extensively, especially to Philadelphia and his Alabama plantation when
school was not in session. He married Catherine Percy (d.1813) in
1808, and they had three children. He died on his Alabama plantation
where he had retired because of poor health. The members of the
Brown and Clark families knew each other. George Rogers Clark and
Samuel's brother John had been friends since the 1780s. Samuel
Brown and Thomas Jefferson were friends, and given the association
of the Clark and Brown families and their circle of friends and acquaintances, William Clark and Brown undoubtedly knew each other,
especially since Clark was going to the trouble of sending him a mineral sample. (Dorman (2), 44–45; *KE,* 131.)

12. The Sioux (or Dakota) Indians were known by whites at this time as
the "bandits" or "bullies" of the Missouri River. The Teton and Yankton groups had migrated southwestward from present Wisconsin and
Minnesota to the northern Great Plains in the seventeenth and eighteenth centuries. The Yanktons were basically a sedentary and peaceful people. Lewis and Clark had no trouble with them. The Teton were
more populous and warlike, and the Corps had strained relations with
the Brulé band of the Teton that almost ended in hostilities. The Teton
Sioux remained the most formidable foe of the U.S. Army on the plains

until almost 1880. Ironically, they were among the first Native American nations encountered by Lewis and Clark, and they were among the last to be subjugated by the U.S government. Ronda gives an excellent account of the Corps' encounter with them. (Lamar, 115–18; Ronda (1), 23–41.)

13. The Cheyenne Indians, like the Sioux, had migrated from present Minnesota to the plains, largely because of Sioux pressure. They settled in the eighteenth and early nineteenth centuries in present Wyoming and eastern Colorado and often spent part of the year farther out on the plains. Because they lived to the west of the Dakota and away from the Missouri River, Lewis and Clark did not encounter the Cheyenne to any significant degree. While visiting the Arikara and Mandan, however, the Corps did encounter Cheyenne-made items and a few Cheyenne visitors and traders. The information the captains gathered on this tribe was included in their reports to the government. On the return trip Clark counciled with a band of Cheyenne while visiting the Arikara. The Cheyenne also resisted Euro-American encroachment, and have the unfortunate distinction of being attacked in two of the most infamous "battles" of the Plains Indian wars, Sand Creek (1864) and Washita (1868). (Lamar, 195–97; Ronda (1), 50, 75, 100, 129, 248–49; Moulton, 3:420–21.)

14. John Shields (1769–1809) was a native of Rockingham County, Virginia. He accompanied his family to Pigeon Forge, Tennessee, in 1784 and learned blacksmithing from his brother-in-law. It is believed that by 1790 he had migrated to Kentucky. At the time of his recruitment he apparently was living in West Point, Hardin County, Kentucky, about twenty miles downstream from Louisville. The Field brothers lived in the vicinity, and they almost certainly knew each other. His date of enlistment was 19 October 1803. Shields recovered from a poor start marred by disciplinary problems to become a valued member of the Corps. He received compliments from Lewis in his post-expedition comments for his smithing abilities. He was also a good hunter. After the expedition, he is believed to have spent a year in Missouri trapping with Daniel Boone, who apparently was a kinsman. He settled near Corydon, Indiana, some thirty miles west of Louisville, apparently because of that Boone connection; Daniel Boone's brother Squire had settled in the Corydon area with several families. Shields was married to a woman named Nancy (maiden name unknown) before the expedition, and they had one daughter. Because of his blacksmith and gunsmith abilities, Clark may have figured he needed him and made an exception to the no-married-men rule that Lewis concurred in. Clark most likely knew Shields before October 1803. A day book kept by

Jonathan Clark, in which he recorded business he transacted for his brother while he was on the expedition, lists providing a Mrs. Shields with twenty-one bushels of corn and four dollars. If this was John Shields's wife, which I think very possible, perhaps William Clark was keeping a promise made to Shields to assist her in his absence or from his concern that his men's families be taken care of if necessary. (Yater (2), 7–8; Cromwell v. Young (ca. 1837–38), Hardin Co. Circuit Court Records, KDLA; Jonathan Clark Day Book, 10 June 1804, 6 July 1805.)

15. York (b. ca. 1772) was William Clark's African American slave and manservant. He was the first African American to cross the United States from coast to coast, and North America north of Mexico. York officially was owned by John Clark until the latter's death in 1799, and then by terms of his will his son William inherited him and other slaves. An examination of the records concerning the Clark slaves leads me to believe that York was the son of Old York but not the son of Rose. M. Lewis Clark states in his family genealogy that York and Nancy (see letter dated 2 July 1808, note 1) were siblings, and Nancy clearly is listed as the child of Old York and Rose. Although York is not listed as being a child of one or both of them, that may be because of a difference in ages. Nancy is associated with Rose in John Clark's 1799 will, but York is not associated with any parents. This is most likely because he already was an adult. My guess is that he was Old York's son from a previous relationship; that Rose had at least two children (Scippio and Daphny) before marrying Old York; and that their union produced at least two children (Nancy and Juba). William Clark's mention of York sending his wife a buffalo robe establishes that he was married at the time of the expedition. Nothing definitely is known of his wife except that she lived in the Louisville area and was owned by someone else. A 15 May 1811 letter from John O'Fallon to his Uncle William reveals that York's wife's master was believed to be moving to Natchez. This slave union and slaveholder attitudes concerning slave marriages were to be the basis for a serious falling out between Clark and York in 1808, as later letters in this collection reveal. As a result of this rift and Clark's apparent acquiescence in allowing York to be near his wife, York spent most of his traceable years in Louisville, either hired out or working for Clark family members. He apparently was working as a waggoner in Louisville as early as 1810. In November 1815 he was the wagon driver for a drayage business that William and John Hite Clark established. That is the last known evidence of York until William Clark's 1832 interview with Washington Irving, in which he related his fate. Clark reported that he had set York free after the expedition

(though not before 1816) and set him up in a freight-hauling business between Nashville, Tennessee, and Richmond, Kentucky, but York was a poor businessman and lost the business, and while returning to Clark in St. Louis he died of cholera in Tennessee. Two theories contradict this, but I do not agree with them. One has York returning to the Rocky Mountains and becoming a chief among the Crow Indians. Another recalls an "Uncle York" who lived at Clay Hill, a Lewis family plantation in Virginia where he was buried, as late as about 1878, and wonders if this may have been the York of the expedition. Clark had no reason to falsely report what he knew about York, and what he did tell Irving coincides with known documentary evidence. If York did attempt to operate a drayage business between Nashville and Richmond, why did he choose these two towns? His experience and family ties would seem to keep him in Louisville. One possibility is that perhaps John O'Fallon misunderstood where York's wife's owner was moving. Slurred together, Natchez and Nashville sound very similar. This certainly would have given York the incentive to leave an area he knew and settle in Nashville. A major road connected Nashville and Lexington, Kentucky, and a spur led to Richmond; so operating a wagon between Nashville and Richmond certainly was plausible. There is one more possibility. In recounting York's fate to Irving, Clark gives an impression (at least to me) that his death had occurred some years earlier. Cholera visited Kentucky and Tennessee periodically during this time, and no one definite year can be pinpointed for the likely year of York's death. One interesting possibility, given Clark's tone and known cholera deaths, is 1822. There are recorded cholera deaths for that year, including Clark's brother-in-law Dennis Fitzhugh, and Clark's implication that it had occurred some years earlier would fit the date. Robert Betts's *In Search of York* is an excellent biography of this famous African American. It has been updated and reissued with an epilogue by me. (O'Fallon to Clark, 15 May 1811, WCP-VMC; MLClark, 90–95; Holmberg (2), 7–9; JCISB, 2:160–61; John H. Clark to William Clark, 14 November 1815, John Hite Clark Papers, TFHS; Betts, 83–170; *EL*, 962; Lewis, 21.)

16. Ben was inherited by John and Benjamin O'Fallon upon the death of their grandfather John Clark in 1799. By terms of the will William Clark retained control of Ben, and actual ownership would transfer to him when the O'Fallons reached twenty-one years of age. Clark apparently considered this to mean he could do what he wanted regarding Ben (unless he had bought him from the estate or the O'Fallons), and perhaps in consultation with his sister Fanny (her sons being too young) decided to free Ben—but with strings attached. On 10 De-

cember 1802, Clark legally freed Ben "in consideration of services rendered me and regarding perpetual involuntary servitude to be contrary to principles of natural justice." The next day, 11 December, Clark and Ben returned to Jefferson County court where Ben bound himself to Clark as a servant for a period of thirty years. In return Ben received one dollar and all necessities of living, and when his indenture expired on 11 December 1832, he was to receive a one-half-acre lot in Clarksville, a plow, an ax, and a hoe. Ben was married to Venos (see letter dated 21 July 1808, note 12), a Clark family slave that William acquired from his brother George. While it is possible that a desire to remain with his family explains why Ben bound himself to Clark, or that Clark wanted to assist him and preferred this arrangement, it should be noted that Clark did not free other slaves at this time. The most likely explanation is that Clark "freed" Ben as a legal means of officially taking him across the river to the nonslave territory of Indiana, and that this was done in preparation for Clark's impending move from slaveholding Kentucky to free Indiana Territory. Legally, former slaves could be brought into Indiana Territory during this period if they had become indentured servants. In reality they still were slaves and, as in the case of Ben, once removed from free territory back to slave territory they were considered slaves again. Slaves were also unofficially, and actually illegally, brought into Indiana and other free territory. An unknown number of Clark's slaves, most likely including York, were unofficially brought across the Ohio to his farm at Clarksville. Ben and Venos apparently remained with Clark for a number of years because M. Lewis Clark, in his 1853 family genealogy, lists them as "Old Uncle Ben" and "Old Aunt Venus." He does not mention when they died, but one would suspect that they were with William Clark until at least 1817 or later in order for his son, born in 1809, to remember them. In an 1868 interview with Lyman Draper, M. Lewis Clark refers to Ben as having the surname McGee. (JCWB, 1:86–90; John Clark will and 1799 tax document, WCP-VMC; JCBPAB, 2:56, 201–2; Thornbrough, 7–18; MLClark, 90; Draper Mss., 2J100.)

17. The commandant of St. Louis Clark refers to is Amos Stoddard. The letter he wrote to Stoddard is no. 145 in Jackson and possibly was written on 1 April 1805. This letter verifies that the recipient of no. 145 was Stoddard. Clark probably was sending the boxes to him not only because of his position in St. Louis but because he was a friend who was acting as his agent there. By the time the keelboat arrived, Stoddard had been transferred, but the boxes for Jonathan were forwarded overland, apparently with no problem or delay, under the possible escort of Corporal Warfington. The shipment of papers and

artifacts for Jefferson and Dearborn apparently was escorted down the Mississippi to the Gulf of Mexico and along Atlantic coastal waters by a Captain M'Clellan. This is probably John McClallen (d. 1810), a captain in the artillerists who resigned on 31 January 1806 and entered the fur trade. Lewis knew McClallen from the army. The Corps of Discovery encountered him on 17 September 1806 leading a party up the Missouri. This is the same man as John McClellan of the mysterious McClellan Expedition. There have been several variations in the spelling of the name. Harry Majors in his articles on the McClellan expedition preferred that spelling but army records list him as McClallen. (Jackson (1), 1:40n–41n, 226–27; *The Western Spy*, 26 June 1805, 3 July 1805; Majors; Heitman (2), 1:655.)

≈

St. Louis 23rd September 1806

Dear Brother

We arrived at this place at 12 oClock today from the Pacific Ocian where we remained dureing the last winter near the entrance of the Columbia river.[1] this Station we left on the 27th of March last and Should have reached St. Louis early in August had we not been detained by the snow which bared our passage across the Rocky Mountains untill the 24th of June.[2] in returning through those mountains we devided ourselves into Several parties, digressing from the rout by which we went out in order the more affectually ∧to[∧] explore the Country and discover the most practicable rout which does exist across the Continent by way of the Missouri and Columbia rivers,[3] in this we were completely successfull and have therefore no hesitation in declaring that Such as nature has permited it we have discovered the best rout which does exist across the continent of North America in that direction.[4] Such is that, by way of the Missouri to the foot of the rapids below the great falls[5] of that river a distance of 2575 miles thence by land passing the Rocky Mountains to a navagable part of the Kooskooske[6] 340. and with the Kooskooske 73 miles Lewis's river[7] 154 miles and the Columbia 413 miles to the pacific ocian makeing the total distance from the confluence of the Missouri and Mississippi to the discharge of the Columbia into the Pacific Ocian 3555 miles. the navegation of the Missouri may be deemed good; it's dificulties arise from it's falling banks, timber embeded in the mud of it's channel, it's sand-bars and Steady rapidity of it's current all which may be over

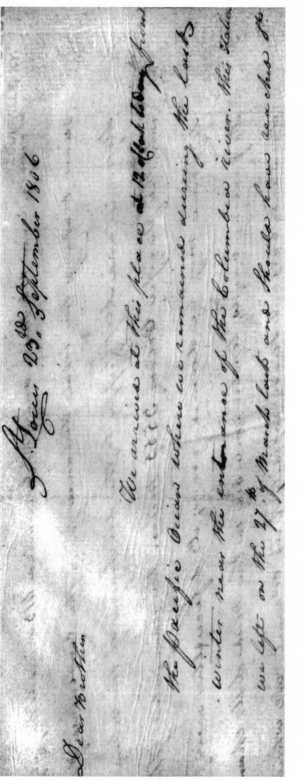

William Clark's letter of 23 September 1806 to Jonathan announcing the successful return of the Corps of Discovery. Courtesy of The Filson Historical Society

come with a great degree of certainty by useing the necessary precautions.[8] the passage by land of 340 miles from the Falls of the Missouri to the Kooskooske is the most formadable part of the tract proposed across the continent. Of this distance 200 mile is along a good road, and 140 miles over tremendious mountains which for 60 miles are covered with eternal Snows.[9] a passage over these mountains is how ever practicable from the latter part of June to the last of September and the cheap rate at which horses are to be obtained from the Indians of the Rocky Mountains and west of them reduce the expences of transportation over this portage to a mere trifle. the navagation of the Kooskooske Lewis's river and the Columbia is Safe and good from the 1st. of April to the middle of August by makeing three portages on the latter river. the first of which in decending is 1200 paces at the Falls of the Columbia 261 miles up that river, the second of 2 miles at the long narrows 6 miles below the falls and a third also of 2 miles at the Great Rapids 65 miles Still lower down.[10] the tide flows up the Columbia 183 miles and within 7 miles of the great rapids. large Sloops may with Safty ascend as high as tide water and Vessels of 300 Tons burthen reach the entrance of the Multnomah River[11] a large Southern branch of the Columbia which takes it's rise on the confines of new mexico with the Callarado and Apostles rivers[12] dischargeing itself into the Columbia 125 miles from it's entrance into the Pacific Ocian._. I consider this tract across the Continant of emence advantage to the fur trade, as all the furs collected in 9/10th. of the most valuable furr country in America may be conveyed to the mouth of the Columbia and Shiped from thence to East indias by the 1St. of august in each year. and will of course reach Canton earlier than the furrs which are annually exported from Montrall arive in Great Britain__.[13]

In our outward bound voyage we ascended to the foot of the rapids below the great falls of the missouri where we arived on the 14th of June 1805 not haveing met with any of the nativs of the Rocky mountains we were of course ignarant of the passes by land which existed through those mountains to the Columbia river, and had we even known the rout we were destitute of horses which would have been indispensibly necessary to enable us to transport the requisit quantity of amunition and other stores to ensure the Success of the remaining part of our voyage down the Columbia; we therefore deturmined to navigate the Missouri as far as it was practicable, or unless we met with Some of the nativs from whom we could obtain horses and information of the Country. accordingly we undertook a most laborious portage at the falls of the missouri of 18 miles which we effected with our Canoes and baggage by the 3rd of July. from hence ascending the Missouri we penitrated the Rocky mountain at the distance of 71 miles above the upper part of the portage and penitrated as far as the three forks of that river a distance of 181 miles further; here the Missouri devides into three nearly equal branches at the Same point. the two largest branches are So nearly of the same dignity that we did not conceive that either of them could with propriety retain the name of the Missouri and therefore called these three Streems Jefferson's Madisons and Gallitin's rivers.[14] the confluence of those rivers is 2848 miles from the mouth of the Missouri by the meanders of that river. we arived at the three forks of the Missouri the 27th of July. not haveing yet been so fortunate as to meet with the nativs alth'o I had previously made Several excurtions for that purpose, we were compelled Still to continue our rout by water. the most northerly of the three forks, that to which we had given the name of Jeffersons river was deemed the most proper for our purpose and we accordingly ascended it 248 miles to the upper forks[15] and it's extreem navigable point, makeing the total distance ~~of~~ ₐto[ₐ] which we had navigated the waters of the Missouri 3096 miles of which 429 lay within the Rocky Mountains. on the morning of the 17th of August 1805 I arrived at the forks of Jeffersons river where I met Capt. Lewis who had previously penitrated with a party of three men to the waters of the Columbia discovered a band of the Shoshone Nation and had found means to induce thirty five of their chiefs and warriors to accompany him to that place.[16] from these people we learned that the river on which they resided was not navagable and that a passage through the mountains in that direction was impracticable; being unwilling to confide in the unfavorable account of the natives it was concerted between Capt. Lewis and my self that one of us Should go forward immediately with a small party and explore the river while the other in the interem would lay up the Canoes at that place and engage the nativs with their horses to assist in transporting our Stores and baggage to their camp,[17] According[ly] I Set out the next day passed the devideing mountain between the waters of the Missouri and Columbia and decended the river which I ~~found~~ since Call the East fork of Lewis's river[18] about 70 miles. finding that the Indians account of the country in the direction of this river was carrect I returned and joined Capt. Lewis on the 29th of August at the Shoshone Camp excessively fatigued as you ₐmay[ₐ] Suppose. ~~after~~ ₐ haveing[ₐ] passed mountains almost inexcesseable ~~haveing~~ and ["and" is written over the word "been"] compelled to Subsist on berries dureing

the greater part of my rout. we now purchased 27 horses of these indians
and hired a guide[19] who assured us that he could in 15 days take us to a
large river in a open country west of these mountains by a rout Some Distance to the North of the river on which they lived and that by which the
nativs west of the mountains visited the plains of ∧the[∧] Missouri for the
purpose of hunting the buffalow. every preperation being made we Set
forward with our guide on the 31st of August through those tremendious
mountains. in which we continued untill the 22nd of September before
we reached the lower country beyond them; on our way we met with the
Ootelachshoot a band of the Tuchapahs[20] from whome we obtained ax-
cession of Seven horses and exchanged Eight or ten others this proved of
infinite Service to us as we were compelled to Subsist on horse beef about
Eight days before we reached the Kooskooske. dureing our passage over
those mountains we Suffered every thing which hungar Cold and fatigue
could impose; nor did our difficuelties with respect to provision cease on
our arival at the Kooskooske for although the Pallotepallars[21] a noumerous nation inhabiting that Country were extremely hospitable and for a
fiew trifling articles furnished us with an abundance of roots and dryed
Salmon the food to which they were accustomed we found that we could
not Subsist on those articles and almost all of us grew Sick on eating them
we were obliged therefore to have recourse to the flesh of horses and
dogs[22] as food to Supply the dificiency of our guns which produced but
little meat as game was scarce in the vicinity of our camp on the Kooskooske where we were Compelled to remain in order to construct our perogues to decend the river. at this Season the Salmon are m[e]agre and
form but ~~little~~ indifferent food. while we remained here I was my Self
Sick for Several days and my friend Capt. Lewis Suffered a Serious in-
desposition.[23] Haveing completed four Perogues and a Small Canoe we
gave our horses in Charge to the Pallotepallors untill we returned and on
the 7th of October reimbarked for the Pacific Ocian. we decended by the
rout I have already mentioned. The water of the river being low at this
Season we experienced much dificuelty in decending, we found ~~them~~
∧it[∧] obstructed by a great number of dificuelt and dangerous rapids in
passing of which our perogus Several times filled and the men escaped
narrowly with there lives. however the dificuelty does not exist in high
water which happens within the period which I have previously mentioned. we found the nativs extreemly noumerous and Generally friendly
though we have on Several occasions owed our lives and the fate of the
expedition to our number which consisted of 31 men.[24] on the 17th of

November we reached the Ocian where various considerations induced us to Spend the winter, we therefore Searched for an eligible Situation for that purpose and Selected a Spot on the South Side of ~~the~~ a little river called by the nativs the <u>Netul</u> which discharges itself ~~into~~ [ˏ]at[ˏ] a Small bar on the South Side of the Columbia and 14 miles within point Adams.²⁵ here we constructed Some log houses and defended them with a common Stockade work; this place we called Fort Clatsop after a nation of that name who were our nearest neighbours. in this Country we found an abundance of Elk on which we Subsisted principally dureing the last winter. ˏwe left Fort Clatsop on the 27th of March &[ˏ] on our homeward bound voyage being much better acquainted with the Country we were enabled to take Such precautions as ~~have~~ in a great measure secured us from the want of provision at any time, and greatly lessoned our fatiegues, when Compared with those to which we were compelled to Submit, in our Outward bound journey. we have not lost a man Sence we left the mandans ~~in~~ a circumstance ~~to~~ which I assure you is a pleasing consideration to me. as I Shall Shortly be with ˏyou[ˏ] and the post is now waiting I deem it unnecessary here to attempt ~~writing~~ [ˏ]minutely to[ˏ] detail the Occurrencies of the last 18 month.²⁶ I am &c. Yr. Offectunate brother,

Wm Clark

Note: This famous letter announcing the successful return of the Lewis and Clark Expedition was believed to have been written to Gen. George Rogers Clark. Donald Jackson questioned the identity of the recipient and theorized that it may have been Jonathan, although he listed George, as former editors had done. Jackson was correct in his thinking. The letter in this series dated 24 September settles the matter. This 23 September letter belongs in this series, although it was not found in 1988 in that Louisville attic. Years earlier, it had passed into the Fanny Clark line of the family. Along with the bighorn sheep horn and other family papers, it descended to her great-grandson, Rogers Clark Ballard Thruston, who gave them to the Filson. Although alienated from the group of letters that descended through Jonathan's line to Temple Bodley and eventually to his grandchildren, it should, I believe, be included with them, and I consequently present it here.

Another point of debate, and one that Jackson sought to answer, is the author of the letter. Was it William Clark or Meriwether Lewis? Perhaps it really does not matter, since the primary objective was to announce the return of the Corps. But it is interesting to speculate about the authorship. Jackson states that Lewis wrote the letter for Clark and that the latter copied it for transmittal to Kentucky, where it would be published. This may be the case, especially if it is theorized that Lewis wrote his letter to Jefferson and the letter to Jonathan Clark for the newspaper in one sitting. A possible hint of this is given in his remark to Jefferson that Clark is with the Mandan chief. The Lewis draft or copy does read very much the same as Clark's actual letter. The letter does, however, lack much of Lewis's usual prose style, such as he used in his letter to Jefferson. Perhaps he refrained from such turns of phrase, but knowing the letter would be printed in newspapers throughout the nation perhaps would have made "waxing poetic" quite tempting. The argument could also be made that Lewis's draft/copy is dated 24 September, while Clark's letter is dated 23 September. Clark's journal entry for 24 September indicates that both his and Lewis's letters of 23 September were actually written on 24 September. Had they decided that it was best to date the letters from the day of their arrival? This would perhaps explain Lewis dating Clark's letter the 24th. But if this is true, how is Clark's letter dated 24 September to Jonathan referencing the letter he wrote him yesterday explained? Is it possible that Clark is off one day in dating his letters, and that his 24 September letter was written on the 25th? Were the letters to Jonathan and the president written very early on the 24th, but from the perspective of the 23rd because they had not yet retired for the night? Clark, recording events in his journal on the 24th, includes all the day's activities, the very early as well as the later. Again, as with many things regarding the expedition and its members, we may never know. I do think it reasonable, however, to speculate that Clark had an active role in writing the 23 September letter. It stands to reason that the captains would have collaborated on such an important document. Clark had been writing letters and keeping a journal of this nature during the expedition and even before it. He did not need Lewis to write it for him. Clark may have in the past simply copied letters Lewis had written, such as the May 1804 letters of introduction for Pierre Chouteau, but the prose of that letter clearly identifies it as being drafted by Lewis. I do not think that is the case here. It should also be remembered that Clark was the more faithful journalist of the two, and that he had written letters reporting on the expedition as early as December 1803. My inclination is that both men worked on the 23 September letter and Clark also deserves credit as its author. (Jackson (1), 1:319–43; Moulton, 8: 370–72.)

1. The Corps reached the Pacific on 15 November 1805 and explored the coast and area for ten days. Clark actually visited the ocean for the first time on 18 November. A vote—that included York and Sacagawea—

determined that the party preferred to cross to the south side of the Columbia to establish winter quarters, and the captains decided to do so. After exploring the southern side of the river in that area, Lewis fixed on a site some three miles up the Netul (now Lewis and Clark) River. Fort Clatsop, named after the neighboring Indian tribe, was established on 7 December. It was a fifty-foot-square (2,500 square feet) log stockade, with two rows of cabins on the west and east sides. The winter was thoroughly miserable, with rain and overcast skies almost every day, poor food, and tense relations with the Indians. Fort Clatsop was about five miles southwest of present Astoria, Oregon, just off U.S. Hwy. 101 (business route). A reconstructed fort is near the site of the original, the remains of which were visible until the 1870s. The Columbia River was known to exist and was called the "Great River of the West" or the "Oregon River." An American sea captain, Robert Gray, discovered it in 1792 and named it after his ship. It was not known how far inland it extended, but common belief was that it and the Missouri River system were within an easy portage of each other. The Columbia rises in British Columbia and flows northwestward, south, and finally westward some 1,200 miles to the Pacific. Lewis and Clark had entered the waters of the Columbia on 16 October from the Snake River. (Appleman (1), 25, 345–49; Moulton, 6:110–11, 114–15n; Lamar, 248–49.)

2. Eagerness to begin the return journey and leave their miserable winter quarters resulted in a premature departure. The Corps actually left Fort Clatsop on 23 March, not 27 March as Clark states. Snows in the Bitterroot Mountains stopped the Corps for some six weeks, which they amiably spent with their hosts of the year before, the Nez Percé. In addition to misstating the date they left Fort Clatsop, Clark also gives dates that conflict with those in the journals for when they arrived at the Great Falls of the Missouri, completed the portage around them, reached the Three Forks (he lists the date Lewis arrived with the main party; Clark arrived on 25 July with a scouting party), and when they reached and saw the Pacific for the first time (see note 1). Perhaps Clark and Lewis were relying on their memories rather than the journals for the dates stated in this letter.

3. The Corps divided at Travelers' Rest, near present Missoula, Montana, on the eastern front of the Rockies. Three Nez Percé braves guided them across the Lolo Trail. The eastward trip across the mountains was much better than their hardship-filled trek westward over the trail the year before. From Travelers' Rest Lewis led a party overland to the Great Falls. On a reconnaissance along the upper reaches of the Marias and Two Medicine Rivers, Lewis and his party of three (George Drouillard and Reubin and Joseph Field) had a hostile confrontation on 27

July with eight Blackfoot warriors, in which one warrior was killed by R. Field and one wounded and possibly killed by Lewis. Clark's party experienced no misfortune other than having their horses stolen by Indians, probably Crows. They retraced part of the previous year's route, then cut eastward from Lost Trail Pass to the Beaverhead River, Jefferson River, and thence to the Three Forks. Sgt. Ordway continued with the boats down the Missouri to Great Falls. Clark traveled overland to the Yellowstone River, journeyed eastward down it by horse, foot, and boat, and reached the Missouri on 3 August. It was along the Yellowstone that their horses were stolen. Lewis's party rendezvoused with Clark's on 12 August.

4. Lewis and Clark may have found the best route across the continent "in that direction," but it was not the most direct or best route. Later explorers and mountain men would blaze better, more direct paths across the plains and mountains. The Platte River valley and South Pass became the preferred route to the Oregon Country.

5. The Great Falls of the Missouri (near present-day Great Falls, Montana) is a series of five cascade-like waterfalls over a ten-mile stretch. The Missouri drops four hundred feet in this distance. The five falls (beginning with the one farthest downstream and the first encountered) are Great Falls (the tallest at some eighty-seven feet), Crooked Falls, Rainbow (originally Handsome or Beautiful) Falls, Colter Falls, and Black Eagle (originally Upper) Falls. Crooked Falls has not been dammed, and Colter Falls usually is no longer visible because of the pool created by Rainbow Dam. Dams have been built at the Great, Rainbow, and Black Eagle Falls. Lewis arrived at the falls with a scouting party on 13 June 1805. The eighteen-mile portage along the south side of the falls was completed on 2 July, and the expedition set out again on 14 July. (Appleman (1), 137–46; Portage Route Chapter, L&CTHF.)

6. The Kooskooske River is the present Clearwater River. Rising in the Rockies and flowing westward in various forks before merging and flowing into the Snake, the Clearwater was the first river of the Columbia River system on which they sailed. The Corps struck the Clearwater on 26 September near present Orofino, Idaho, after the most grueling travel of the expedition northward through the Bitterroots and then westward across the Lolo Trail. (Appleman (1), 277–83.)

7. Lewis's River is the present Snake River. Clark also named the Salmon River Lewis's River, mistakenly thinking that it and the lower Snake were the same river. On their return journey he realized his error, but for some reason the correction was not made on his map of the West, and the two rivers appear with the same name on Samuel Lewis's map (which was based on Clark's map) in the Biddle edition of the expedi-

tion history. Both the Salmon and upper Snake were unnavigable to them, thus necessitating a grueling hike overland through the mountains. The Corps canoed the stretch of the Snake from its confluence with the Clearwater at present Lewiston, Idaho/Clarkson, Washington to its confluence with the Columbia at Pasco, Washington. (Appleman (1), 165–66; 372–73.)

8. The Missouri of Lewis and Clark's day was significantly different from what it is today. Only in its very upper reaches, and along certain stretches of its course does the river now resemble the Missouri of two hundred years ago. Flood control, hydroelectric, navigational, and recreational projects have changed it from its former meandering and dynamic self into a much more controlled waterway.

9. Here Clark must be referring to the route Lewis's party took on their return. The Lolo Trail was still a grueling march, even with knowledgeable Nez Percé guides. The route from Travelers' Rest to Great Falls spanned a transition from mountains to plains. Although Clark had not experienced the latter part of this land route, Lewis and others had no doubt described it to him, and he had read the journal entries after the two groups linked up on 12 August. (Moulton, 8:290–91.)

10. These falls and rapids were serious obstacles to Columbia River navigation. The four primary falls/rapids (going downstream) were known as Celilo (or Great) Falls, the Short and Long Narrows (together known as The Dalles), and the Cascades. They stretched from present Celilo, Washington, to Cascade Locks, Oregon. (Moulton, 9:243–48.)

11. The Multnomah River is the present Willamette River. Flowing northward to join the Columbia, it is Oregon's major river and population center. Lewis and Clark missed the Willamette's mouth on both their outward and homeward journeys because of poor weather conditions and islands that shielded the river's mouth. Local Indians had told them of the river, and Clark returned with a party to explore upstream on 2–3 April 1806 when informed they had again missed it. They went as far as present Portland. The river flows through a wide, fertile valley between the Coast and the Cascade ranges. The captains correctly predicted the area would become an important center for future settlement. It became the western terminus of the Oregon Trail. (Moulton, 7:55–70.)

12. The Colorado is one of the West's major rivers, flowing over 1,400 miles from its source at Grand Lake in Rocky Mountain National Park in Colorado to the Gulf of California. The Spanish named it in the 1770s for its reddish color. In the early nineteenth century there was speculation that its headwaters might be near those of the Missouri and other major western rivers and possibly provide the water route to

the Pacific. Jefferson specifically addressed this in his instructions to Lewis. The Apostles River, or Rio de los Apostolos, was more myth than fact. It appears on Nicholas King's 1803 map which the captains carried with them, and they obviously are speculating that the un-marked Multnomah River coming from the south may rise in New Mexico in the area of the Colorado and Apostles Rivers. While the Apostles River does not actually exist, it is conceivable that a river in that region flowing southward, such as the San Juan River, or confu-sion over the course of the Colorado formed the basis for this belief. (Jackson (2), 130–31; Allen, 100–101, 115–16, 297.)

13. One of the objectives of the expedition was to determine the existence and feasibility of a water route to the Pacific from the Missouri River system. If one was found, and if it was economically feasible, Jeffer-son's plan was to use this route as a major trade link between the United States and the Orient. An important part of the trade would be in furs, an item prized not only for eastern and European markets but in China as well. Shipping furs from the Rockies and the Northwest di-rectly to Canton and the Asian market would be much more efficient and lucrative than the then-current procedure of shipping them to eastern ports such as Philadelphia and New York and thence overseas. The British shipped their furs eastward to Montreal. U.S. officials and businessmen dreamed of dealing a serious blow to the British fur trade if this could be done. It was not. No such practical route existed, and the vast majority of furs were shipped eastward. The furs that were shipped directly to the Orient usually came from the British.

14. Some 2,500 miles from its mouth, the Missouri is formed by the con-fluence of the Jefferson, Madison, and Gallatin Rivers at Three Forks. They were named for the then-president, secretary of state, and secre-tary of the treasury, respectively. The Jefferson rises in the mountains of southwestern Montana, the Madison in Montana just west of pres-ent Yellowstone National Park, and the Gallatin in the northwest cor-ner of Yellowstone National Park. Lewis and Clark both deduced that the westward Jefferson was the route that would take them deepest into the mountains. This area was prime fur country and became a fo-cal point of early American fur trapping efforts in the West. It was also the place where some of the Corps' members, such as George Drouil-lard and John Potts, were later killed by Blackfoot Indians. (Apple-man (1), 148–52.)

15. After initially turning westward up the Big Hole River, the captains re-traced their route and traveled up the Beaverhead River (near present Twin Bridges, Montana). The Corps followed that river toward the southwest. The forks or upper forks that Clark refers to are the conflu-

ence of the Red Rock River and Horse Prairie Creek, south of present Dillon, Montana. This is where Camp Fortunate was established on 17 August. The party then headed westward up Horse Prairie and Trail Creeks. (Appleman (1), 152–62; Moulton, 5:110.)

16. "That place" was the Forks of the Beaverhead where Camp Fortunate was established. The Corps' meeting with the Shoshone and trading for the horses they needed to cross the mountains allowed the expedition to continue. By a great stroke of luck—a serendipitous connection that even Hollywood would hesitate to script—the leader of the Shoshone band, Cameahwait, was Sacagawea's brother. The three men with Lewis when they finally made contact with the Shoshone were Drouillard, John Shields, and Hugh McNeal. The Shoshone lived in central Wyoming and southern Idaho in four bands at the time Lewis and Clark encountered them. Sacagawea was a member of the Lemhi band, which was the band that the Corps encountered. Until about 1800 the Lemhi Shoshone had been among the Shoshone that lived on the eastern side of the Rockies in Montana and southern Alberta, but a 1781 smallpox epidemic had decimated them, and subsequent fierce attacks by the Blackfeet had driven them into the mountains. The Lemhi were settled along the upper Salmon River and dared to make only seasonal hunting trips eastward. The Corps of Discovery were the first white men to visit Shoshone country and are believed to be the first white men the Lemhi Shoshone saw. (Appleman (1), 163–67; Moulton, 5:133–74; Lamar, 1107–9.)

17. Clark and a party reconnoitered along the Lemhi and Salmon Rivers and determined they were not navigable. Upon their return he helped Lewis barter for horses from the Shoshone. The Shoshone village was to the west, across the Continental Divide, in the Lemhi Valley.

18. The Salmon River. See note 7 to this letter.

19. The guide was Old Toby, an elderly Shoshone who had been over the Lolo Trail to the Clearwater River apparently only once years before, but he was somewhat familiar with the country to the north and west that the Corps had to traverse. Following the faintest of trails, he got lost at least once but did succeed in guiding the Corps to Weippe Prairie and the Nez Percé Indians. He also guided Clark's party on their reconnaissance along the Lemhi and Salmon Rivers. His name may have been a derivation of Tosa-tive koo-be, Tobe for short, meaning "furnished white white-man brains" (as opposed to black white-man, meaning York), since he guided them. His real name may have been Pi-kee queen-ah, "Swooping Eagle." (Appleman (1), 167–76; Moulton, 5:3, 131n.)

20. Also spelled Eoote-lash-Schute and Oat la shoot, and Tushepau and

Tushepaw, these were the Flathead Indians. This tribe did not actually practice head deformation but were known as such either because of the sign language symbol for them or because they had gotten confused with and consequently were included with Northwestern tribes that did practice head flattening. The name preferred by the tribe is Salish. "Ootelachshoot" may be a Salish term for "those down below." "Tushepaus" may have been the Shoshone term "tatasiba," meaning "the people with shaved heads." Clark estimated this band's numbers at about thirty-three lodges totaling some 400 people. He estimated the entire tribe at 450 lodges. In testimony to the persistent myth of the Welsh Indians, some members of the Corps thought the Salish language had characteristics of the Welsh and theorized that the Flatheads might be descendants of the Welsh colony which legend stated had been founded by Prince Madoc on the east coast of North America in the twelfth century. The Salish were encountered at Ross's Hole near present Sula, Montana, in the Bitterroot Valley. Originally living on the plains east of the Rockies, they had been forced into the mountains by the Blackfeet. They were allied with the Shoshone and made annual forays onto the plains to hunt buffalo, despite the danger of Blackfoot attacks. (Moulton, 5:187–88n, 189, 9:218–19; Ronda (1), 154–56; Appleman (1), 168–70, 326–27.)

21. The Pallotepallors are the Nez Percé, also called the Chopunnish. All three names refer to the tribe's practice of piercing their noses. There is some question whether they actually practiced nose piercing but contemporary accounts and evidence indicate they did. The sign language for them indicates piercing the nose, perhaps the origin of the name. Remember that the Flathead were known by a misleading name in part because of the sign language symbol for them. The Nez Percé were friendly to the explorers and provided desperately needed food. Clark's Pallotepallors may be "tsoopnitpeloo," meaning "piercing people." (Moulton, 5:224–25n; Ronda (1), 157–62; Appleman (1), 175–79.)

22. Eating horses was a new dietary experience for most of the men. Food was indeed so scarce that they had to eat some of their horses during their trek across the Bitterroots. Dog was not a new food. They had been served dog by various Indians tribes since ascending the Missouri in the summer of 1804. Puppy was considered a special delicacy. Lewis acquired a certain liking for dog meat, but Clark never did.

23. Going from a diet based on meat, and then suffering through near starvation rations, to fish and camas root wreaked havoc with the men's digestive systems. Many, including the captains, developed severe cramps, gas, and diarrhea. Lewis suffered so badly at one point that he barely could ride a horse. Their systems gradually adapted, and fish

and camas root, along with the preferred meat, remained an important part of their diet until they passed back onto the plains the next summer. The Corps constructed its dugout canoes to descend the Clearwater at Canoe Camp, near present Orofino, Idaho. (Ronda (1), 157–62; Appleman (1), 280–85.)

24. There are various ways in which Clark's statement of thirty-one men on the expedition can be reconciled with the official count. Sacagawea and Jean Baptiste obviously are not included. Charles Floyd, John Newman, and Richard Warfington, who appear on expedition rolls, including the compensation list, cannot be counted here. Counting those men who traveled all the way to the Pacific, including the captains and York, yields the stated thirty-one, and reaches the permanent party number of thirty-three, which includes Sacagawea and Jean Baptiste.

25. Point Adams, still its name today, is the southern headland at the mouth of the Columbia. It was named by Robert Gray in 1792, most likely in honor of John Adams, fellow Bay Stater and vice president of the United States at the time, though it is possible that he named it in honor of Samuel Adams, another Massachusetts patriot. Gray also named Cape Disappointment (the cape extending from the northern side at the mouth of the Columbia) Cape Hancock, but that name was not adopted into general use. (Moulton, 6:51n.)

26. Clark is referring to the time since they left Fort Mandan, the last time they had sent reports back, including his letter to Jonathan. His mention of the post raises the question of who carried this important letter eastward. Would the captains have trusted this communication to the regular mails or dispatched a courier? Clark's reference to the post would seem to indicate the regular mails. However, in 1866 and 1867 Patrick Gass reported to Lyman Draper that in 1806 he carried a letter about the expedition, which was published, to Captain Clark's brother George Rogers Clark at the Falls of the Ohio. That letter must be this 23 September letter. The recipient was Jonathan, so Gass must either have forgotten which brother he delivered the letter to, or possibly have delivered it to George (whom he had met in 1793) with the request that he pass it on to Jonathan. The address leaves for both William Clark's letter and Lewis's are not present, so it is not known if they were sent by regular mail or special courier. Gass's biographer J. G. Jacob recorded that Gass and a couple of companions were waiting for Lewis and Clark in Vincennes, and when they learned that the captains had changed their route to Louisville and bypassed that town they joined them in Louisville. If Gass and a couple of others (possibly other expedition veterans?) did carry the 23 September letter to Louis-

ville, it would be reasonable to think that they then returned westward as far as Vincennes in order to wait for Lewis and Clark and their party. Both captains had stated their intention to take the Vincennes-to-Louisville route. Gass and his companions perhaps planned to meet the party there and then accompany them on their triumphal procession eastward. Jacob reports that Gass was back home near Wellsburg, West Virginia, by late 1806. This is logical since by early 1807 David McKeehan of nearby Pittsburgh had acquired Gass's journal for publication. (Patrick Gass to Lyman Draper, 1 December 1866 and 11 January 1867, George Rogers Clark Papers, Draper Mss., 34J61–62; Jacob, 108–10; Jackson (1), 2:390–91, 399–408.)

∼

St. Louis September 24th 1806

Dear Brother

    I wrote you a letter last night giveing you a Sumerey Sketch of our Journey & c. untill our return to the Rocky mountains[1] Since that time maney interesting accurrences has taken place, which I hope to have the pleasure of relateing to you in the Course of about 18 days.[2]

 Capt. Lewis and my Self will be detained here for the purpose of Settling with ∧& Dischargeing[∧] our men which will delay us ~~here~~ eight or ten days, when we Shall Set out with a Great Chief[3] of the Mandan nation his family and an interpreter[4] through the Country by the way of Vincennes, and expect to reach the falls about the 9 or 10 of next month. Capt. Lewis will proced on with the Indians to Washington City after remaening a fiew days in the neighbourhood of Louisvill. as I Cannot here any certain information of my frends near you, I know not who is liveing or dead and must therefore request you to prosent me most cincrely to them all. I have not time to write more as the ~~time~~ post is waiting at the dore. present me most effectunately to my Sister and the family and be-lieve me to be yore Sincere friend & brother.

           Wm Clark

My friend Capt. Lewis presents his Compliments
most respectfully to yourself and lady & also my
brother Edmund

     Note please to have ~~the~~ my letter to you of yester
      published if you think proper[5] WC.

THE PALLADIUM,

FRANKFORT:

THURSDAY, OCTOBER 9, 1806.

WE congratulate the public at large and the particular friends of Messrs. Lewis and Clark and their enterprizing companions, on the happy termination of an expedition, which will, doubtles, be productive of incalculable commercial advantages to the

Article from the 9 October 1806 Frankfort, Kentucky, *Palladium* in which Clark's letter to Jonathan was reprinted. This was the first detailed printed report of the expedition's return and soon was circulated in papers throughout the United States. Courtesy of The Filson Historical Society

1. This, of course, is the preceding letter of 23 September. The identity of the recipient of that famous letter announcing the successful return of the Lewis and Clark Expedition had been in doubt prior to the discovery of this letter: historians and editors previously had listed George Rogers Clark, rather than Jonathan, as the recipient. Although both men were generals, George was famous and apparently came to mind before Jonathan. Donald Jackson theorized that Jonathan may have been the recipient but listed George with a question mark. See the appropriate notes for the 23 September letter for more information. (Jackson (1), 1:325, 329–30; Thwaites (1), 7:338.)

2. Clark was being optimistic regarding settling expedition affairs in St. Louis and returning to Louisville. After settling accounts, making dispositions for surplus goods and equipment, discharging the men (10

October 1806 is the official date of discharge from expedition service), and making arrangements concerning expedition artifacts and records and their own party's trip eastward, it was actually some three weeks later, on 5 November, rather than about 10 October, that he, Lewis, and their party arrived at the Falls of the Ohio. (Appleman (1), 235–36; Jonathan Clark Diary, 5 November 1806.)

3. Sheheke, or the Big White, was the principal chief of the lower Mandan village Matootonah, the one that Fort Mandan was located across the Missouri from during the Corps' winter stay. The name Sheheke is commonly translated as "Coyote." White traders had named him Big White because of his light complexion and obesity. He, his wife, and son accompanied the Corps downriver and then went on to Washington with Lewis. After they returned to St. Louis in 1807, the government's attempt to escort them back to their home under the command of former sergeant, now ensign, Nathaniel H. Pryor, failed when the Arikara attacked and prevented them from proceeding farther upriver. Sheheke and his family lived at Cantonment Belle Fontaine at the mouth of the Missouri River until 1809, when a large trading party under Pierre Chouteau was paid by Lewis to escort them home. This attempt succeeded, but Sheheke failed to reap the influence and prestige upon his return that he undoubtedly thought such a trip would bring him. The Mandan refused to believe much of what he told them he had seen among the white men. His position in the tribe consequently suffered, a status possibly already eroded by his three-year absence. The date of Sheheke's death has often appeared as 7 January 1832. The source cited is a journal entry dated 7 January 1835 by Francis Chardon, a fur trader who kept a journal from 1834 to 1839, while at Fort Clark on the Upper Missouri. In that entry, Chardon wrote that the "Old Mandan Cheif (The White Head)" had died three years ago that day. Annie Heloise Abel, editor of Chardon's journal, identifies this chief as Sheheke. This might be correct, but I think there is a better date, one that has begun to be cited in recent years. The name White Head is certainly different from Big White and may refer to a different Mandan chief. Abel's reference to Thwaites for this identification is a journal entry by Clark in which he mentions the Big White. A more immediate source, and one that well may establish Sheheke's date of death, is John Luttig's journal of 1812–1813. He reported on 3 October 1812 that news had been brought them of the Big White and Little Crow (or Little Raven) being killed by the Big Bellies (Gros Ventre of the Prairie, or Atsina Indians, I believe, rather than the Big Bellies or Gros Ventre of the Missouri, the Hidatsa, since the former were enemies and the latter were allies). Luttig's closeness to the situation, and likely familiarity with some

of those involved, especially knowing about Big White and his connection to the Lewis and Clark Expedition, makes it unlikely that he would have gotten the name wrong. Therefore, I am inclined to believe that Sheheke was killed in a battle with the Atsina Indians in late September or early October 1812. John Bakeless in *Lewis & Clark: Partners in Discovery* gives the 1812 date but does not list the source for it. St. Mémin drew portraits of Sheheke and his wife while they were in the East at the request of Lewis (who also paid for them). Lewis apparently intended to use them in the expedition book. Patrick Gass's biographer J. G. Jacob states that Gass believed the Big White was the "best looking Indian he ever saw." (Moulton, 3:206–7n, 213–14n; Jackson (1), 2:408n; Abel, 20, 294; Thwaites (1), 1:262; Luttig, 82–83; Lamar, 471–72; Bakeless (2), 179, 407; Jacob, 108.)

4. René Jusseaume (or Jessaume) was a French-Canadian trader who had lived among the Mandan since approximately 1790. He was not well thought of by Lewis and Clark and earlier explorers, and despite having lived with the Mandan for some fifteen years, he was not considered a good interpreter. He told Clark when they met on 27 October 1804 that he had served as a spy for George Rogers Clark during the Revolution. Necessity likely forced Lewis and Clark to hire Jusseaume as the interpreter to accompany Sheheke to Washington in 1806. His wife and two children traveled with them. In Pryor's 1807 attempt to return the Sheheke party home, Jusseaume was seriously wounded during the battle with the Arikara. He was still alive in 1834. (Moulton, 3:203, 205n.)

5. From a practical standpoint, one of the primary reasons Clark wrote Jonathan was to have the letter published. Both Clark and Lewis knew that a letter to Jonathan would be received and made public (including published)—thus circulating the news of the Corps' successful return—much sooner than Lewis's report to Jefferson in Washington. Clark must have realized with some anxiety that he had not specifically requested Jonathan to have his 23 September letter published in order to achieve that objective. Thus the reason it is specifically mentioned here. Jonathan did indeed see that it was published. It appeared in the 9 October issue of the Frankfort *Palladium*.

~

Washington City January 22nd 1807

Dear Brother

I arived here on Sunday evening[1] and Sence that time have been engaged in formal visits to the heads of departments and partakeing of the Sumptious far of maney of the members, maney of whome I have become acquainted with. my old western friends do not forsake me and appere happy that ~~that~~ they have it in their power to pay me much respect which appers to be the general disposition of every member of Congress with whome I have become acquainted.[2] Congress is doeing very little at present ~~a~~ the bridge across the Potomac has taken up Several days in the Senit and appears to be a Subject of great anxiety. a Bill has been brought forward to raise a regiment of Infantry and four Companies of Cavelry. and ~~one is refured to~~ a Commite is appointed to bring in a bill giveing Compensation to the Party on the late Expedition. I think the Comite will report 2 Sects. of Land to Capt. Lewis and my Self each, and half a Section and half pay to the men, the most of the members appear favourable to a liberal appropriation tho' I believe we Shall not receive any more than I have mentioned.[3]

Your leters of the   & 23rd of Decr. I have received, one of which I have Shewn to the president it contains Some information respecting Mr. Burrs Expedition[4] which he wished to See or know. the Expedition of Mr. B. has excted the greatest allarm and his views as are maid known to the Exctve. (and which will be laid before Congress tomorrow or the next day) are of the most desperate and violent ~~nature~~ aspect [(]and little Short of a Second Boneparte to the Nateal Convention.) Genl. Wilkinson has been giveing information to the Government for Some time and Genl. Eaton[5] has opened the whole plan yesterday, which appears to be of Such a violent nature that it is scrcely Crediable that a man in his proper Sences could be possessed of Such mistaken ~~principals~~ idea of the desposition of the american people. I Should be very glad to have heard from brother Edmund on the Conell business. Majr. Hite tells me that you will certainly be at richmond in march if So another letter will not meet you. I Shall leave [this] place in a Short time and possiably meet you, at any event wish to doe So. I Shall go the Southern rout[6] by Colo. Handcocks[7] near Findcastle and the family of the Prestons.[8] I wished I had 20 minits Conversation with you on Some points which I am much at a loss. The letter you mention I wish much that you have fowarded on to

PROSPECTUS

OF

LEWIS AND CLARK'S TOUR

TO THE

PACIFIC OCEAN

THROUGH

THE INTERIOR OF THE CONTINENT OF NORTH AMERICA,

Performed by order of the Government of the United States, during the years 1804, 1805 & 1806.

THIS work will be prepared by Captain Meriwether Lewis, and will be divided into two parts, the whole comprized in three volumes octavo, the first containing at least seven hundred pages, the second and third from four to five hundred each, printed on good paper, and a fair Pica type. The several volumes in succession will be put to press at as early periods as the avocations of the author will permit him to prepare them for publication.

PART THE FIRST: IN TWO VOLUMES.

VOLUME FIRST.

WILL contain a narrative of the voyage, with a description of some of the most remarkable places in those hitherto unknown wilds of America, accompanied by a map of good size, a large chart of the entrance of the Columbia river, embracing the adjacent country, coast and harbours, and embellished with views of two beautiful cataracts of the Missouri; the plan, on a large scale, of the connected falls of that river, as also of those of the falls, narrows, and great rapids of the Columbia, with their several portages. For the information of future voyagers, there will be added in the sequel of this volume, some observations and remarks on the navigation of the Missouri and Columbia rivers, pointing out the precautions which must necessarily be taken, in order to ensure success, together with an itinerary of the most direct and practicable route across the continent of North America, from the confluence of the Missouri and Mississippi rivers to the discharge of the Columbia into the Pacific Ocean.

VOLUME SECOND.

WHATEVER properly appertains to geography, embracing a description of the rivers, mountains, climate, soil and face of the country, a view of the Indian nations distributed over that vast region, showing their traditions, habits, manners, customs, national characters, stature, complexions, dress, dwellings, arms, and domestic utensils, with many other interesting particulars in relation to them: also observations and reflections on the subjects of civilizing, governing and maintaining a friendly intercourse with those nations. A view of the fur trade of North America, setting forth a plan for its extension, and showing the immense advantages which would accrue to the mercantile interests of the United States, by combining the same with a direct trade to the East Indies through the continent of North America. This volume will be embellished with twenty plates illustrative of the dress and general appearance of such Indian nations as differ materially from each other; of their habitations; their weapons and habiliments used in war; their hunting and fishing apparatus; domestic utensils, &c. In an appendix there will also be given a diary of the weather, kept with great attention throughout the whole of the voyage, showing also the daily rise and fall of the principal water-courses which were navigated in the course of the same.

PART THE SECOND: IN ONE VOLUME.

THIS part of the work will be confined exclusively to scientific research, and principally to the natural history of those hitherto unknown regions. It will contain a full dissertation on such subjects as have fallen within the notice of the author, and which may properly be distributed under the heads of Botany, Mineralogy, and Zoology, together with some strictures on the origin of Prairies, the cause of the muddiness of the Missouri, of volcanic appearances, and other natural phenomena which were met with in the course of this interesting tour. This volume will also contain a comparative view of twenty three vocabularies of distinct Indian languages, procured by Captains Lewis and Clark on the voyage; and will be ornamented and embellished with a much greater number of plates than will be bestowed on the first part of the work, as it is intended that every subject of natural history which is entirely new, and of which there are a considerable number, shall be accompanied by an appropriate engraving illustrative of it.

THIS distribution of the work has been made with a view to the accommodation of every description of readers, and is here offered to the patronage of the public in such shape, that all persons wishing to become subscribers, may accommodate themselves with either of the parts, or the entire work, as it shall be most convenient to themselves.

** Subscriptions received by C. and A. Conrad and Co. (late John Conrad and Co.) No. 30, Chesnut-street, Philadelphia.

Detached from this work, there will be published

LEWIS AND CLARK'S MAP OF NORTH AMERICA,

FROM LONGITUDE 9° WEST, TO THE PACIFIC OCEAN, AND BETWEEN 36° AND 52° NORTH LATITUDE, WITH EXTENSIVE MARGINAL NOTES,

DIMENSIONS FIVE FEET EIGHT INCHES BY THREE FEET TEN INCHES,

EMBRACING all their late discoveries, and that part of the continent heretofore the least known. This Map will be compiled from the best maps now extant, as well published as in manuscript, from the collective information of the best informed travellers through the various portions of that region, and corrected by a series of several hundred celestial observations, made by Captain Lewis during his late tour.

FOR the convenience of subscribers, these several works will be delivered at the most respectable commercial towns, and at the seats of government of the respective states and territories within the Union: no advance is required, nor will payment be demanded until such delivery is made.

THE price of part the first, in two volumes, will be ten dollars, and that of part the second, in one volume, eleven dollars, delivered in boards. Price of the Map, ten dollars.

** ANY persons who may have subscribed for these works, to lists which contained no stipulated prices for the same, and who may be dissatisfied with the terms now proposed, are at liberty to withdraw their names from such lists, at any time prior to the 1st day of December next.

Philadelphia June 3d, 1807.

M. LEWIS.

SUBSCRIBERS' NAMES.	PLACES OF RESIDENCE.	LEWIS AND CLARK'S TOUR. No. of Copies. PART 1st.	Lewis & Clark's Map of North America. PART 2d. No. of Copies	SUBSCRIBERS' NAMES.	PLACES OF RESIDENCE.	LEWIS AND CLARK'S TOUR. No. of Copies. PART 1st.	Lewis & Clark's Map of North America. PART 2d. No. of Copies.

Prospectus that Meriwether Lewis had printed for his proposed history of the Lewis and Clark Expedition in 1807. This copy belonged to his and Clark's friend William Preston. Courtesy of The Filson Historical Society

me, I do not know the Contents, perhaps I may find them out as I Shall Spend this evening with the god of War.[9] I am told that the President made his comunication to Congress to day, you will See them published nearly as Soon as you receive this letter. Several propersitions has been made, as they are Confidential I will not trust them in a letter, I fear I shall displese the ____ by my timidity as maney may term it, however I am Sincere in my desecions. I most probably will return to your house in Public Servece, but what Situation I Shall be in is not yet deturmined on.[10] I Shall write you in a fiew days a confidential letter in the mean tim I mest beg you to present my most respectfull [wishes] to Sister & the family & Subcribe my Self you Sincer & offectunate brothr

Wm Clark

note

pleasee to ∧tell[∧] Sister Clark that I have an object in view that I flatter my Self will extort from her that old promis, at ~~any~~ all events it is almost time to put up the Chickens & ducks to fatten and prepare Sugar and plumbs for the pies.[11]

1. 18 January 1807. In a letter to William Croghan dated 14 December 1806 Clark stated that he intended to leave the Louisville area the next day, proceeding as far as Col. Anderson's, and then going eastward by way of Danville, where he planned on visiting nephews who were in school there. From Danville, he, and most likely York, took the long-established Wilderness Road southeastward through the Cumberland Gap into northeastern Tennessee, and then turned northeastward down Virginia's Great Valley. Clark was in Fincastle, Virginia, by 8 January, where he, and Lewis *in absentia,* were honored by its citizens. While there he renewed his acquaintance with Julia Hancock and seriously courted her. Meriwether Lewis and most of the party that had come from St. Louis to Louisville left Louisville about 10 November, and reached Frankfort, Kentucky, on 13 November. There the party split up. Lewis and the Mandans turned southward to the Wilderness Road while Chouteau and the Osage traveled on to Lexington and took a more northerly route to Washington. Lewis reached Washington on 28 December, having spent Christmas with his family at Locust Hill near Charlottesville. Chouteau's party had reached Washington before 24 December. (Clark to Croghan, Croghan Papers, Historical Society of Pennsylvania, Philadelphia; Jackson (1), 1:358–60; Appleman (1), 236–37; *The Palladium* (Frankfort, Ky.), 20 November 1806.)

2. Clark, Lewis, the Mandan chief Sheheke (Big White), and others did

indeed partake of the sumptuous fare they were treated to in Washington. Clark actually missed some of the celebrations, including a 14 January affair in the captains' honor (which already had been postponed once), due to his delay in arriving at the capital city. His "old western friends" serving in Congress had an obvious interest in the expedition, its success, and the wonderful opportunities the vast new territory presented. While particulars of Clark's connections with these senators and congressmen are not known for the most part, he undoubtedly knew some of them. His closest connection probably was with Kentucky senator Buckner Thruston, the brother of his late brother-in-law Charles Mynn Thruston and late neighbor and militia commander John Thruston. He also knew Benjamin Parke, delegate from Indiana Territory, and Daniel Clark, delegate from Territory of Orleans. Clark also probably knew Representative George M. Bedinger of Kentucky, who had served as an officer in some of the same Indian campaigns in which George Rogers Clark and William had participated. A definite Lewis connection was Representative David Meriwether of Georgia, a cousin. (*Biographical Directory of the American Congress* (hereafter cited as *BDAC*), 84–88, 1556, 1649.)

3. Lewis and Clark's supporters did well by them and their men in rewarding them for their services on the expedition. The act compensating the Corps of Discovery exceeded Clark's expectations. The captains both received 1,600 acres of land and double pay for the period of the expedition. The other official members of the Corps received 320 acres and double pay also. The act required that the land be located west of the Mississippi River, and a petition by some of the men to allow the grants to be east of the Mississippi was rejected. York and Sacagawea received nothing. (Jackson (1), 2:377–82.)

4. The Aaron Burr Conspiracy is one of the most sensational episodes in early nineteenth-century U.S. history. Historians differ as to what Burr's exact intentions were, and even at the time there was debate about just what he planned to accomplish. Aaron Burr (1756–1836) was a native of Newark, New Jersey, graduated from the College of New Jersey (Princeton) at the age of sixteen, and served as an officer in the American Revolution. In 1782 he began the practice of law in New York and became involved in politics on the state and national level. He served as vice president during Jefferson's first term but was not renominated for the second term. He killed Alexander Hamilton in a duel on 11 July 1804. While vice president and after leaving that office Burr was involved in a scheme to seize or acquire Spanish land. The scheme unraveled in 1806–1807 when his fellow conspirator James Wilkinson informed on him to U.S. officials. Burr had recruited Ken-

tuckians for his scheme. Jonathan Clark did not support Burr and apparently had acquired information about Burr's possible activities and contacts in Kentucky. Clark's mention of Jonathan's letter to him containing information on Burr that he showed to Jefferson apparently led to a request from the U.S. attorney general for information from Jonathan about Burr and his conspiracy. Burr avoided indictment for treason, and in 1808 moved to England for four years. Upon his return to New York he reestablished his successful law practice. (*DAB*, 3:314–20; *KE*, 144–45; Caesar Rodney to Jonathan Clark, May 1807, Edmund Clark to George Tompkins, 17, 18 July 1807, Bodley Family Papers, TFHS.)

5. William Eaton (1764–1811) was a native of Connecticut. He gained distinction for his army service on the frontier, and was considered a hero by many for his actions while consul in Tunis during difficulties with that kingdom. He was implicated in the Burr Conspiracy but was able to clear himself. His statements against Burr were quite sensational and apparently are what Clark refers to in this letter. After the initial shock of them wore off, most of them were discounted. Following the Burr affair, Eaton served one term in the Massachusetts legislature and retired to Brimfield, Massachusetts. (*DAB*, 5:613; see the entry for Aaron Burr also, 3:318.)

6. The southern route was via the Cumberland Gap, the route stated in note 1.

7. George Hancock (1754–1820) was William Clark's future father-in-law. He was a native of Chesterfield County, Virginia, served in the militia during the Revolutionary War, and by 1782 had settled in Fincastle, Botetourt County, Virginia. He practiced law, farmed, and served in various political offices, including two terms in the U.S. Congress, and as colonel of the county militia. He married Margaret "Peggy" Strother (1763–1834) in 1781. They had five children, including Caroline and Julia (see, respectively, note 8 to this letter, and letter dated 6, 7 June 1808, note 5), and George (1798–1875) (see letter dated 26 August 1809, note 11), who married William and Lucy Clark Croghan's daughter Eliza in 1819. About 1805 Hancock completed a mansion on a 295-acre estate on the southern outskirts of Fincastle that he christened Santillane. He also owned a 598-acre estate named Fotheringay, near Elliston in Montgomery County. It was here that Julia Hancock Clark died and was buried in 1820. The references to visiting the Hancocks in this and other letters refer to Santillane outside Fincastle. Clark was going to Hancock's to court his daughter Julia with the intention of becoming officially engaged to her. Jonathan Clark was coming east to Virginia on business and a visit. Clark may have been correct about this

letter not reaching him before he left Louisville, and they may have encountered each other on the road, although Jonathan does not mention it in his diary. Jonathan left for Virginia on 14 February and took the southern route (via the Wilderness Road and Cumberland Gap), reaching Richmond on 7 March. On his return he left his brother-in-law Maj. Hite's near Middletown on 19 June and reached home on 5 July, having taken a southwesterly and then westerly course through the mountains and present central West Virginia into Kentucky. (*BDAC*, 1262; Bond, 242–43; Jonathan Clark Diary, 14 February–5 July 1807.)

8. The Preston family was prominent in Virginia and Kentucky. The Clark-Preston family friendship may have begun in the 1790s when William Clark and William Preston (1770–1821) served in the army together under Anthony Wayne. Preston was a native of Botetourt County, Virginia, served as a first cornet of cavalry and an ensign in the Virginia militia, was commissioned a captain in the regular army in 1792, and served on the frontier. He resigned in 1798 but served in the Virginia militia, rising to the rank of major. Following his resignation from the army, he resided in Botetourt and Montgomery Counties, but by late 1803 he had removed to Robinson's Tract in Wythe County, Virginia, developing that extensive inherited property. On 24 March 1802 he married Caroline Hancock (1785–1847), daughter of Col. George Hancock and older sister of Julia Hancock. In 1815 they moved to extensive Preston family property in Jefferson County, Kentucky, that his father Col. William Preston (1729–1783) had acquired through his service as surveyor for Fincastle County, Virginia, (which included most of Kentucky at one time). Maj. Preston was a leading citizen of Louisville. He died in Virginia while on a visit there, and was buried on the Preston family estate, Smithfield, in Montgomery County. His friendship with William Clark extended to other members of the Clark family. William's brother-in-law Dennis Fitzhugh and nephew-in-law James A. Pearce were named executors of his estate. (Dorman (2), 57–61; Heitman (2), 1:806.)

9. Henry Dearborn (1751–1829) was a native of New Hampshire, Revolutionary War veteran, militia general, and U.S. congressman. He served eight years as secretary of war in Jefferson's cabinet. His leadership and campaigns as one of the U.S. Army's highest ranking generals during the War of 1812 were complete failures, and he was honorably discharged in 1815. In 1822 he was appointed minister to Portugal, a post he held for two years before retiring to Massachusetts. (*DAB*, 5:174–76; Heitman (2), 1:363.)

10. It is not known what propositions were made to Clark, or why he

termed himself as acting in a timid manner. He did indeed return to Jonathan's house in public service. On 9 March he was appointed superintendent of Indian affairs for Louisiana Territory (excluding the Osage, who already had Pierre Chouteau as their agent), and on 12 March he was commissioned a brigadier general of militia for the territory. (Jackson (1), 1:376, 2:382–83.)

11. A reference to Clark's engagement to Julia Hancock. Sarah Hite Clark apparently had been urging him to enter the marital state and had promised him a feast upon his doing so. He wrote Meriwether Lewis in the latter part of March that he was officially engaged and that the wedding was set for next January. (Jackson (1), 2:387–88.)

~

Big Bone Lick[1]   9th Sept. 1807

Dear Brother

      By Mr. Banks[2] you will recve this letter which will do little more than inform you that I am well;

I arrived here Sunday and Comenced monday morning, found that Trools [tools] were not to be precured here and Sent to Cincinnati, to day I have 8 hired hands in the mud, have found maney bones of the mammoth[3] none of much Consequence except a Tusk taken out to day 9 feet 11 [ᴧ]In.[ᴧ] long & 17 incehs around, Several Teeth of two different animals. ___ Bro. G.___ D___ and has given me Some uneaseness but he appears to be more thoughtfull to day[4]___ I find that this business will Cost more ready Cash than I have brought along, and must precure Some from the falls[5] or Cincinnati. if you Should meet with any person Comeing this way please to Send the money in my Desk___ perhaps brother Edmund may Come by this way on his trip to the State of Ohio- if he does it will be a good oppertunity to Sind me Some money[6] ___ and the news papers ___ please to Send up my Great Coat or Cloak _ I am in a Camp and live verry pore. in hast I am your most offecctunate Brother

Wm Clark

[Letter carried by Mr. Banks.]

1. Located near the Ohio River in present southwestern Boone County, Kentucky, Big Bone Lick contained many fossil remains. Euro-Americans

were aware of the lick and its mysterious bones as early as 1739. Explorer Thomas Bullitt and his party explored the lick in 1773. In 1781 Thomas Jefferson requested George Rogers Clark to search for fossils there. A December 1783 and February 1784 exchange of correspondence between them indicates that Clark apparently had gathered some fossils for Jefferson, but it is not known whether they ever reached him. Jefferson's continued interest in acquiring fossils from there would seem to indicate that perhaps they did not. Meriwether Lewis visited the lick in October 1803 after leaving Cincinnati for Louisville to rendezvous with William Clark. He collected a number of specimens for Jefferson, but the boat carrying them sank in the Mississippi River at Natchez, and none apparently ever reached Jefferson. Clark agreed to oversee a dig there for Jefferson in 1807 (see note 3). Big Bone Lick now is a state park. (See Jackson (1), 1:126–32 and 2:654–55 for additional information. Of particular interest is Clark's eleven-page report on his dig, dated 10 November 1807, in the Jefferson Papers, Library of Congress.)

2. Mr. Banks has not been definitely identified. He may be the John Banks who is listed as living in Jefferson County in the 1800 census or possibly the C. Banks living in Lexington whom William Clark stayed with on 30 October 1809 on his trip eastward. (William Clark Memorandum Book, 1809, Breckenridge Collection, State Historical Society of Missouri.)

3. The mammoth, which ranged through North America, Europe, and Asia, was one of Jefferson's major paleontological interests. More than three hundred fossilized bones and teeth that Clark's crew of ten (according to sources) men dug up were sent to Jefferson via New Orleans, and they eventually made their way to the American Philosophical Society, the Musée Nationale d'Histoire Naturelle in Paris, and Jefferson's home, Monticello. Examination of the teeth by the authorities of the day revealed them to be from mastodons (similar in appearance, but larger and with distinctive teeth) as well as mammoths. Therefore, William Clark was instrumental in a breakthrough in paleontology. Jefferson and Clark corresponded about the fossils from this dig as late as September 1809. Several of the fossils are on exhibit at Monticello. At least some of those sent to the American Philosophical Society are now in the collection of the Academy of Natural Sciences in Philadelphia. Clark arrived at Big Bone Lick to start the dig on Sunday, 6 September 1807. (See appropriate correspondence as it appears in published versions of Thomas Jefferson's papers; Lipscomb, 11:403–5, 12:15–16, 83–88, 309–11; Stein, 80–83; Large (2); Jackson (1), 2: 654–55.)

4. George Rogers Clark's problem with alcohol abuse is documented. This

letter indicates that he still suffered from alcoholism in 1807. It is interesting to note that he did definitely make it to Big Bone Lick regarding a fossil dig for Jefferson, even if it may have been twenty-five years after Jefferson had initially proposed it.

5. Falls of the Ohio, meaning Louisville. Other towns at the Falls in 1807 were Shippingport on the Kentucky side at the foot of the falls and Jeffersonville above and Clarksville below the falls in Indiana Territory.

6. Clark did receive his money. An undated [September] entry in Jonathan Clark's previously cited day book states that $85 of William Clark's own money and $20 of Jonathan's were sent to him at Big Bone Lick. An amount for £6.0.0 also is listed. An entry for October lists a cash advance to Clark of "(£90) $— 300." (Jonathan Clark Day Book, fl. 178.)

3

"I Wish You to See & Know All"

Life in St. Louis, 1808–1809

William Clark's life changed forever after his trip to the Pacific. Whether he thought ahead to what those changes might be is not known. Perhaps he believed he would return to the Louisville area and life would go on as it had before the expedition. If he did, it did not take him long after his return to know that this was not to be. His comment to Jonathan in his 22 January 1807 letter indicates that perhaps he had not anticipated the attention and honors an admiring nation would bestow upon him. The rewards included the brigadier generalship of the Louisiana territorial militia and the position of chief Indian agent for the territory.

By the late spring of 1808 William Clark was ready to move permanently to St. Louis and take up his new responsibilities. With him were his new wife, Julia, many of his slaves, including York, and friends and associates who were either traveling partway with them or also going to St. Louis. Clark knew this move marked a significant change in his life. It was only a year before he left for the Pacific that Jonathan had moved to the Louisville area. The separation from his family had lasted for three years, and since his return he had been able to visit them only periodically. Now, with this move to St. Louis, even that infrequent coming and going would be reduced to visits only every year or two. The conversations with Jonathan that William cherished so much would almost be at an end. Now he must communicate news of importance and interest to Jonathan primarily by letter. By doing so he maintained that important familial connection and kept Jonathan sufficiently informed so that he could still give the advice William so much desired. William truly did want Jonathan to be "possessed of the knowledge of all our intentions, views, & prospects, & receive your advice & oppinion," and he warned his brother that he "must not expect either Connection grammar & good Spelling in my lettrs as I write to You without Reserve & at Such tims as I can find leasure."

William Clark was a mature adult, almost thirty-eight years of age, when he moved to St. Louis. Any sense of adventure and challenge he felt was surely balanced by losing the joy and sense of closeness that having his family around him brought. His letters from St. Louis make this feeling very evident, and to counter it he wrote Jonathan long, newsy letters full of the important and the "diverting" happenings in his life. His reports on his activities, on Julia's—and his—homesickness, and on the people and events around them provide excellent information about St. Louis, frontier affairs, and himself and others. Clark confesses in one letter that "I beleev I have Said all I can think of." He wanted his family in Kentucky to know what life was like for Julia and him, from the move to St. Louis in June 1808 and the newlyweds settling down in their new home to his troubles with his slaves—including York—and the headaches of territorial and Indian administration. Whether it is their joy in the birth of a son and seeing him bathed, or the frustration and concern Clark feels about having exceeded his authority in signing a treaty with the Osage, he reports it to Jonathan.

His letters are a treasure trove of information. His 9 November 1808 letter provides the reason for his serious falling-out with York, a subject he commented on frequently during this period. Two weeks later, in a letter seven and one-half folio-size pages in length, Clark confesses his hurt and anger at some family members thinking he might have acted dishonestly as administrator of his late brother-in-law's estate. Yet, leaving his distress over the "Snears of the ungreatful," he also reports on current prices for a variety of produce, livestock, and other items in St. Louis. He writes that fortunes are to be made in the mercantile trade and hopes that Jonathan's son and he will be among those enterprising enough to act on the opportunity. He confesses that Meriwether Lewis has delayed writing the expedition history for so long that he fears they will not make much money on the book when it finally is published. All this leads him to "wish to See you [Jonathan] much verry much indeed." His request for Jonathan to "ride over and See us" would go unfulfilled. But with this hope disappointed, the next best thing was communicating through letters. William Clark was a faithful correspondent and the letters he wrote from frontier St. Louis in 1808 and 1809 are a significant addition to knowledge about him, his contemporaries, and their times.

~

Aboard my Boat near the mouth of
Tradewater[1] Monday 6th June 1808.

Dear Brother

I take the liberty of incloseing part of Mr. C. & Toms. Bullitts[2] account against me which I wish you to give to Mr. Brock[3] and tell him that I have paid Mr. Bullitt for those articles Charged in this little account — we have proceeded on this far well verry well indeed, all well and in high Spirits[4] — The misquitors is excessively troublesom near Shore, and have tormented Julia[5] and Miss Ann Anderson[6] very much dureing the time we lay at Bro Edmunds which was from about 9 A.M. yesterday untill 2 PM to day. Bro E. appears to have every thing about him in abundance except open land and house roome — he is not Satisfied & I do not think will Continue ~~here~~ verrey long.[7] his girl Philes[8] cannot live verry long, and it was reported as we Set out that one of his horses was Stolen last night. he tels me that he Shall Set out to youre house in about two weeks. — I also inclose you Mr. Fitzhughes receipt for Baseys[9] bond £30.6.0. which I wish you to put with the papers. Majr. Croghan[10] will give you every information which you may wish to know and which I have not mentioned. Julia Joins in the most Sincerre Effection for your self Sister Clark & nancy.[11] I am yor Sincere and efft. Brothr

Wm Clark

7th in the evening

Sence writeung you, we have descended to the mouth of Cumbarland[12] and Majr. Croghan, George[13] and the doctr.[14] is about to leave us, I sent my Horses Carrage & Cart with Mr. Charless[15] York, Ja. & Easters[16] family across to Kasskasska I have just heard that Mr. Pryor[17] & about 20 men with 2 boats is watting at the mouth of the ohio for me. The D.__r is unsucksessful in his C.___p to Miss N. A__n. and both appear a little displeased.[18] Prey write to me & beleve me to be your Sincere friend

Wm Clark

N.B. J. Markill[19] was to have married last friday had not Mr. Gilcrist[20] required a letter of apprebation from his father which he is to get.
[Letter carried by William Croghan.]

1. The Tradewater River rises north of Hopkinsville in Christian County, in southwestern Kentucky, and flows northwestward between the Green and Cumberland Rivers, forming the border between various counties, including Crittenden and Union, where it empties into the Ohio near Caseyville. The name apparently derives from the Indian trading posts located along its course in early times. (Fowler, 32:291.)

2. Cuthbert Bullitt (1774–1825) and his brother Thomas (1777–1823) were natives of Virginia. They lived in Moorefield in present Hardy County, West Virginia, where they operated a tavern, and by 1802 they had moved to Louisville, quickly establishing themselves as successful merchants and prominent citizens. At one time they were among the wealthiest citizens and largest landholders of Louisville. They also built and operated Spring Mill (now a state park near Mitchell, Indiana) and are considered the developers, if not the founders, of Terre Haute, Indiana. Cuthbert married Ann Neville (1780–1854), daughter of Gen. Joseph Neville; Thomas married Diana Moore Gwathmey (1782–1853), daughter of Clark sibling Ann Clark Gwathmey, in January 1803. Thomas and Diana Gwathmey Bullitt had thirteen children. Their oldest child, Mary Ann (1803–1862), married Gen. Henry Atkinson (1782–1842) of frontier fame, and her sister Diana Moore (1819–1906) married (and divorced) Gen. Philip Kearny (1814–1862) of Mexican War and Civil War fame. Cuthbert Bullitt's will details an extensive estate, including houses in Louisville; his country estate, Walnut Hill, south of Louisville; Richmond, near Jeffersonville, Indiana, which Robert K. Moore had once owned; and a great deal of property in Terre Haute, Vigo County, Indiana. Their uncle was the explorer Thomas Bullitt who in 1773 surveyed the site that would become Louisville, and their first cousin was Alexander Scott Bullitt (see letter dated 22, 24 November 1808, note 1). (Bullitt (1), 139–45, 162–65; Bullitt family file, TFHS; JCWB, 2:289–304.)

3. Thomas Brock (d. ca. 1833) was a resident of Jefferson County in the early 1800s. The account books of Edmund and John H. Clark's mercantile firm list Brock collecting money due him for rent and receiving

money owed him by Jonathan and George R. Clark. He may have owned a tavern and adjacent building where the firm of E. and J. H. Clark operated. By 1810 he had moved from Jefferson County; possibly to St. Louis. In 1830 he was living in St. Louis. (Edmund and John H. Clark Papers, TFHS.)

4. The party made good time down the Ohio. They left Louisville on 2 June and had reached the mouth of Highland Creek (in present Union County) by the morning of 5 June, a distance of approximately 230 miles. Jonathan noted in his diary entry for 2 June that "my brother William, this day moved from Louisville – to St. Louis – parted with him at Shipping Port." Shippingport was at the foot of the Falls of the Ohio. (The "lower landing" was at Shippingport and the "upper landing" at Louisville.) Shippingport eventually was annexed by Louisville but retained its community identity. The 1937 flood essentially destroyed Shippingport, however, and it no longer exists. Clark family friend George Rogers Clark Sullivan reported that William was "accompanied to the river landing by many ladies and gentlemen . . . and I suppose many tears will be shed when they part." William Clark's account with merchants Fitzhugh and Rose provides good information on his preparations for his 1808 move to St. Louis. During May 1808 he purchased a great many supplies, household materials, and a boat. He also paid and was paid various debts. Given the number of people in the party and the amounts and kinds of things taken, I assume that Clark's boat was a flatboat. (Jonathan Clark Diary, 2 June 1808; Sullivan to John O'Fallon, 2 June 1808, John O'Fallon Collection, MHS; Account Journal, Fitzhugh and Rose Account Books, vol. 6, in Charles W. Thruston Collection.)

5. Julia Hancock Clark (1791–1820) was the daughter of George and Margaret Strother Hancock. She was born in Fincastle, Virginia, on 21 November 1791 and christened Judith, but she apparently preferred Julia and went by that name (although her father often called her Judith). She knew William Clark before the expedition. Family tradition states that he was taken with her after rescuing her from a balky horse during a visit with the family about 1802. On 29 May 1805 he christened a river in Montana the Judith in her honor, proving that he knew her. On his trip from Louisville to Washington in December 1806–January 1807 following the expedition, and then on his way back, Clark visited the Hancocks, courted Julia, and by the end of March they were officially engaged with the wedding date set for January 1808. Clark returned from St. Louis and Kentucky by early January 1808 and on or about 5 January (the date of the marriage bond) he and Julia were married (she is listed as Judith on the marriage bond). By May they were in

the Louisville area visiting Clark's family and preparing for setting up housekeeping in St. Louis. William and Julia had five children (from January 1809 to July 1818), and by 1820 Julia's health was failing. Complications from giving birth to their fifth child two years earlier, cancer, and consumption, or perhaps a combination of these maladies, have all been mentioned as the cause of her illness. While on a visit to her parents at Fotheringay, in hopes of regaining her health, she died on 27 June 1820. She was buried in the Hancock vault there. Her father died three weeks later (by one account from his grief over the death of Julia) and joined her in the vault. (Bond, 178, 189–90, 242–43.)

6. Ann Clark Anderson (1790–1863) was the daughter of Col. Richard C. and Elizabeth Clark Anderson. Elizabeth (1769–1795) was a Clark sibling. She died 15 January 1795 as a result of childbirth. In 1810 Ann Anderson married John Logan (1785–1826), son of Gen. Benjamin Logan and Shelby County's representative in the Kentucky legislature in the 1820s. After his death she married Benjamin A. Riggs in Shelby County in 1829. Ann Anderson created quite a stir in St. Louis. Lewis already had spread word that Clark was bringing some of his nieces with him (only Ann came), and anticipation of their arrival apparently was quite high among the town's bachelors. Ann was described as "beautiful and accomplished" and apparently was so sought after that one person jokingly suggested a town meeting in order to dispose of her by lot to some lucky suitor. Unfortunately for her suitors, Ann apparently did not find St. Louis to her liking or she grew homesick, and she soon decided to return to Kentucky. (William Croghan to Edmund Clark, 1 February 1795, and John Clark to Jonathan Clark, 4 February 1795, Draper Mss., 2L38–39; Jefferson Co. Marriages, 1:67; Rogers Index; Hasskarl, 134; Loos, 819–21.)

7. Edmund Clark did not continue long in Henderson County (where he lived is now part of Union County). He located there in 1807, but moved back to Jefferson County by 1809 (possibly even late 1808) and entered into a mercantile business with his nephew John Hite Clark. The 1808 Henderson County tax list includes Edmund, and lists him as owning 667 acres of third-rate land on Lost Creek, four slaves, and two horses. Letters to him were addressed to Highland Creek (near the Ohio). A letter he wrote to Jonathan in 1808 locates his plantation along the Ohio some five miles below the mouth of Highland Creek. (Henderson Co., Ky., Tax List, 1808; Ann Clark to Isaac Clark, 6 June 1807, and Edmund Clark to Jonathan Clark, 26 March 1808, Bodley Family Papers.)

8. Philes was one of Edmund's slaves, though not one of the slaves he inherited from his father's estate. Both the death of one of his slaves and

the theft of his horse would have been serious blows to Edmund economically and perhaps emotionally.

9. Edmund Basey (ca. 1745–ca. 1825) came to Jefferson County, Kentucky, in 1787 and settled near the Bullitt family, with whom he had been acquainted in Virginia. Basey was a tailor. The debt Clark refers to was due him from Basey and two partners for the hire of Robin, his wife Franky, and their four children, all slaves belonging to the estate of Charles M. Thruston of which Clark was administrator. Clark hired the family out on 1 January 1807, and was to be paid by 1 January 1808. Basey failed to pay, and Clark brought suit against him and his partners Thomas Joyes and James McCasland in Jefferson County Circuit Court. The jury found in Clark's favor in February 1809 and awarded him $108.07 in damages. The name also appears as Basy and Basye. (Basye, 208–11; Clark v. Basey et al., case no. 7964, Jefferson Co. Circuit Court Records, KDLA.)

10. William Croghan, his son George, and Dr. Richard Brown had accompanied William Clark's party to the mouth of the Cumberland River. To travel part way with a party was a common practice. In Clark's 2 March 1802 letter to Jonathan he states that he would meet him somewhere on the Ohio upstream from Louisville if he knew when he would be coming. Croghan also may have had business in the area. He and the Clarks had extensive landholdings in the vicinity. In 1805 he had founded the town of Smithland at the mouth of the Cumberland River. (*EL*, 233; Sullivan to O'Fallon, 2 June 1808, John O'Fallon Collection.)

11. Ann "Nancy" or "Nany" Clark (1792–1833) was Jonathan and Sarah Hite Clark's daughter. She married James Anderson Pearce (1777–1825) on 30 September 1810, in Jefferson County (most likely at Trough Spring). They resided near Russellville after their marriage but later moved to Trough Spring. They were buried at Mulberry Hill, but like Jonathan and some of the other Clarks buried at the old home place, they were reinterred in Cave Hill Cemetery in 1868. (Jonathan, wife Sarah, sons John Hite and Isaac, and brother Edmund were reburied at Cave Hill on 1 May 1868. James and Ann Clark Pearce were transferred there on 3 August 1868.) As stated earlier, it was through this line of the Clark family that this group of William Clark letters descended. Julia was always eager to have her relatives visit, especially those young Clarks who were about her age. Nancy Clark was less than a year younger than her Aunt Julia. (Dorman (1), 29; Cave Hill Cemetery Records, Cave Hill Cemetery.)

12. The Cumberland River rises in the mountains of southeastern Kentucky, flows into north-central Tennessee, and then northward back

into Kentucky, entering the Ohio at Smithland. Along with the Cumberland Gap and Cumberland Mountains, it was named for the Duke of Cumberland by explorer Thomas Walker in 1750.

13. George Croghan (1791–1849) was the son of William and Lucy Croghan. He was born at Locust Grove, grew up there, and graduated from William and Mary in 1810. Following in something of the family tradition, and inspired by that tradition, he pursued a military career, serving with distinction as an aide-de-camp to William Henry Harrison at the Battle of Tippecanoe in November 1811, and receiving a captain's commission in the regular army in 1812. He served with the Northwestern army during the War of 1812 and gained fame as the commander of Fort Stephenson, Ohio, when he successfully defended it against an overwhelming force of British and Indians in August 1813. The "Hero of Fort Stephenson" was breveted a lieutenant colonel as a result of this action, which was the high point of his career. He was postmaster at New Orleans in 1824, and during the Mexican War he served with General Zachary Taylor (a neighbor and friend while he was growing up) and as inspector general of the army. He married Serena Livingston (of the famous New York Livingston family) in 1816. He suffered from alcoholism and died of cholera in New Orleans in January 1849. (*DAB*, 4:557.)

14. Dr. Richard Brown of Louisville. No other information has been found about him. In the previously cited letter dated 2 June 1808 from George Rogers Clark Sullivan to John O'Fallon, Sullivan reported that Maj. Croghan, George Croghan, and Dr. Richard Brown were accompanying Clark's party as far as the mouth of the Cumberland. (John O'Fallon Collection, MHS.)

15. Joseph Charless (1772–1834) was a native of Westmeath, Ireland. He came to America in 1796, following the failed Irish Rebellion of 1795, and settled at Philadelphia, where he worked as a printer for Mathew Carey. In 1800 he moved to Lexington, Kentucky, and six years later to Louisville, practicing the printing trade in both towns. In 1807 he published the *Louisville Gazette.* He accompanied Clark's party to St. Louis, apparently with the intention of establishing a newspaper there. This he did in July 1808, christening it the *Missouri Gazette.* Lewis and Clark were both supporters of Charless's efforts. It was the first newspaper published west of the Mississippi. In 1809 Charless changed its name to the *Louisiana Gazette,* and in 1812 to the *Missouri Gazette and Public Advertiser.* Charless continued its publication until September 1820 when he sold it to James C. Cummins, who in turn sold it in 1821 to Charless's son Edward, who changed the paper's name to the *Missouri Republican.* Charless married the widow Sarah Jordan McCloud

(1771–1852) in 1798. She already had one child, and their union produced four more. (Scharf, 2:1390–91; Billon, 229–31; Yater (1), 32.)

16. James and Easter and their children were slaves of William Clark.
Easter was listed as being between twelve and fifty years of age on
William Clark's list of taxable property compiled on 9 August 1799.
Clark consistently spells her name Easter, but her name appears as
Easther and Esther on a contemporary copy of John Clark's July 1799
will. Given Clark's phonetic spelling I am inclined to think her name
was indeed Easter. By terms of John Clark's will and the 1799 property document, she was willed to John and Benjamin O'Fallon, but
under the control of Clark's executors (his sons, sons-in-law, and
friend Benjamin Sebastian) until the O'Fallons reached twenty-one
years of age. It is understandable that she may have remained on the
Mulberry Hill estate in William's service. His control apparently extended to removing her and her children to St. Louis, unless he had acquired her from his O'Fallon nephews. She did not yet have any children in 1799. There is some uncertainty about James. He may be the
James listed as being over fifty years old on the 1799 tax document.
John Clark's will lists an "old negro" named Jane inherited by William, but I think a mistake was made in copying the will and the name
should be James, given the tax document list. This would mean that by
1808 he was sixty or older and married to the much younger Easter
and that they had had children in the nine years since John Clark's
death. They are not listed by M. Lewis Clark in his family genealogy
regarding the family slaves, which seems to indicate that they no
longer were owned by William Clark or had died by the time M. Lewis
Clark was old enough to remember the family slaves. (William Clark
tax document, 1799, and John Clark will, 1799, WCP-VMC; JCWB,
1:86–90.)

17. Nathaniel Hale Pryor (1772–1831) was a veteran of the Lewis and
Clark Expedition. He was a native of Virginia and moved to Jefferson
County, Kentucky, with his parents John and Nancy Floyd Pryor by
April 1782. His mother was the sister of Robert Floyd, so therefore
Nathaniel Pryor and Charles Floyd of the expedition were first cous-
ins. Pryor and his brother Robert were bound out as orphans in July
1791, but given the former's age he would not have stayed so for long.
On 17 May 1798 he married Peggy Patten (or Patton), daughter of
James Patten, who was one of the original settlers at the Falls in 1778
with George Rogers Clark. Patten was a Falls pilot at this time, and it
is quite possible that he piloted the keelboat through the falls.

By the time Pryor officially joined the expedition on 20 October
1803 he was a widower. He was one of the Nine Young Men from Ken-

tucky, served throughout the expedition as a sergeant, and was highly thought of by Lewis and Clark, as evidenced in his being recommended for and receiving an ensign's commission in the army following the expedition. It is believed that he kept a journal during the expedition since the sergeants were ordered to do so, but it has never been found. He led the failed effort to return Sheheke in the summer of 1807. He resigned from the army as a second lieutenant in 1810, obtained an Indian trader's license from William Clark, and operated a lead-smelting furnace at the mouth of the Galena River in northern Illinois. A party of Winnebagoes attacked the Galena mines in revenge for the Indian defeat at Tippecanoe in November 1811, and Pryor barely escaped, eventually making his way back to St. Louis in the spring of 1812. He rejoined the army in 1813 and served as a captain at the Battle of New Orleans. When his regiment was disbanded in 1815, he returned to the Indian trade, this time along the Arkansas River, in present northeastern Oklahoma, among the Osage. He married an Osage woman and lived with the tribe until his death. Clark "heard" that Pryor, twenty men, and two boats were waiting for him at the mouth of the Ohio probably from Lewis's letter of 29 May, which apparently had reached him at the mouth of the Cumberland and informed him that Pryor's party would be meeting him at either Fort Massac or the mouth of the Ohio. Clark had requested help be sent to assist his party in ascending the Mississippi. In addition to his family and personal baggage, he also was carrying many government supplies. Lewis requested Col. Hunt at Cantonment Belle Fontaine to approve the escort and he did so, even doubling the number of privates from ten to twenty. (Yater (2), 6–7; Moulton, 2:514; Loos, 818–19; Smith and Swick, 124.)

18. A reference to Dr. Brown unsuccessfully courting Ann Anderson. His desire for the "beautiful and accomplished" Miss Anderson's hand in marriage may well have been his reason for accompanying the party down the river.

19. This could be John Markwell who lived in Jefferson County at this time. No record of his marriage has been found. A John Marcum was living in Henderson County in 1808, but nothing else is known of him, and it is not known if this might be the person to which Clark was referring. (Henderson Co., Ky., Tax List, 1808.)

20. Robert Gilchrist (d. 1837) was living in Jefferson County in 1802 and in Henderson County by 1807, where he was a friend and neighbor of Edmund Clark. He apparently remained in Union County (formerly part of Henderson County) in the area of Morganfield because his will was probated in that county in 1837. He was associated with Dennis

Fitzhugh and possibly Edmund and John Hite Clark in their various mercantile enterprises. In 1816 Fitzhugh brought suit against Gilchrist on behalf of Edmund Clark's estate to recover two young female slaves named Nancy and Harriet (or Harriot), who belonged to Clark at the time of his death, but whom Gilchrist had had in his possession. Gilchrist apparently had hired the two girls from Edmund, and after Edmund died he sold them to a Mr. Poole near Morganfield. His authority to do so was disputed, and the court ordered the return of the slaves to Fitzhugh as administrator for the estate. Fitzhugh still was trying to recover the two girls in 1819, and William Clark assisted in this effort. While traveling east to Louisville and Virginia in March 1819, he commented in a letter to Dennis Fitzhugh that he had unsuccessfully attempted to collect the two girls from Poole; however, if Fitzhugh should get them soon Julia Clark would like to take one of the girls with her to Virginia. Evidence indicates that the girls' mother was Daphny (also spelled Dafney, Daphney, and Daphne). She was the daughter of Rose, Old York's wife. Edmund inherited her from his father. Daphny was between twelve and fifty years of age in July 1799 and had no children, so Nancy and Harriet were under sixteen years of age. In fact, they, along with Daphny, her other three children (Rose, Samuel, and Juba) and a woman and her three children, were advertised to be sold on the courthouse steps on 13 November 1815 at Edmund's estate sale. All the children were listed as being under thirteen years of age. Rose was purchased by Richard C. Anderson, Jr. The results of the sale apparently were never filed in the court house, so it is not known who purchased Edmund's other slaves. (*Kentucky Census,* 180, 1830; Heffington, 64; Edmund Clark Papers, fl. 13; JCISB, 3: 136–40; *Louisville Correspondent,* 6 November 1815; WCP-VMC; Tischendorf and Parks, 44.)

~

St. Louis July 2d. 2pm 1808

Dear Brother

I am hapy to anounce to You our Safe arrival at this place our time was more agreeable than I expected, we are all well, on our way we lost Nan[c]ys[1] Child, and Bens[2] horse. I have hired out most of my negrows and Shall if possible live in a littl Snug way,[3] I have not heard from one of my friends near you Since my arrival here.

Portrait of Julia Hancock Clark by John Wesley Jarvis. Julia was very close to William Clark's family and called Jonathan's wife Sarah her "Kentucky mother." Courtesy of the Missouri Historical Society

I take the liberty of inclosing to You a lettr to John[4] & one for nany,[5] The letter to John I wish ~~only~~ you to give him it is a propesition from me to join in trade at this place & Camp &c.[6]

The post is waiting prey excuse the hasty Scraul. my love to Sister & nancy. Julia Joins in love and ads a kiss to you both, her effection for Nancy ~~dis~~ is equal to that for her Sister.[7]

Yr. Offct. Brother

Wm Clark

1. Nancy was the daughter of Old York and Rose and sister (probably half-sister) of York. She was inherited along with her parents and brother by William Clark in 1799 by the terms of John Clark's will. William Clark's 1799 tax document lists her as under twelve years of age. At this time she would not have been older than twenty-one. It is not known whether she was married, and if she was, whether her husband was one of Clark's slaves or a slave owned by someone else. It is also not known whether her child that died was her first. M. Lewis Clark, in his family genealogy, states that Nancy had four children: Rosella (possibly Rosetta), Phoebe, Harriet, and Alexander; he also states that Alexander ran away in 1840 and became an editor in New York state. It would seem likely that these four children were born after the move to St. Louis. Neither Nancy nor her four children, with the possible exception of Rosella or Rosetta (Rosella in MLC's genealogy, but there is a Rosetta in William Clark's will), are listed in William Clark's will written in April 1837. It would seem that Clark would have owned more slaves than the nine plus a few children listed in his will, and further research probably would answer this question. (Clark tax document, 1799, WCP-VMC; JCWB, 1:86–90; MLClark, 90–95.)

2. The Ben referred to here could be either Clark's former slave, then bound to him, or his nephew Benjamin O'Fallon (1793–1842). Although it is rather unlikely that the former would own a horse or have such control of one that it would be referred to as his, this may be the case. In a letter written by George Rogers Clark Sullivan to John O'Fallon on 16 July 1808 he mentions that John's stepfather Dennis Fitzhugh had received a letter from Clark since his arrival in St. Louis and that he reported they had lost one of the children (Nancy's child) and his best horse. Therefore, ownership of the horse appears to be Clark's, but Ben's use of it is such that it is identified with him. One must wonder if the dead horse was really his best one. It is unlikely that Ben would have been allowed to use one of Clark's best horses, let alone his best one, to such a

degree that it was thought of as his (Ben's). If the horse was Ben O'Fallon's one would think that Clark would not refer to it as his, especially to O'Fallon's stepfather, who would have a special interest in his stepson's property, unless Clark just let Ben use it—which again would seem unlikely. (Sullivan to O'Fallon, 16 July 1808, John O'Fallon Collection.)

3. William and Julia Clark's first house in St. Louis had been rented for them by Meriwether Lewis, and he planned to share it with them. It was on Main Street and was described in a letter Lewis wrote to Clark on 29 May 1808. Clark apparently found the house inadequate because he soon rented a different house and then purchased one to his liking (as related in subsequent letters and notes). (Loos, 819–20.)

4. John Hite Clark (1785–1821) was the son of Jonathan and Sarah Hite Clark. He was born and raised in Spotsylvania County, Virginia, and moved with his family to Jefferson County, Kentucky, in 1802. He went into the mercantile business and operated a store in Louisville until his death. From 1809 until his Uncle Edmund's death in 1815, the two were partners in the firm of Edmund and John H. Clark. (John Hite Clark Papers; Edmund and John H. Clark Papers; Dorman (1), 27.)

5. Jonathan's daughter Ann Clark.

6. This is the first of many statements by Clark about establishing what he believed would be a very profitable store in St. Louis in partnership with his nephew John Hite Clark. He envisioned the Louisville store supplying the St. Louis store, which he or his manager would oversee, and a lucrative trade being established in the town and with the army at Cantonment Belle Fontaine. Clark was fated to be frustrated in his dreams of mercantile wealth. He may have engaged in some trading on a personal basis, but he certainly was involved in government and Missouri Fur Company trade with the Indians. While he did engage in some business ventures with John, the partnership in the hoped-for St. Louis store with its anticipated financial rewards apparently never materialized.

7. This reference is believed to be to Julia's sister Caroline Hancock Preston, wife of William Preston, Clark's old army comrade. I do not think Julia is referring to her other sister, Mary Hancock Griffin (1783–1826), and certainly not to Jonathan's wife Sarah, her sister-in-law, who was some thirty years older and whom Julia looked upon as her "Kentucky mother" rather than as a sister.

~

St. Louis July 21st 1808

Dear Brother

      I think I requested you in my memorandom to pay the bal-
lance which may be Due to the estate of C. Thruston,[1] and all other
money you may Collect to John[2] please to write and inform me what
Suckcess in receiving the amount of the Bill on S. G.[3] and Bond on E.v.
C.[4] as also the prospects of a Settlement with the estate. I have wrote to
John Several times, but have not rceived a letter as yet, but expect to get
one on Saturday, John I suppose has made you acquainted with the purpote of my letters. I Should be glad to have an evenings talk with you on
the Subject. Can't you make it Convenent to ride down to See us, we
Should be exceedingly hapy to See you with us in our new abode. Julia
inquires of every person from Kentucky for nany[5] with a view to find out
if they heard of her Comeing on, her attachment appears to increas, and
if She Should not come on with John the desapointment will be great. I
Shall Set out about the 15th. augt. up the Missouri and Shall be absent a
fiew [∧]2 or 3[∧] a fiew weeks   my businss is to lay out & direct the
building of a fort,[6] on that river, one Compny. of regular troops Sets out
in a few days by water I Shall proced by land with about 80 militia. one
other fort is to be built imediately on the Mississippi Some distanc up under the direction of Col. Hunt[7]

      I have inclosed a little receipt of Evd. Clarks,   only 2$ is my riteful
property the balance ought to be the propty. of W. Clarks heirs.[8]

      Julia Joins in most effectunate and Sincere respects to your self
Sister & nany __ and beg you accept of our best wishes for your helth &
hapiness.

Yr. Sincr. Bro.

Wm Clark

I have Directed Mr. Charless to Send you his paper, that You may see
what is going on here.   at this time I am much pestered with Indians,
101 Socks foxes & Ioway are here waiting the result of the trial of 4 of
ther men who have been given up as murderers, ther Trial is now pending.[9]

      Julia tels me to ask her "old mama Clark[10] to have her Some Garden
herbs dried, particularly time & Sage, as none is to be got at this place"

I have hired out Sillo, nancy, Aleck, Tenar, & Juba,[11] _ Ben is makeing hay, York employd in prunng[?] wood, attendng the garden, Horses &c. &c. Venos[12] the Cook and a very good wench Since She had about fifty, indeed I have been obliged [to] whip almost all my people. and they are now beginning to think that it is best to do better and not Cry hard when I am compelled to use the whip. they have been troublesom but are not at all so now ____

1. Charles Mynn (also spelled Mynne or Minn) Thruston (1765–1800) probably was a native of Gloucester County, Virginia. He was the son of the Rev. and Col. Charles Mynn Thruston (1738–1812), a Revolutionary War veteran known as the "Fighting Parson," and Mary Buckner (1732–1765). Charles was raised on the family estate Mt. Zion in present Clarke County, Virginia (then part of Frederick County), was a merchant in Bladensburg, Maryland, ca. 1784–1787, came to Kentucky with his brothers John and Buckner in 1788, and by 1789 he and John had settled in Jefferson County. He was a partner in the 1790s of the mercantile firm of McDonald and Thruston of Louisville, and had relocated by 1800 to a plantation about thirty miles upstream from Louisville near Westport, Kentucky. He married Fanny Clark (see letter dated 2 March 1802, note 31) on 20 January 1796. They had two children, Charles and Ann (see letters dated 13 August 1801, note 13, and 2 March 1802, note 31, respectively). He was murdered by his slave Luke on 8 December 1800. William Clark was the administrator of his late brother-in-law's estate after the first administrator, Charles's brother John, died in 1802. Settling the estate caused Clark a degree of financial trouble and resulted in strained relations with some family members. (Charles W. Thruston Papers; Thruston family file.)
2. John Hite Clark, Clark's nephew. He was going to St. Louis for a visit, and apparently planned on carrying money collected for Clark with him.
3. Samuel Gwathmey, Clark's nephew.
4. Everard Clark (1780–1829) was born in Lunenburg County, Virginia, and was William Clark's first cousin. His father was Benjamin Clark (1730–1806). His brothers were Marston Green, Jonathan, William, and Benjamin Wilson Clark. He and some of his siblings had settled near Edmonton in Barren County (now in Metcalfe County), Kentucky, by the early 1800s. Many of their Rogers cousins also settled in the area. Edmonton was named for William Clark's first cousin Edmund Rogers. Everard Clark married Lucinda Courts (d. 1823) on 10

December 1822 and served as Edmonton's first postmaster from 1826 to 1829. (Clark family file; Simmons, 32, 43–44.)

5. Ann "Nancy" or "Nany" Clark, Jonathan's daughter.

6. Fort Osage, near present Sibley, Missouri. Clark selected the site and supervised the construction of the fort and related buildings in 1808. While ascending the Missouri in 1804, Lewis and Clark had noted the site on the south (or west) side of the river with its seventy-foot banks as an ideal location for a fort and trading factory. Clark left St. Louis on 24 August for St. Charles, where he picked up the eighty mounted militiamen. Capt. Nathan Boone, son of the famous frontiersman Daniel Boone, served as their guide. They left St. Charles on 25 August and arrived at their destination near Fire Prairie on 3 September. The company of regular troops mentioned set out from Fort Bellefontaine (or Cantonment Belle Fontaine), at the confluence of the Mississippi and Missouri, on 7 August as the escort for six keelboats carrying the supplies and trade goods for the fort. At the time it was built, Fort Osage was the farthermost outpost in Louisiana Territory. It was built to establish a military and trade presence among the Osage Indians. It was abandoned in June 1812 in order to shorten the defensive line of the frontier but was reoccupied in the spring of 1816. As other posts were established farther upriver, Fort Osage's importance declined, and in 1819 the garrison was removed. The trading post continued to operate until 1822 when a law was passed abolishing the federal trade factory system. Clark kept a journal of his Fort Osage expedition, which provided the first detailed description of the overland route across present central Missouri (I-70 largely parallels Clark's route), and he wrote detailed letters about his mission to the secretary of war. He apparently never visited the fort again, and it primarily is associated with the government Indian factor George C. Sibley. Today a reconstruction of Fort Osage provides visitors with an idea of what life at the post was like. (Gregg; Lamar, 390–91.)

7. Thomas Hunt (d. 1808) was born in Massachusetts and served as a sergeant in a company of Minute Men at Lexington and Concord in April 1775. He received an ensign's commission the following month and rose through the ranks of various Massachusetts and regular army regiments to the rank of captain. He was wounded at Stony Point in July 1779 and at Yorktown in October 1781. He was commissioned a captain in the regular army in 1791 and rose to the rank of colonel, serving in the Second Infantry, Second Sub-Legion, and First Infantry. At the time of his death on 17 or 18 August 1808, he was the commandant of the First Infantry and commander of Cantonment Belle Fontaine. He was eulo-

gized in the 31 August 1808 edition of the *Missouri Gazette*. His wife died
a few months later on 15 January 1809 and was eulogized in the 25 January edition of the *Gazette*. The fort mentioned was Fort Madison on the
Mississippi River in present Lee County, Iowa. Second Lieutenant Nathaniel Pryor was second in command of the company dispatched to establish the fort and trading factory among the Sauk and Fox Indians in
August 1808. It was abandoned and burned in 1813. A reconstruction of
the fort is in the town of Fort Madison. (Heitman (1), 309–10; Jackson
(1), 2:383n, 642n.)

8. William Clark (d. 1791) was the son of Benjamin Clark and first cousin
of William and Jonathan Clark. He was a native of Virginia (possibly
Lunenburg County) and moved to Kentucky by 1780, serving as a lieutenant in the Illinois Regiment from 1780 to 1782. He settled in Clarksville and was a town trustee, a surveyor, and a commissioner for Clark's
Grant. Shortly before his death, he moved across the river to Jefferson
County, and reportedly died at Mulberry Hill. He never married and
had been a member of the Society of the Cincinnati since 1787. Both his
commission as a militia captain, dated 8 January 1790, and his member-
ship in the Society of the Cincinnati are sometimes mistakenly attributed to his younger cousin of the same name. As mentioned earlier (see
letter dated 13 August 1801, note 11) the Clark cousins had various
dealings with each other, especially regarding land in Clark's (or the
Illinois) Grant and Clarksville. Cousin William Clark left no direct descendants, and according to his will his heirs were his brothers Marston
Green, Jonathan, Benjamin Wilson, and Everard Clark, his sister Lucy
Clark Pool, and his cousin Elizabeth Clark Anderson. His estate was
not settled until 1812. (Heitman (1), 158; Gwathmey, 154; Rogers Index; Hening, 11:335–36; JCWB, 1:36–38.)

9. Clark mistakenly reports four instead of three Indians being on trial for
murder, but he was indeed much "pestered" by Indians. The first issue
of the *Missouri Gazette* reported on the trials. The two Iowa braves were
found guilty of killing Joseph Tibbeau and Joseph Marshall (or
Marechal) at the mouth of Grand River, and they were expected to receive the death penalty. In what apparently was a surprise move, the
judges ignored the cries of "Hang them!" and granted the two defendants a new trial. They were again found guilty, but this time the matter
was referred to the president for a decision. The trial of the Sauk brave
accused of murdering a white man at Portage de Sioux was to begin on
26 July. The Sauk also was convicted, but it was reported that Governor
Lewis granted him a reprieve, pending a decision by the president.
Large numbers of Sauk, Fox, and Iowa Indians were in St. Louis during
the trials, just as Clark reports. They even had a section reserved for

them in the courtroom so that they could observe the proceedings. The paper reported that the Indians "incessantly harassed" both Lewis and Clark to pardon the defendants and that they were kept busy counciling with them and maintaining control. A seemingly never-ending procession of relatives also pleaded for their lives into the next year. The paper did not report on the outcome of the appeal to the president on behalf of the Iowas (or the Sauk), but the answer, whatever it may have been (and if received) for the Iowas, apparently was moot. The 19 July 1809 issue of the *Gazette* reported that the two Indians escaped from jail a couple of days earlier and had not been seen since. Lewis demanded that the Iowa chiefs return them. Until they did so, he ordered that all trade with the Iowa be suspended as punishment for their refusal. They refused, reasoning that the two braves had been given up once and that they should have been punished then. Before further action could be taken, Lewis left on his fateful trip eastward. Frederick Bates canceled Lewis's order when he assumed the duties of acting governor in Lewis's absence. No other mention was found of the matter, so Bates apparently let the matter rest. The Sauk received a presidential pardon on 5 February 1810. (*Missouri Gazette* (St. Louis), 26 July 1808, 2, 10, 17 August 1808, 19 July 1809, 4 October 1809; Loos, 822–24, 828–30, 862, 885–86; Scharf, 1:120.)

10. Jonathan's wife Sarah Hite Clark. This is another example of the closeness that not only Clark but his bride Julia felt toward Jonathan and his family.

11. Sillo is Priscilla (also referred to as Sillow and Sill). She was between twelve and fifty years of age in 1799. She would have been a young woman, because she had one child (I believe Molly) in 1799, and had at least one more later. She was left to John and Ben O'Fallon by their grandfather John Clark, but William Clark retained control or possession of her and apparently would gain ownership of her when the O'Fallons reached twenty-one years of age. Nancy was the daughter of Old York and Rose (see letter dated 2 July 1808, note 1). Aleck has not been positively identified. He may be Nancy's son Alexander, but that seems unlikely. He would have been under ten years old in 1808 and rather young to be hired out, unless as part of an agreement with Nancy. He may have been a slave that Clark had purchased or one that Julia had brought into the marriage. Tenar (also spelled Tener, Tenor, and Tanner) was Venos's child. He was under twelve years of age in 1799. Inherited by George Rogers Clark from John Clark, he was acquired along with his mother and sibling Frankey (also spelled Franie) by William in 1800. Juba (also spelled Jubia and Jubar) was the son of Old York and Rose and inherited by Clark from his father. In 1799

he was under the age of twelve (see letter dated ca. 1 March 1809, note 7, for more information on Juba). Priscilla, Tenar, and Juba may not have remained with Clark for a long period of time. M. Lewis Clark does not list them in the family genealogy, indicating, I think, either that he does not remember them at all or that they were not with the family long enough after he was born for him to remember them as part of the family. Therefore, possibly by 1820 or so they had either died or been sold or freed. (Clark tax document, 1799, WCP-VMC; JCWB, 1:86–90; JCBPAB, 2:56; MLClark, 90–95.)

12. Venos (also spelled Venus and Venice) was married to Ben (see letter dated April 1805, note 16). In 1799 she was between twelve and fifty years of age. Her children at that time were Peter, Frankey (or Franie), and Tenar (or Tenor or Tanner). She had at least one more child, Gilbert, after 1799, according to M. Lewis Clark's family genealogy. Venos and her children Frankey and Tenar were inherited by George Rogers Clark by the terms of John Clark's will, but William Clark gained title to them in January 1800 because of the debt owed him by George (he acquired adult male slaves Lew and Kitt in the same transaction). Peter was left to Edmund Clark. This may be the Peter who was owned by Dennis Fitzhugh and apparently later by John O'Fallon and who was hired out for some years in the Louisville area. He was living in the Louisville area into the 1820s, being hired out by Dennis Fitzhugh and after his death by Charles W. Thruston. Thruston described him in 1827 as a fine servant who was opposed to leaving the Louisville area. This is the first mention by Clark of trouble with his slaves. The problems stemmed from their unhappiness with moving to St. Louis and the changes it brought. (Clark Tax Document, 1799, WCP-VMC; MLClark, 90; JCBPAB, 2:56; Charles W. Thruston Papers.)

∼

Saint Louis 22nd August 1808

Dear Brother

       I observe in a LeuiSville paper[1] Several tracts of my land advertised for Sale in the name of G. R. Clark, for the Tax due on them |No. 62, 163, 84 ∧ pd. by Mr. W. Pope[∧]|[2] & 223 ∧ of this No. 250 in the name of Newcock[?][∧] are mortgaged to John Holker,[3] if I pay the mortgage those lots are to be mine, I observe that a part of No. 62, 84 & 163 are Sold to the amount of 150 acrs, I must requist you to attend at the

Sale which is to be wednesday the 21st of Septr. and purchase those lands for me if you Can for the Tax, I wish the Tax paid for then at all event. If you Cant purchase those lands for the Tax, will you be So good as to enquire about the mortgage to Holker, & Should you think the lands worth more than the mortgage please to enquire how the mortgage Could be Settled, perhaps it might be paid with a part of the land __ No̶. 312 acres in No. 276 ∧ pd. by Mr. S.[amuel] G.[wathmey] [∧] belongs to me. 100 acres in No. 30 letter **B** advertised belongs to M̶a̶j̶r̶.̶ C̶r̶o̶g̶h̶a̶n̶ [∧]Mastn [Marston] G. Clark[∧] (I believe) the half of letter C in the Same N̶o̶. ∧ pd. by Mr. S.G[∧] to me, the other M. G. Clark __

John has not yet arrved and I have not heard from him for two weeks. The anxiety of Julia & ann anderson has been So great for his arival, that Scercely a man has passed on horse back for ten days past without their running to the window to See if it was not John. I fear I Shall not See him, as the day after tomorrow I Shall Set ∧to[∧] out [to] fix the establishment on the missouri and Shall be absent more than 3 weeks

we have nothing verry interesting. Col. Hunt who Comd., [∧]in[∧] this quatr died a few days ago. Julia Joins in Sincere wishes for the health and hapiness of yourself & Sister Clark yrs. most affectunately

Wm Clark

Since I wrote you this lettr John has arrived, and handed me you[r] letter, which makes me much more anxioues to See you than I was, John has gratified all. I am just about Seting out up the missoire

If you See Mr. Capron[4] ask him if he has any intention of Coming here_ if three hundred & Sixty fair or 400 dollars a year would induc him.

one more adieu perey write me full letters & [I] Rmn. yr. Sincr

Broth WC.

John patly promises to Stay with his aunt untill I return.

1. The *Louisville Gazette* (1807–1812) or *Farmer's Library* (1801–1810) most likely; they are the only known newspapers published in Louisville in 1808. Joseph Charless was the publisher of the *Louisville Gazette,* and he was in the midst of relocating to St. Louis. He was associated with the paper until at least April 1809. Jared Brooks (d. 1816) was listed as the publisher in an 1810 issue. Brooks is better known for his work as a surveyor and cartographer. Clark owned extensive property in the Illinois

or Clark's Grant in southern Indiana, especially in Clarksville. The sale that Clark refers to was indeed held on 21 September in Jeffersonville, and Jonathan attended it. (Brigham, 1:170–71; Lathem, 48; Yater (1), 32; Jonathan Clark Diary, 21 September 1808.)

2. This is either Col. William Pope, William Pope, Jr., or Worden Pope of the prominent Pope family of Louisville. The Popes were friends and associates of the Clark family and later became connected through marriages. The nature of Clark's mention of W. Pope, his use of Mr. rather than a military title, and the kind of business Pope did for him, leads me to think that he is referring to Worden Pope (1776–1838). A native of Westmoreland County, Virginia, Worden Pope came to Kentucky in 1779 with the Pope clan. He was raised in Shepherdsville, twenty miles south of Louisville, and attended Mr. Priestley's school in Bardstown until 1792. In 1794 he began working in the Jefferson County clerk's office and in 1796 became clerk of the county court, a position he held until his death. He also served as clerk of the circuit court from that time until late 1832 or early 1833. He practiced law and was known as one of the best land lawyers in Kentucky. In 1804 he married Elizabeth Taylor Thruston, daughter of the late Col. John Thruston. They had thirteen children. A date of 1772 also is given for his birth but 1776 seems more likely. (Johnston, 2:606–7, 645–46; Robert E. McDowell Collection, 7:417, 12:342, TFHS; Jefferson Co. Minute Order Book, 18:15–17.)

3. John (or Jean) Holker (1745–1822) was the son of an expatriate Englishman, born and raised in France. He was something of a protégée of Benjamin Franklin while Franklin was in Paris and came to the United States in 1778 as a French official. He settled in Philadelphia and soon gave up government service to become a merchant and speculator in paper money and land. By 1798 he had settled in Frederick County, Virginia. While living there and in Philadelphia he became associated with the Clarks and some of their family and friends. (Rice, 267–71, 282–91; CCDB 37:82, 85, 95–99, 121–30; JCBPAB, 254–55; Michael Lacassagne Miscellaneous Papers, TFHS.)

4. Henry Capron was an accomplished violinist who lived in Philadelphia in the 1780s and 1790s. He was a music tutor of George Washington's stepdaughter in the 1790s. By the early 1800s he had settled in Louisville, possibly coming from Maryland. A suit filed against Capron in November 1808 sought payment for bringing three slaves from Maryland to Louisville for him in May 1808, and expressed the fear that Capron was preparing to remove himself and property from Kentucky without paying the debt. This was just one of seven suits filed against him from 1805 to 1809. While in Louisville he became associated with the Clarks. It is not known whether Clark's suggestion that he relocate to

St. Louis influenced Capron, but he did move there. In 1810 Capron
was licensed to operate a tavern in St. Louis, and in 1811 he led an effort
to establish a public library there. (*The Pennsylvania Magazine of History
and Biography* (2), 31:70, 69:108, 112–13; Wayman v. Capron, case 8114,
Jefferson County Circuit Court Records, KDLA; *Louisiana Gazette*, 14
February 1811; Houck, 3:60, 72.)

≈

St. Louis October 1st 1808.

Dear Brother

I have but just returned from the Fire prarie[1] to which
place I have been to build a Fort, all went on nearly as I expected, and
prety much as I wished, I was lain [lame?] on my way out and, Sick when
Fixing and building the Fort and on my return with a ~~desentary~~ which
has with the assistence of medesin Sinc my return been nearly Cured[2]

I found a letter and Small memorandom of yours in my desk which I
inclose in this letter to you if you do not want those papers there will be
no expense in Sending them.

The Bearer of this letter is Mr. George Shannon[3]   [one or two words
lost due to the seal tear] unfortunate fellow who lost his leg by a wound
received in the action at the Ricaras, he is going to lexington to go to
School, with the veiw of acquiring Some knowledge to fit him for an employment to get his liveing, he is Studious, and ambitious, and a man of
impeachable [impeccable] Charector. I Shall Continue to pay him his
~~wages~~ Salerry untill ordered to the reverse by the Secty. of War, which
will enable him to pay his board and Schooling —[4]

Julia and Miss Ann Anderson are both in perfect health and join
ₐin[ₐ] ther love to you Sister & nancy.

I will write you by the mails a long lettr in the mean tim _ I am yer of-
fectinatly ys.

Wm Clark

[Letter carried by George Shannon.]

1. Fire Prairie was located in the area of present Sibley, Jackson County,
Missouri. As the name indicates, the area was named for a prairie fire or
fires that had occurred there. Fire Prairie River (now Fishing River)
entered from the north side of the Missouri and Fire Prairie Creek from
the south. Lewis and Clark noted that the bluff on the south side of the

river was an ideal location for a fort, and this is where Clark returned in 1808 to build Fort Osage. Lewis initially referred to the fort as Clark, but its commanding officer Capt. Clemson dubbed it Osage instead, and that became its official name. Clark returned to St. Louis late in the evening of 22 September. (Moulton, 2:316–17; Loos, 849, 853.)

2. I am assuming that Clark means lame for "lain," rather than lain or laid up. Although ill, he kept going and did not stop for any period of time; thus he was not really "laid up." I do not know what this malady was, but it sounds similar to the ill health he suffered in the fall of 1803. An apparently different health problem that struck him and some of the other men was dysentery, which was, of course, a common malady of the day. While different from the constipation problem that Clark had suffered from in 1803, the dysentery he suffered from on this trip may have been related to the intestinal problem that periodically plagued him, or it could have been the result of local conditions, water, etc. He kept a journal of the trip and recorded that he and other men suffered from dysentery. (Gregg; Loos, 840–41, 845.)

3. George Shannon (1785–1836) was the youngest member of the Corps of Discovery and one of the famous Nine Young Men from Kentucky. He was a native of Pennsylvania (possibly Washington County) and moved with his family to Ohio in 1800. He may have joined at Pittsburgh or Maysville, Kentucky (the latter is usually cited), and was officially enlisted at the Falls of the Ohio on 19 October 1803. In September 1807 he was a member of Ens. Nathaniel Pryor's party which unsuccessfully attempted to return Sheheke and his family to the Mandan. Shannon was wounded in the leg (which one apparently is not known) in that battle with the Arikara, and the leg became gangrenous. It was amputated above the knee by Dr. Bernard G. Farrar after the party returned to St. Louis. He wore a peg or wooden leg the rest of his life and acquired the nickname "Peg Leg." He explored saltpeter caves with Meriwether Lewis for a short time, and turned down an offer from Clark to become involved in the fur trade, deciding instead to pursue an education and acquire a profession more suited to someone with his physical limitations. Thus the purpose of this letter. In the fall of 1808 Shannon enrolled in Transylvania University in Lexington, Kentucky, and remained there until 1810 when Clark asked him to assist Nicholas Biddle with the editing of the official account of the expedition. He spent part of the next two years in Philadelphia assisting Biddle and then returned to Lexington in 1812. He apparently read law during this period, and by 1815 he was practicing law and was involved in politics. He served in the Kentucky legislature, 1820–1823, and was appointed a circuit court judge in 1824. In 1828 Shannon resigned his judgeship and

moved to St. Charles, Missouri. In Missouri he was appointed U.S. attorney for the District of Missouri, 1830–1834, and briefly served in the state legislature. He married Ruth Snowden Price of Lexington in 1813. They had seven children. He died in Palmyra, Missouri, while trying a case there. He is buried in an unmarked grave (like so many of the members of the Corps of Discovery) in the Massie Mill Cemetery one mile north of Palmyra. (Denton, 15–24; Jackson (1), 1:125n, 2:438n, 620n; Moulton, 2:521–22.)

4. Clark continued to pay Shannon's salary until ordered to stop. He then assisted him in getting a pension from the government based on the loss of his leg. Henry Clay assisted with this and also with renewing Shannon's land warrant in 1814 for his service on the expedition (which he then bought from Shannon). (Denton, 19; Jackson (1), 2:620–21.)

≈

Saint Louis October 5th 1808.

Dear Brother

On my return from building a Fort up the Missouri found your letter of the 3rd of September by John Sullivan[1] and was happy to hear of the health & hapiness of your Self & Sister, but must lament a little the loss of her peaches which has been distroyed by the Rains. I hope they are not all distroyed.

I have never Seen John Sullivan untill yesterday he was verry Sick when he first arrived and Sence he got better has been rideing about, he talks of Comeing to this Country to farm if he Could get land, I have offered him a part of my purchase Six miles from Town as long as he wishes to tend it. he is like a great maney others in this Country in Serch of Some employment or Situation to better their circumstances. if John was a little more experienced I could employ him in the Indian department _ or he might be employd in the Salt peter or Lead mine business. but his youth and wont of experienc and a Sufficent Knowledge of mankind, prevents me placeing him in a Situation in which he might not do Credit to himself; if he Coms here as a farmer, I may get him in as a Surveyor ʌ when the p.[ublic] Lands are Surveyed[ʌ] or Something of that Sort After a while. Talk to the old Capt.[2] on this Subject if you think proper. _ I have letters by every post and applications from maney persons is waiting in this Country, for Situations advice & assistance. indeed

I am much pestered in that way as you may Suspect from my public Situation. The multiplicity of buseness which has been heeped, upon me has employed and Still Continues to employ So great a po[r]tion of my time that I have not leasure to attend to my private affairs — You were made acquainted with my business up the Missouri, I have partly built a butifull Fort 300 miles up the missouri, and Fixed a Tradeing establishment Collected the Little & Great Osage, formed a Treaty with them extinguished their Claim to the lands for 300 miles back between the Missouri and Arkansaw, fer a verry Small Sum, caused them to move and build their villages under the protection of the Fort established peace between the Osage ^excep a Band on arkansaw[^] and other nations up the Mississppi brought the vicious Lawless Kanzas to Seek terms and they now also Settled near the Fort &c.[3] [a pointing finger drawn here] [( ]~~I am not glad that I have caused those things to be done without any Sort of instructions, it is too much for one man like me to do and the pie must have a new Crust and more plumbs put in by partcular fingers to be engraved to make it palaleable)~~—[4]

I was very unwell for About 2 weeks on my trip up the Missouri, but have nearly recovered, Miss A Anderson's expressing a wish to return, disconcerts me virery much as Julia is not in a Situation to be left alone, the length of time necessary for me to accompany Miss An A to Kentucky, and I know it is [not at?] all convenient for Colo. Anderson to leave home and Come for her,[5] I Shall write to him to day on the Subject — John Clark and my Self Could not have as much talk a[s] I could wish on the Subject of Trade. he will tell you all we have Said and Shew you my letters I hope as I wish you to be possessed of ~~all~~ the Knowledge of all our intentions views & prospects, & recve your advice & oppinion — I am So frequently enterupted by whisspersins that I fear I Shall not Say to you half I at first intended, four times I have been disturbed Since I commencd this letter and the dores are again Cracking.— what you have done for me in my affrs. business mar [matters?] &c. deserves my greatest thanks, indeed I wish I was blessed as much with your Council as with your good wishes for my interest & prosperity — do Just as you please in all my business which you may have in your Ciare. I have wrote to Bro: Edmund about Sippo[6] the man would not pay without a Suit and Mr. Fitzhugh expressed a wish that the business Should be arranged in Some way imediately. I hope Bro: Edmund does not think I wish'd to get the fellow back from the man in opposition to his will, I did not know the fellows Crime nor do I at this time know it. he Shall be delt with just as

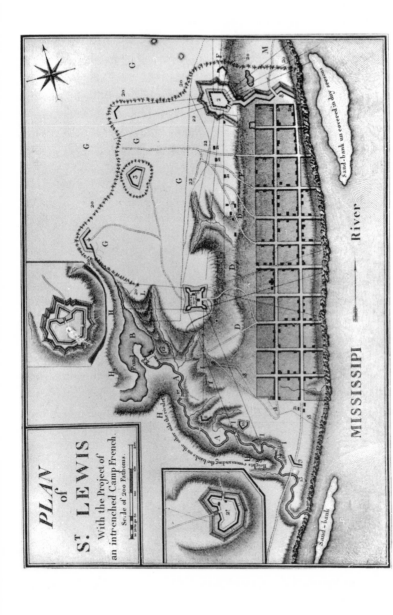

Plan of St. Louis as it appeared in the 1790s at the time of Victor Collot's visit. The town had not significantly changed by the early 1800s, when Lewis and Clark visited and then settled there to take up their government duties. From Victor Collot, *A Journey in North America*

he ∧Bro Edmund[∧] wishes I am not ~~much~~ in want of a fellow, as I cannot attend to a farm at Present ‒ but Should have kept him ∧& employed him[∧] Cutting wood Baaling [hay? or boating?] &c. if My Bro: had not expressed to Mr. Fitzhugh a disapprobation to his returning to any branch of the Family.

you Say Maj. Preston has been with you, I wished he had brought his fat Sides this way.[7]

I inclose you Davis Floyds[8] letter on the Subject of the mill Seat, please to let the Subject be known to bro George and for him to act in the business as he thinks best and most to his advantgee with your approbation.

I have just recved a lettr from John, and find he has been verry unwell and not yet recoverd, and that Mr. Brooks[9] has also been Sick & his business Suffering, I hope and prey they have both recovered

I have moved into a larger house, and rented out the one I lived in to Webster,[10] the house I reside in is large Spacious has large Cellars and rooms for public Stores, which will Save the most of the Rent of the house to me, and a more pleasent Situation ‒

I have not time to reade over this lettr and must Conclude by a request that you and Sister Clark will accept the assurances of my best wishes & Sincerust affaction, Julia Joins in love to you Sister, nany John and Mr. & Mrs. Temple if they are with you. Julia Still looks out for nancy — John done ~~them~~ ∧Julia & Ann[∧] a great pleasure by Continun as long as he did with them and I feel much gratifyed my Self for his atuntion & delay ‒ but Could have wish he had enjoyed more health.

You must not expect either Connection grammr & good Spelling in my lettrs as I write to you without reserve & at Such tims as I can find leasure.[11]

Yor Sincr Broth
Wm Clark

I have just heard that near 4,000 Inds. men
women & children at the fort I built and others
on their way to Trade.
[note written vertically in the margin of page two] Julia requests you to tell nany to Send her the long Lawn[12] which She wrote to her for, John will pay for it. if it is to be ~~had~~ found in the Town

1. John Campbell Sullivan (1788–1830) was a native of Jefferson County, Kentucky, and the son of Capt. James Sullivan. Sullivan relocated to St.

Louis in 1808. While Clark may have doubted his prospects initially, Sullivan proved capable in his pursuits and no doubt benefited from Clark's interest in him. By 1814 Sullivan was serving as collector of revenue for St. Louis County, and in 1820 he served as a delegate from that county to the Missouri Constitutional Convention. He married Nancy Morgan Smith (1798–1871) on 18 January 1821, and they had four children. (Sullivan family file.)

2. James Sullivan, William's former and Jonathan's current neighbor along Beargrass Creek. He moved to St. Louis by 1810, and lived with his son John. (Sullivan family file.)

3. The treaty Clark discusses transferred nearly half of Missouri and a good portion of Arkansas to the U.S. government in return for the standard annuities, etc., but it was quickly objected to by several Osage chiefs and never ratified by the government. A similar one, however, written by Lewis and negotiated by Pierre Chouteau two months later, was ratified (see letter dated 22, 24 November 1808, note 20, for information on this treaty). The Kansa Indians belonged to the Southern Siouan Indians, which included the Osage, Ponca, Omaha, and Quapaw. They had migrated from the southern Atlantic seaboard through the Ohio Valley to Missouri, Kansas, and Nebraska long before whites began entering the region. The Kansa were a much smaller tribe than the Osage but actively engaged in warfare with rival tribes and occasional opportunistic raiding against whites. They lived in semi-permanent villages of earth-covered lodges and depended on hunting and agriculture for subsistence. (Lamar, 391, 1114–15; *American State Papers: Indian Affairs*, 4:763–64; Loos, 849–54.)

4. This part has been marked out in the letter with vertical slashes ("\") but is easily readable. It is not known whether Clark, Jonathan, or someone else marked it out. Despite not having orders to negotiate the treaty he did, William Clark sought to achieve the maximum he could for the government and to worry about any consequences of exceeding his authority later. Taking advantage of opportunities certainly was one of Clark's characteristics; it was something he had done his whole life to the benefit of both himself and the government. He obviously was not unaware of the benefits accrued to the government because of his actions, and comments—if not exactly complains—to Jonathan that he should receive proper compensation for his actions. In his official report to Secretary of War Dearborn, he apologized if he overstepped his bounds but stated that he was only seeking to do everything he could in the government's interest and that he believed the treaty was fair to the Osage. (Loos, 847–48.)

5. Clark was periodically troubled by some kind of intestinal malady, its origin or cause unknown. His reference to illness here likely is to the dysentery he and others suffered from on the trip. Ann (or Nancy) Anderson's desire to return home to Louisville came at a bad time and upset Clark because Julia was some six months pregnant with their first child. The longer Ann Anderson had stayed, especially as the birth of the child neared, the happier he no doubt would have been. Always happy to have family around him, he would have been even more so at this time because he and Julia were newly settled in St. Louis, and Julia was pregnant and still very homesick for her Kentucky and Virginia relations. Clark apparently meant to indicate that it was not or might not be convenient for Ann's father Col. Richard Anderson to come get her at that time. The predicament soon was solved when a party with an appropriate female chaperon traveled to Louisville.

6. Sippo is Scippio (also spelled Scipio, Seppo, Sep, and Pipo). He was the son of Rose, and was twelve to fifty years old in 1799. He was inherited by Edmund Clark following John Clark's death, but it is not certain whether Edmund took actual possession of him until he moved to Jefferson County in 1802. It is very possible that Scippio continued to live at Mulberry Hill until then. He worked for Edmund in the mill he bought from Clark in 1803, keeping the accounts of grain ground and whiskey due. By mid-1807 Edmund and Scippio had had a serious falling out, and Edmund sold him. In a 17–18 July 1807 letter to George Tompkins, Edmund refers to "S" (meaning Scippio, I believe) as the "vilest creature that exists on the face of the earth," and writes that he is "determined to ship" the "vilian." Clark, as indicated in this letter, was unaware of the problem between the two men or of Edmund's desire for the Clarks to have nothing to do with him, and bought Scippio from a Mr. Howell (see letter dated 2 January 1809, note 4). In deference to Edmund's wishes and because of his own subsequent unhappiness with Scippio, yet balancing his financial investment, Clark tried to sell him, but apparently did not do so for a number of years. M. Lewis Clark lists Scippio in his family genealogy, indicating that he was still with the family ca. 1818, when Lewis would have been old enough to remember the family's slaves. Although he was Rose's child, I believe that Scippio was not a sibling of York's. Given the documentary evidence I have previously cited, I think that Old York and Rose had families prior to their union that produced Nancy and Juba. Scippio and Daphny were Rose's children from an earlier relationship(s). York was Old York's son, which was generally assumed, but this seems to be confirmed by M. Lewis Clark listing Nancy (whom records verify as the daughter of Old York and Rose) as York's sister (actually half sister, I believe). (Clark tax doc

ument, 1799, WCP-VMC; JCWP, 1:86–90; Clark to Tompkins, 17, 18 July 1807, Bodley Family Papers; MLClark, 90.)

7. Maj. William Preston. Clark's reference to Preston's "fat sides" is accurate. A portrait of Preston painted by Joseph Bush dated from the period 1815–1821 (but possibly done posthumously) reveals the major to be rather portly. (Whitley, 428–29.)

8. Davis Floyd (ca. 1772–1831) was the brother of Sgt. Charles Floyd of the Lewis and Clark Expedition. He was born in Virginia and came to Kentucky as a child. He was a long-time friend and associate of the Clarks, including William. Floyd held a variety of government positions in Clark and Harrison Counties, Indiana, and engaged in a variety of business endeavors. He and his father operated a ferry from Clarksville to the Kentucky side of the river in the early 1800s, and he also was a licensed Falls pilot. He was involved in the Burr Conspiracy, and while found guilty he received a mild punishment. In 1794 he married Susanna Lewis and after her death Elizabeth Robards in 1816. He had four children. (*EL*, 299–300; Yater (2), 4–6; Floyd family file, TFHS; Clift (1), 39; Baird, 287–288; *BDIGA*, 1:129.)

9. It is difficult to determine from Clark's writing if this name is Brook or Brock. It may be Thomas Brock, who worked for Edmund and John H. Clark.

10. Resin (or Rezin) Webster (d. 1810). A native of Massachusetts, Webster served from 1791 to 1802 in the army, being promoted from sergeant up to captain during that time. He opened the Eagle Tavern in the fall of 1808 in the house Clark had just recently vacated. By January 1810 he had declared bankruptcy. The *Gazette* listed an R. Webster, formerly of the U.S. Army, dying in Herculaneum later that year, and I assume this must be Resin. (Heitman (2), 1:1013; *Missouri Gazette*, 2 November 1808; *Louisiana Gazette*, 1 February 1810, 7 November 1810; Houck, 3:60.)

11. A wonderful reference by Clark to his writing style, grammar, and spelling. All those familiar with his journals from the expedition and from reading his letters know how uninhibited and creative he could be with the English language.

12. A plain-woven cotton or linen fabric used for clothing.

Saint Louis November 9th 1808

Dear Brother

It has been a verry long time Since I have had the pleasure of hereing from you by letter, not Since you commenced distilling.[1] I beleve the last letter was about the time you were collecting your froot to make Syder, and Sister lost all her froot prepared for drying by the rain. John was verry Sick most of the time he was here, and dureing his journey through, & he writes me that he has not recovered his health & Strength Since._ he has told you, I hope of our Cormercial plans, and my ideas of that business, prey give us a little of your instructions or advice _ This place has presents flattering advantages at this time and I think it will increas as the population increases, which is beginning to be considerable, at this time, the whole Town of St. Louis has not as maney Goods as John has in his Store at Louisville. Miss Nancy Anderson is about to Set out on her return home, with Mrs. Farrow [Farrar], The doctr.[2] Judge Coburn[3] & Mr. Harry[4] will form the party, they will pass by the way of the Seline & red banks,[5] I Should have accompanied Nancy my Self, if it was possible. Govr. Lewis leaves us Shortly and we Shall then be alone, without any white person in the house except our Selves I Shall Send york with nancy, and promit him to Stay a fiew weeks with his wife. he wishes to Stay there altogether and hire himself which I have refused. he prefurs being Sold to return[ing] here, he is Serviceable to me at this place, and I am deturmined not to Sell him, to gratify him, and have derected him to return in John H. Clarks Boat if he Sends goods to this place, this fall. if any attempt is made by york to run off, [∧]or[∧] refuse to provorm his duty as a Slave, I wish him Sent to New Orleans and Sold, or hired out to Some Severe master untill he thinks better of Such Conduct ∧I do not wish him to know my deturmination if he conduct[s] [himself] well[∧] (This Choice I must request you to make if his Conduct deservs Suverity)[6] The hores [horses] which I Send I wish Sent back to this place if an oppertunity offers. I [s]hall write John on the Subject and impower him to Sell them if he can get a Saveing price for them.

The wind has been verry high for Several days past and the praries & woods on fire, the last night all my Hay Some rales boards &c. was burnt entirely up at a place I have purchased 6 miles distant and on which I have Settled Ben, Several farms in the neighbourhood have receved much injury from the fire. —

I wrote to you Some time ago about Sippo and a knowledge I had of Bro: Edmunds dislike to that fellow, I have never had him about me, nor Shall I have him near me, I have tryed to Sell him but no one will give me the $400 I gave and am accountable to my bro for as yet. If Sep was a good and honest fellow he would Suit me better than any fellow of his age I know but as he has behaved badly (as I am informed) to my brother he Shall never come in my familey at this place without it is perfectly pleasing and agreeable to him [Edmund]. —

Part of this day has been taken up in beholding a prosession of the Freemasons of this place, and attending to an oration given by Mr. Bates,[7] which will be in the papers of this place – The Govr. was Instolled as master last night[8] —

I have a bad Cough and a bad head ake fer Several days. yesterday I took Salts which acted —— also as a puke and made me very Sick fer the greater part of the day. Julia complain[s] a little every day but I must Say that we are Generaly very healthy.

Sam Gwathmey formerly wrote to me verry often but Since I came here he has wrote me one letter, I Shall have to Call on him again I fear, — I assure you that the maried State makes a great me look about my Self and excties a disposition to accoumilate a little for a future day— can this be a good or bad disposition in a man who is pore and ambitious to live—

I wish verry much to See Some of you, Majr. Christy[9] has just now told me that Bro. Edmund is with you please to give my best wishes to him, and ask him if he cant Come and See us, take a ride to the lead mines and Some Salt Springs _ Tell him I know of 2 Springs of Salt water nearly equal to Kings.[10] The Country on both Sides of the Missour 150 mil up abounds in Salt licks & Springs of Salt water, Some of which I have Seen. Majr. Christy has taken a Lease of one near the missouri 160 miles up amensly Strong and wants a partner. I think If bro Edmund is fond of business of thiss kind, or the lead business or Salt petr businss, this Country afferds a field fer him.[11]

I am much imployed in my public business with Indians agents & Interpreters, Those people are much Scattered & require a goodell of attention. I believe I have told you all I recollect of at present and must Conclude by a request that you will give the best wishes of Julia and my Self to Sister Clark and nancy, and accupt your Self with them of our Sincerust affections.

> Yr. Sincr Brother
> Wm. Clark

[Letter carried by Mr. Harry.]

1. The still was a commonplace item on early nineteenth-century farms. The Clarks operated stills at Mulberry Hill and Trough Spring. The product produced (generally whiskey) not only provided refreshment, but could be used as a trade item or form of currency. During periods of rapid change in the value of hard money and local currency and economic uncertainty, the barter of standard-value items like distilled beverages helped give some stability to the local economy. The freedom to distill beverages was deemed particularly important by Kentuckians and other people on the frontier as a means of turning excess corn or other grains into a desirable commodity that also could be easily transported long distances. Taxing such products became a source of revenue for the government and at times a source of conflict (such as the Whiskey Rebellion of 1794).

2. Dr. Bernard Gaines Farrar (1784–1849) was a native of Goochland County, Virginia, who was brought to Kentucky as an infant when his parents Joseph Royal and Jane Ford Farrar relocated to Fayette County. He studied under Dr. Selmon (possibly his brother-in-law Dr. John Selman) in Cincinnati and Dr. Samuel Brown in Lexington before attending medical school at the University of Pennsylvania in 1804. He graduated from Transylvania University in Lexington, Kentucky, in 1806. He opened a practice in Frankfort, Kentucky, but at the urging of his brother-in-law Judge John Coburn (see note 3), and no doubt others, he removed to St. Louis about June 1807. He has the distinction of being the first American physician to permanently establish his practice west of the Mississippi River. It was Farrar who amputated expedition member George Shannon's gangrenous leg in October 1807. He was a friend of Clark's and maintained his office in Clark's house in 1808–1809. In conflict with his dedication to the healing arts was his active participation in dueling (see letter dated 31 January 1811). Farrar was a member of the first Missouri territorial legislature, was active in civic affairs, and served in the Missouri militia as a surgeon and soldier during the War of 1812. He married Sarah "Sallie" Stubbs Christy (b. 1793), the daughter of William Christy (see note 9), in 1811. He married second Ann Clark Thruston, daughter of Clark's sister Fanny, in Louisville in February 1820.

I could not identify Mrs. Farrar. I initially thought that the Mrs. "Farrow" referred to was Bernard Farrar's first wife, Sarah Christy Farrar, but the date of their marriage is given as 1811, and in 1808 she would have been only fifteen. It could not be his mother because she had remarried and had a different surname (Rogers). The only possibilities seem to be a sister-in-law (he did have a brother who was married), an unidentified first wife, or an incorrect marriage date for him and Sallie Christy. The Farrar name apparently was pronounced with an "o" or "ow" sound at the end, because the 1810 Kentucky census lists a number of Farrars (including B. G. Farrar's brother William) spelled Farrow. Census, tax, and other records often spelled names phonetically. (Scharf, 2:1518–19; Billon, 240–41; *Missouri Gazette*, 6 September 1809; Rogers Index; Charles W. Thruston Papers; MLClark, 60.)

3. John Coburn (1763–1823) was a native of Philadelphia and was educated and read law there. He moved to Lexington, Kentucky, in 1784 and, rather than practice law, engaged in the mercantile business. In 1794 he relocated to Mason County, Kentucky, and continued in the mercantile trade. Soon after settling there he was appointed judge of the Mason District Court, and later of the Mason Circuit Court. In 1796 he was appointed one of the commissioners to run the Kentucky-Virginia state line. He was active in politics as a Jeffersonian Republican. Coburn was appointed judge of the Superior Court of Louisiana in 1805 (after first declining the judgeship of Michigan Territory) and relocated to St. Louis. In 1809 he resigned the judgeship and returned to Kentucky. In a letter to William Clark dated 23 November 1809 Coburn reported that while in St. Louis that fall he had been approached by prominent citizens regarding his interest in serving as territorial governor (this was before the news of Lewis's death was known). Coburn stated his interest in the position and requested that Clark put in a good word for him and make known his willingness to serve to the appropriate officials in Washington His wife was Mary Moss, half sister of Dr. Bernard Farrar. (Collins, 2:578–79; *Biographical Encyclopedia of Kentucky*, 114–15; Houck, 2:401; Coburn to Clark, 23 November 1809, WCP-VMC.)

4. Probably Jacob Harry, a St. Louis merchant and respected citizen.

5. The Saline River is in southeastern Illinois. It empties into the Ohio nearly opposite the mouth of the Tradewater River some twenty-five miles downstream from the mouth of the Wabash River. Its name indicates the presence of salt springs in the area and, indeed, a saltmaking industry was based in the area. Red Banks was the original name of Henderson, Kentucky. It was named for the color of the banks of the Ohio in that area just as Owensboro's initial name was Yellow Banks.

6. This is the first in a series of letters in which Clark discusses his difficulties with York. What he writes is a sad and tragic commentary on the relationship of these two men and on the abhorrent institution of slavery. York no doubt expected to settle again in the Louisville area near his wife (who was owned by someone else), and possibly children, after an absence of three years on the expedition. However, when Clark permanently relocated to St. Louis in 1808 and York and some of his other slaves went with him, York faced indefinite separation from his family. Clark's letters to Jonathan discuss problems with a number of slaves, but York is his primary concern. For Clark to threaten to sell York—whom he basically grew up with and who had been a life-long companion—because of his behavior and to treat him as nothing more than a piece of property (which York legally was) illustrates the evils of slavery and the attitudes and beliefs it engendered.

7. Frederick Bates (1777–1825) was a native of Goochland County, Virginia. He moved to Detroit in 1797, where he worked for the army's quartermaster department. He was also a merchant and served as a judge for Michigan Territory. In November 1806 he was appointed secretary of Louisiana Territory and served as acting governor until Meriwether Lewis arrived in St. Louis to take up the duties of governor in March 1808. Bates was a conscientious and able administrator, but he clashed with Lewis on some matters, and his complaints helped lead to Lewis's downfall. His role in Lewis's demise has cast a permanent shadow on him. Donald Jackson theorized that Bates's animosity toward Lewis may have had its foundation in 1801 when Jefferson selected Lewis as his private secretary rather than Bates, his brother Tarleton, or their father Thomas. Ironically, Bates's compilation of the laws of Missouri in 1808 was a contributing cause in Lewis's troubles. Lewis's authorization to spend government money to print the laws was one of the vouchers the government protested, which precipitated a personal crisis and his fateful trip to Washington in 1809 to settle his accounts and clear his name. Bates also complained about Clark to government officials. This, together with Bates's part in Lewis's downfall, caused a falling-out between the two men. Bates was appointed secretary of Missouri Territory when it was created in 1812 and served in that office until Missouri became a state. He was elected governor of Missouri in 1824 and died in office. (*DAB*, 2:50–51; Houck, 3:50; Jackson (1), 1:134n.)

8. Meriwether Lewis was quite active in the Masons throughout his adult life. He joined Virtue Lodge Number 44 in Albemarle County, Virginia, on 28 January 1797 and quickly climbed in degree, achieving the degree of Past Master Mason by 3 April 1797 and Royal Arch Mason by

October 1799. He named several western rivers for attributes (Philanthropy, Philosophy, and Wisdom) prominent in Masonic ritual. He was one of the founders of a Masonic lodge in St. Louis and was installed as its Master on 8 November 1808, as Clark states in this letter. Various Clarks also were Masons, including some of William's brothers and nephews. William Clark joined the Masons in 1809. Why he had not done so sooner—assuming he had the opportunity—is not known. (Chuinard, 12–15; Ambrose, 47, 443.)

9. William Christy (1764–1837) was a native of Carlisle, Pennsylvania, who came to Kentucky about 1780, settling in Louisville. He served in the Jefferson County militia and under St. Clair and Wayne in their Indian campaigns. He rose from adjutant (1791) to major (1799) in the Kentucky militia, preceding Clark as captain of a troop of cavalry in the First Regiment. He operated a saltworks in Jefferson County, Kentucky, prior to 1800, and he also owned and operated Christy's Inn "at the sign of the Eagle" in Louisville in the early 1800s. In the spring of 1806 he advertised the inn for lease because of his imminent move to St. Louis; that same year he received a license as a tavernkeeper and liquor retailer in St. Louis. By 1809 he also operated a livery, and in 1810 he reopened Webster's Eagle Tavern (using that same name) in Clark's former house and later opened the Missouri Hotel. Christy was actively engaged in politics, serving as a town trustee, judge of the court of Common Pleas and Quarter Sessions, auditor, and registrar of the land office. In April 1809 he was placed in command of the "Louisiana Spies" by William Clark as brigadier general of the militia when Indian hostilities threatened. In 1792 he married Martha Taylor (1777–1849), and fathered fourteen children. Their oldest child, Sarah "Sallie" Stubbs Christy (b. 1793), married Dr. Bernard G. Farrar. The salt spring Clark mentions Christy leasing is in Cooper County, Missouri. Edmund Clark did not become a partner in the venture; a John G. Heath did. It was the first saltworks in that part of Missouri. Clark described the salt-making and lead-mining potential of the area in some detail in his 1808 report and journal on his Fort Osage expedition. (*The Farmer's Library*, 23 April 1806; Clift (1), 39, 104; Charles W. Thruston Papers, fl. 2; Houck, 3:49n, 146; Scharf, 1:193–95; *Missouri Gazette*, 12 April 1809; *Louisiana Gazette*, 19 April 1810, 30 August 1810; MLClark, 60.)

10. Kings salt spring was not located in Kentucky or Missouri. Given the nature of the reference, it must be a salt spring familiar to both Jonathan and Edmund. Since they were unfamiliar with Missouri springs, and it apparently was not in Kentucky, it must be in Ohio, Indiana, or Illinois. The brothers owned property in Indiana and Ohio, as well as

Kentucky, and my guess is that Kings salt spring probably was in Indiana or Ohio.

11. Edmund Clark never did become involved in any of the promising salt and mining ventures that Clark was so enthusiastic about. Neither did Jonathan or his sons. William's enthusiasm for Missouri and its opportunities may have found fertile ground among some of his Kentucky associates, but his Kentucky family was generally immune to his boosterism.

~

Saint Louis November 2̶2̶ 4 [22, 24] 1808.

Dear Brother

I received your kind letters by yesterdays mail of the 9th and 12th inst. with greater pleasure than you can amagine. I do assure you that advice was never given to one who receved it with more Satisfaction, and red the letters of another with more real pleasure than I do yours. The letter from Col. Bullits[1] was dated the 12th of October, and not Signed by you, but I know your hand, and the references agreed with your other letter of the 9th _ you were at a wedding[2] at the time and they were danceing finely at the time you wrote, I am sorry that wedding was as Soon, as Miss N.A. wished much to be at it, She Set out with Mrs. Farrow, Doctr. Farrow Judge Coburn &c. last thursday week, by the way of Brother Edmunds & the red banks, on monday they left Kasskaska. I hope they have, or will reach Col. Andersons in Safty. I have had much uneasiness about nancy['] s getting home, on my return from up the missouri, I found that I could not leave my family the length of time necessary for to accompany her home, and She being deturmined to return, I wrote the Colo. expressing a wish for him to Come on to this place if he could not agree for N. to remain with us this winter, Stateing to him the impossibility of my accompan'g her through this fall, he objected to come farther than vincennes and Seemed anxious for her return, I did not know what to do, Majr. Christy Docr. F. and others Seeing my Situation, provailed on Mrs. Farrow to accompany her through; I fear I am rong in Suffering her to go without my own protection which I had promised, but knowing dispositions I thought it best.

as to polotics I learn but very little all we have is from news papers, if we are to judge from them, The Courts of England and France are involved in a Species of madness that is unacountable, god only knows when or where their frenzy will end; I have Strong hopes from the election of Mr. Madison. I belevee the British ministry think they are playing a deep game. that as they believe our god to be mercantile avorece and the oppositionists to the Embargo will in a Short time Supplant the present Administration, and bring in a Junto more Compliant and Consestant with their views. I observe they persist in their orders in Council, and I have not a doubt, that they are Sanguine, that their persiverance will defeat the election of Mr. madison_[3] (So much for politics) now for the affairs of this Country. we are peace and tranquillity with the Indians at present, a maomi killed a man near Kasskia this Summer and took refuge on this Side, he was delivered up and is Condemed, the Three Indian persons, are yet in jole at this place waiting the presdt. deturmonation, live or Die,[4] a very Considerable imigration to this Territty this fall, the[y] have went mostly up the missoure above St. Charles, a verry valuable Lead mine has been descovered nearly west of this place about 60 miles, Several people are Contending for this mine to rent or Lease it_.[5] Would it not be possible for to provail on Bro Edmund to brake up, Sell out or give away that grave yard of a place of his and either live near you ar come to this Country, and engage in fur Trade, Lead business, Salt peter, Salt or mercantile persuits _ The Lead would Suit his tast best, The fur businss would Suit his Constitution but the Salt peter, or Salt would be most certain _ The Government wish Salt peter, and will make advances, Some good Caves are known in this Territory _ The Countrey about 150 miles up the missouri contains maney valueable Springs of Strong water, which might be precured from the Government _ Majr. Christy has one and wants a partner. I have Settled Ben & venos on a place 6 miles west of this place on Som land I purchased. he had Collected a Suffeceny of Hay to winter a horse & 2 Cows & Calves, the other night the praries Cought fire and burned his hay rales & Some poles which has distressed Ben verry much, and disapointed me a little._ I have not Sold Seppo as yet, he is imployed in bringing down wood from an Island above this village _

I am exceedingly happy to find you are pleased with the mercantile plans which John & myself is about to commence, if we can keep up two Stores one at Louisville and one at St. Louis, we Shall Certainly make money, the one at this place to be under my directions, kept by such a man as Mr. Brock, and the one at Louisville under the directions of John, who will have to lay in the goods for both places, and the one at this place furnished occasionally from that at Louisville with Such articles as will be necessary to keep up the assortment at this place, of merchendize as also, Several articles of Country production Such as, Iron, Cartins, Flour, meal, Conntry Linen, Thread, Cider, apples, Salt, whiskey, Soap and Several other articles which are Sometimes in great demand here _ and as I Shall keep one or two public boats here which I can apply occasionally to my use, the expens up the river will only be the hands & provisions _ The S[t]ores at this place is only Supplied once a year, and great part of the year they have Scercely any goods calculated for the Consumption of the Country. Some money Circulates here, The Indian department pays out a large Sum, the offices of government, and the Troops cause much Caish to circulate, & we may as well as others Ceatch a little. I think 4 Compy. will move this way before long if they do I Should wish a few goods Sent to their Camp, which draws in ready Cash, from a Store of not more thane 10 or 1100 Dollars worth of Such articles as are Calculated for Solders, mostly Licquors, groceres & fancy articles. Those troops will most probably assend the missouri next Summer. This is only Conjecter in me founded on Comuncations from the Government &c. _ you may rest assured that we Shall not attempt to run with the rich french merchents of this place, I have reasons to beleve that we Shall receve aid from Some of them if required. we Shall go on our own gate [gait] with the veiw of permonance. I wish that our goods could have been here this fall as we Should had the most of the trade, there being no goods Suteable in the place, a Small assortment has arrivd laterly and one expected which will not last long if we may be judge from what has taken place in the Sale of merchendize at this place _ . _

I am Sorry for the loss of my mare, more because She was the property of Julia than the amoent of her value to me, the Coalt I do not Calculate any great things from, but wish to try what it may Come to.

I received a letter from Mr. Fitzhugh the other day by Mr. Manuel[6] in which he mentioned he had been appointed guardian for C. & A. and talked about the trouble he had, frequently with Sendry persons with fee bills and the like, and wished Something to be done with the estate, he mentioned that he had paid for John['] s schooling, and intended to pay Mr. Fry for Ben & Charles, that he had pd. £10 for C. & Nanys Schooling, and £21. odd for Bro George, and that money was hard to be got &c. all of which I believe Sencerely. I have answered his letter and told him that you would Deliver up the estate as Soon as possible, that you were impowered to Settle the estate for me & could & would do it better than if I was myself present. the £10 he had paid for C̲ & A̲. must be discharged from money Colected from the bonds of the estate (Some of which I beleve are in his hands) The money due for John Schooling I requested him to pay, and I well [will] repay what he pays to Mr. Fry, as to the £21 which he paid for Bro G_ I cannot Say any thing about, I did not request it. I only intended to appropriate Lamptons bond to the finishing [of] his house. you think that the amount of the work about that house will be more than $105_ it must be much more as Mr. F[itzhugh] paid $70_ John 50, and ~~I sent 50 by Manuel to bro G~~ which will bring the expence very high is [as] more is to be paid. I wish this account Setled fer the workmen, and Shall write to John to pay agreeable to your Setlement of that account. (I hope my friends will excuse me but I cant pay much more for __ [brother George?] I have a family now and must attend a little to my Self ₐthe bals. of[ₐ] my act. agasnt him allowing every credit ₐwith venos & children included,[ₐ] & exclusive of my forther['s] debt which was paid by lands in the Grant) is $1432.31½ Cent _ my Fathers act. Settled by that Land was abt. 1650 Do. 56 cent, the interest on the last Sum to this time would be $759. adding those two Sums to this Interest will be $3841.96. I make this Statement mearly to Shew you howe I Stand on this Score, and if anything is ever Said on this Subject as May have been Said on others; you may if you please, Say for me that I will deduct 20 pctg. and give all the lands ₐto my Bro.[ₐ] I obtained in the Grant under my fathers will, and four lots in Jeffersonville ₐin addition, negrows Stock & every thing at the point[ₐ] for the ballanc of the money __) This part of my letter you will please to keep to your Self except you wish to use it in Answer or reply &c. [The preceding sentence is written vertically across the preceding four sentences regarding the estate.] I Suspect verry much Some person has been Saying more than was necessary about my Conduct in the management of the estate, perhaps it is my Security Genl. B.[reckinridge] if it is his Charector is much altered from what I had expected it was, at all events let them Say or think what they may I feel conseontiously Cleare of any dishonest transactions, and must attribute their errorr to either peevishness, disappointment or a missconseption of <u>facts</u>. It has always been my intention to pay to the estate any ballance which was due, and expected that Mr. Ev. Clark would have payed you in time. I delayed paying up, it is Certain, when I ought to have paid, but as I intended to give the estate my Serveces, I thought they were, or had been worth the interest. If any thing has been Said by the relations of the Children respecting the business unfavourable to my acts, I may as well have what I am entitled to, it will assist ~~to enable~~ me to

bear the Snears of the ungreatful a little, and under this view of the business must request you to Charge a Commission.   {I am a little displeased
& perhaps I am rong in charging a commission [This sentence is written
vertically in the left margin with the bracket for the preceding sentence
regarding the commission pointing to it.] please to pay up for me, and
add what Interest you think right, if you have not Collected from our relation, I will Send you the money I hope you will do for me in this business as you would for yourself, I know you will, and therefore feel more
Scure than if I had the Settlement to make my Self, but at all events do
not Suffer me to owe one half a cent _ I have no account of advances
made ~~Mr. Fitzhugh~~ that I know off I think all has been Charged, I do not
recollect haveing made use of any money or bonds of the estate Sence we
Settled our private account, at which time we Charged all The bonds. I
have credit on my private account with Mr. <u>Fitzhugh</u>. Mastin G Clarks
Bond, John Loftons bond £12 _ R. Murpheys £8.2 of Tho Winn £15.
John Speed £21. of Mrs. Fitzhugh (May 21st 1807) £15. on Speeds
£16.7. (Bals.) the others which he has, he must be accountable, I gave an
order to him for a judgmt. I think it was Mr. Crutchfields, just before I
came off _ I Shall rejoice when I hear that I am Clear of the admn. it has
given me much uneasiness and you a great deel of trouble _ I hope none
of my relations in your neighbourhood thinks that I have Cheeted or attempted to Cheet the Children or injur the estate, you know that if I am a
little indebt to C & N: and my Sister, J. & Ben is greatly in debt to me,
they owe me £128.s6.d3$\frac{3}{4}$ & by Jany. they will $_\wedge$owe me near $<u>600</u>[$_\wedge$] af-
ter allowing them the hire of their negrows this year.[7]

as to my bro. G's plans about the Slip, I am desirious that he Should
carry them into execution if he can profit by them, but he has not been
fortunate in maney of his plans, I wish you make any arrangement you
think will be to his interast respecting the Slip and I will confirm what
you do as far as I can, I do not wish to give up the Slip lower than Mrs.
Fitzhughs lot above the point. The Slip was intended for bro. G_ and I
wish him to have the advantages, even if it Should not Sell for more than
$1000, I did wish to have Some little prospects but now I cear little about
it, prey pay Some little attention to this Slip and his interest in it. I requested Fitzhugh to Sell two peces of land of mine in the grant to raise
money fer Bro. Geo.'s use for a low price. 312 acres, part of No. 276 fer $\frac{1}{2}$
a Dol. pr. acre, and a 50 acre pece up Silver Creek about a milee from the
Town lands for 3 Dollars. If he gets any thing from the Slip, or for his
[$_\wedge$]ner 4000 acre[$_\wedge$] Locust Creek lands or his 1500 acre military lands

on Cumbarland he will have no need of the Small Sum from those 2 Tracts _ my principal object in Selling those lands was to ~~have~~ complete the house and leave a little money in my bro: hands to purchase a little Coffee & Sugar, flour &c.[8] I will never with my [word loss due to seal tear] consent give up my appointment as a <u>Trustee</u> for Clarksv[ille] [word loss due to seal tear] ever wheter [word loss due to seal tear] one inch of property in that place, if I am Superseeded I [letter loss due to seal tear] [sha?]ll remonsterate. I know how Trustees are appointed, and know the Critical Situation of my property under Such as may be appointed, Brother I begin to think that every Speces of property will become usefull one day or other. I have not heard from Mr. morrison as yet respecting his Son,[9] but most probably Shall by next post, he wrote me last august that he had mad[e] arrangements with Mr. Charless to discharge those debts, I have lost his letter and do not at this time recollect exactly the mode of payment he mentioned. _ I wish to See you much verry much indeed can't you arrange your matters So as to ride over and See us, I wish much to Know how all friends drive on, I am told that great works are going on about your Town, nael [nail] factores duck [as in textile] factores Tobacco factores and a great many other factores; I hope they may all Suckceed, how does our brother Denis [Fitzhugh] com on among them. Manuel tels me that Congress is held every night at John Gwathmeys[10] and as their business is only in the money way, they have only use for a Treasurer. _ I here nothng about Jeffersonville, how does Mary. & Coz Samy. and little polly[11] Come on, I fear Sam is mad, he has not wrote fer a long tim, I Shall have to write to him for fear he forgets me. I wished I could do without troubleing the worthey little fellow, but you may depend that a Dollar is more valueable to me now than 2 formerly. _ <u>please</u> Tell John Sullivan if you See him that I have got a place this next year for him to work on near this place and adjoining my land he had best come on with his negrows imedeately, a good house out houses & garden and 40 acrs under fence, on the edge of a prarie where 40 more might be inclosed without much Trouble. I Shall write to John by the post _ what has become of the old Captn.[12] where does he mean to live. _ I have Said So much that you must be a little tired I must not Say much more. butt to give you Some Idear of what John S. _ Could make on his farm if industerous I will give you the prices of different articles of produce at this time _ and which are Commonly in demand Beef, grass fed on the foot ——— 3 cents a pound & in demand Pork corn fed from 3 to 4 cent by the Quantity – Pigs Cleaned 9/. on the foot 6/–

without being fed at all in demd. Mutton about 5 cents not much in demand, Veele high _ Turkey taim $3. Taim ducks 1 Dol. a par wile [wild]
duck verry low Venison from 9/. to 2 dollars a carcus other wild meat in
propn.[proportion?] Chickings 9d. & 1/– a peer and Sometims 1/6 great
demand Chees 1/6 Eggs from 9d to 1/2 and _ _ _ &c _ _ _&c &c milk
25 cts. qt. Butter at 1/6 ~~and~~ not long Since at 9d. and will be at 3/– Prarie
Hay in the Sumer 2 dol. & 2-1/4 a load of about 900 lb. in winter $5. Corn
by the quantity 1/6 in the Sumer 3/– & a great favore to get it oats about
the Same if dilivered _ wheat $1. not much for Sale Flour of the Country
3 Dol. a Hd. [hogshead] Sometims hier, ground at Horse mill meal one
Dol. a Bus: [bushel] and Scerce, 1/4 given fer grinding at the Horsmills.
Irish potatoes, 2 Shillings a bushel and in demand often 3/– Sweet potatoes 6/_ but fiew to be Sold – Turnips 3/– will fall to 1/– Apples Small
3/– a hundred, large apples double _ Cyder _ none to be Sold, Bear of
Some demand in Summr whiskey from 3/. to 4/6, Sometims 6/. per gallon Tobaccor Carroted 9d. a pound Standing price. Hog lard in demand
wood delivered on the river bank $2 a cord and Sometins $3. Tallow 9d.
a pound and Sometines much higher 3/. a day for Labourers milch cows
with a calf first rate 15$. 2d. rate $12. 3d rate 10 Dollars horses about the
Same price they are in Kentucky and plenty Salt is 3 dollars and in demand, bar Iron Sometims Sells for 20 cents apd. Soap a Shilling and 1/6
a pound. Tar 1 Dollar and in no demand cabbage $3\frac{1}{2}$ dollars a hundred.
plank high and Scerce in this Country Lead at the mins 5 cents retail
here 10 and $12\frac{1}{2}$ Cents a pound Beaver fur from Missouri high up 2 dollar cash a pound. low down 1 1/– deer Skins, Small furs are low and not
much demand for them. Furniture of every kind high and in demand.[13] I
beleev I have Said all I can think of

Julia has broke out all over with Small red bumps which itches verry
much, and for my part I have a verry bad cough which I have had for
about ten days, I am about to take Some tea and go to bed which I hope
may be of Service to me.

Govr. Lewis is here and talks of going to philadelphia to finish our
books this winter, he has put it off So long that I fear they will [not]
bring[?] us much.[14] I wrote you the other day about york, I do not wish
him Sold if he behaves himself well, I directed him to come with John's
goods if he Sent them, & to call on John & See if he had any thing fer him
to do __ he does not like to Stay here on account of his wife being there.
he is Serviceable to me here and perhaps he will See his Situation there

more unfavourable than he expected & will after a while prefur returning to this place. (Novr. 22d.)

I have been for Several day[s] trying to buy a house and Lot and give Seppo in part pay, but we will not Conclude the bargain I as the man is disposed to underrate the <u>boy</u>. he wavers and may yet come to my offer, if he dose I Shall make a good purchase as the lot is well Siteated for trade and [has a] tolerable house on it, & on the bank of the river.[15]

Last night <u>Hinkle</u>,[16] Mr. Charles[s's] printer Son to the old man in Louisville left this place with his family without takeing leave, he acted a verry honest part by me, as you will observe by the following Statement I hired a Girl to him Since last June, lent him a Small Sum to purchase necessaries on his way to this place, gave himself and familey a good birth [berth] in one of my boats, and Several other little favours had been Shewn his family by Julia & nany Anderson, for which he returned us our own negrow, by Sending her home without any Clothes more than She had on.[17] This morning Charless Comes with a Sour Countinonce and tells me Hinkle is run off in his debt $240, I walked down [the] Street, Saw Several persons at the printing office, Sone had Hinkles notes others accounts, he has got money but has Contrived to clear out about $1000 in debt. maney of these Chaps visit this place, and I am a lit-tle Supprised that this fellow Should have been So Suckcessfull — I must Conclude as you must be fateegued befer you read this far. Julia has Sent by Docr. Farrow [Farrar] to Lexington for lace. She Says nancy was to have written to her often often She has only recved two Short letters from her, She is much concerned fer fear Sister and nancy will forget her before She has it in her power to See them agan. and re-quests that you will just, mention to them, that her Love is not tempurary or chilled by absincee, but permonant, and hopes Sister & nancy and youself will aceept it with half the real pleasure which She now offers it to you.

I must request you Sister, & nany, and Mr. & Mrs. Temple Isaac Willm. & George[18] if they are with you to accept of my ∧Love &[∧] best wishes and remain ever affectunately —   your Sincear Brother
                                              Wm. Clark

as I have in all cases Sought your advice and good Councils, words can-not express the pleasure which I feel in receving it unasked ___ " ___

I receved a letter from Bro Edmund by Mr. Manuel and would write to him but do not know how a letter is to reach him, as he must have left your house before this, he Said in ten days, and it is now, 19 days, he must be at his place at this time, I wish verry much to See him, he talks of Coming at Chrstmass. I hope he may Come Sooner. we both wish to See him I wished much that I knew Mr. Tompkins[19] intention to come here, a man has [word loss due to seal] [come?] here to teach and has commenced teaching with 12 Schoolers, and will get all in the Town if Mr. T does not come, Some of those that are entered with him are inten'd for T_ if he com's. They do not like this man much and I have given him no incuragement. Ben [O'Fallon] has just arrived and tells me that he beleves that Tompkins has given out Coming I Should like to know.

Yesterday Mr. P. Chouteau returned from the establishment up the missouri, every thing does not go on exactly right there but will mend. a Second Treaty has ben made with the Osage, framd. by the Govr. and Sent up by Chouteau to get Signed, it has been Signed [and] takes in the Same Country of [as] mine.[20] I will write you agin

our long letters ought not to [be] much examined I write without much reserve, and Some people might not be fond of my Stile &c. [This appears vertically in the left margin of page 7, as a carryover from the last page.]

1. Alexander Scott Bullitt (1762–1816) was born at Dumfries, Prince William County, Virginia, the son of the legislator and judge Cuthbert Bullitt (1740–1791) and Helen Scott Bullitt (1739–1795). He was a member of the Virginia House of Delegates in 1783 and was commissioned a major in the Prince William militia in May 1785. He apparently made some trips to Kentucky in connection with land acquisition before settling in Jefferson County in 1785. He was appointed county lieutenant of Jefferson County in May 1786. Bullitt lived at Oxmoor on the Middle Fork of Beargrass Creek in eastern Jefferson County; his house (much modified) still stands today. He was active in politics, serving in the state legislature and state constitutional conventions, and he was Kentucky's first lieutenant governor, being elected in 1800 when that office was established by the state's second constitution. Bullitt also was a colonel in the Kentucky militia. He married Priscilla Christian (1770–1806) about 31 January 1786. Her father was William Christian (1743–1786), who was killed by Indians near present Jeffersonville, Indiana, in April 1786, and her uncle was Patrick Henry. After her death Bullitt married the widow Mary Churchill Prather (1777–1817) in 1808. He was the half first cousin of Louisville merchants Thomas and Cuthbert

Bullitt. His uncle was the soldier, explorer, and surveyor Col. Thomas Bullitt (1730–1778), who in 1773 first laid out a plan for a town at the Falls of the Ohio. (Bullitt (1), 124–28, 139–41, 162–63; *EL*, 141.)

2. Alexander Scott Bullitt's daughter Helen Scott "Nellie" Bullitt (1790–1871) married Henry Massie (1768–1830) on 11 November 1808. They lived at Ridgeway, about three miles west of Oxmoor, and like Oxmoor the house still stands today. Following Massie's death, she married John Lewis Martin, and after his death she married Marshall Key. The thrice-widowed Aunt Key, as she was lovingly called, never had any children and took great interest in her nieces and nephews. Joseph Bush's portrait of her is in the collection of The Filson Historical Society. Clark must be mistaken about the date of the letter or Jonathan misdated it. Given the references, the letter would have to date from either 11 or 12 November. (Jonathan Clark Diary, 11–12 November 1808; Jefferson Co. Marriage Book, 1:62; Bullitt (1), 140, 164.)

3. Reporting of foreign affairs was a major feature in newspapers of that day, including the *Missouri Gazette,* which Clark read regularly. The reference to the courts of England and France refers to the Napoleonic Wars. The embargo was a major foreign policy matter at this time between the United States and Great Britain, with each restricting the other's goods and access to ports. It was one of the differences between the two countries that helped lead to the War of 1812. James Madison was elected president in November 1808, which Clark did not know yet.

4. The *Missouri Gazette* made no mention of the Miami Indian's trial but did devote coverage to the trial and fate of the two Iowa and one Sauk Indians (as detailed in letter dated 21 July 1808, note 9). The Indians were indeed in the St. Louis jail at this time, awaiting President Madison's decision concerning their fate. As reported in the earlier note, the two Iowa took their fate into their own hands, escaped from the jail, and apparently were never apprehended. The Sauk was pardoned.

5. This would have been another of many lead mines in the area. This area of Missouri, especially to the southwest and south of St. Louis, as well as along the Mississippi River from the mouth of the Ohio northward, was known for the lead it contained. Lead mines had operated in the country along the Mississippi, Meramec, and St. Francois (or St. Francis) Rivers since the early eighteenth century.

6. Manuel Lisa (1772–1820) was a native of New Orleans and of Spanish descent. He had settled in St. Louis about 1790 and became well established in the fur trade. Lisa was one of the earliest traders to follow the trail the Corps of Discovery had blazed up the Missouri beyond the Mandan and to begin exploiting the rich fur country of the Rocky Mountains. He, along with Clark and others, were founders of the St.

Louis Missouri Fur Company, and he and Clark's paths crossed often in personal and official business. In fact, Clark may have known him as early as the 1790s when Lisa operated a store in Vincennes and spent part of each year there. He also visited Louisville on business and had dealings with the Clarks. From 1807 to his death Lisa made twelve or thirteen trips up the Missouri, totaling some 26,000 miles. He was married three times (having a white wife and an Indian wife simultaneously) and died in St. Louis. He is buried in Bellefontaine Cemetery. The account books for Fitzhugh and Rose contain accounts for Lisa. Entries support, as Clark mentions in the letter, that Lisa had been in Louisville in November 1808 and carried Jonathan's and no doubt other letters to St. Louis. Lisa is believed to be the Mr. Manuel mentioned in some of these letters. John Luttig, in his 1812 journal, refers to Lisa as both Lisa and Mr. Manuel. (*DAB*, 11:291; Luttig, 116; Oglesby, 9–13; Fitzhugh and Rose Account Books, 6:14.)

7. There are a number of names needing identification in this section of the letter. "C. & A." are Clark's nephew and niece Charles and Ann or "Nancy" Thruston. Ben and John are his O'Fallon nephews. Joshua Fry (1759–1839) was a native of Albemarle County, Virginia, educated at William and Mary, and he served in the militia during the Revolutionary War. He married Peachy Walker (b. 1767), daughter of Dr. Thomas Walker, in 1783. In 1788 or 1789 he and his family moved to the Danville, Kentucky, area where he soon opened a school. His school became one of the finest and best known in Kentucky, and many future leaders of the state were pupils of Fry's. Several members of the Clark family were his students. In November 1809 he moved the school to Lexington, but it is not known if he kept it there. His children married into other prominent Kentucky families, including the Speeds and Bullitts. Mark Lampton apparently was the contractor for George Rogers Clark's house at The Point in Clarksville. The information William Clark gives regarding The Point, as well as other information I have gathered, leads me to believe that he also lived at The Point when he moved across the river to Clarksville in early 1803. It is likely that he and George lived in the same house, very possibly the one still being worked on in 1808. It must be remembered that Clark expected to return to Clarksville after the expedition and that he lived there off and on after his return until permanently moving to St. Louis earlier that year. John Loftin, Robert Murphy, Thomas Winn, John Speed, and Thomas Crutchfield were all Kentuckians, and several, if not all, were residents of Jefferson County financially involved regarding the estate of Charles Thruston, which Clark was still in the process of settling. Loftin apparently was a carpenter and perhaps builder. He built the boxes for Clark

in October 1807 in which the fossils from the latter's Big Bone Lick dig were shipped to Jefferson. Thomas Minor Winn was the late Charles Floyd's brother-in-law; in 1790 Winn married Floyd's sister Elizabeth. He jointly purchased a plantation along the Middle Fork of Beargrass Creek with his father-in-law Robert Floyd in 1791 and remained in the area after Floyd moved his family to the Clarksville area. John Speed (1772–1840) was a native of Mecklenburg County, Virginia. His father settled near Danville, Kentucky, in 1782 with his family. By the mid-1790s he had settled in Jefferson County. Speed operated the saltworks at Mann's Lick, which Thruston had had business with, and owned Farmington (another historic home that still stands), about five miles southeast of Louisville. He was a farmer, businessman, and judge. He married Abby Lemaster in 1796, and after her death in 1807 he married Lucy Gilmer Fry (1788–1874), a daughter of Joshua Fry, in 1808. Two of his sons (James and Joshua Fry) would play important roles in Abraham Lincoln's life and presidency. This passage of the letter makes clear the difficulties Clark was having with the settlement of Thruston's estate and his fear that it was creating family discord. (*DAB*, 11:291; Frye, 35–39; Collins, 2:625, 687; Fitzhugh and Rose Account Books, 5:405; JCP-CHC; Yater (2), 4–5; Speed, 93–94; Heywood, 11–23; Jefferson Co. Marriage Records, TFHS; Robert E. McDowell Collection, 1:149, 5:288–91, TFHS.)

8. Clark remained involved in his brother George's affairs until the latter's death in 1818. Their affairs were intermingled in various ways, especially regarding land, such as the "Slip." The slip was a parcel of land that stretched along the Ohio River between Jeffersonville and Clarksville. It apparently had belonged to George at one time but by 1808 it was owned by either William or both the brothers. It was of particular interest to them, not only as valuable riverfront and millsite property, but also because of plans to build a canal at the Falls of the Ohio. George was a member of a canal company that proposed a canal on the north side of the Falls. This slip of land was foreseen as being crucial to the project and thus extremely valuable. By late 1808, however, hopes for a canal on the Indiana side had faded, so, while it was still considered prime real estate, Clark was willing to sell some of the slip for funds to assist his brother. They both had extensive landholdings in Clarksville, and his determination to continue as a Clarksville trustee indicates his interest in the town and in protecting his and his family's investment there. He still owned many town lots at the time of his death in 1838. Silver Creek empties into the Ohio below the Falls and forms much of the boundary between Clarksville and Clark County to the east and New Albany and Floyd County to the west. The Locust Creek property

was in Bracken County, Kentucky. The Cumberland tract was at the mouth of the Little River and the Cumberland River in present Trigg County, Kentucky. Clark's wish to help supply George with coffee, sugar, and flour illustrates in part the pitiable state that the Conqueror of the Northwest had been reduced to by financial and legal difficulties, poor health, and alcoholism. (Draper Mss., 35J13; *The Courier-Journal,* 23 June 1912, 6; JCWB, 3:423; JCTL, 1801.)

9. Clark was involved in arrangements for the education of Morrison's son, William, Jr., with Joshua Fry in Danville, Kentucky. Some of Clark's nephews also attended Fry's school.

10. John Gwathmey (1774–1824) was the son of Owen and Ann Clark Gwathmey, a nephew of William and Jonathan Clark, and the brother of Samuel Gwathmey. He was a native of Virginia and moved to Louisville about 1797, apparently at the same time his parents did. He engaged in business and civic affairs, including the planning and construction of the Jefferson County courthouse and jail. He was the proprietor of the Indian Queen tavern, one of Louisville's finest early hotels and taverns, and he built one of Louisville's best known early houses (since destroyed). He married Ann Booth (1782–1862) on 22 July 1800, and fathered seven children. As noted previously, his brother Samuel married Ann's sister Mary in 1807, and the women were also the nieces of Jonathan's wife Sarah (see letter dated 13 August 1801, note 4). (Gwathmey family file.)

11. Nephew Samuel Gwathmey and his wife Mary Booth's first child was Mary (or Maria) Ellen, nicknamed Polly. She was an infant in November 1808. Polly died unmarried in December 1865 and is buried in Cave Hill Cemetery with her parents. Clark consistently refers to Sam Gwathmey as a cousin rather than a nephew. His concern that Gwathmey is angry with or has forgotten him is another example of his strong family attachments.

12. Captain James Sullivan. See letter dated 2 March 1802, note 5.

13. Although this information may exist in other sources, Clark's listing of the prices various goods, livestock, etc., were bringing in St. Louis at this time is a wonderfully concise and detailed source reflecting the town's economy. Other information he imparts in his letters regarding mercantile affairs is also extremely enlightening on St. Louis and frontier economic history.

14. This is Clark's first reference to his concern with Lewis's delay in preparing the official published account of the expedition. Although he did not mention it again for almost a year, when, following Lewis's death, publication of the journals was dropped in his lap, Lewis's failure to make progress on the project undoubtedly distressed Clark dur-

ing the next year. From the nature of his comment here (and particularly from one made in a later letter), it appears evident that Clark was unaware of how little progress Lewis had made on the book.

15. This may be the house at the southeast corner of Main and Vine. The original house was of wood on posts. At a later time, Clark apparently had it torn down and replaced with a two-story brick one that he lived in for the rest of his life. In 1820 it was considered one of the finest houses in St. Louis. Clark's "Indian Museum" was attached to the south end of the house. It was not uncommon to include slaves as part of a deal in real estate or other transactions. See letter dated 2 January 1809 for Clark's description of the property (I think this property) he purchased. (Scharf, 1:315.)

16. Jacob Hinkle (1785–1862) was the son of John Hinkle, a Revolutionary War veteran and early Louisville settler. He was born in Pennsylvania, but he came to Louisville with his parents while still a young child. Hinkle was a printer by trade and moved to St. Louis in 1808, helping Joseph Charless publish the early editions of the *Missouri Gazette*. After leaving St. Louis he lived in Illinois, Indiana, and Louisville at various times. He apparently followed the printing trade throughout his life, but in 1811 he was granted a license to keep a tavern at his house in Louisville. He died in Louisville, and was buried in the old Western Cemetery. He married Nancy Kennedy (1789–1869), daughter of Presbyterian minister John Kennedy, in Chillicothe, Ohio, on 24 September 1805. She was a native of Ireland and came to the United States about 1795.

In the 23 November 1808 and several subsequent editions of the *Missouri Gazette*, Joseph Charless printed a notice headed "*CAUTION ! ! !*" warning the "Printers of the United States, & the public in general" about Hinkle. Charless reported the method of financial chicanery the "speculating *genius*" used and his practice of giving his "creditors *leg bail* for payment." The obviously furious newspaperman described "*The Villain*" in unflattering physical terms, including his sallow complexion and cross-eyes. Clark states his unpaid debts at being some $400 more than Charless does. It is not known whether Hinkle was ever brought to justice, but by either avoiding paying his debts or turning around his financial fortunes he became a property owner and apparently a respectable citizen in the Louisville area. In 1824 he bought a lot in Louisville from the Bank of the United States. The deed was signed by none other than Lewis and Clark historian and bank president Nicholas Biddle. (Hinkle family file, TFHS; Jefferson Co., Ky., Minute Order Book, 9:204; *Missouri Gazette*, 23 November 1808.)

17. It is possible that the slave hired out was either Nancy, York's sister, or

Priscilla, given Clark's mention of having hired them out in his 21 July letter. It was a customary inclusion in "hiring out" agreements for slaves that they be returned with a new set of clothes at the expiration of the term. Not to do so under normal circumstances was looked upon with disfavor; thus Clark's mention of it to Jonathan. Given Clark's mention of having hired the female slave out to Hinkle since June and having given him a place in his boat, etc., it is likely that Hinkle was part of Clark's party in June 1808. If not, he must have been in St. Louis by late summer.

18. Clark adds a few more members of Jonathan's family to whom he wants to be remembered to this letter. Benjamin and Eleanor Clark Temple apparently were visiting, and for the first time he adds Jonathan's sons Isaac (1787–1868), William (1795–1879), and George Washington (1798–1883). Isaac was born in Spotsylvania County, Virginia, and moved to Kentucky with his parents and siblings in 1802. He lived at Trough Spring and then Mulberry Hill, where he was a farmer and operated a mill. In 1863, stating that he could no longer operate the farm because his slaves were required to work for the Union Army and the Louisville & Nashville Railroad, he moved in with his brother William and lived the rest of his life with him. William also was born in Spotsylvania County, and came with his family to Jefferson County. He graduated from Jefferson Medical College in Philadelphia, but he practiced only briefly in Florence, Alabama, before removing to a country estate outside Lexington, Kentucky. About 1835 he settled near his brother Isaac on a farm and remained there until about 1865, when he moved to a house in Louisville. On 17 February 1825 he married Frances Ann Tompkins (1807–1852) in Jefferson County. The Clarks and Tompkinses were old family friends. George Washington, like his brothers, was born in Spotsylvania County and moved with his family to Jefferson County. In 1822 he settled in Fayette County, Kentucky, near Lexington and apparently farmed. He married Martha A. Price (1804–1831) in 1822. (Dorman (1), 27, 30–31.)

19. George Tompkins apparently did not arrive in St. Louis and open a school until 1810. He announced in the 1 May 1810 edition of the *Missouri Gazette* that he would open a school in the house of Mr. Alvarez on 7 May. He taught for four years. In the 10 June 1814 issue of the *Missouri Gazette* it was announced that he "declines keeping school any longer." The teacher recently arrived in St. Louis whom Clark apparently did not care for was Christoph Friederich Schewe, formerly a professor at the Lycée Academy in Paris and a minister in Pittsburgh. He placed an announcement for his school in the 11 January 1809

Gazette, and located it in Mr. Alvarez's house on Market Street before Tompkins's arrival. In 1810 he was offering only French lessons and working primarily as a candlemaker and later as a painter and glazier. (Scharff, 1:824–25; *Missouri Gazette,* 11 January 1809, 22 February 1810.)

20. This treaty, framed by Meriwether Lewis and negotiated by Pierre Chouteau, was signed on 10 November 1808. (The Arkansas Osage signed it 31 August 1809 in St. Louis.) It essentially was the same as the one Clark had drafted and gotten the Osage to sign in September. Clark's treaty had been set aside because of Osage objections that Clark and Lewis both believed were orchestrated by Pierre Chouteau for selfish reasons (to protect land interests in the ceded area). Clark maintained officially that his treaty had been conditional and that Lewis's revised one negotiated by Chouteau accomplished the goal. Lewis's 15 December 1808 letter to Thomas Jefferson states that he doubts the validity of the objections, that friction exists between Clark and Chouteau, that the latter may be jealous of the former, that Frederick Bates claims to be unacquainted with Indian affairs and does not want to assume Indian duties in his (Lewis's) absence (he was talking about returning to the East on business), and that Clark should have responsibility for all Indian affairs in his absence. The incident created chilly relations between Clark and Chouteau that lasted for some months. This latter treaty became the official one and was ratified by the U.S. Senate on 28 April 1810. See letter dated 5 October 1808, note 3. (Loos, 849–55; *American State Papers: Indian Affairs,* 4:763–67.)

~

Saint Louis Decr. 10th 1808.

Dear Brother

I had the pleasure of receiving your letter of the 26th novr. day before yesterday by the mail, which gave us much Satisfaction. you will have received before this time a long letter from me, at the time I wrote that letter my State of mind may have been the cause of my Saying more than you may think necessary, if I have you will excuse me I know, I keep no Copies of letters I write to you, and do not exactly recollect all I ded write, what ever it may have been it was <u>trooths</u> and every thing I recollected on Several Subjects[1]—

we are verry glad to heare of Miss Nancy Andersons Safe arrival at her fathers. I have been verry uneasy about her getting home Since my return down the Missouri. Julia at the time Could not be left alone, and nancy verry anxious to return. ___

In my last letter I have Said much about the proposd. mercantile Connection between John and my Self I Shall Say to you more on that Subject. I assure you that I am much pleased to find that the plans which John and my Self have been talking of ~~carries~~ meets your approbation, without which we Should most certainly form no Connection _ my mode of carrying on this trade was, fer John Should lay in the goods in Baltimore or Philadelphia on the best terms possible, waggon them to the Ohio, purchase Kentucky Boats[2] and take them down to the falls, take out all but Such as were necessary for this place, Send them on with Certain other articles of Kenty. produce to the mouth of the Ohio, write to me by post when the boat would arrive at the mouth. I would Send one or more <u>barges</u> (two or three of which I Shall have on hand public) with a Suffcent number of hands to bring up the goods &c. _ Those hands are to be precured at $20 the trip and found pork and Corn and Some Grens which will make the expence amout <u>$5:</u> Cents a hundred pounds &c. from the mouth up, and if John Contracts, (as I wish him) to bring on the public Stores from Pittsburgh the expence will be much lower, allow the expence to be double, it will not amount to as much as the waggonage from the falls to ~~d~~ Lexington and back _ Louisville is the proper place and no other places will doo to establish a Store to Supply one at this place. I have wrote to John a little on this Subject pointed out my Situation & prospects and if we cant precure goods Sufficunt fer to Commence and keep up two Stores one at Louisville and the other at this place my principal plan will be k[n]ocked in the head, as we cannot calculate upon haveing any advantage of the merchents that are now here who recieve their goods but once a year, and nearly half of the time without goods Soutable for the Country.[3]

I approve your plan of John's being ready to purchase his Goods Soon after the embargo is taken of[f] verry much and your advice in this Case is Such as must be followed if we enter into this business ___ I fear that my fun[d]s and prospects for cash are not Sufficent to join with John's to make the necessary purchase of good[s] without a good deel of Credit my prospects and Situation are truly those, The expence of my family from virginia to this place, the purchases of furniture provisions &c. on the way and Sence my arrival together with $400 which I gave [∧]as[∧] half the payment of 1400 acrs of Land, leaves me in debt which is not increasing but dimenishes in the Same preportion as I make my Sellery

over goes [to] my expenditures _ (this Salery may as well be in trade as
to pass thro' my hands in cash) ___ I think I can venter [venture] to bor-
row by anticipating my pay to the amount of 500 or 1000 Dollars, and
Cozen S ___ and Cozen E⁴ _ &c. perhaps Could pay me a little, which
would do me more good now than it may hereafter _ indeed I almost
wish my old Stock of negrows were with good masters and I had the
money to put in trade _ I cant Calculate on more than a thousand dollars
and perhaps this will be too little with Johns Credit (which I do not wish
[to] risque if there is the Smallest danger[)] to precure a Sufficeincy of
Sueitiable goods for both places, if it is not and a Suffeceny cant be Collected in time, perhaps it will be best for us to decline the Connection for
the present _ nothing Could induce me to join in [a] project [which]
whould make it necessary to breake up Johns business in Louisville or
change it to any other place _ will [you] ask Cozen Sam, if you can bring
it about, when he can pay a little, I hope Cozen Everit has called on you.
I must have my money I want it from both, and no Sum much Smaller
than the whole amount will be of much Service to me, if any money of
mine Comes into your hands after discharging the estate amount, I must
request you to Give it to John, ~~and for any~~ I Shall [∧]Sell[∧] Seppo if I
can even if I get ⅔ds. of what I took him at I fear I will be put to it to Sell
him, I have been trying fer Some [time] to exchange him in part payment
for a Lot in town.

I think I wrote you pretty fully about the Estate, I Sencreely wish I
was Clear of it, all Such employments are unthankful, I never thought I
was a verry great deel in debt and am a little Supprised how Such an idea
Should get ~~to town~~ [∧]afloat[∧] and that all my trouble and your trouble
for me Should not have givn Satisfaction, ~~I hope my own blood has not~~
~~deceved me, no they Can't think me a lier~~ In answr to your 1st. en-
qurey I gave Sister fitzhugh every debt and articles which She has not ac-
counted with me for and mentioned on the papers. 2nd. Enqr. Mr.
Crutchfields accounts assignd to Mr. Fitzhugh, This and the othr accounts &c. I have mentioned in my last letter 3rdly I paid Mr. Fry fer
Charles an advance of £5._0_0 when he went of[f] 4th.ly. I for got
about Angella⁵ but have Some faint recollection that her Clothes were
furnished by Fanny, but do not recolect about her provisions & Tax, as I
cant remember I can Say nothin about the Charge ___

I wrote you in both of my last letters about York, I did wish to do well
by him _ but as he has got Such a notion about freedom and his emence
Services, that I do not expect he will be of much Service to me again; I do

not think with him, that his Services has been So great (or my Situation would promit me to liberate him[)]_ I must request you to do for me as Circumstances may to you, appir best, or necessary and will ratify what you may do — he could if he would be of Service to me and Save me money, but I do not expect much from him as long as he has a wife in Kenty. I find it is necessary to look out a little and must get in Some way of makeing a little, you will not disaprove of my inclinatuns on this Score, I have long discovered your wish (even beforee I went [on] the western trip) to induc me to beleve that there might be a raney day, Clouds Seem to fly thicker than they use to do and I think there will be a raney day[6] _ I must conclude as my paper will Surely fold

Julia joins ∧me[∧] in Love to you Self Sister Mrs. Temple & nancy and belev me to be

yr. affactnate Bro: Wm Clark

P.S. Julia Says in those words _ ["]ask you brother to tell my Kentucky mother that I am out of Sage, that She must Send Some to her Child in this wild Country." and tell Nancy to write her a long letter, not Such a Short one as the last,[7]

40 Indian men Came down the Mississippi to this place to day from high up the <u>winabagoes</u>, their business in mearly to tell ther poverty and State the bad Councils they have receved from the British _ I have been in Council all day with them,[8] I have a long Story to tell you Shortley in the public way _ it is not ripe yot & paper full[9]

I have not timee to read what I have wrote as it is late at night [This last sentence of the postscript is written along the left margin of the first page.]

1. This is quite an enlightening passage for two reasons. First, it shows yet again how open William Clark was with Jonathan, holding back little if anything regarding his feelings and affairs from him. Second, Clark states that he retained no copies of his letters to Jonathan; therefore the original letters edited here are the only ones in existence and thus even more historically priceless.
2. "Kentucky boat" was another name for a flatboat, the river craft commonly used on the Ohio and other rivers. The name is a reflection of the westward traffic on the Ohio. Many of the boats were built in the Pittsburgh area and traveled downriver to Kentucky. The term also had a

derogatory connotation because the boats, being intended for a one-way trip and not for reuse, were of inferior quality; they were broken up for various uses, or their lumber was sold upon reaching their destination. The flatboat is considered an ancestor of the houseboat.

3. Clark's description of his mercantile plans states not only his ambitions to engage in the lucrative trade but also the method and route used to bring goods from the East across the mountains to Kentucky and farther west. The accepted mixing of public business with private pursuits also is evident. But, again, Clark was destined to have his plans "k[n]ocked in the head," as far as establishing a mercantile business with his nephew John Hite Clark. He did become involved in the mercantile trade in St. Louis through his Indian Department duties and participation in the St. Louis Missouri Fur Company, but he apparently never formed a partnership with any family members. His belief that Louisville was the best place to base the enterprise reflects the town's thriving character in the first two decades of the nineteenth century. Other comments he makes in his letters indicate the rapid population increase and strong commercial growth Louisville experienced during this period. (Casseday, 138–55.)

4. The oft-mentioned Samuel Gwathmey and Everard Clark.

5. Angella and her two children were inherited by Charles Thruston under the terms of John Clark's will in 1799. It is likely that John Clark gave them to Fanny Clark for her use either before or upon her marriage to Thruston. Under the law at that time, property would be inherited by the male in-law, rather than the female, although it really was intended for her and was often unofficially considered hers. Angella and her two children were in Thruston's possession in 1799 when Clark died. In dealing with Thruston's estate William Clark had hired out Angella but does not remember the details. Jonathan's day book reveals that Angella had a child in the fall of 1803 and that she was hired out each of the three years Clark was absent on the expedition. (JCWB, 1:86–90; Jonathan Clark Day Book, 16 June 1804, January 1805, 1 January 1806.)

6. This passage is a bit disjointed, but what I believe Clark was writing was that contrary to York's belief that his services (especially those on the expedition) merited his freedom, Clark did not think so, and that if he did believe his services warranted it he would free him. But, alas, he does not expect York to be of enough economic and financial benefit to him to achieve the level of service deserving manumission, primarily because of his attitude resulting from being separated from his wife. In addition, Clark was trying to heed Jonathan's advice, apparently given for a number of years, to save his money for a "rainy day." Clark's mood must have been either rather low or unoptimistic since he believed that

clouds were gathering and there would soon be a rainy day. This passage provides an excellent example of the evils of slavery and the pernicious effect it had on the humanity of the master as well as the slave.

7. Another wonderful insight into Julia Clark and her closeness to William's family, especially Jonathan's family, and her loneliness and homesickness in St. Louis.

8. The Winnebago Indians are a Siouan tribe that inhabited east-central Wisconsin in generally prehistoric times. By the late eighteenth century they had extended their territory to the lower Wisconsin and Rock Rivers near the Mississippi. Although of Siouan stock, they remained in the Wisconsin region when their kin moved farther west and gradually were surrounded by Algonquian tribes such as the Sauk and Fox, Menominee, and Potawatomi. They had good relations with these neighbors and often cooperated with them militarily. They were actively allied with the French against the British, and then with the British against the Americans. As white pressure for their lands increased, they were uprooted in a succession of transfers to Iowa, Minnesota, South Dakota, and finally Nebraska. A small number eventually returned to Wisconsin. At the time Clark wrote this letter, the Winnebago were allied with the British and would support them against the United States a few years hence in the War of 1812. This delegation of Winnebagoes to St. Louis was unexpected and created quite a stir until the settlers were convinced of their peaceful intentions. Clark apparently questioned their true motives also and did not respond generously to their request for presents. He instead distributed presents sparingly, and spoke to the Winnebago delegation quite sternly about the conduct expected of the tribe. (Lamar, 1275–76; Loos, 861–62.)

9. It is not known what this story in the "public way" was. Clark does not relate a lengthy story of that nature in any of his letters in this collection. One can speculate that it concerned Indian affairs, especially his views on the Chouteaus and the Osage treaty or perhaps even the deteriorating relations between Lewis and Frederick Bates. It is unfortunate for researchers that Clark apparently did not commit the "story" to paper.

∼

St. Louis Decr. 17th 1808

My Dear Brother

I have not time to write you a long letter by this mail, I have employed all my time writing to bro Edmund & John and the time is aproaching fast for the mail to close, John Sullivan Came here yesterday and gave me your letter of the 6th instant _ I think it would be well to take up Capn. Oldhams[1] bond if it Should have to be paid by my Self provided it does not amount to a large Sum, I forget the amt.

I believe I mentioned every thing to you about the estate, my hint respecting G. _ B _ge[2] was not founded on the Smallest intimition of any person, Some person had been Saying Something and I could not Surmise whome it could be and mearly Sayed him, as being most Concerned in the Suckcess of my Settlement &c. God forbid I Should be the means of Sentioring [censuring] an inocent man, as I beleve him to be.

I am happy to here of the health of Sister & family, I wished they Could be with Julia a fiew days and give her new Spiruts She talks of tham often, She recveed a letter from nancy, and a very devirting one it was, as She explained the adventures at a late play in Louisville.[3] John Sullivan was here yesterday _ and a verry unfortunate accurence like to have happened, I had just introduced John to Col. Chouteau[4] & Mr. Bates and we were talking about getting John a Surveyors place, which would be verry profitable, at that moment John Saw the Tavern keepers boy rideing his horse by my winder [window] from water, rose in a violent passion, damed a little & thretened what he would do with the Tavern keeper &c. a went out, Col. C. went out Mr. Bates Steaed and Said the young man was patnt. [passionate] and would Say nothing more about recomending him. I shall talk to John on the Subject but I fear the place will be given to another. I have got a plantation for John to work one Clear of rent from the Govr. what a pity John was pationate he was in five minets of a place to make his fortun[5] I must request you to Send my [horses] to Some Convenent place and have them put in good order Govr. Lewis will take one or both of my horsees and the public horse with him to the Eastward and Sell them I have made my arrangements with him and he wants the horses fatuned _ I do not wish the horses nor do I cear for Yorks being in this Country. I have got a little displeased with him and intended to have punished him but Govr. Lewis has insisted on my only hireing him out in Kentucky which perhaps will be best, _ This I leave entirely to you, perhaps if he has a Severe master a while he may do Some Service, I do not wish him again in this Country untill he applies himself to Come and give over that wife of his _ I wish'd him to Stay with his family four or five weeks only, and not 4 or 5 months _ please to have all those three horses fattened at my expences.[6] Dear Bro. I give you a great deel of Trouble about my Concerns shall I ever compensate you

Brother Edmund writes me that he has joined John & wishus me &c. in Trade this Connection in trade would be verry pleasing indeed to me, it would be the verry thing I wish, and Shall be much pleased to here that I am as a cupt. [acceptable] to them both as they are to me _ I have wrote Bro Edmund and John both a long letter as I write nothing I wish kept from you, I wish you to See & know all, _ the distance we are, makes it necessary that they both write freely to me without any Sort of reserve or fear of hurting my feelings _ they are not to be hurt by a friend who Speecks on what may concern our Suckcess & prosperity &c.

Julia Joins [me] in love to yourself Sister nancy and family with you and hope you will of acupt of our unalterab[le] affuctions   yr

Wm Clark

1. Samuel Oldham (1749–1823) was a native of Prince William County, Virginia, and also lived in Frederick and Berkeley Counties. He served as a seaman in the Virginia State Navy, and in 1783 he moved to the Louisville area, as had other Oldhams, and settled on an estate named Fairhope south of Louisville near the Churchills. He served in several civil offices in Virginia and Kentucky. Oldham married first Jane Cunningham and second Ann Lipscomb. Several of his children married into prominent Louisville families. His son William married Elizabeth Field, the daughter of Capt. Reuben Field, a Revolutionary War veteran of the 8th and 4th Virginia regiments. He apparently was the great-uncle of Joseph and Reubin Field. The Kentucky Fair and Exposition Center is located on the site of Oldham's farm, and the family cemetery is still extant. (Oldham family file, TFHS; Thompson, 131–33.)

2. General Robert Breckinridge. Various disputes were occurring regarding Charles Thruston's estate, and accusations both real and rumored were circulating. Breckinridge had claims against the Thruston estate.

3. The play was Shakespeare's *The Taming of the Shrew*. Actors found a receptive audience in Louisville. Louisville's first theater was established as early as 1808 in a three-story brick building on the north side of Jefferson Street between Third and Fourth Streets. The Clarks enjoyed the arts, and Jonathan records attending various plays, concerts, etc. The Clark interest in the arts was carried to St. Louis by William. Amateur theater had been active, and in 1819 when a professional troupe under N. M. Ludlow settled in St. Louis, Clark welcomed them and discussed the advantages he believed were "derived in any community from well-regulated dramatic performances." (Jonathan Clark diary, 8 December 1808; Yater (1), 33; Ludlow, 184–85.)

4. René Auguste Chouteau (1749–1829) was a native of New Orleans. He assisted his stepfather Pierre Laclede in founding St. Louis in 1764. He gained wealth through the Indian trade, primarily with the Osage, the fur trade, and other businesses, and became the wealthiest citizen and largest landholder in St. Louis. Although having little interest in public office, he served as a justice of the first territorial court, colonel of the St. Louis militia, chairman of the St. Louis town trustees, commissioner in negotiating Indian treaties, and the U.S. pension agent for Missouri Territory in 1819–1820. He married Marie Thérèse Cerré on 26 September 1786. They had seven children. (*DAB*, 4:94–95.)

5. This is an informative insight not only into how business was done by the leaders of St. Louis—no different, really, from how it was done in most places—but as to how important one's horse was considered. Horse theft during the time when horses were a major means of transportation can be likened to the seriousness of car theft today. It is understandable that John Sullivan would have become alarmed and passionate when he saw his horse unexpectedly being ridden down the street by a stranger. This unfortunate episode did not harm Sullivan's long-term success in St. Louis (see letter dated 5 October 1808, note 1).

6. Clark had sent these horses to Louisville to help carry Nancy Anderson back home. Like many slaveholders, Clark has a disturbing tendency to discuss livestock and slaves together, indicative of the mindset in which they often thought of their slaves.

~

Saint Louis 2nd January 1809.

Dear Brother

A happy new ~yer~ year! Julia also wishes you Sister and nancy a happy new year &c. &c. __ Every person in this village appear at this time to be gay and barley amuseing themselves visiting Slaying [sleighing] and the like, excupt my Julia. She is verry domestuc, Stays at home and works, when She finds herSelf ~a~ loneson talks of nancy and _ B. G &c¹ takes a little cry and amuses herself again with her domestuc concerns

I purchased a Lot and house &c. near the Center of this town of about one acre, Situated between the main Street and the River bounded on both, the best Situated lot in town for Commerce and Storehouses, a Corner lot, and a good harber at all Stages of the water it has on it a large old low house & kitchen, the house has a passage, a bar, 2 Small lodging rooms & a parlour tolerably well finished, also 2 Small lodging rooms and a large hawl not finished piaza on either Side, a [ᴧ]hewd[?][ᴧ] log kitchen, a log Stable, part of a Stone wall on the River & Street Side, with Severel apple trees – fcr this lot I am to give $300 in march or april, and $1200 in October next this is thought a great bargin on my Side — I intend to build a Store house of Stone on the main Street, and houses for public Stores on the River Side, and if I find it to my advantage I Shall move the present buildings on another Lot for Indian purposes, all those last arrangements depinds on the disposition of the Secretary of war; as I must See my interest in those measures before I enter into thm, at all events it answers my purpose as Commerce is my Object.[2]

I am frequently much vexed & perplexed with Indian interpretrs Indians, and verry frequently with my fiew negrows, who wish to go on [in] the old way, Steel a little take a little, lie a little, Scolw a little pout a little, deceive a little, quarrel a little and attempt to Smile, but it will not all answer— I have not leasure to attend to them and gave the Chastizement Some of them may diserve, and have a Sort of a disposition to Sell all but about four, all the Old Stock except Ben,[3] I wish I wais near enough to Council with you a little on this Subject, will you write a fiew lines about this inclination of mine, to turn negrows into goods &c. — Seppo is yet with me and I am verry much afraid I Shall not get as much as I gave [ᴧ]Mr.[ᴧ] Howell[4] for him. – I got a letter from Sam G –[Gwathmey] the other day, before I recved it [I] had wrote him a long letter and mentioned that I wished him to pay John who I was much in debt to &c. &c. Sam is not mad with me, but thinks I am ~~mad~~ displeased with him – I write you So often ~~you~~ that I have not much to Say at this time, I am just killing 19 fat Hogs and 2 Beevees for my years provisions that I expect to Sell Some bacon ᴧand have Sold one Beef[ᴧ]– The weather is exsessively Cold, the river Closed and hav been So for a long time we have not recved the mail but once for a long time Seven weeks — every Sunday we anxiously wait the arrival of the mail to hear of our freinds —. Julia complains very much this evening I fear She has Caught a Cold. John Sullivan is about to Set out by him I Send this letter, I have paved the way for John to get into the Surveying line, if he will make use of his time, he will do well, I have talked to John about – you know what,[5] Govr. Lewis has agreed to let him have one of his places to work his negrows next year, — Slays waggons & horses are driving across on the Ice in every Direction – Some hores Slip in but, none have been lost as yet.

—   I think Mr. Fitzhugh had Some wish to purchase my black nancy, if
he wishes her he Shall have her, She is the best of the old Stock[6]

Julia joins me in best wishes for your helth and hapiness and Sencere
Love to Sister, Mrs. Temple if She is with you nany & the family.
You[r] Eft. Bro

Wm Clark

1. Julia had reached the "time of her confinement," a term then commonly
used for the last stage of pregnancy. She would give birth to their first
child on 10 January. I am not sure who B.G. is. It might be her younger
brother George Hancock (1798–1875), whom she had been separated
from for less than a year, but I am inclined to think she is referring to two
people, Jonathan's two youngest sons, William, or Billy, (B) and George
Washington (G). It seems rather unlikely that Julia would be referring
to, much less missing, George Rogers Clark, with whom she probably
had had little contact. For Clark to use initials, it must have been someone Jonathan readily would have known. (MLClark, 98–99.)

2. This most likely is the lot Clark mentions in his letter of 22, 24 November 1808. From his statement of the terms and what he says later in the
letter, he had been unable to include Seppo (Scippio) as part of the deal
(see letter dated 22, 24 November 1808, note 15). Clark hoped that the
War Department would pay for part of the costs he incurred in the purchase of the lot and buildings since he would in part be using them in his
duties as Indian agent. William Eustis, the new secretary of war, told
Clark that he needed specific cost estimates, and later wrote him that a
decision would have to wait until Clark's visit to Washington in October. Funds eventually were allotted to support the costs of these buildings and operations associated with Indian affairs. Clark did not know it
when he wrote this letter, but two days earlier the superintendent of Indian Trade had written him, offering him the post of agent of the Office
of Indian Trade in St. Louis. Clark accepted the position, so he consequently would need even more room for his operations. (Loos, 863–64,
883, 888–92.)

3. This is a rather puzzling comment about Ben. Clark had freed Ben in
December 1802, and then Ben had bound himself to Clark for thirty
years. Unless Ben's official status had changed, Clark would not have
been able to legally sell him because he was no longer a slave. Clark of
course would have been well aware of this, and perhaps that is why he
was tempted to sell all the "old stock" except Ben. It should also be kept
in mind, however, that since Ben's freeing in 1802 had apparently been
a legal maneuver in order to settle him in a free territory, having brought

him back into slave territory might have led Clark to again consider Ben a slave (even though he had been freed in a slave state) and thus able to be sold. Clark's use of the term "stock" for his slaves was common, and is another indication of the mindset with which slaveholders viewed their human chattel.

4. This may be Daniel S. Howell. He was a hatter in partnership with Henry Duncan in Louisville in 1815, and by 1823 he was living in Bardstown, Kentucky. He married Sally G. Shipp, the daughter of Edmond Shipp, Sr. (d. 1816), in Louisville, on 26 July 1808. Shipp's son Edmond, Jr., died in St. Louis, probably in 1822, and named Howell and John Gwathmey his executors. Another possibility is Lemuel (or Samuel) Howell who was living in Henderson County, Kentucky, in 1808. He is not listed as owning any slaves, but it is possible that if he did purchase Scippio from Edmund Clark and resell him to William Clark the timing was such that it was not recorded in the tax lists for 1808 (the 1807 list is missing). (*Western Courier* (Louisville), 20 July 1815; JCWB, 2:32, 201; Jefferson Co., Ky., Marriage Book, 1:62; Henderson Co., Ky., Tax List, 1808–1809.)

5. The "you know what" may be the incident involving the tavernkeeper's boy and Sullivan's horse that Clark recounted in his 17 December 1808 letter. Clark apparently had smoothed over any problems created by the incident with Bates and Chouteau, and again "paved the way" for Sullivan to get a lucrative surveying appointment.

6. It is doubtful that Clark sold Nancy to Dennis Fitzhugh. If she had left the family that early, even before Meriwether Lewis Clark was born, it is very unlikely that he would have listed her in his family genealogy, much less have known the names of her children. If she was sold to Fitzhugh or someone else, Clark apparently got her back, and she was with the family long enough for M. Lewis Clark to remember her. By 1837, however, she had apparently been sold, given to someone else, freed, or had died, since she was not listed in Clark's will. This second mention of the "old stock" in reference to those slaves who had belonged to the Clarks for many years and had come with William Clark from Kentucky implies that he had purchased additional slaves since his return from the expedition and perhaps since settling in St. Louis. See letter dated 2 July 1808, note 1. (MLClark, 90; William Clark Will, 14 April 1837, WCP-VMC.)

Saint Louis January 21st. 1809.

Dear Brother

I Set down to write you without haveing much to
say, on the 10th inst: Julia gave me a fine Son,[1] a Stout portly fellow with
Strong longues and well formed, he is beginning to break out, which the
old womin Say is a good Sine _ Julia is tolerably well tho' feals great
want of Sleap. Miss Polly Nicholes[2] has been with her for about a week,
~~day b~~ untill day before yesterday   Majr. Christy became So danjerously
ill of his Old Disorder that Miss Polly was obliged to go home, the Majer
begins to mend, but Mrs. C. is gitting into the Suds, and we may not expect Miss P. _ companey any more[3] _ negrows are Such Sleepy creatures
that Julia Can put no dependance in them, nancy is best, but She Sleeps
verry Sound _ and to hire a woman we cant think of the expence even if
we Could trust them, So you See it is best for us to deprive our Selves of
Some Sleup, _ I assure you that the old Town Lady[4] has recved of me a
good deel of ready Cash. Some time in the fall, She gave out that She
would go to New Orleans if a house was not built for her, as She was the
only woman of experiencd knowledge, a Subcription went about among
the Ladies who were in a Certain way for money to build this Skillful old
Lady a house. Julias proposion was $12 which can only be Considered
as a Bribe and $17 as a fee, and a fee for nancy of $6 _ is 35 Dollars, and
She is now in the kitchen attend.g on Easter which will be 6 Dols. more[5]
_ I do not know if I Shall have to pay Easters 6 Dollars as Soon as She
wishes me or not, about four days ago She Cut a fiew Capers which had
been repeeted for Several days, I gave her a verry genteel whipping
which made her verry good for on[e] Day and a half, finding She Could
not vent the violence of her Disposton. She thought it best to <u>lay by</u> and
this morning Sends for assists.

I fear you will think that I have become a Severe master it is not the
case _ but I find it absolutely necessary to have business done, and to
Check a Slanderrous desposition, which has for a long time Suffered to
rage, in nancy and Sillo I have had but little trouble, but Easter & venos
much, and have only Chastised E- 3 times & V. twice, and they appear
Something better fer it _ . Seppo I have not Sold as yet, he has heard of
my intention and makes fair promessis, and begs Stoutly to continue with
me. I Shall fatigee you with negrow acurrencs _

You will know that I not only experence a degree of Satisfaction but improve by your advice an[d] councils, in respecting my own afforres, and to get from you Some Ideas on those Subjects, I have been So manute that I fear I have been troublesom; but I will not be So much So again, and will just mention to you how I go on [in] the money way this is a matter [in] which I feel more interested, and Shall at all times feel So —when I was at washington the Secty. of war advanced me about $1100 dollars of my pay to assist in fixing my Famly. in this placee _ my pay is Due from the 1st. of this month, and I am in debt to the U.S. $1287– of which I have paid for Lands $450 – paid Govr. Lewis, my part of expences incured about our book &c. about $300[6] – and the bals.[balance] of about 537 Dollars has been expended in prcureing provisions, cows hogs and Such articles of merchendize as we have purchased at this place ∧of which 120 Ds. to Charely [Charless?] & 23 to the old woman[∧][7] – how do you think I drive on, I assure you I go to no unnecessary expence, if I do err it is on the other hand —

I wrote to John last post a Short Letter, we have not heard from you [in] a long time but hope in a fiew days to here. my Julia Joins me in love to yourself Sister nancy and the family. Julia is So pleased with her Son that She thinks that every body else must be pleased also, and expresses much anxiety to have nany here to help her corress the little Boy

Yr. Affct. Bro

Wm Clark

my little Son Sends his love to his uncles
aunt & cozen nancy ——

in hast

1. Meriwether Lewis Clark (1809–1881) was the first of William and Julia's five children. In his family genealogy he stated he was born at Maj. William Christy's house at the southwest corner of Walnut and Main Streets. He was educated in St. Louis and graduated from the U.S. Military Academy at West Point in 1830. Soon after graduation he resigned from the army and settled in St. Louis. M. Lewis or Lewis, as he was known, was interested in the arts, and was one of the founders of the St. Louis Theatre Company in the 1830s. He served as a major in the Mexican War, participating in Kearny's Southwestern campaign. When the Civil War began, M. Lewis sided with the Confederacy and was commissioned a major of artillery. He was promoted to colonel in the CSA

and to brigadier general in Missouri state Confederate forces. After the war, he settled in Louisville and later in Frankfort, Kentucky. His first wife was Abigail Prather Churchill (1817–1852) of Louisville. They married at her father Samuel Churchill's home, Spring Grove, on 9 January 1834. She died in St. Louis on 14 January 1852 from complications of delivering their seventh child. He married Julia Servos Davidson (1826–1907) in Louisville on 30 December 1865. M. Lewis apparently was a rather spoiled, self-indulgent person who liked to live extravagantly. John O'Fallon complained about his activities and attitude, and the problems, especially financial, that he caused. Following his wife Abby's death he "gave" five of his six surviving children to relatives to raise. He died of consumption in Frankfort on 28 October 1881. His body was immediately shipped to St. Louis, and he was buried at Bellefontaine Cemetery on 29 October. His son Meriwether Lewis Clark, Jr. (1846–1899), was the founder of Churchill Downs and the Kentucky Derby. Like the man for whom his father had been named, he committed suicide. (MLClark, 98–99; Bond, 189–90; John O'Fallon Papers; Bellefontaine Cemetery Records; *EL*, 198–99.)

2. There are two possibilities as to the identity of Polly Nicholes. She may be Matilda Nicholas Christy (b. 1798), the daughter of William and Martha Christy. She would have been not quite eleven at the time but mature enough to help the Clarks. The way in which Clark refers to her certainly indicates that she was related to the Christy family and considered the Maj. Christy household her home. She married Dr. David Verill Walker (1786–1824) in St. Louis, 20 November 1816. Walker was a native of Buckingham County, Virginia. He settled in St. Louis in 1812 and became the partner of his future brother-in-law Bernard G. Farrar. The other possibility is that Polly's surname was Nicholas (or Nicholls, Nichols or Nicholes) and that she may have been a relation of the Christys, perhaps a niece, living with them. This would then be the Polly Nicholls (Nicholas?) who married John Campbell of the First U.S. Infantry in St. Louis in 1810. Campbell entered the Clark-Christy circle through that marriage. He mentions in an 1811 letter that he is happy to hear that his wife was with the Clarks and in an 1812 letter regrets that he does not have time to write Maj. Christy and Dr. Farrar. In his genealogy, M. Lewis Clark lists a Julia Clark Campbell (b. 1811) as living with the Clarks and later with the Christys. This almost undoubtedly is the daughter of John Campbell and his wife. A positive identification is further complicated by references to Campbell being Farrar's brother-in-law as early as December 1810. Unless the birthdate for Matilda "Polly" Nicholas Christy is late by some six years, which seems rather unlikely, I am at a loss to determine the relationship. (MLClark,

60–62, 66; Houck, 3:76, 80; John Campbell to Clark, 30 July 1811 and 10 March 1812, WCP-VMC; Scharf, 1:315n.)

3. It is not known what Maj. Christy's "old disorder" was that required Polly to return home, but Clark's comments, including the reference to Martha Christy's over-indulgence in beer ("gitting into the Suds"), provide interesting information concerning the Christys and their relationships.

4. The "Town Lady" or midwife could not be identified.

5. Clark's further comments about the midwife who attended Julia and his pregnant slaves reveals her importance in St. Louis and the fees she could command. It is interesting to note that she attended slaves as well as whites and that she charged almost three times as much for white deliveries as she did for black. The child Nancy was going to have might have been Rosella (or Rosetta). Nothing is known about Easter's child. (MLClark, 90.)

6. Although Meriwether Lewis had done essentially nothing personally as far as the writing up of their expedition journals for publication, expenses were being incurred for such things as the printing and distribution of the prospectus, the purchase of John Ordway's journal, and work done by various people on the scientific and printing aspects of the project. Lewis and Clark apparently were splitting the expenses evenly. On 21 August 1809 Clark and Lewis settled their account, balancing what each owed the other at $554.43. Apparently the $300 Clark paid Lewis in January for his share of expenses was included in this account, although the August account lists only $271.50 in book expenses due Lewis. At the time of his death, Lewis owed Clark $100, so he apparently borrowed some money before setting out for the East. (Jackson (1), 2:462–63.)

7. The identity of Charely is unknown. Clark may be referring to Joseph Charless, but his writing, and meaning, are indistinct; "the old woman" refers to the midwife.

∾

[no place, no date – St. Louis, ca. 1 March 1809][1]

Dear Brother

I have not heard from you for a long time, and have been trying to recollect what I could have written, – I can't recollect of any thing that I have Said to you out of the way – I keep no Copies of letters I write to you and have and Shall feel no restraint either in Stile or grammer.[2] I Should be verry glad to know how every thing goes on in the neighbourhood, what has become of Tompkins, if he does not chuse to excupt of the $600 a year it would Save my feelings verry much for him to write that I might laey his decision before the Trusteees, Two men are now waiting to be employed, and the place is kept for Mr. Tompkins.[3] —

we have formed a Company to hunt and Trade up the Missouri to be Called the St. Louis Missour fur Compny.[4] — of 10 Shares, and 140 men with the view to hunt & Trap th Beaver &c. Mr. Wilkinson [written above "Beaver & c." with no indication where it should be placed][5] on this Subject I must refur you to my lettr to Bro. E. & John for particulars —

I wish, the Side Saddle Bridle &c. which Miss nany anderson was furnished with, asso the portmanteu, tent, umbrella &c. by Some oppertunity which may offer.

Julia requests Sister Clark to Send her Some Seeds, the rats has eat all hers —

Genl. Mason[6] Supr. intd. of Indn. Trade has thought proper to apt. me his agent at this placee to recve & transport all publick Goods to the factores abov and the reterns in peltres & furs to New Orleans or Sell them — indeed brother I have my hands full of public business. I have not time or I could fille a Sheet with Something, prey excuse this Scraul,

Our familey are well I have advrtised Sep & Jubia for Sale,[7] Jubia has becom the worst fellow in town, has Broke open a Desk and Stole money with a boy of Majr. Penrose s,[8] been whiped run away, and [become] the greatest lier in the Territory I am Deturmined to Sell him, do you think I can get a tolerable price for him near you, Sep I cant Sell for a tolerable price.

Julia Joins me in love to you Sister and family and remain affectunately

Yrs. Sinceerely
Wm Clark

Easter is bad and I have trounced her three times I
wish to hire her but cant as so as yet, indeed I have
been Obliged to trounce all except Sillo Ben & Sip Since
I came here, they are troublesom creatures but I think
are getting much better Since they have been whiped a little.
what has becom of york? and the horse. — ever yrs.

WC

[Letter carried by Benjamin Wilkinson.]

1. Although this letter is undated, Jonathan docketed it as being about January 1809, but it was actually written in late February or early March 1809. Internal evidence supports the ca. 1 March date because William Clark placed an ad offering two slaves for sale in the 22 February edition of the *Missouri Gazette* (see note 7) and the establishment of the St. Louis Missouri Fur Company basically was accomplished by the end of February (see note 4).

2. A very important passage because it confirms the statement in his 10 December 1808 letter that he did not keep copies of these letters to Jonathan. Therefore, the letters edited here are unique. His comment regarding no restraint in "Stile or grammer" further confirms how much William Clark wrote these letters from the heart.

3. Clark returns to this topic mentioned in his 22, 24 November 1808 letter regarding Tompkins teaching in St. Louis (see note 19 of that letter). Not only does it again reflect Clark's immediate standing and influence in St. Louis but also shows how interested he was in finding his Kentucky friends and associates positions in St. Louis and encouraging them to move there. One of the two men waiting to be employed may have been Christoph Schewe (see letter dated 22, 24 November 1808, note 19). The other might have been Isaac Septlivres, although it was not until November 1809 that he advertised to teach. (Scharf, 1:824.)

4. The St. Louis Missouri Fur Company was officially founded in 1809. It had begun to be formed in the latter part of 1808, and it was sufficiently established by the end of February to enter into an agreement (on 24 February) with Meriwether Lewis as governor of Louisiana Territory concerning returning Sheheke to the Mandan. Its articles of incorporation were signed on 7 March 1809. Among its founders were Manuel Lisa, William Morrison, Pierre Menard, Benjamin Wilkinson, William Clark, Pierre Chouteau, Sr., Auguste Chouteau, Jr., and others. Clark was an original stockholder, and he tried to get Jonathan, Edmund Clark, and Dennis Fitzhugh to invest in the venture also, wanting his family to benefit from what he believed would be a lucrative enterprise. He may have succeeded in persuading Fitzhugh to invest in the company, although his letter of 28 May 1809 casts doubt on this. Internal dissension and hostilities with the Blackfoot Indians forced the company to reorganize in 1812 as the Missouri Fur Company. That company was dissolved in January 1814. A successor company of the same name operated until 1825, when it became defunct because of competition and the massacre of one of its major trapping parties by the Blackfeet. It was the St. Louis Missouri Fur Company and Missouri Fur Company, under the leadership of Manuel Lisa, that helped open up the Rocky Mountain region and establish the importance of St. Louis in the

fur trade. (Chittenden, 1:137–39; Lamar, 760; Jackson (1), 2:446; Loos, 896.)

5. A Mr. Wilkinson carried the letter to Louisville. I think Clark intended to say that Jonathan could ask Wilkinson for information on the St. Louis Missouri Fur Company but neglected to write more than his name. This must be Benjamin Wilkinson (d. 1810), a native of Maryland who had moved to St. Louis from Jefferson County, Kentucky, and who was one of the founders of the fur company. He was a partner in the mercantile firm of Wilkinson and Price (Risdon H. Price) and served as a captain of a St. Louis militia company. Wilkinson would have made trips to Louisville and other places in order to buy supplies for his store. Billon states that it was on such a trip from New Orleans to Baltimore that he died at sea. Wilkinson also was acting as the agent of the fur company in preparation for its expedition up the Missouri that spring to return Sheheke, and he went to Louisville to recruit men for the expedition. Clark's letters to brother Edmund and John H. Clark giving details on the formation of the company have not been located. (Jackson (1), 1:349n; Clift (2), 319; *Missouri Gazette*, 24 August 1808; Billon, 269–70; Loos, 896–97.)

6. Gen. John Mason was a Georgetown, D.C., attorney, banker, and farmer. At this time he was superintendent of Indian Trade. Meriwether Lewis knew him from his time in Washington as Jefferson's private secretary. Clark may have known him before the expedition because of his work on his brother George's legal affairs or have become acquainted with him after the expedition when he visited Washington. Mason invited Clark to become the agent of the Office of Indian Trade in St. Louis on 31 December 1808. Clark accepted in letters dated 4 and 26 March 1809. His compensation was to be $250 annually—more, Mason wrote, if Clark's responsibilities warranted it. His duties were to be just as he reported to Jonathan: the receiving and forwarding of trade goods to the U.S. factors at Forts Osage and Madison and in turn receiving, storing, forwarding, and sometimes selling the furs and peltries they sent to St. Louis. (Jackson (1), 1:170, 172n; Loos, 888–93.)

7. Clark first advertised Scippio (or Seppo) and Juba for sale in the 22 February 1809 edition of the *Missouri Gazette*. The ad read "I wish to SELL two likely NEGRO MEN, for Cash. WILLIAM CLARK." He ran the same ad in a number of subsequent editions. Juba apparently was not sold until 1816 or later, or may have even escaped. Beginning in April 1816, and running into 1817, Clark ran a reward notice in the Louisville *Western Courier* for Juba. The notice stated that Juba (spelled Jubar) had run away from Benjamin O'Fallon's mill near the Missouri. He was about twenty-four years old; 5'9" or 5'10" tall and "strongly

formed." The ad also stated that he stuttered a little when confused and that he had a new shotgun, and it gave other details of his appearance. It was believed he may have gone to Louisville because his mother (Rose) and relations (probably including his half brother York) lived there. If he did not go to Kentucky, Ohio was believed to be his destination. Clark offered either a $100 or $50 reward depending upon where he was captured. (*Missouri Gazette,* 22 February 1809; *Western Courier,* 6 June 1816.)

8. Maj. Clement Biddle Penrose (1771–1829) was a native of Philadelphia and a member of the wealthy Biddle family. He was a nephew of Gen. James Wilkinson; his mother Sarah Biddle Penrose was the sister of Wilkinson's wife Ann Biddle. In the late 1780s he was commissioned an officer in the Pennsylvania militia. In 1804 Jefferson appointed him one of three commissioners to settle land claims in Louisiana Territory, and he moved from Philadelphia to St. Louis in 1805. He served as a St. Louis town trustee with Clark. His rank of major probably came from service in the Missouri militia. He lost his fortune in bad land investments. (Houck, 3:41; Billon, 216–17; *Louisiana Gazette,* 7 March 1811.)

∾

Saint Louis 28th May 1809.

Dear Brother

I have not wrote you for Some time it is not been from neglect, but for the want of as much time as to Collect my Ideas on those pleasing Subjects I wished to Comunicate, I Say pleasing, because it is at Sometimes pleasing to me to Comunicate even on disagreeble Subjects —

You have been at more trouble about the estate of C. Thruston than I could have wished to have put you to, you must be pleased at getting me Clear, if you knew what pleasure it gives me to reflect that I am Clear, even with the unwarrented Snsure [censure] which has been attached, it would give you Some Satisfaction to See So hapy a man as I am on that Score _ I Say nothing to you about the perticuelrs of the Debts &c. because I know you will do for the best, and much better for my interest than I could have done my Self _ I wish very much to See you and would ride over this Spring if it was possible, I have Somuch to do in the Indian and Factory Departments, and laterly in the Military department that it is impossible for me to leave this place at present, I am deturmined to visit you in the fall, and will if possible go on with my family to virginia from your house, and will most probably return imedeately leaving Julia with her relations untill Feby. I am not deturmined on the rout, perhaps by way of Ressells vill [Russellville] _ if we can get that way Could Sister yourself & nany meet us there when the roads are fine and weather a little Cool towards fall.[1] I am told Bro George is mending fast, what well [will] he wish to do how and where will he live, will he return to the point of rocks do you know? pore fellow I wish it was more in my power to assist him than it is.[2]

York brought my horse, he is here but of verry little Service to me, insolent and Sulky, I gave him a Severe trouncing the other Day and he has much mended Sence Could he be hired for any thing at or near Louis ville, I think if he was hired there a while to a Severe master he would See the difference and do better.[3]

Tell Sister ∧that[∧] Julia has recved Several good things in a Box laterly by a Boat which She dose not prise as a Small acquisiton I assure you _ She Says She wants to Shew her Boy to Sister verry much, he is a fine fellow, just getting well of the Cow pox[4] _ we had him Soused in a tub of water this morning, which is a piece of amusement he is fond of provided he is washed with whiskey after he Coms out _ I think the little man is yet nomely [gnomely or perhaps homely] his head gits reader, we have named him M. Lewis.[5]

I have given up one Shere in the fur Company which I had taken fer Mr. Fitzhugh or John &c.[6] but have been oblige[d] to retain the other which I calculate on makeg. a prophet [profit]. The goods which have been put in to the company was generally as it was purchased by the quantity at this place _ I wish my horses wase here Govr. Lewis talks of Going on but I think he will not untll July. if you meet with an oppertunity prey Send thum on to me partcularly the publc Horse.

a man has just Come down the missouri who informs us that one man was killed by the Blackfoot Inds. last fall on the head of Jeffersons River and others robed &c.[7] we have been thretened by the Indians Some time ago, but every thing is like to turn out well, as Soon as ther plans and intentions was well understood, the Govr. ordered out the militia, and the regulars garresoned at Bellfontain near this place moved, those movements, Confused the Stimulators (British) of the Indians flusterated their plans and the most of the bands broak of[f] from the Connection and well [we] Shall have tranquility. 100 Militia is Still out up the Mississippi at the fort on that river placeing it in a complete State of Defence.[8] they will be down in a fiew Days.

Sillow[9] is in a Danjerous way, yesterday morning the doctor was oblige to take from her a dead Child we are all well except Sillo and her little boy he was Scaulded the other day —

Julia Joins me in love to your Self Sister nancy and all the family and hope to See you all in a few month.

You aft. Bro.

Wm Clark

1. Clark proposed meeting Jonathan and family in Russellville because that is where Jonathan's daughter Eleanor and her husband Benjamin Temple had recently settled. The brothers also had cousins Benjamin and Jonathan Clark living in the area. Also, once they had visited family in Russellville, William's and Jonathan's families could travel together to Jefferson County. William and family did indeed visit Russellville, but Jonathan's did not. Russellville had been laid out in 1795 and was the county seat of Logan County. (William Clark Memorandum Book, 1809; Jackson (3), 14.)

2. In March 1809 George Rogers Clark suffered a stroke in his house in Clarksville at the Point of Rocks and fell near the fire. (Another theory is that he was drunk and passed out, falling into the fire.) His right leg was severely burned and became gangrenous. Consequently, it was amputated on 25 March in Louisville by Dr. Richard Ferguson while a fife and drum played martial music at Clark's request. Thereafter he lived with his sister and brother-in-law Lucy and William Croghan at Locust Grove, which Clark obviously did not know at the time he wrote this letter. William Clark's reference to his once-idolized big brother as a "pore fellow" illustrates how the relationship between them had changed and how even he viewed George with pity. (Jonathan Clark Diary, 25 March 1809; George Rogers Clark Sullivan to John O'Fallon, 24 April 1809, Clark Family Papers, TFHS; *EL*, 197–98.)

3. York apparently had stayed five or six months in the Louisville area visiting his wife and family, instead of the month Clark had intended. The poor relationship between the two men is clear from Clark's remarks. It is believed that York "mended" his attitude/ways after his trouncing rather than needing to mend physically.

4. Clark must have had his son vaccinated with the cowpox virus as a preventive measure against the dreaded smallpox, and the infant was re-

covering from the mild infection caused by it. Dr. A. Saugrain of St. Louis ran an ad in the 7 June 1809 edition of the *Missouri Gazette* announcing the availability of the smallpox vaccine, and giving information on smallpox and the benefits of the vaccine and inoculation. (*Missouri Gazette*, 7, 14 June 1809.)

5. Clark obviously is proud of his son and takes delight in observing his activities, such as being bathed and getting a whiskey rub (the equivalent of a modern alcohol rub). Yet he also is objective and comments that he thinks his son is still rather misshapen (gnomely) or homely, and that his hair is getting redder. Whether William and Julia Clark delayed naming their first born for a time is not known, but this is the first mention Clark apparently makes to family in Kentucky as to what his son's name is, some four months after his birth. Naming him for his good friend and partner in discovery, Meriwether Lewis, Clark stresses that they call the child Lewis. He was known as Lewis or M. Lewis throughout his life.

6. Anticipating his brother-in-law Dennis Fitzhugh or nephew John Hite Clark possibly wanting to invest in the St. Louis Missouri Fur Company, Clark bought extra shares in the company for them. The Clark family's enthusiasm apparently did not match his, and he disposed of some of the extra stock.

7. It is unfortunate that Clark does not mention the name of the man killed and those robbed, assuming he knew them. It is likely that the names had been reported to him. The *Missouri Gazette* does not mention the report.

8. The spring of 1809 brought heightened fears of an Indian uprising along the upper Mississippi and surrounding territory, particularly to the east in Illinois and Indiana. Both Clark and Meriwether Lewis devoted much of their time to Indian affairs, and both were convinced that the British were responsible for Indian hostility. Lewis ordered army regulars from Cantonment Belle Fontaine to Fort Bellevue (soon to be replaced by Fort Madison) at the Des Moines rapids. He also set about strengthening and readying the militia (with limited success). Clark believed that the Prophet or Shawnee Prophet, brother of the great Shawnee leader Tecumseh, was to blame for the Indian threat east of the Mississippi. The situation soon calmed down, but intermittent hostilities and threatening situations would continue for the next two years until the fall of 1811, when war broke out between the Americans and Indians beginning at the Battle of Tippecanoe. Actual war between the United States and the British was declared in June 1812, and many of the tribes in the upper Mississippi and Great Lakes region officially allied themselves with Great Britain. (Loos, 865–74; *Missouri Gazette*, 5, 12, 26 April 1809, 14 June 1809.)

9. Priscilla was one of Clark's slaves. He had hired her out upon arriving in St. Louis, but from what he writes here, it sounds as if she is living in his house. Perhaps that agreement no longer was in force or the terms allowed her to spend some time at Clark's, or her pregnancy had required her to return to the Clark household. Her little boy may be the child she already had in 1799. See letter dated 21 July 1808, note 11.

~

St. Louis July 22nd 1809.

Dear Brother

I have not had the pleasure of hereing from you for a long time, I Should be glad to know how you all wase, Bro Edmund has wrote to me Several times laterly and favered me with the genl. State of my friends about you. I wrote you Some time a go on the Subject of my affairs which are at this time nearly as they were at that time. I have taken york out of the Caleboos and he has for two or three weeks been the finest negrow I ever had.[1] I lost my favorite horse a fiew days ago, which is all the misfortune I have recved laterly[2] _ The Missouri Fur Company has met with Several disertions, I have now Six men in joil who deserted from the Compy 250 miles from this, I have jost herd of the Company they are now going on verry well[3]— I am not positive as to the rout I Shall take to virginia, my present object is by way of Russellvill & thro Jefferson, but if the U.S. will Bear my expencess which I have Some expectation that they will, I may go round by Philadelphia & Washington and See you on my return, This Change will depend altogether on what I may hear on that Subject, The Govt. ~~will~~ has in my possession about 80,000 lb. of furs & peltres, which I expect they wish Shiped around. I wish much to See John

Please to acupt yourself and Sister Nan & The famly with you of the aft. Love of Julia any [and] my Self, and be assured that our wish is for you[r] helth & hapiness   yr. Bro

Wm Clark

1. It is not known what York did to be jailed. It may have been for his reported continued "insolent and Sulky" behavior, or it could have been for a more serious offense. One story regarding York tells of his relating adventures from the expedition and spinning yarns about it in St. Louis

saloons, frequently getting drunk and being tossed into jail to sober up. Possibly he was jailed as punishment also. (Betts, 73–76.)

2. Yet another example of many slaveholders' troubling tendency to associate their slaves and livestock. Clark routinely discusses or associates the two together. Clark's favorite horse that died may have been Gellart, although he and his nephew Benjamin O'Fallon differ as to when the horse may have died. O'Fallon reported in a 25 June 1809 letter to his brother John that Uncle William's finest horse Gellart had died about three weeks earlier while on loan to a man moving his family to St. Charles. (John O'Fallon Papers, TFHS.)

3. This was the large expedition mounted by the company with the objective not only of trapping and trading for furs but of returning Sheheke to the Mandan. Meriwether Lewis agreed to pay the company $7,000 to return the chief and his party, which it did. William Eustis, the new secretary of war, reluctantly agreed to this payment but protested two additional drafts totaling $940 related to the expedition, along with other expenses Lewis had submitted. This protest was what caused the run of Lewis's creditors on him and helped lead to his financial and mental collapse, and thus his death. Ironically, the additional $940 was not needed, and in an even more cruel irony, the secretary of war decided in 1812 that the two bills totaling $940 should not have been protested and reimbursed Lewis's estate $636.25 after deducting government expenses. (Chittenden, 1:138–39; Jackson (1), 2:446–65; Jackson (3), 3–11, 21.)

4

"What Will Be the Consequence?"

A Good Friend Lost, 1809–1810

On 26 August 1809 William Clark wrote Jonathan in an agitated state of mind. His letter marks the beginning of a series of eight letters written to Jonathan from late August to early the following March that relate to the tragic death of his friend and partner in discovery, Meriwether Lewis. Four of the letters are particularly significant because they chronicle Clark's reaction to Lewis's death and pass on information he received about his friend's suicide. Although whether Lewis committed suicide or was murdered is still debated today, historians almost unanimously concur that the great explorer died by his own hand. Significant evidence in support of this belief is in the letters Clark writes Jonathan.

In the summer of 1809 Meriwether Lewis's world seemed to be collapsing. After the expedition Lewis was rewarded with the governorship of Louisiana Territory. While he had many talents, those of a territorial administrator and politician were not among them. He achieved successes in governing the huge territory, but he also made enemies who resisted his decisions and wishes. His second-in-command, Territorial Secretary Frederick Bates, was a political enemy sending negative reports about the governor to officials in Washington. Lewis overextended himself financially in land speculation and was unsuccessful in his quest for a wife. To this was added what must have been a guilty conscience because of his failure to write the official account of the expedition; a book for which he had been under contract since 1807. The proverbial last straw came in August 1809 when Lewis learned that the War Department had protested several of his vouchers and refused to authorize their payment. When word of this embarrassment became public, the result was a run on Lewis by his creditors and rumors that he had conducted himself improperly as governor. Lewis was humiliated and upset. He turned to his good friend William Clark in this difficult time. He also turned to the solace of alcohol.

Clark reported this distressing situation to Jonathan on 26 August. The sense of foreboding he had is palpable. Lewis had left the day before, Clark reported, not only to go to Philadelphia to write their expedition book, but especially to go to Washington regarding the protested vouchers. A day after parting with his friend, Clark still could not get Lewis out of his mind. Lewis had expressed the depths of his distress to Clark "in Such terms as to Cause a Cempothy [sympathy] which is not yet off." William Clark defended his friend's honor, declaring that there was never an "honest er man in Louisiana nor one who had pureor motives than Govr. Lewis. if his mind had been at ease I Should have parted Cherefully." Part of Clark's unease may have been caused by the fact that Lewis had turned over all his landed property to him and two other friends to be used to pay his debts. The thought may have crossed Clark's mind that his friend did not intend to return, though he wrote that he was sure everything would be settled and Lewis would "return with flying Colours to this Country."

Tragically, Lewis would never return to St. Louis. On the evening of 10 October Governor Lewis stopped for the night at Grinder's Stand some seventy miles southwest of Nashville on the Natchez Trace. He had been delayed on his journey east at the U.S. fort at Chickasaw Bluffs because he was in a "State of Derangement." Capt. Gilbert Russell reported to Clark and later to Thomas Jefferson that Lewis had already tried to kill himself twice by the time he reached the bluffs. Russell detained him for fifteen days and kept him off hard liquor, he wrote Clark, until he thought Lewis had recovered sufficiently to continue his trip. But Lewis again sank into the depths of depression. Overcome by his seemingly insurmountable problems and a ruined reputation, he mortally wounded himself with pistol shots to the head and body. He lingered through the night and died on the morning of 11 October. The Nashville *Democratic Clarion* carried the first printed word of Lewis's death on 20 October. Word quickly spread to other newspapers.

William Clark headed east with his family on 21 September. He needed to take care of some of his own business in Washington, and he and Julia looked forward to a visit with their families in Kentucky and Virginia. They arrived at Jonathan's on 12 October and left on 26 October. Two days later they stopped in Shelbyville, where William Clark read the numbing newspaper report that Lewis had killed himself. That night, and periodically over the next month, Clark wrote Jonathan about this tragic event, relaying to him the details he learned of Lewis's death and his own distress at the terrible news. It was an event that Clark rarely spoke of afterward, but in those first weeks after he learned of Lewis's death he could hardly think of anything else. His best friend was dead. What was he to do about the publication of the expedition book? He must get the expedition journals and papers that Lewis had with him at the time of his death. The letters to Jonathan detail all this information and his emotions. Clark's tortured declaration "I fear O! I fear the waight of his mind has over come him, what will be the Consequence?" still evokes his distress today. On 30 October he mentioned a letter he received from Lewis that his friend had written at New Madrid. Clark thought it would help explain his friend's state of mind and actions. That important letter is not known to exist today. About a week later at Bean Station, Tennessee, Clark was still reeling mentally and emotionally. "I am at a loss to know what to be at his death is a turble [terrible] Stroke to me, in every respect. I wish I could talk a little with you just now."

As he had done for some years now, Clark turned to his brother Jonathan for counsel. The shock of Lewis's death, the responsibilities concerning the publication of the expedition book and preservation of expedition manuscripts, and the turbulence of Louisiana politics and the role he would play in them all preoccupied Clark's mind. He heard speculation that he might replace Lewis as governor. Knowing what had happened to his friend, he was loath to subject himself to such troubles, confessing to Jonathan that "I am afraid, and Cannot Consent if I was [nominated] . . . I do not think mySelf Calculated to meet the Storms which might be expected." Clark may have relayed his reservations to the president and secretary of war, which may be why he was not named to replace Lewis.

From Virginia and Washington Clark continued to pass on information about Lewis's death as he received it. He makes reference to receiving letters from Gilbert Russell detailing Lewis's behavior and attempted suicide and to Lewis's servant John Pernier's account of the governor's disturbed state of mind in the days before his death. Those important letters also are not known to exist today. Clark voices his frustration at being unable to find out what has been done in regard to publishing the journals and his fear that nothing had been done. Two months later he is able to report the progress he has made in getting the journals published. While he is relieved, he also resents having the responsibility placed on his shoulders. In one of his strongest statements expressing his displeasure toward Lewis and his procrastination in writing the journals, Clark writes "his neglecting to write our Journal has given me a great deel trouble and expence _ and will give me Still more." But William Clark soldiered on, doing what had to be done to prepare the journals for publication and to wrap up government business before returning westward.

∼

St. Louis August 26th 1809.

Dear Brother

        I have not time to write a verry long letter tho' I will write all the time I have _ your letter of th 2th June I thought I had answered. The lands of bro. G in Brucking County and on Little river & Cuembarland I paid taxes for in the County of Jefferson untill the year 1803 they are entered in the name of G R. Clark. I have also paid the Taxes for the lands $ [value] 3000 acres in Frankling on Severn Creek in the name of John Clark also in the County of Jefferson[1] _ Majr. Croghand did not pay the Taxes, and I do expect the lands have been left off the List, please to enquire of Ransdel Slaughter[2] _ I wish Mr. Hardin[3] to attend to the business of Col. Hancock if he has not appointed another atty. to do that business within your knowledge _ I hope Cozen E. has troubled you a little lately with a little Caish in hand &c. &c. you Speak of Compensation I do assure you that it tw[as] Small for the risk and trouble I am at, I have not 2 hours in the day to appropriate to my private use, it will not do I cant Stand Such Confinement for $1750 your hint is a good one, but I assure you I have been perticular, but not with standing I lose a little in the throngs of business. _ Govr. L. I may Say is r—d by Some of his Bills being protested for a Considerable Sum. which was for moneys paid for Printing the Laws and expences in Carrying the mandan home all of which he has vouchrs for, if they Serve me in this way what ___[4] I have Sent on my accounts to the 1st of July with vouchers for all to about $1800 which is not yet expended in totl. I am under no apprehention, they Settled my Acts. to the 30t. Decr. laist and a ballance was in my faver of $17.68 ___ but we anticipate much pleasure in Spending a fiew days with you on our way to virginia, I expect we Shall go by Russels ville last post I receved a letter from Mr. Temple, all was well he expected to go up to See you about this time. ___ Since I confined york he has been a gadd fellow to work; I have become displeased with him and Shall hire or Sell him, on the 5 of next month I [shall] Set him off in a boat to wheeling as a hand, on his return to the falls I wish much to hire him or Sell him[5] ___ I cant Sell negrows here for money ___ I have Offered my Share in the missouri Company for what it Cost me $3000 and wish much to get it, but Still keep up good hopes and use flattering expressions if you have not Sent my horses please to keep thm for me to ride to virginia ___ I find all the people about Louis ville is building and going on finely ___ as to my Self I do but little for my Self and have the name of a hard hand to bargain

I have not Spent Such a Day as yesterday fer maney years, busily employed untill Dinner writing my Dispatches, and then took my leave of Govr. Lewis who Set out to Philadelphia to write our Book,[6] (but more perticularly to explain Some matter between him and the Govt. Several of his Bills have been protested and his Crediters all flocking in near the time of his Setting out distressed him much. which he expressed to me in Such terms as to Cause a Cempothy which is not yet off ___ I do not beleve there was ever an honest er man in Louisiana nor one who had pureor motives than Govr. Lewis. if his mind had been at ease I Should have parted Cherefully.[7] he has given all his landed property into the hands of Judge Steward[8] Mr. Carre[9] & myself to pay his debts. with which we have Settled the most of them at this place, Some yet remains and Some property yet remains ___ his property in this Country will ___ pay his ___ by a Considerable amount, tho' I think all will be right and he will return with flying Colours to this Country ___ prey do not mention this about the Govr. excupt Some unfavourable or wrong Statement is made ___ I assure you that he has done nothing dis honourable, and all he has done will Come out to be much to his Credit ___ as I am fully purswaded.[ )][10]

Julia is verry pore and not in good health, She anticipates much pleasure in with Sister & nancy and Says that She can make finer with you than with any [of] my relations except John who [she] does not Care more about than her little brother[11] – Bro: Edmunt She Says thinks more about us than any of our relations as he writes us oftener he must think more of us.

She joins me in love to your self and Sister nancy and friends & beleev me to be yr. afft. Brother

Wm Clark

1. Clark is referring to Bracken County in northern Kentucky; the Little River southwest of Hopkinsville, Kentucky, and a tributary of the Cumberland River; land along the Cumberland River in Pulaski County in south-central Kentucky; and Franklin County, Kentucky. He is listed in the 1802 Jefferson County tax list as paying the taxes.

2. Francis Ransdell Slaughter (1767–1831) was a native of Fauquier County, Virginia. He settled in Jefferson County, Kentucky, in 1792 where he was a farmer, and served as a tax commissioner. He married Frances Latham on 28 May 1795 in Nelson County, Kentucky. (Rogers Index.)

3. There were several Hardins practicing law in Kentucky during this time, but Benjamin Hardin, Jr. (1784–1852), may most likely be the Mr. Hardin to which Clark refers. He was a native of Westmoreland County, Pennsylvania, and moved to Kentucky as a child in 1788. After studying law under his cousin Martin D. Hardin and Felix Grundy, he opened his own practice in Elizabethtown in 1806, and in 1808 moved to Bardstown. He quickly earned a reputation as an able lawyer and orator and became one of the foremost trial lawyers—for both the defense and prosecution—in antebellum Kentucky. John Randolph of Roanoke, who knew something about oratory, characterized Hardin as a "vigorous but unpolished speaker" who was "like a kitchen-knife when whetted on a brick, he cuts roughly, but cuts deep." Randolph's remark earned Hardin the nickname "Old Kitchen Knife." He served eight years in the Kentucky legislature, five intermittent terms in the U.S. House of Representatives, 1815–1837, and as Kentucky's secretary of state, 1844–1847. He married Elizabeth Pendleton Barbour in 1807.

   Martin D. Hardin (1780–1823) was the son of Clark's old commander and associate Gen. John Hardin. He was a successful attorney and state legislator and official. He practiced in Richmond, Kentucky, and Frankfort. He was in Louisville periodically, and it is possible that Clark is referring to him. (*KE*, 403–4; Capps, 73:359.)

4. Jackson prints the letters and documents regarding Lewis's financial Waterloo. The letter from Eustis to Lewis of 15 July 1809 and Lewis's response of 18 August 1809 are of particular interest. While no specific mention is made of the protested voucher for the printing of the laws of the territory, a list of protested drafts compiled in 1811 lists an amount of $1,410.75 due Joseph Charless, the territory's printer. Clark's deep concern is obvious in the statement he leaves hanging about if "they Serve" him in that way. (Jackson (1), 2:446–65, 730.)

5. Clark seems to contradict himself by writing that York is a "gadd fellow," while just a month earlier he had reported that he was the "finest negrow" he'd ever had. (Gad is a mild oath.) Apparently, York would improve his behavior after being punished but as time passed would again become "insolent and Sulky." York's service as a hand on a boat (for which he had plenty of experience) to what was then Wheeling, Virginia, on the Ohio, demonstrates that despite their problems, Clark apparently still had a degree of confidence in York's abilities and was not worried that he would run away. Of course, a strong incentive for York not to run away was his wife and family in Louisville. Despite Clark's stated intention to sell or hire him in Louisville, something York himself had requested, York apparently was willing to take his chances in hope of remaining in the Louisville area. Clark never sold York but did hire him out, including to a drayage business he was partners in with his nephew John H. Clark. The letters to Jonathan in this group continue for another two years, but this is the last one mentioning York. Either Clark washed his hands of him as far as discussing him in letters to Jonathan, or subsequent letters mentioning him are unlocated. Also, with York now being in Louisville, Clark would (and did) receive reports concerning him, but not necessarily have much to write himself. York is mentioned in other sources as late as November 1815. (John Hite Clark Papers, fl. 36a, TFHS; Holmberg (2), 6–9; Betts 163–67.)

6. There is some confusion as to when Meriwether Lewis left St. Louis for the East. Clark clearly states it was 25 August. However, Frederick Bates stated that it was 4 September. The difference of ten days is significant because it would indicate a much longer travel time, with unexplained delays, from St. Louis to Chickasaw Bluffs, where he arrived 15 September, and thus indicate the kinds of difficulties and illness mentioned by Lewis and Russell. Clark's comment regarding Lewis going to Philadelphia to "write our Book" indicates that he was aware by this time of his friend's failure to accomplish much, if anything, concerning their expedition book. It is not known if he expected Lewis to be absent from St. Louis until that was accomplished, which would have to be

sometime in 1810 at the earliest. (Jackson (1), 2:464–68, 573–75; Marshall, 2:86–87.)

7. This is a very important passage concerning Lewis's state of mind at this time. For Clark to be so obviously concerned about his friend's distress and relay it to Jonathan indicates the extent of his worry for him and the degree to which Lewis's mind was unsettled.

8. Alexander Stuart (1770–1832 or 1833), a native of Virginia, was a lawyer and practiced in Kaskaskia as early as 1807. He settled in St. Louis about 1808. In 1809 he was appointed a judge for the newly created Illinois Territory, and served in that position from 1810 to 1813. He served as judge of the St. Louis Circuit Court from 1823 to 1826. He died while on a visit to Virginia. Lewis owed him $750 at the time of his death. (Houck, 3:10–11; Billon, 244–45; Jackson (1), 2:729; *Louisiana Gazette,* 15 February 1810.)

9. William C. Carr (1783–1851) was a native of Albemarle County, Virginia. His father Walter Carr was a friend of Thomas Jefferson. William was educated and studied law in Virginia, and in March 1804 moved to Louisiana Territory. After a brief stay in St. Louis, he moved to Ste. Genevieve, where he remained a year and then settled permanently in St. Louis. He was a successful attorney and prominent citizen. In 1805 he was appointed U.S. land agent in St. Louis, and became involved in a dispute with James Wilkinson regarding lead mines in the area. In 1817 he was appointed a trustee of St. Louis's first public school system, and in 1826 was named Alexander Stuart's successor as judge of the St. Louis Circuit Court, a position he held for eight years. He married first Anna Marie Elliott (ca. 1788–1826), daughter of Dr. Aaron Elliott, in Ste. Genevieve in 1807, and after her death he married Dorcas Bent, a daughter of Silas Bent, in 1829. (Houck, 3:14–15; Billon, 201–2.)

10. This entire section of the letter, from the parenthesis after "Book" (note 6) to "wrong" has been crossed out with three large Xs, but is completely legible. The rest of the comment undoubtedly was also intended to be marked out, but it was on the next page and apparently overlooked. The color of the ink marking out this passage is slightly different from the color Clark used to write the letter, and it is not known whether William, Jonathan, or someone else crossed it out. If Clark marked it out he apparently did so for added emphasis as to its sensitive nature or had second thoughts about putting it in the letter. If the latter is true, he either did not really try or want to obliterate the passage or did not want to discard this letter and write another. I interpret the lined gaps in the phrase "his property in this Country will _

pay his — by a Considerable amount," to mean his property will not pay his debts by a considerable amount. The fact that Lewis turned his property over to friends and agents in this manner is rather irregular and certainly can be seen as an indication that he did not intend to return to St. Louis. Such an intent can be interpreted several ways: One, he wanted to settle the debts he could to defend his honor and prove his good intentions and honesty. Two, he undoubtedly had heard the rumblings about him not being reappointed governor and thought he would not be returning for some time, if at all, because of his removal from office and his working on the book. Three, he was in such a distressed mental state that he already was thinking dark thoughts of suicide and wanted to begin settling his affairs. All three of these scenarios are speculation on my part, and may or may not reflect Lewis's reason.

11. George Hancock (1798–1875), a native of Botetourt County, Virginia, graduated from Yale in 1818, served one term in the Virginia legislature, and then moved to Jefferson County, Kentucky. He apparently served in the military (most likely the Kentucky militia), rising to the rank of colonel, but his major occupation was farming. He believed in agricultural improvement and was a founder of the Jefferson County Agricultural and Mechanical Association in 1852. He married Clark's niece Eliza Croghan (1801–1833) at Locust Grove in September 1819. Following her death he married Mary Holliday Davidson in Alexandria, Louisiana, in December 1834. Mary Davidson's younger sister Julia married Meriwether Lewis Clark in 1865. Hancock died at his estate Glencony in Jefferson County, and is buried in Cave Hill Cemetery. (Rogers Index; MLClark, 40–41; Johnston, 1:391–92.)

~

Saint Louis Septr. 16th 1809.

Dear Brother

    It is a long time Sence I heard fron you; bro Edmund favers us with letters which is all the letters we receve from our friends about you. I intended to write you a long letter at this time but realy I have not as much time, three or four persons are now waiting to do business. I have a great deel to Say to you and much of what I have to Say is diverting and ought not to be Commited to paper.[1]

  I am about Shipping the last of the public Pelteries and Closeing my businss to this time. Indian Department must be left with Mr. Bates, I Shall pay up to the date all public Demands.

The present Secretary of W.[ar][2] has thrown all the Indian department on me, derected me to Displace Several agents Interpretrs Smiths
&c. &c. which is a little disagreeable, as those appointments were made
by my friend[3] and not by me _ no more on this Subject untill I See you _
we Shall Set out about Thursday next[4] and go by Russles ville, all of our
furnitur is moved to our own house except a Bed & a fiew Chears & my
writing Desk.

a man is to be hanged to day fer murder, and the Town is full of people[5]
Julia joins me in love to yourself Sister nancy and family

Yr. Affectinate

Wm Clark

1. This is one of several instances in which Clark mentions people or
events which he wants to tell Jonathan about, but thinks it better to do
so in person rather than in writing—unfortunately for present readers.
If Clark had committed the news and observations to paper, even more
information would have been revealed about the man, his contemporaries, and their times.
2. William Eustis (1753–1825) was a native of Massachusetts. He graduated from Harvard in 1772, studied medicine under Dr. Joseph War-
ren, and served during the American Revolution as a surgeon. After the
war he resumed his medical practice in Boston but gradually gravitated
to politics. He served in the state legislature, 1788–1794, and the U.S.
House of Representatives, 1801–1805 and 1820–1823. A longtime supporter of Republican politics, he was appointed by James Madison to
be secretary of war in 1809, succeeding Henry Dearborn. He attempted
to prepare the army for the War of 1812, but made little progress, and
resigned in December 1812 under criticism. He served as minister to
Holland, 1814–1818, and governor of Massachusetts, 1823–1825, dying in office. He married Caroline Langdon in 1810. (*DAB*, 6:193–94.)
3. Governor Meriwether Lewis. Eustis, in a letter dated 7 August 1809,
had complained that Indian Department positions for Louisiana had
been filled with neither War Department approval nor appropriated
funds, and he directed Clark to dismiss a number of employees (including expedition veteran Alexander H. Willard—one of the mentioned
blacksmiths). He also announced that George Shannon's disability pension should not be paid from Indian Department funds. It is understandable why Clark found such instructions distasteful. (Loos, 878–84.)
4. William and Julia Clark and their party did indeed leave St. Louis the
following Thursday, 21 September. Known members of the immediate

party, in addition to them, were M. Lewis Clark and two slaves named Scott and Chloe (or Cloe). M. Lewis Clark in his genealogical record states that Chloe was born an African princess, married Mark Wideman, and had at least three children (a girl named Berry and two boys, Alexander and Anthony). Wideman may have been a second husband, which means that Scott may have been her first husband. Chloe (and possibly Scott) may have had a child named Rachiel (Rachel), who drowned on the return trip (see letter dated 3 July 1810, note 6). Chloe was inherited by M. Lewis Clark by terms of his father's will. She died in St. Louis in 1849. (Jackson (3), 13; William Clark Memorandum Book, 1809; MLClark, 90, 96.)

5. John Long, Jr., or the younger, was hanged in St. Louis on 16 September for the murder of George Gordon. The 16th was a Saturday, the preferred day of the week for a public hanging. It was a social event, often taking on a festive air, with whole families attending and picnicking. In the 6 September edition of the *Missouri Gazette* Long published a letter unsuccessfully pleading for mercy and bemoaning how his death would affect his wife and two small children. The 20 September 1809 edition of the *Missouri Gazette* reported the execution. The condemned was reported to pray and sing hymns fervently on the way to the gallows and ask Jesus to have mercy on him. His hands were tied behind him and he accepted a cap (hood). When he mounted the chair in the cart under the gallows he did not wait for the cart to pull away. Instead he kicked the chair out from under himself and "launched into eternity." His estate, which included three slaves, was being settled by Gabriel Long in March 1811. (*Missouri Gazette*, 6, 20 September 1809; *Louisiana Gazette*, 7 February 1811, 14 March 1811.)

∼

Mr. Shanons[1]   Octr. 28th 1809

Dear Brother

I proceded on verry well to Mr. Smiths[2] and arrived there about an hour after dusk, and this day have Come on verry well to this place – The man boy is not well, tho' not wors than he was when you parted with us[3] –

when at Shelbyville[4] to day I Saw in a Frankfort[5] paper called the Arguss[6] a report published which givs me much Concern, it Says that Govr. Lewis killed himself by Cutting his Throat with a Knife, on his way between the Chickaw Saw Bluffs[7] and nashville,[8] I fear this

Letter dated 28 October 1809 from William Clark to Jonathan on the day he learned that Meriwether Lewis might have killed himself. Clark himself was traveling eastward to visit family and settle government business when he read the report in a Kentucky newspaper. Courtesy of The Filson Historical Society

report has too much truth, tho' hope it may have no foundation— my reasons for thinking it possible is founded on the letter which I recved from him at your house, in that letter he Says he had Some intintion of going thro' by land ∧ & his only objection was his papers[9][∧] The Boats I Sent down with the pelteres [peltries], under the derections of Mr. James McFarlane[10] must have over taken the Govr. between new madrid[11] and the Chickasaw Bluffs, and if he was Still dis posed to go through, I is it not probable that he might have intrusted his papers to McFarlane who is a pertcular friend of his and on his way to the City of Washington? and Set out from the Bluffs with a view to pass thro' the most derect rout, which is by nashville _ I fear O! I fear the waight of his mind has over come him, what will be the Consequence?[12] what will become of ~~my~~ [∧]his[∧] paprs? I must write to Genl. Robinson[13] or Some friend about nashville to enquire about him, and Collect and Send me his papers, if he had any with him _ I am quit[e] distressed about this report.

I have left all my letters which I receved from defferent persons at your house' or lost them, they are not with my baggage. will you be So good as to examine and enquire for them, and if you get them Send ~~me~~ them to me by John,[14] or John Croghan.[15] I have also missed my ∧ Corduroy [∧] bag of Small money of forty odd Dollars, I thought I had put the bag in my paper trunk, but I may have placed the bag with the papers in Some Draw[er] or place intending to put them up & for got them— The last recollection I have of the Bag is when I put it in my paper trunk in the little room before I went to Brackfast, leaving it open for Julia to fill with Some of her ~~thin~~ Clothes. She does not not recollect Seeing the bag in the Trunk when She put in her Clothes and locked the Trunk.

I am Sorry to [∧]tell[∧] you that I am not only forgetfull but neglectful & inattentive, I hope you will excuse me, and parden this hasty Scraul which is written in a room Crouded with different descriptions of people. Some drunk[16]_

Julia joins me in Love to you Sister nancy and belev yrs to affly. [be]

yr Frend & Bro

Wm Clark

Note: This letter was known to exist only in typescript until 11 September 1998. Even after the initial cache of William Clark letters was found in 1988 and presented to The Filson Historical Society and made public in 1990, this and several other letters remained undetected in the large collection of Bodley family papers in the possession of the family. That collection was given to the Filson in 1998 and preprocessed immediately because it was believed that more Clark letters might be among the papers. Of particular interest was this letter. The original typescript is at The Filson Historical Society in the Temple Bodley Collection. Bodley hired Minnie Cook of Milwaukee and Madison, Wisconsin, to type historical letters and documents he collected regarding his research. This letter is part of that group. The source, or repository, of the originals is noted, and for this letter the source is given as the "Bodley Papers." Therefore, the original or a copy of it was in Temple Bodley's possession. The typescript carries the corrections in pencil that Bodley made in proofing it. Obviously he must have had the original to compare the copy with. The typescript follows perfectly in both style (with some probable differences in punctuation), creative spelling, and the facts about William Clark's trip eastward, and I had no doubt that it was a copy of the actual letter Clark wrote to Jonathan. But where was the original? Apparently what happened was that it was separated from the rest of the Clark letters in the trunk (possibly when Bodley had it copied) and, therefore, was not found with them. Although I believed the typescript to be a true copy of a William Clark letter, this was not absolutely certain. Now, with yet another emergence of several Clark letters from that trunk, there is no doubt.

1. The place where Clark wrote this letter has consistently been misidentified. Past and present writers have stated that Clark was staying with George Shannon, but this is incorrect. George Shannon was attending Transylvania University in Lexington and was not living some thirty miles to the west in the vicinity of Graefenburg. I believe Mr. Shannon was John Shannon of Shelby County. He lived near present Peytona about three miles west of Graefenburg on the waters of Tick Creek and had a tavern license. Peytona is about ten miles west of Frankfort and nine miles east of Shelbyville. The route and distances normally traveled made Shannon's tavern a frequent stop for dinner, refreshment, or lodging. Jonathan's diary records stops at Shannon's when he traveled through the area. The Clarks had known the Shannon family for over twenty years. In addition, Clark's note that his party made sixteen miles from Smith's to Shannon's corresponds perfectly with the approximate distance between Smith's tavern (see note 2) near Simpsonville and Shannon's tavern in the vicinity of Peytona. In listing his expenses for the trip, Clark noted that he paid $3.25 at "Mr. Shannons." An additional bit of evidence that these are two different Shannons is that he lists paying "Shannon," meaning George Shannon, $40 when in Lexington on 30 October. Clark's route eastward from Middletown to southeast of Frankfort followed the present US 60. Not far outside Frank-

fort he left the Versailles Road (U.S. 60) and took the Frankfort Pike (now the Old Frankfort Pike, present Kentucky 1681). The party spent the night of 29 October at William Dailey's (also Daily/Daly and Clark's Daley) tavern at present Nugent's Crossroads. The little town was known as Leesburg in the 1800s. The Offutt-Cole Tavern, as Dailey's inn later became known, still stands today. (Shelby Co., Ky., Tax List, 1807–1809; Jonathan Clark Diary, 23 November 1802, 16 February 1807; William Clark Memorandum Book, 28–29 October 1809; Munson and Parrish, 44–46.)

2. This most likely is George Smith, a tavern owner who owned property east of Simpsonville and also had a lot in the town. Jonathan also records stopping at Smith's in his diary. (Shelby Co., Ky., Tax List, 1808–1809; Jonathan Clark Diary, 15 February 1807.)

3. "Man boy" refers to nine-month-old M. Lewis Clark. Jonathan had accompanied William and family to Richard C. Anderson's, where they spent the night of 26 October. (Jonathan Clark Diary, 26 October 1809.)

4. Shelbyville is the county seat of Shelby County. It was officially established in 1792 when William Shannon donated land for the courthouse. It is located between Louisville and Frankfort. Clark and his party made a stop in Shelbyville on 28 October. Although he does not record incurring any expenses there (perhaps they dined with a friend), the stop was long enough for Clark to glance through a copy of the *Argus*. (*KE*, 817; William Clark Memorandum Book.)

5. Frankfort was founded in 1786 on the Kentucky River by the infamous James Wilkinson. It pledged the largest contribution for the construction of a statehouse when Kentucky became a state in 1792, and it was consequently selected as the state capital. In 1800 it was Kentucky's second largest town, with 628 residents. (*KE*, 352.)

6. The *Argus of Western America* was established in Frankfort in 1806 and published until 1838. For twenty-five years it was one of Kentucky's most influential papers, particularly under the editorship of Amos Kendall (1816–1829). (*KE*, 31.)

7. The site of present Memphis, Tennessee, Chickasaw Bluffs was where Fort Pickering was located. The fort was actually located in Chickasaw Indian country at the southern end of the Fourth Chickasaw Bluff, which was two miles long and rose sixty feet above the river. Fortescue Cuming described the fort as a "small stoccado" with a stair of 120 cut logs leading up to it from the landing. It was the major American post on the Mississippi in that area. Lewis had commanded a troop of infantry at the post in the late 1790s, and William Clark had negotiated with the Chickasaw Indians at the Bluffs in the mid-1790s. Memphis would be

founded ten years later, in 1819, by Andrew Jackson and John Overton (see letter dated 30 October 1809, note 2) and named after Memphis, Egypt, because of the Nile-like appearance of the Mississippi
there. (*DAB*, 14:115; Thwaites (2), 292–95.)

8. Nashville was the major town in central and western Tennessee in
1809 and was considered to be the northern terminus of the Natchez
Trace. It officially was founded 1 January 1780 by James Robertson
(see note 13) and a party of settlers on the Cumberland River. Robertson and a party had planted a crop of corn there in the spring of 1779.
It had earlier been the site of a French trading post. Originally christened Nashborough (it soon became Nashville), it was named for Gen.
Francis Nash, a North Carolina Revolutionary War hero. In 1807 it
replaced Knoxville as Tennessee's capital. (Burt, 145–46.)

9. The letter Clark refers to has not been located, and may no longer exist. Apparently it revealed a great deal concerning Lewis's mental state
in the last weeks of his life, and was one of the major reasons Clark immediately believed the report that his friend had killed himself. One
wonders if the letter revealed so much of Lewis's troubled mental state
that Clark may have even destroyed it to protect his friend. Another
possibility is that the letter was destroyed in the Minoma "junk" fire
previously described (see letter dated 2 September 1792, note 18). The
papers Lewis had with him and wanted to protect were his financial
papers needed for his defense of his expenses and, most important, the
journals and associated papers of the expedition.

10. James McFarlane (also appears as McFarland) lived on a farm on the
Monongahela River about fifteen miles south of Pittsburgh. His father
was James McFarlane, a Revolutionary War veteran, ferry operator,
and a leader of the 1794 Whiskey Rebellion. The younger McFarlane
and his brother John had moved to the St. Louis area by 1807. (There
also was a Lewis McFarlane involved with the saltpeter cave exploration who probably was a brother or relative.) There he became involved in the Indian trade along the Mississippi and Missouri and
worked for Lewis concerning Indian matters and the exploration of
saltpeter caves. He had a claim against Lewis's estate for $718.45,
which with interest of $56.25 totaled $814.90. The arithmetic does not
balance, and possibly another claim was not recorded. William Meriwether complained to William Clark in a letter dated 22 January 1810
that McFarlane already had "duned" him for Lewis's bond of $780 plus
an additional amount of $25.50. That apparently was incorrect be-
cause the $718.45 and $814.90 amounts are recorded in 1812 regarding the settlement of Lewis's estate. A letter to Frederick Bates in 1809
reported that McFarlane was uncouth, undisciplined, and sometimes

cruel, and that he had "produced universal terror" in Arkansas (where Lewis had sent him to council with the Osage). (Colter-Frick, 348, 454–55, 475–77; Jackson (1), 2:471, 490, 729; Marshall, 2:54–59.)

11. New Madrid, located on the western bank of the Mississippi River some 250 miles downriver from St. Louis and some 70 miles downstream from the confluence of the Mississippi and Ohio, was known by the French as L'Anse à la Graisse, meaning "cove of fat" or "cove of grease." There was a large Delaware Indian village in the area when French-Canadian fur trappers and traders François and Joseph LeSieur established a trading post there in the 1780s. In 1789 the Revolutionary War veteran, former Indian agent, and land speculator Col. George Morgan of New Jersey arrived, and he chose the site for what he hoped would be a major city. He named his town New Madrid in honor of the capital of Spain and began promoting it. His grand plans were frustrated by Spanish governor Don Estevan Miró, who, apparently influenced by James Wilkinson, limited Morgan's power and opportunities. Morgan returned to New Jersey in disgust, but his town survived and grew, the first American town in Missouri. Its population primarily was French and American. It soon became the most important river landing and town on the Mississippi between the Ohio River and Natchez. Henry M. Brackenridge's *Sketches of the Territory of Louisiana* (published in book form as *Views of Louisiana*) was serialized in the *Gazette* beginning in January 1811. The 21 March 1811 edition of the paper carried his description of New Madrid, which would accurately reflect the town and its situation at the time Clark wrote these letters. Brackenridge stated the town had about 400 inhabitants, one-third of them Americans, and while it was "low" at present it was expected to "improve greatly." He noted that its position on a half-moon bend of the river caused serious erosion, which in the last fifteen years had claimed 300 yards of land, three forts, and a number of large and spacious streets. The New Madrid earthquakes of 1811–1812, floods, and falling river banks destroyed the original town, the one Lewis visited, and it was relocated nearby. (Bagnall, 5–20; *Louisiana Gazette,* 21 March 1811.)

12. This is the strongest known statement that William Clark ever made that he believed Meriwether Lewis committed suicide. The news understandably was a great shock to him and very distressing, as this and the next several letters clearly demonstrate. No evidence has come to light revealing the specifics of what he said to the Lewis family, Thomas Jefferson, the Clark family, and others concerning the death of his friend. It is known that the subject was discussed, but what was said is not known. The subject was very painful for Clark, and after the initial

shock passed and several months had gone by, he apparently rarely, if ever, spoke of it. However, Clark's immediate reaction that his friend was capable of suicide, and may indeed have killed himself, is telling and lends strong support to the belief that Lewis's death was self-inflicted and not the result of murder. If William Clark—Lewis's comrade, best friend, and staunchest defender—had believed for one moment that foul play was involved in Lewis's death, he most certainly would have demanded that it be investigated. I also believe that he would have expressed such concerns to Jonathan.

13. Clark writes Robinson, but apparently means Robertson. James Robertson (1742–1814), a native of Brunswick County, Virginia, was raised in Wake County, North Carolina, settled on the Watauga River in 1771, and served as an agent for the Cherokee and in the militia. He was the leader of the party that founded Nashville in 1780, and he served as a Tennessee leader and military officer for the rest of his life. He died at Chickasaw Bluffs while serving as Indian agent to the Chickasaw. (*DAB*, 16:24–25.)

14. John Hite Clark was traveling eastward, most likely to Baltimore, to acquire supplies for his and Edmund Clark's store.

15. John Croghan (1790–1849) was the son of William and Lucy Clark Croghan. Croghan would have been heading east to attend school. He graduated from William and Mary and then attended the University of Pennsylvania medical school, graduating in 1813. He practiced medicine briefly but then turned his attention to farming at Locust Grove and to business, sometimes combining the latter with medical enterprises. In 1839 he purchased Mammoth Cave, developing it as a tourist attraction but also trying (unsuccessfully) to treat tubercular patients in its cool, damp interior. He was also one of the first to discover oil in the United States, striking it in 1829 while drilling for salt along the Cumberland River. (*KE*, 242.)

16. An additional strong piece of evidence that Clark and his party were in a tavern rather than a private home is this last line of his letter, which is rarely quoted. It is not likely that Clark would have described a stay in George Shannon's, or someone else's, private home as being in a "room Crouded with different descriptions of people. Some drunk _"

~

Lexington Octr. 30th. 1809

Dear Brother

We arrived here this evening all in the Same State of health we were when we parted with you, but not in the Same State of mind, I have herd of the Certainty of the death of Govr. Lewis which givs us much uneasiness.[1] I have wrote to judge Overton[2] of Nashville about his papers, _ [I] have Some expectation of their falling into the Care of the Indian agent[3] who is Said to have Come on imediately after his death &c. _ I wish much to get the letter I receved of Govr. Lewis from N. madrid, which you Saw it will be of great Service to me. prey Send it to Fincastle as Soon as possible, I wish I had Some conversation with you about our Book. [and] the plans of [the] Govr.[4] write me to fincastle if you please.

we Shall Set out at Sun rise tomorrow and proced on Slowly _

our love to Sister & nany &

acup [it for] yor Self [also]

Wm Clark

Julia requst John to bring on 12 pockons[5] for her & more if Convenent.

1. Clark recorded in his journal/memorandum book on 29 October that Mr. Fitzhugh (probably his brother-in-law Dennis Fitzhugh) told him of the death of Lewis. They met Fitzhugh on the road west of Frankfort, Kentucky. He probably meant that Fitzhugh confirmed Lewis's death, since Clark already had read the *Argus* report of it. Also, by the night of 30 October, he may well have read additional reports confirming it. (William Clark Memorandum Book, 1809.)
2. John Overton (1766–1833) was a native of Louisa County, Virginia. He taught school in Virginia for several years and in 1787 moved to Mercer County, Kentucky, where he studied law for two years. In 1789 he moved to Nashville, where he met and became friends with Andrew Jackson, with whom he established a successful law practice. He and Jackson also were partners in successful business ventures, particularly concerning land. In 1794 they purchased the tract that included part of the Chickasaw Bluffs and in 1819 founded Memphis. Overton was a political promoter, supporter, and adviser for Jackson until his death. In 1804 he replaced Jackson as judge of the superior court of Tennessee,

serving until 1810. He served as a judge of the Tennessee state supreme court from 1811 to 1816. Given his position and influence, it is under-standable that Clark would write to him about Lewis's papers. (*DAB*, 14:115–16.)

3. James Neelly served as the Chickasaw agent from July 1809 to June 1812. He probably is the James Neelly who served as a cavalry officer in the Tennessee militia under Andrew Jackson in the War of 1812. His militia service must have been of some duration, because he was already known by the title of Major in 1809. Murder and conspiracy theorists often impugn Neelly's character and motives, and suggest—even claim—that he played a sinister role in Lewis's death. This is very un-likely. There were a number of Neellys living in the vicinity south of Nashville. It is quite possible that James Neelly had family there and was simply traveling from the Chickasaw country to the Nashville area for a visit and to possibly take care of some business. (Jackson (1), 2: 468; Sistler, 268.)

4. The publication of the expedition journals and Lewis's plans regarding them obviously weighed heavily on Clark's mind. With his partner in the enterprise dead, he immediately knew that the responsibility of their publication lay with him. In his typically practical, tackle-the-problem approach, he set about achieving the task within months.

5. "Pockons" are most likely puccoons, any of several species of North American herbs in the borage family, which could be eaten, used to fla-vor beverages, and used medicinally. Julia most probably wanted the plants for medicinal purposes.

∾

Beens [Bean] Station.[1] Wednesday 8th: oct. [Nov.] 1809.
Dear Brother
We arrived here this evening much fatigued, all quit[e] as well as when we parted with you, Lewis has a verry bad Cobld which does not decrease. The leathers which Support be [the] body of our Carriage broke on the way which detained us half a day, and the rain of last Friday was So constant and Cold that we lay by at Rockastle[2] that day, which is ~~every~~ all the detention we have had — The roads are verry bad thro' the wilderness and more perticularly on the Turn pike of Clinch mountain,[3] we have been all day Comeing 16 miles, over what they Call a turnpike road, whor [for] which pleasent traveling I payed $162\frac{1}{2}$ cents — You have heard of that unfortunate end of Govr. Lewis, and probably

more than I have heard, I was in hopes of hearing more perticular[s] at this place, but have not — I wrote from Lexington to Wm. P. Anderson,[4] to Send the Govrs. paipers to me if they were yet in his part of the Conntry —

I am at a loss to know what to be at his death is a turble Stroke to me, in every respect. I wish I could talk a little with you just now.

John Allen[5] talked a little to me about filling his [Lewis's] place, when at Frankfort and injoined it on me to write him on the Subject which I must do tomorrow, and what must I Say? — to have a green pompous new englandr[6] imedeately over my head will not do for me — ! —.

We Shall leave this in the morning and proceed on without loss of time.

Julia joins me in love to all and beleve me to be yr. Afft. Bro

Wm Clark

1. Bean Station, Tennessee, was founded by William Bean (or Been) of Pitt-sylvania County, Virginia. Bean is credited with establishing the first permanent white settlement in Tennessee in 1769, when he and a group of settlers pushed down the Holston River. He was a member of the Committee of Thirteen of the Watauga Association and a captain in the Washington County (Virginia) militia. He spelled his name Been, but his son spelled it Bean, which has become the official spelling. (In this instance it may be that Clark actually was on the mark with his spelling.) Bean Station is on the southeastern side of Clinch Mountain, southeast of Cumberland Gap. The original site of Bean Station is under Chero-kee Lake. Clark and his party spent the night at James Kennedy's (Clark spells it Keneday and Cannaday which I assume to be Kennedy) for a cost of $3.82. (*Tennessee,* 35; Folmsbee (1), 52; William Clark Memo-randum Book, 8 November 1809.)

2. Rockcastle apparently is the Rockcastle River area north of present London, Kentucky. It was common for the area to be referred to in this manner during this period. From Lexington, Clark and party traveled to Lancaster, Stanford, Crab Orchard, and on to Rockcastle. One of the carriage leathers broke in the vicinity of Lancaster on 1 November. His memorandum book entries indicate they may have stayed at or near present Mount Vernon, Kentucky. They lodged with a Mr. Faris. There is a Fariston south of London, but that would seem to be farther than they could have traveled in two days from Crab Orchard over bad roads in poor weather. (William Clark Memorandum Book, 1–3 November 1809.)

3. Clinch Mountain is part of the Appalachian range, running from south-

western Virginia in a southwesterly direction into northeastern Tennessee. Like many of the "mountains" in this region, it is not particularly high or wide, but it is long. The turnpike over Clinch Mountain was opened around 1785 as an alternate route of the Wilderness Road. It branched from the Holston Road at Bean Station across Clinch Mountain to the Clinch Valley, over Powell Mountain to the Powell Valley, and then to the Cumberland Gap. (Folmsbee (2), 1:371.)

4. William P. Anderson most likely is the Nashville attorney of that name. Both William P. and William Preston Anderson appear in Davidson County public records, and they may well be the same person. He was a resident of the area as early as 1798 and as late as 1811. If his middle name was Preston, interesting possibilities of a kinship relation with Clark are presented. He must be the William C. Anderson listed in Jackson. He married Nancy Bell in Davidson County in February 1800. The death of Nancy Anderson, wife of Maj. William P. Anderson, is noted in the 17 November 1809 edition of *The Democratic Clarion.* It reported that she had died about a week earlier in the twenty-fifth year of her life and left a husband and four small children. This probably is the Col. William P. Anderson (1775–1831) listed as a resident of Winchester, Tennessee, where he died. Clark was correct in thinking the papers might have been placed in Anderson's care. A memorandum of Lewis's effects made in Nashville by Thomas Freeman on 23 November states they were left in Anderson's care and lists him as one of the witnesses to the inventory. For Clark to assume that Anderson had the papers or had some control over them indicates either that he had received additional information or that Anderson was a friend of Lewis's and possibly Clark's and that he consequently may have taken custody of them. (Fischer, 4–5; Clayton, 256; Jackson (1), 2:470–73; Eddlemon, 1; *The Democratic Clarion* (Nashville), 17 November 1809.)

5. John Allen (1771–1813) was a native of Rockbridge County, Virginia, whose family migrated to Kentucky in 1779. He received a good education under James Priestly in Bardstown and studied law in Staunton, Virginia, returning to Kentucky in 1795 and establishing a successful law practice in Shelby County. In 1798 he married Jane Logan, daughter of early Kentucky leader Benjamin Logan. He served in the Kentucky House of Representatives from 1800 to 1807, and the state Senate from 1807 to 1812. He and Henry Clay had been Aaron Burr's defense attorneys in 1806. He lost the 1808 gubernatorial election to Gen. Charles Scott. He raised the first militia regiment for service in the War of 1812, serving as its colonel, and he was killed at the Battle of the River Raisin. Clark met with Allen, Governor Scott, former governor Christopher Greenup, and other acquaintances while in Frankfort. Allen's re-

mark indicates that there already was speculation about Clark's replac-
ing Lewis as governor of Louisiana Territory. (*KE,* 14–15.)

6. Secretary of War William Eustis (see letter dated 16 September 1809,
note 2). Clark's low opinion of him was shared by others, and Clark undoubtedly believed he was partly to blame for Lewis's death. Clark's
opinion apparently moderated as time passed, but by the time he accepted the governorship of Missouri Territory in 1813, Eustis had resigned under pressure as secretary of war.

∾

Colonel Hancocks November 26th 1809

Dear Brother

We arrived her on the 22nd. on a Cold and Snowey day
without any material accidents. Col. H. met us about forty miles from
this and Came down with us and on our arrival and Sence much joy have
been apperent in the Countenancs of all, Lewis is much broke out in
Sores, but Continues helthy otherwise[1]

I expect to leave this [place] for washington on Sunday morning I
have delayed this week expecting to receive Govr. Lewis papers by
Mr. Whitesids,[2] a Seneter from Tennessee, whome I am in formed by
Mr. W. P. Anderson, will take Charge of those papers for me and bring
them on __ I have just receved letters from Capt. Russell[3] who Com-
mands at the Chickasaw Bluffs that Govr. Lewis was there detain by
him 15 Days in a State of Derangement most of the time and that he had
attempted to kill himself before he got there _ [∧]his Servent[4] reports
that[∧] "on his way to nashvill, he would frequently "Conceipt[con-
ceive] that he herd me Comeing on, and Said that he was certain [I
would] over take him, that I had herd of his Situation and would Come to
his releaf" _ [∧]Capt. rusell Sais[∧] he made his will at the Bluffs and left
Wm. Merrewether[5] & myself Execeters and derected that I Should dispose of his papers &c. as I wished _ pore fellow, what a number of Con-
jecturral reports we hear mostly unfavourable to him. I have to Contre-
dict maney of them _ I do not know what I Shall do about the publication
of the Book, it will require funds which I have not at present. perhaps I
may precure them[6] _ I have just herd that one of my Bills drawn on the
Secty. of War for the quarterly pay of Docr. Robinson[7] a Sub Indian
Agent of the Osage apt. by Govr. Lewis have been <u>protested</u> for $160,

Photograph of Meriwether Lewis Clark and his six sons, ca. 1855. Named after his father's good friend Meriwether Lewis, Clark was known as Lewis and was said to bear a strong resemblance to his father. Courtesy of The Filson Historical Society

which alarms me verry much. if this Should be the Only one I Shall be easy, as I am convenced that explanation will Cause the Secty. to pay this Bill which was drawn previous to the late arrangemt. made by the Secty. in respect to those appts. __

Maj. Preston Doct. Floyd[8] and maney others in this quarter have got the Louisiana fever verry hot and will vesit that Country next Spring _

Crops are fine about here but below the Blue ridge I am told are very bad _ I hope to See John [Hite Clark] this week before I Set out, as he had expectations of getting here about this time ___ The Small Change [purse] which I thought had been left at your house was found Since we Came here among our Clothes _

Julia joins me in love to yourself Sister nancy Bro Edmund & Isaac, acupt of our preyer for the helth and hapiness of you all

Yr

Wm Clark

1. This might be an indication that M. Lewis Clark had been inoculated against smallpox and was suffering from the mild outbreak of the virus generally associated with such vaccinations (but see letter dated 28 May 1809, note 4). If the sores were not related to vaccination, perhaps they were caused by the chicken pox or other malady.

2. Jenkin Whiteside (1772–1822) was a native of Lancaster, Pennsylvania. He was educated and admitted to the bar in Pennsylvania but soon thereafter moved to Knoxville, Tennessee. He was elected to the U.S. Senate in 1809 to fill a vacancy, was reelected that same year, and served until October 1811, when he resigned. He relocated to Nashville and was recognized as an expert on land law. He never married. (*BDAC*, 2006; Clayton, 99–100.)

3. Gilbert Christian Russell was the commander at Fort Pickering at Chickasaw Bluffs and detained Lewis there when he arrived in mid-September 1809 in a "deranged" mental state. As with many military men of the day, not much apparently is known of Russell. Heitman lists him as being from Tennessee. He was commissioned an ensign in the Second Infantry in November 1803 and for that time gained rapid promotion, rising to major by May 1809 and ultimately to colonel during the War of 1812. In mid-1813 Russell was in New Orleans. He was honorably discharged in June 1815, apparently a result of the army being reduced following the war and possibly also of ill health. Russell's statements concerning Lewis's behavior during his last days are among the most detailed and crucial. Prior to the emergence of this letter, the known statements Russell made regarding Lewis's death were in two letters to Thomas Jefferson, dated 4 and 31 January 1810, and a written statement dated 26 November 1811 made for an unstated reason, though possibly in regard to army records or the publication of the journals. Proponents of the murder theory have criticized Russell and questioned his motives and the validity of his statements, often citing the de-

lay of a written statement until late 1811. However, the letters he wrote to Jefferson in January 1810, and this previously unknown letter of William Clark's, provide detailed information soon after Lewis's death that is consistent with his 1811 statement. Some murder supporters have gone so far as to theorize that Russell was somehow involved in the murder, served Lewis poorly, and was trying to gain something by his death. The facts simply do not bear this out. (Heitman (2), 1:853; Jackson (1), 2:573–75, 728, 732, 748.)

4. John Pernier was a free mulatto serving as Lewis's servant. He was with Lewis when the governor died and provided crucial information regarding his death. Murder theorists often include Pernier as the possible murderer or accuse him of withholding important information. The most cited source for this belief is William Clark Kennerly's memoir *Persimmon Hill,* in which he states that the family believed Pernier had killed Lewis and robbed him and that this was borne out years later when Lewis's sister and brother-in-law encountered Pernier in Mobile, Alabama, wearing Lewis's watch. *Persimmon Hill* is fraught with inaccuracies, and this is one of them. Lewis's watch was not stolen. It was listed by Thomas Freeman in the memorandum of Lewis's effects and is mentioned in letters of James Neelly, Isaac Coles, and William Meriwether. The details of Lewis's behavior in his last days as reported by Pernier apparently came to Clark in a letter from someone in Nashville, possibly William Anderson, who is known to have written him. Pernier continued eastward and was interviewed by Jefferson at Monticello in November; in fact he was with Jefferson at Monticello the day Clark wrote this letter to Jonathan. The information that Clark relates to his brother about Lewis's mental state during the last weeks of his life supports his mental collapse and likelihood of committing suicide.

The story Pernier told of Lewis hallucinating that Clark was coming to his rescue had never before been reported. In all fairness to Lewis, such hallucinations may have been caused by a spell of malaria with its fever and resultant effects. The *Missouri Gazette* reported that Lewis had been ill at New Madrid and Chickasaw Bluffs and that while on his way to Nashville was stricken with "extreme mental debility," and shot himself in the head and chest with a brace of pistols. The paper's conclusion: "The governor has been of late very much afflicted with fever, which never failed of depriving him of his reason, to this cause we may ascribe the fatal catastrophe!" The Nashville *Democratic Clarion* carried the first printed account of Lewis's death. Dated 20 October 1809, it reported that Lewis had shot himself twice and cut himself with a razor on the neck, arm, and ham; that he had been "under the influence of a deranging malady for about six weeks" the cause of which was unknown, unless it was the protested draft on the war department. An epidemiologist claims that mental and physical illness caused by *neurosyphilis paresis* was the major cause of Lewis's committing suicide. He even goes so far as to name the likely date on which he believes Lewis contracted syphilis (13–14 August 1805 from a Shoshone woman). This theory is not generally accepted. The more accepted belief is that Lewis suffered from manic-depressive (or bipolar) disorder and that this together with his financial, political, romantic, medical, alcohol, and expedition book difficulties combined to result in his killing himself. (Jackson (1), 2:468, 471, 475–76, 487–88; *Missouri Gazette,* 4 October 1809, 2 November 1809; *The Democratic Clarion,* 20 October 1809; Ravenholt, 372, 377–78.)

5. William Douglas Meriwether (1761–1845), a native of Albemarle County, Virginia, was the son of Nicholas and Margaret Douglas Meriwether of Cloverfields, near Charlottesville. He was a cousin of Lucy Meriwether Lewis Marks, and after the death of her second husband he served as a guardian for her children, including Meriwether Lewis. He was a state representative in the Virginia legislature from Albemarle County from 1809 to 1810, and was in Richmond at this time attending the legislature. He did serve as an executor for Lewis's estate and received two trunks containing his personal effects while in Richmond. These he carried home to Albemarle County for the family. He also received various papers and accounts of Lewis's that had been sent to the government, which were forwarded by Isaac Coles. (Anderson, 115–16, 153; Jackson (1), 2:472–74, 490.)

6. The conjectural reports unfavorable to Lewis that Clark believed he must contradict concerned charges of dishonesty, malfeasance, etc.— not the report that Lewis had committed suicide, which he did believe. Clark initially investigated whether the government would pay for the publication of the journals, but upon the rejection of that possibility he returned to Lewis's original plan of paying for it privately and recouping his investment through sales of the book.

7. Dr. John Hamilton Robinson (1782–1819) was a native of Augusta County, Virginia, and nephew of Alexander Hamilton. He settled in St. Louis by mid-1805, served as the surgeon at Cantonment Belle Fontaine, and was a member of Zebulon Pike's southwestern expedition. After his return he served as an Indian agent and merchant at Fort Osage. Robinson went back to Mexico by 1814 and rose to the rank of general in Mexico's revolutionary forces, but he returned to the United States in 1817 before independence from Spain was achieved. He married Sophie Marie Michau (ca. 1786–1848) in St. Louis in December 1805. He died of yellow fever in Washington, Mississippi, in 1819. His

father David and two brothers also were on the frontier. A David Robinson reported on an herb to cure snake bite in the 30 August 1809 issue of the *Missouri Gazette*. The herb was sinakle and may be the root and plant that Clark reported cured the bite of a mad dog and rattlesnake in his April 1805 letter to Jonathan from Fort Mandan. (Jackson (4), 1:290n, 2:192–93, 206n, 382–87, 392–93; Billon, 191–92; Colter-Frick, 419–32; Jackson (1), 1:258.)

8. Dr. John Floyd (1783–1837), a native of Jefferson County, Kentucky, was the youngest son of Col. John Floyd, who was killed by Indians two weeks before he was born. He and Charles Floyd were first cousins. He was educated locally and at Dickinson College in Carlisle, Pennsylvania. He graduated from the University of Pennsylvania medical school in 1806 and practiced briefly in Lexington, Virginia, but by mid-1807 had settled in Christiansburg, Virginia. He served in the militia, the state legislature, 1814–1815, the U.S. House of Representatives, 1818–1829, and as governor of Virginia, 1830–1834. He was a candidate for president in 1832, finishing a distant third. He married Letitia Preston, sister of Maj. William Preston, on 13 May 1804, in Franklin County, Kentucky. (*DAB*, 6:481–82; *BDAC*, 1167; Dorman (2), 68–69.)

~

Washington 12 Jany. 1810.

Dear Brother

I received your favor of the 11th novr. and have posponed answering it with a view to Collect Some information worth informing you of but have Collected nothing of a political nature, which you will not be as well or better informed thro' the news papers than I can relate. I recved your package with the letters I had left, but find nothing of the agreement of the Missouri Company which I fear I have lost,[1] will you ask bro Edmund if he has it, perhaps I may have left it with him.

I have receved my journals and maps but not the Botanical and Calculations or Selestial observations, expect they are in Phila: to which place I Shall Set out tomorrow, to get them and inquire what Can be done, and what has been done, I fear nothing has been done, I can find out nothing which has been done, _ I am trying if Congress will ~~not~~ print this work at their expence and allow me a part of the aprudiments [appurtenants?] &c.[2] _ no nomonation for Govr. has taken place – maney and a great maney of the ferst Standing has offerard ther Interest and expressed a wish fer me to be appointed, but I am afraid, and Cannot Consent if I was, no doubt would remain _ I do not think mySelf Calculated to meet the Storms which might be expected.[3]

I fear I cant' Suckced with Bro Georges Claim, but have flattering hopes of getting him a pention[4] _ My accounts are all Settled without much dificuelty. I find the president & Secty. of war reather favourably disposed towards me & in place of my haveing lost Confidence, I feel flattered from their attention & refurences that I am reather a faverite. I have hot [not] the good wishes of the anl. [animal?] who I treat like a puppy _ as he is.[5] I wrote to Bro Edmund Some time ago to recvee from Cozen Sam a little money and Send with an additionl. Sum to Mr. Comegys[6] at St. Lous, I hope he has Sent Some, a less amount is Sufficunt than I wished at that time, as the ballance against me is but Small and not thought of much Consequence.

There is a Bill before the house of Congs. to refit the Frigits, and another Bill to raise 20000 volunters for a Short period,[7]

and I beleve that Some arrangements will be made to meet any diffacuelties which may probably take place in the Country on our western borders, on my plan I write you in hast & in Confidenc[8]

I recved a letter from Mr. Temple he tels me that nany & Isaac is with him, _ I have not Sold my Share in the missouri Compy. as yet but am Trying

please to present me affuctinately to Sister and beleve me your Sincer Brothr

Wm Clark

Julia & the manboy was well about ten days ago

1. This most likely would have been the package of letters Clark requested Jonathan to send him while en route to Fincastle and Washington. It may be assumed that Meriwether Lewis's New Madrid letter, which Clark deemed so important concerning his state of mind and intentions, was included since he makes no mention of it. If that letter had not been in the packet it would stand to reason that he would have mentioned the fact in his letter to Jonathan. But whether or not he did receive the letter, it has since disappeared (see letter dated 28 October 1809, note 9).
2. This comment illustrates just how little Clark knew about what Lewis had done—and not done—regarding the expedition book. This and earlier comments indicate that he knew Lewis had done very little, but he may have been unaware that his friend had not written even one page

of their expedition narrative. He also could be referring only to the astronomical and other scientific data collected on the expedition. Clark was correct in thinking nothing had been done to prepare it for publication. There is some question what, if anything, Benjamin Smith Barton had at this time. Lewis and Barton had discussed Barton's preparing the botanical aspects of the expedition records for publication, but there was some disagreement between them, and little if anything had been done at the time of Lewis's death. The astronomical and other scientific findings of the journey seem to have been misplaced or lost, at least in part, by early 1810. Clark apparently did not find them in Philadelphia. He stated to Thomas Jefferson in October 1816 that those records had been lost before he assumed direct involvement in the project in the fall of 1809. We know that some of the records were extant because they have since been published, and Clark even mentions copying this information for Barton, but it seems that perhaps this information was being extracted from the journals, rather than coming from the "lost" astronomical and other scientific records. Clark's attempt to have Congress print the book failed. It was printed by Paul Allen of Philadelphia, and Clark did not reap any financial rewards from it. In fact, it was more than two years after the book's publication before he even acquired a copy. In a letter dated 3 February 1810 from Jonathan Clark to George Rogers Clark, in the Draper Manuscripts, Jonathan cites this letter of William Clark's and relays the main points to George. Historians have referred to the apparent existence of this letter and its contents citing Jonathan's letter. (Jackson (1), 2:561–62, 624; Draper Mss., 55J71.)

3. Clark's reluctance to fill the position that he believed was largely responsible for Lewis's destruction is understandable. The passage of time and Clark's own greater experience and confidence overcame such doubts by 1813 when he accepted the governorship of Missouri Territory. Benjamin Howard was nominated for governor of Louisiana instead, and Frederick Bates served as acting governor until Howard's arrival in St. Louis and at other appropriate times.

4. George Rogers Clark still hoped to receive some compensation from the government regarding his Revolutionary War debts, and his brother William and others continued their efforts on his behalf. In 1812 he began receiving an annual pension of $400 from Virginia. (Thomas (1), 52.)

5. It is unclear who Clark means. The most likely possibilities are Frederick Bates and William Simmons. Clark was not fully aware at this time of Bates's actions against him and especially against Lewis. By mid-1810, after his return to St. Louis, he learned of the extent of Bates's actions against them both and refers to him as a "little animal," comment-

ing on the matter in his 16 July 1810 letter to Jonathan. William Simmons was the accountant of the War Department and played a major role in reviewing and either approving or disapproving payment requests. He and Secretary of War Eustis had been responsible for protesting some of the bills of Lewis and Clark and were thus in part blamed by Clark for Lewis's death. Given the nature of the reference, I think that Clark means Simmons. (Jackson (1), 2:408–9, 416–17, 419, 576.)

6. John G. Comegys was a St. Louis merchant and partner in the firm of Falconer and Comegys and later of John G. Comegys & Co. The former firm also had a store in Ste. Genevieve. They did business with the Corps of Discovery on both official and personal levels. In the 21 March 1811 edition of the *Louisiana Gazette,* Comegys announces he will be leaving soon for Baltimore and requests that everyone settle their debts with him. On 20 August 1810 he purchased the 320-acre land warrant that John Colter had received as a member of the Corps of Discovery. Comegys surrendered the warrant to the land office in late 1824. (*Missouri Gazette,* 24 May 1809; Colter-Frick, 112–14.)

7. This action was in response to the threat of war with Great Britain.

8. It is not clear whether Clark meant that his plan for western defense was to be adopted or whether he was writing Jonathan in haste and confidence about his plans as discussed in this letter. The latter would appear to be his most likely meaning.

~

Fincastle [Va.] 8th [March] 1810

Dear Brother

I have not had the pleasure of hereing from you for a long time, Julia recved a letter from Nancy at Russleville by the last post which mentioned you were all in good health at the time She herd from Jefferson [County, Ky.] _ I have wrote to you Several times and related what I was about and my probable Suckcess _ I have not much reason to Conplain of my Suckcess or prospects, they are as flattering as I expected and not more So. my public accounts were all Settled _ Govr. Lewis's gave me Some trouble _ and his neglecting to write our Journal has given me a great deel of trouble and expence _ and will give me Still more[1] _ I have made a bargain with Messr. A. Conrad & Co. Booksellors[2] in Philadelphia [to] publish the work, they are to pay all the expences & to receve 20 pr.Cent _   Docr. Bartin[3] will write the Scientific part, and I expect to get a Mr. Biddle[4] to write the naritiv _ The map I Shall improv on my Self

_ I am not very well (have rhumitism in my Sholdrs) but am Continualy employed writing from the Books Such parts as are intended for the natural history part for Dr. Bartin to Compile from.

On my way from Washington I passed thro' Fred.bg. Thos. Rogrs Saml. Reds Mr. minors, Sun in Law to Mr. Hurndon Mr. Jeffersons by the friends of the late Govr. Lewis[5] _ Mr. Rogers is about to Set out to Kentucky, Mr. Hurndon is in the old way _ Dick Tompkins wishes to Send one of his Sons by me to Louisiana _ Bennet does not appear to have made much, Sam Red is thriveing. Jo Pollard & Dick Tompkins wishes to go to Louisiana[6] Jo. wants an apt. as his property has failed him &c. his purchase of the old mill lost him $500 10 negrows & ₍ₐ₎his half of[ₐ] the mill which was Sold laterly. I wish Dick Tompkin's Could get out, he is anxious, and would go if he had contrivance or in other words Could make arrangements to leave the Old fields.[7] Mrs. Fitzhugh[8] is quit[e] anxious to go to Kentucky to See you all as She Sais _ a letter is in the post office fron Louisville derected to John at this place, we have been looking for hin for a week past with great anxiety —

The Secty. of War has no objection to my Delaying here untill April to prepare my papers for the work to be written ~~but~~ I feel anxious to get to my place of residence and Shall Set out as Soon as I can fix and get off after the 1st. of april my rout will be land to the Canhaway,[9] there take water and decend to the mouth of Ohio and assend the Mississippi _ Julia has enjoyed hea[l]th and Says She begins to want to See her ~~Kent~~ Kentucky mother again, and her friends and relations in you[r] neighbourhood. The man boy begins to walk and tryes to talk he has enjoyed good health laterly — Majr. Preston is going to your neighbourhood this Spring and I do believe he will move his family to his part of that Tract adjoining you which he has laterly recovered of his Brother Frank[10] _

as to news I can inform you of none worth your attention. Col. Hancock has Settled his business with Robinsons Heirs to his Satis faction ₍ₐ₎assd. Mays[11] Deed of trust[ₐ], if you See Mr. Hardin,[12] be pleased to inform him.

I have told you all that I can recollect of and must request you and Sister to accupt of the wormest affection of Julia & my Self

yr. Bro. Wm Clark

I have just rceived a letter from Bro Edmend of the 17h. Feby. which mentioned John Setting out from your house that day, we are looking with much anxiety for him.

1. This is perhaps the strongest statement critical of Lewis that Clark makes in the letters. His frustration with him is evident. By this time he had received and had time to review the expedition journals and other records that Lewis had with him at the time of his death, and Clark fully realized that Lewis had done essentially nothing concerning the journals' publication. In typical William Clark fashion, he promptly set about getting the work accomplished.

2. C. and A. Conrad and Co. was the Philadelphia printer that had originally contracted with Meriwether Lewis to publish the journals. John Conrad had his own printing and bookselling business as early as 1795. In early 1807 the firm's name was changed from John Conrad and Co. to C. and A. Conrad, the initials being for brothers Cornelius and Andrew Conrad. The firm experienced financial difficulties and was dissolved in mid-1812 before the journals were published. John Conrad was back in business the following year, but no longer had the contract for the journals. They were finally published in 1814 by Bradford and Inskeep of Philadelphia. About April 1807 Conrad's had issued the first of at least three versions of a prospectus for their publication. Clark had a copy of the prospectus with him when he went to Philadelphia in early 1810 and listed names and addresses of people he needed to see on it, especially regarding expedition matters and the journals project. In order to reannounce the project and rekindle public interest in it, Nicholas Biddle had Conrad publish another version of the prospectus about May 1810. (Jackson (1), 2:393–97, 547–48.)

3. Benjamin Smith Barton (1766–1815) was a native of Lancaster, Pennsylvania. He received an excellent education in Pennsylvania and abroad and settled in Philadelphia in 1789, practicing medicine and teaching at the University of Pennsylvania, and also pursuing his interest in the natural sciences and Native Americans. He was one of the men who tutored Lewis before the expedition, and he was Jefferson's choice to edit the scientific portion of the journals, which was to be issued as volume three. Unfortunately, because of other responsibilities and poor health, he never produced the work. It was not until after his death, when Biddle was gathering the journals for placement with the American Philosophical Society, that those records were reunited with the journals. The failure to publish the scientific portion of the journals deprived Lewis and Clark of the scientific legacy they would have otherwise enjoyed. Since scientists of the day and the general public did not have access to the information recorded by the Corps of Discovery, later expeditions and travelers were often credited with discovering and identifying many of the species of flora and fauna and geographic features that the Corps had earlier observed and recorded. Few of the names assigned by

the captains were perpetuated and survive today. (*DAB*, 2:17–18; Jackson (1), 2:607–18.)

4. Nicholas Biddle (1786–1844) was a native of Philadelphia. He is an acknowledged genius who attended the University of Pennsylvania at age ten, and became one of the country's foremost litterateurs, scholars, and financiers of his day. His greatest fame lay in his tenure as president of the Second Bank of the United States. During the expedition he was in Europe in the diplomatic service. Upon his return in 1807 he became a successful attorney and an established part of Philadelphia's cultural and social life. He was a regular contributor to the *Port Folio* (the leading American literary periodical at that time), and his reputation as a man of letters led Clark to request that he edit the narrative of the expedition. (Clark initially asked William Wirt of Richmond, Virginia, to edit the journals, but he declined.) Biddle initially declined, but then he reconsidered and traveled to Virginia, staying with Clark at Fincastle and interviewing him for the project. He carried the journals and other records back to Philadelphia (delivering the astronomical observations, etc., to Barton) and plunged into the project. Clark had George Shannon go to Philadelphia to assist Biddle and answer questions. Biddle essentially completed the manuscript by July 1811, but difficulties in getting the work printed by Conrad delayed the project further. Biddle became editor of the *Port Folio* in early 1812 and was active politically, and Conrad's failure left the project in limbo. In the spring of 1813 when Clark visited Philadelphia, it was decided to turn the project over to Biddle's associate Paul Allen. Allen was a native of Providence, Rhode Island, an editorial assistant at the *Port Folio*, and by 1816 a newspaper editor in Baltimore. It was Allen who made the final revisions and arrangements for publication and whose name appears on the title page. Biddle maintained an interest in the project, acted as Clark's agent, and helped retain Bradford and Inskeep to print the book, but he declined being named in association with the work. Thus the man who did so much to make the book of the official expedition account a reality does not have his name appear in it. Despite this, the 1814 edition of the journals is recognized as chiefly his work and commonly called the "Biddle edition." The book failed to be the lucrative project Clark had hoped, and he had failed to even receive a copy of it as late as October 1816 (he had borrowed a copy that had reached St. Louis by September 1814). (*DAB*, 2: 243–45; Jackson (1), 2:489–91, 494–97, 577–605, 615–30.)

5. The names mentioned here were friends and relatives of the Clarks in the old Clark neighborhood around Fredericksburg, Virginia. Thomas Rogers (1766–1851) probably was the son of Ann Rogers Clark's brother George Rogers and his wife Frances Pollard and thus a Clark

first cousin. Samuel Redd (1764–1841) lived in Caroline County and also was a first cousin. His mother Lucy Rogers Redd was Ann Rogers Clark's sister. Redd was further related to the Clarks through his sister Lucy Redd Fitzhugh, the mother of Clark brother-in-law Dennis Fitzhugh. Dabney Minor, Jr. (b. 1779), lived in Spotsylvania County and was married to Lucy Herndon, possibly the daughter of Joseph Herndon of Spotsylvania County, an old friend and neighbor of Jonathan Clark's. In mentioning Mr. Jefferson, William Clark probably is referring to Thomas Jefferson and friends of Meriwether Lewis in Albemarle County. He stopped and visited with Jefferson and others in the Charlottesville area on his way to Washington, and most likely did so on his return to Fincastle. In his 1809 memorandum Clark reports visiting several of those mentioned. (Rogers Index; William Clark Memorandum Book, 1809.)

6. Richard Tompkins and Joseph Pollard also were Clark friends and relatives. The Tompkins family bought the Clark plantation when the latter moved to Kentucky in 1784. The Bennett mentioned is Bennett Tompkins. William Clark records visiting Richard and Bennett on his way to and from Richmond (and then on to Washington) in December 1809 in his memorandum of his trip eastward. Members of the family moved to Kentucky and Missouri, including George Tompkins, whom Clark was so interested in having teach in St. Louis. Joseph Pollard was undoubtedly related to Clark's aunt Frances Pollard Rogers. Louisiana refers to the St. Louis area.

7. The "Old Fields" was the name of the area where Lucy Fitzhugh lived in Caroline County.

8. Lucy Redd Fitzhugh of Caroline County, Virginia. She was the daughter of Lucy Rogers Redd, Ann Rogers Clark's sister. Her son Dennis married Clark's sister Fanny and was their first cousin once removed. Her late husband was John Fitzhugh, and their estate was named Locust Grove. (Fitzhugh family file, TFHS; Rogers Index.)

9. The Kanawha River is formed by the New and Gauley Rivers in Fayette County, West Virginia, and flows ninety-seven miles northwestward to where it meets the Ohio at Point Pleasant. It is sometimes called the Great Kanawha to distinguish it from the Little Kanawha River. The route Clark mentions taking was a standard one. Travelers would go overland through the mountains to the Kanawha and travel either along it or down it to the Ohio, where they would continue their trip by boat. (Comstock, 2597.)

10. Francis Preston (1765–1835) was a native of Botetourt County, Virginia, and the second son of William and Susanna Smith Preston. His brother was William Preston, William Clark's friend and brother-in-

law. Francis graduated from William and Mary in 1787, studied law under George Wythe, and began practicing in Montgomery and surrounding counties that same year. He served in the militia (rising to major general), state legislature, U.S. House of Representatives, 1793–1797, and other posts. He also served as an agent of the Loyal Land Company and had extensive land interests. On 10 January 1793 he married Sarah Buchanan Campbell (1778–1846), daughter of Gen. William and Elizabeth Henry Campbell. Shortly after their marriage they moved to Salt Works in Washington County which his wife had inherited, and he helped develop the salt operation there in addition to his other activities. It would be another five years until William Preston moved his family to Jefferson County, Kentucky. (Dorman (2), 52–56.)

11. This may be a reference to one of the May brothers of Virginia: John, George, William, Richard, David or Stephen. The first four listed were very active in Kentucky land surveying and speculation. Two of them, John and Richard, were killed by Indians, but this could be a reference to land matters still pending. In addition, John, Richard, Stephen, and David all lived in Botetourt County at one time. John May had been clerk of Botetourt County before plunging into land speculation on a massive scale. His land affairs were still in the courts some forty years after his death. Given his connection to Botetourt County it is possible that the reference is to him. He and brother George became two of the largest landowners in Kentucky, owning hundreds of thousands of acres. (Coke, 240–67.)

12. Probably Benjamin or Martin Hardin (see letter dated 26 August 1809, note 3).

5

"We Are Striving to Get Along as Well as We Can"

Territorial Leader and Entrepreneur, 1810–1811

When William Clark and his family returned to St. Louis in July 1810 after an absence of almost ten months, his world had changed in many respects. The death of Meriwether Lewis in October 1809 had deprived him of a close friend and political ally. Not only did he face the changes that a new governor might bring, but he now knew he had a political antagonist in Frederick Bates. His responsibilities as superintendent of Indian affairs were expanded to include territory east of the Mississippi as well as Louisiana Territory, which he already administered. Indian unrest was increasing and would become a major concern of Clark's through the War of 1812. Clark also still was trying to achieve financial success and security through trade-related business enterprises.

The eight letters in this chapter reflect those responsibilities and activities. Before he even reached St. Louis after leaving Louisville, William Clark wrote Jonathan reporting on their difficult journey to Kaskaskia. First low water, then high water, bad weather, loss of life, and "Tormenting musketers" all conspired to make the trip so unpleasant that a "disheartened" Julia feared she would never again attempt to journey eastward to visit family. Perhaps Clark's encounters with ravenous mosquitoes on the expedition had increased his tolerance for the "tormenting insects," but their assault apparently was something Julia was reluctant for herself and their son M. Lewis Clark to experience again. Clark reported that the "Stings of the muskeetous had made Julia So lame that she Could Scarcely walk" and that the "little manBoy is nearly Covered with Sores."

His terming Bates a "little animale whome I had mistaken as my friend" and "have neither love nor respect for" were statements that could not be made lightly. Duels were a common feature of society at that time, and a statement deemed damaging to someone's honor or reputation could result in a confrontation to the death if the other party learned of it. William Clark was no dueler, but he apparently believed in the *code duello*. In January 1811 he reported on a duel in which he acted as a second, between his friend Dr. Bernard G. Farrar and James Graham in the closing days of December 1810. Clark's account is the most detailed report of the encounter known and contradicts some printed accounts of it. Lt. John Campbell apparently was jailed for the part he played in the duel (he offered the initial challenge to Graham), and in a tribute to Jonathan, verifying that his reputation for sage counsel reached from Virginia to the frontier west of the Mississippi, Clark reported that Campbell wished Jonathan were there to give him advice. Clark and Bates's differences did not result in a duel. Despite Clark's contempt for the man, they worked together in territorial and state government until Bates's death in 1825.

William Clark's discussion of his mercantile pursuits provides additional information on that facet of his life. The exact nature of his involvement in trade on a personal level has apparently never been determined. While his letters to Jonathan and those to Edmund and John H. Clark (in the Appendix) do not definitively settle the matter, they do shed more light on it. Clark apparently took in stride his disappointment at failing to get his brother Edmund and nephew John H. Clark to join him in a mercantile endeavor in St. Louis, and hoped for success in the lucrative but fickle field of trade through his connection to the St. Louis Missouri Fur Company and possibly on his own.

There are many sources available to chart the decline of U.S.-Indian relations leading up to the outbreak of the War of 1812. Clark's own reports and correspondence in government archives are an excellent source. The letters he wrote to Jonathan, however, provide another source of information. He faithfully reported news of Indian affairs. Whether it was Indians visiting St. Louis or an alarm on the Illinois frontier, Clark informed his brother about Indian activities. Having lived on the frontier since he was a teenager, where Indian affairs were of great importance, he perhaps reported such news from habit. He was an excellent Indian superintendent, instinctively knowing how to interact with the Native Americans. He knew when to threaten and when to persuade, when to praise and when to admonish them. He was prescient in stating in August 1811 that "the prophets party must be despursed they do much harm." Three months later an army commanded by William Henry Harrison did just that at the Battle of Tippecanoe, striking a serious blow against Tecumseh and his confederacy of Indian tribes.

The last letter is dated 14 September 1811. Two months later Jonathan died suddenly. There undoubtedly would have been many more letters to the beloved eldest brother. William Clark confessed that it was a "pleasure to write to you." Right to the end of their correspondence he continued to express the love of family that was so important to him. In January 1811 Clark lamented that they had not heard from Jonathan and other Kentucky relatives and friends and feared that they "are begining to forget us as they do not write." In August of that year he chided Jonathan that it had been a long time since he had the pleasure of hearing from him and worried that Jonathan was ill or overworked. He also lamented that the family was scattered, wishing "we were all to gether Some where." Clark also wished to see Jonathan, no doubt, to discuss any number of subjects as the country edged toward war and his own duties increased. Almost the last words he wrote to Jonathan in this correspondence were "I wish much to See you and if I had the time would ride over this fall." Unfortunately, he did not have the time and in a couple of months Jonathan would be dead. William Clark lost a brother, friend, confidant, and adviser when Jonathan died. History lost a continued source for the study of William Clark and his world.

∾

Opposit Kaskaskia July 3rd. 1810

Dear Brother

After parting with you we proceeded on very well to the mouth of Ohio, as the river was low we went on but Slowly. above the mouth of Green river, we come up with Mr. Tompkins,[1] Called at red banks & Saw Genl. Hopkins[2] and give him the linen Sent by Messr. Ed. & J. H. Clark, also left Mr. Gilkarists[3] articles at Mr.   Sent my Carrage & Horses from Lusks ferry[4] by Mr. Tompkins.   The horse I left at that place has never been able to travel Sence I left him, he has a new Set of hoofs which is nearly hard. when I arrieved at the mouth found that the men I wrote for, to be Sent from St. Louis had not arived, which obliged me to hire three which was not Sufficent, and 23 miles up this river hired 2 more, at a Dollar pr. day and forceed back. _ yesterday morning the men I had Sent to St. Louis for met me, and I discharged those I had hired. __ The letter I wrote from Louis ville Saturday before I left [∧]9th[∧] it, had not reached St. Louis on the 28th. _ Mr. Tompkins got there with the 27th. and told them & that I expected hands and next morning they Set out and were in Such anxiety to meet me that they passed me on the 28th. behind an Island and decended to Cape Girridoux[5] where they heard I had pass, they then passed thro' the wood & Struck the river above me yesterday _ we have been verey unfortunate in decending the Ohio, head wnds the heat & low water, and a fiew minets after me [we] arrived at the Mississippi rachiel[6] fell between the boats and Drowned, from that place we have been assending 13 days 11 of which we have had rain, and three violent Storms of wind Such as pass from the S.W. and tare every thing up by the roots. Trees & Banks falling in in differnt directions about us, I had had Chose my Situation, the best which Saved us from those Trees & Banks. we have also had the Tormenting musketers to Contend with, they have Caused Sores on Julias Ancles and the little manBoy in [is] nearly Covered with Sores – This river is very high and riseing fast from the fresh up the Missouri, which is the Cause of our Slow progress[7] _ Julia is much disheartened & Says She "Shall never go to See you all again She feares"_ She gives her love to you Sister nancy & all. I must beg you to give my best wishes to Sister nan: & all friends

Your afftly.
Wm Clark

1. Mr. Tompkins could be one of several men. George Tompkins apparently had relocated to St. Louis by this time, having announced in the *Missouri Gazette* that he was opening a school in May 1810. It is possible that he had delayed the opening or opened it briefly, left town on busi-

ness, and was returning when Clark and party encountered him on the Ohio. Other possibilities include Richard and Bennett, whom Clark mentioned in his March letter from Fincastle and who apparently were contemplating a visit to St. Louis and Louisiana, or a William Tompkins who would be working for Clark in St. Louis that summer (see letter dated 16 July 1810, note 8).

2. Samuel Hopkins (1753–1819) was a native of Albemarle County, Virginia. He served as an officer in the First, Sixth, Tenth, and Fourteenth Virginia Regiments, rising to the rank of lieutenant colonel. He fought in a number of battles, was wounded at Germantown, and captured at Charleston, and was a comrade of Jonathan Clark, Richard C. Anderson, and other Clark family members and friends. He was an original member of the Society of the Cincinnati. He moved to Kentucky in 1796 and in 1797 settled near Red Banks in Henderson County, Kentucky, on an estate christened Spring Garden. He practiced law, served as a judge, 1799–1801, represented his district four times as a state representative between 1800 and 1806, was a state senator, 1809–1813, and a U.S. congressman, 1813–1815. As a major general of Kentucky militia during the War of 1812, he led two campaigns against Indians in Illinois and Indiana. He married Elizabeth Branch Bugg on 18 January 1783. Red Banks was an area along the Kentucky side of the Ohio in Henderson County characterized by the red color of the high bluffs. The town of Henderson (laid out by Hopkins and Thomas Allin) was established in 1797 on the site of the small settlement known as Red Banks. (*KE,* 439; Gwathmey, 391; *BDAC,* 1329; *DAB,* 9:218–19; Rennick, 137.)

3. Robert Gilchrist, a Clark family friend living in Henderson County (see letter dated 6, 7 June 1808, note 20). Clark apparently either had forgotten the name of the man he gave the articles to for Gilchrist or intentionally left him unnamed.

4. Lusk's Ferry was one of the two great crossing places on the Ohio River for emigrants to Illinois and farther westward during this period. The road north of the river connected to the old French military road between Fort Massac and Kaskaskia. Travelers who wanted to cross southern Illinois using the overland route could boat down the Ohio or travel by way of Kentucky roads to Lusk's Ferry and cross there. Those traveling eastward similarly crossed at Lusk's. It was most likely at Lusk's that Clark sent York and others cross country to Kaskaskia when he moved to St. Louis in 1808, and where on 29 September 1809 he crossed when traveling eastward. James V. Lusk (d. 1803) was the proprietor of the ferry. He and others moved to Livingston County, Kentucky, from either North Carolina or the Waxhaw District of South Carolina (sources differ) in the early 1790s. Lusk soon began operating

this major ferry. In 1798 he may have moved across the river to Illinois (sources again differ). It is possible that he maintained residences on both sides of the river, but his primary residence apparently was Kentucky because that is where his will was probated. He was buried at Carrsville, Kentucky. Lusk's widow Sarah was licensed to operate a ferry on the Illinois side in 1804, and she established one opposite the Kentucky Lusk's Ferry. This ferry apparently soon supplanted the Kentucky-based ferry. In 1805 Sarah Lusk married Thomas Ferguson, who became prominent in Pope County, Illinois, affairs. Ferguson's brother Hamlet established a ferry opposite Smithland, Kentucky. Lusk's Landing, as the Illinois-based ferry was known, was renamed Sarahsville (after Sarah Lusk Ferguson), and in 1817 was named Golconda after the city of that name in India. The Kentucky side Lusk's Ferry eventually became known as Berry's Ferry, but no town is there today. In 1810 the area was still very much on the frontier and subject to Indian troubles. The *Louisiana Gazette* reported that a party of Indians stole a barge loaded with whiskey near Lusk's Ferry; they were pursued and four of them were killed in the ensuing fight. (Trail, 239, 247, 257, 267–69; Bigham, 34; Collins, 2:479; William Clark Memorandum Book, 1809; *Louisiana Gazette*, 26 July 1810.)

5. Cape Girardeau is on the west side of the Mississippi River about thirty-five miles above the confluence of that river and the Ohio. The district predates the founding of the town by that name. The land encompassed by a bend in the river possibly was named after a French soldier named Girardot who settled in the area in the early 1700s. It was identified on maps as early as 1765 as Cape Girardot. In 1793 the French-Canadian Louis Lorimier (b. 1748) established a trading post and settlement there that became the town of Cape Girardeau. Lorimier had had a trading post among the Shawnee in Ohio and was active against the Americans during the Revolution. George Rogers Clark and his Kentuckians burned his store during their 1782 campaign against the Shawnee, and Lorimier drifted westward. Several towns of Shawnee and Delaware, who had moved across the Mississippi in the 1780s and 1790s, were near Cape Girardeau. Henry M. Brackenridge in his *Sketches of the Territory of Louisiana* serialized in the *Louisiana Gazette* in 1811 gives a description of the town that conflicts with the evidence of a mixed ethnic population. He stated that the town had about thirty dwellings and 300 inhabitants, all American. The men and boats dispatched for Clark's party could have been either from the government or from the fur company. (Houck, 2:167–77; *Louisiana Gazette*, 21 March 1811.)

6. Rachiel (or Rachel) is assumed to have been a slave. She is not mentioned in any other letters or other sources checked. She may have been

a child, possibly the daughter of Chloe (or Cloe), a slave who accompanied the Clarks on their eastern visit (see letter dated 16 September 1809, note 4).

7. This was very late in the season for a flood. Clark's mention of this and of all the rain and violent storms they encountered indicates high precipitation for that part of the country in 1810.

~

Saint Louis 16th: July 1810

Dear Brother

We arrived here on the 7th in the evening all in tolerable health excupt the Stings of the muskeetous had made Julia So lame that She Could Scercely walk The Boy was also much worited by those tormenting insects.

Julia has been very Sick, and under the Doctr.[1] for five days, She is better and I hope recovering we have three negrows & two hired men Sick at this time. the State of health, with the unfavourable prospects of the Missouri Company is a little discourageing, they have Sent down no fur and I am Called on for money for the Goods purchased of Manuel $2400 my Share. it is too late to repint of my bargain when thing[s] are going on badly. it is then time to Scuffle and try to get out of the dificuelty.[2] I find that Mr. Bates has disapproved of the proceeding[s] in the Indian departmt. and in addition to his Complaints against Govr. Lewis he has laid in Complaints against me to the government, the amount of which he has not Shewn me, but Sais he is ready to do it at any time I am at Some loss to determine how to act with this little animale whome I had mistaken as my friend, however I Shall learn a little before I act. he must be verry much Surprised to find that the Goverment has not taken notice of his information and he tells me they have not answered his letter on that Subject but has on other Subjects of a later date. This information was Sent on last fall and must have reached the war Dept. before I got there, and accounts in Some measure for Simmons[3] Conduct, it is Singular that the Secty. Should not have mentioned to me this information, I asked him if any information had been lodged against Gov L. he Said "he had rceved Some information" and insinuated that it had no wieght. I little thought that the information Could have included myself. I will not pester you more about this triffleing matter.[4]

I wish the land Sold if possible in ∧& about[∧] Clarks ville & Get as much Cash as will pay off my debts, I Shall Send my land warrent to Orleans to Sell for what I can get. I have already wrote to Mr. D. Clark⁵ on the Subject.

The people of the Terrutory I am told are extreemly anxious for the arrival of the Govr:⁶ maney Changes have been made Since Lewis death, and the Indians have Considerable dificuelty among themselves.⁷

Julia Joins me in love to you Sister nane Isaac John & B. Edmd. and our friends about you

yr. Bro.
Wm Clark

I have ben Sicik but gettng better. Julia is well & at work and all the family is better. Mr. Wm. Tompkins⁸ at work covering the old house I live in   Ben is [word loss due to paper being torn away] Bisy[?] writ [word loss due to paper being torn away]⁹

1. Most likely good friend Dr. Bernard G. Farrar, whose office was in Clark's house. (*Missouri Gazette*, 6 September 1809.)
2. Another wonderful common-sense saying by Clark. Such statements reflect his practical, get-on-with-the-job, attitude.
3. William Simmons was the accountant of the War Department. See letter dated 12 January 1810, note 5, for more information on him and his role in the matter.
4. Clark's anger and disgust with Bates is evident in his remarks to Jonathan. The sense of betrayal that Clark felt can be understood, especially in light of Lewis's death. His sense of vindication and being in better standing with Washington officials than Bates is also evident. It is obvious that the matter has upset Clark, and one wonders how "triffleing" he really considered it. The two men reached some kind of understanding because they both continued in the territory's administration.
5. Daniel Clark (1766–1813) was a native of Sligo, Ireland. He settled in New Orleans in 1786 where he and his uncle of the same name were successful merchants and landholders. Their property interests reached to Baton Rouge and Natchez and their mercantile interests to the upper Ohio and Philadelphia. Clark also served as a Spanish official and later as an American one. He actively supported American interests, served as American consul at New Orleans, and was a delegate from Orleans Territory. For some twenty years he was associated with James Wilkin-

son, and charges were made that he was part of the Burr Conspiracy. This apparently was not true, and he provided important information concerning Wilkinson's intrigues. William Clark had known Clark since the 1790s, when he visited New Orleans. They were not related. It is not known whether Clark actually sent his land warrant for 1,600 acres from the expedition to Daniel Clark to sell. Sources checked dealing with the disposition of the warrants the members of the Corps of Discovery received did not list any information about his warrant. William Clark did sell some of his land in and around Clarksville but still owned a number of parcels at the time of his death. (*DAB*, 4:125.)

6. Benjamin Howard (d. 1814) was a native of Virginia, grew up in Botetourt County, studied at William and Mary, and moved to Fayette County, Kentucky, by 1801. He served in the state legislature and the U.S. Congress. In 1811 he married Mary Thomson Mason (d. 1813). Howard was in Congress at the time he was appointed governor in place of the deceased Lewis. He resigned the governorship in 1813 upon being appointed a brigadier general in the U.S. Army, and Clark succeeded him. Clark knew Howard. He was the first cousin of his good friend and brother-in-law William Preston, and Clark had met with him in Washington while there in late 1809 and early 1810. (Dorman (2), 5, 24–28, 84–85; *BDAC*, 1335; *DAB*, 9:274–75; William Preston Miscellaneous Papers, TFHS.)

7. Bates, as acting governor in Lewis's absence and then until a replacement was named, had run the territory as he saw fit and had made a number of changes. Clark had been absent from St. Louis for over nine months. As in the past, there were a number of issues concerning Indian affairs that demanded Clark's attention. The major problems at this time were sporadic Indian-white conflict and the threat of hostilities between tribes such as the Osage and the Shawnee and Delaware in the area. There also was serious concern about the intentions of the Wabash tribes in Indiana, especially fears that the "Shawanoe Prophet" was inciting them to war. (*Louisiana Gazette*, 19 July 1810.)

8. William Tompkins probably was yet another of the Tompkins clan of Caroline County, Virginia, and Kentucky. There was a William Tompkins in the family, but no biographical information has been found for him. It is possible that he was the Mr. Tompkins that Clark's party encountered on the Ohio on their way back to St. Louis.

9. This part of the postscript extended over to another page, part of which has been torn away, leaving only an incomprehensible fragment. Ben most likely is either their nephew Benjamin O'Fallon, or Clark's former slave Ben, indentured to him. My guess is that the reference was to

O'Fallon, who was becoming actively engaged in Clark's business affairs by this time.

~

St. Louis Decr. 14th. 1810

Dear Brother

I received you[r] favor of the 27th. of October & 5th Novr. the press of business and the uncertinty of a Conveyanc has prevented my answering those letters and doing my Self the pleasure of writeing to you I assure you it is a pleasure to write to you but much greater to recvee a letter fron you. if the farm is broken up whuch I think well of I must draw your attention a little to the old negrows at the point, they must not Suffer when they have become infirm, may I beg of you to doo the best you Can with them So that they may not Suffer I will with much pleasure pay for expences which may be incured by them under your directions[1] _

Inclosed I Send you two powers of attorney to Sell my lands, one to Sell with Mr. Fitzhugh the other your Self,[2] Those lands which I purchased at the Sale of the lots in Clarks ville and with those I purchd. of Davis floyd with the Ferry[3] I would Sell provided a high price Could be had for them altogethr they are [∧]out Lots[∧] No. 4. 5. 6. 35. 36. 42. 43. 44. 47. 48. & 50 _ In lots purchased of D Floyd No. 23. 24. 25 & 54. and one purchased by myself imedeately at the point No. 138[4] _ in all containing 153 ¼ acres exclusive of a tract purchased of D. Floyed of which Mr. S. Gwathmey has the deed. If the other lands, that is to Say the lands included in the power of attorny to you and Mr. Fitzhugh, is Sold tolerably well, there will be no absolute necessity for you to trouble your Self more to Sell my lands _ if you meet with a Big offer for them I wish you to act for me just as you would do for yourself, and I can [say] that my familey will not Say you have done wrong. I wish the lands which Came fron Bro. G to be Sold and my account Settled, it will be Sufficnt to pay more than I owe _ if I retain the lands I purchase[d] at the Sale of lots, out lots No. 2 of 19½ & No. 3 of 15¼ acres Should be anexed as they all join and would be emencely valueable to the othr Lands and I must have them &c. if I own the lots I must have a Check on that mill which over flows my land. Bro Geo. Conveyed half of one of the 100 [acre] Lots in No. 30, previous to the deed to my father to Wm. Clark,[5] ~~and~~ I beleve Bro George owns 4 half acre lots in Clarks ville Nos 19. 48. 77. 78 I have the Deeds except the last purchase[d] of Floyd

I hope Bro George is in a better State of health than when you wrote in Octr. _ Govr. H.[oward] and myself agreed uncommonly well. Mr. B[ates] and my Self Speak to each other when we meat and that is all, for I have neither love nor respect for him_ he has lately put an Indian Speach in Charles[s] papers which has made little noise here, the people Say it is unlike an Indian Speach, to me it is quit[e] Clear, it is intended to answer one which Charlus put into his paper not long Since made to me, and to Sound the importance of Mr. Chouteau abroad to whome he is under maney ob ligations &c. &c.[6] _ we have had Some very Coald weather the river runig with ice Several boats frosen up below. I am much engaged Seldom go to bead [bed] before twelve oClock. please to give our love to Sister John Isacc nelly & nancy and acupt the assurrunc of our fervent preyers for your health and happinss, and that of you[r] familey we are all in health except [word loss due to paper being torn away] eyes. Julia Sais to Nancy that [word loss due to paper being torn away] to learn fron her how to Spell[7] [paper torn away]

[signature torn away]

1. This statement exhibits Clark's, and many slaveholders', seemingly contradictory attitudes in treating their slaves with severity while also being concerned for their welfare. Clark believed he had certain responsibilities to his slaves, just as they did to him, and wanted to fulfill those obligations. This included taking care of the old and infirm slaves he owned. Clark's earlier letters indicated that he must have left some of his slaves in the Louisville area, and this statement confirms it. It is not definitely known whether he actually even still owned these slaves. It is possible that they had been sold to another family member, but that Clark still felt a sense of responsibility toward them. Indiana Territory was free territory, but this did not always stop slave owners from taking their slaves there, especially during its early years; however, the overall number of slaves was small. Slavery there basically ended once Indiana became a state in 1816. It also is possible that Clark had freed the "old negrows" living at the Point by this time. The Bond and Power of Attorney books for Jefferson County for this period are missing and apparently no longer exist, so any record of their manumission is not available. It is possible that he had freed them, and they in turn bound themselves to him, as Ben had done in 1802, or just lived and worked there. The old

slaves living at the Point may have included Old York, Rose, Harry, Cupid, and others. The four named were over fifty years old in 1799. Whether all of them were living is not known, but Rose definitely was because she is mentioned in Clark's 1816 runaway slave ad for her son Juba. The farm at the Point is where Clark and his brother George lived when they moved across the river to Clarksville. After George had his leg amputated in 1809, he moved in with his sister Lucy Croghan at Locust Grove. By late 1810 the family apparently was contemplating disposing of the farm or at least ceasing active farming there.

2. The original of the power of attorney designating only Jonathan as his legal representative is dated 10 December 1810. It was found with additional William Clark letters in the Bodley Family papers in the summer of 1998. It, like the other Clark items found, was placed with the Jonathan Clark Papers—Temple Bodley Collection.

3. A ferry ran between Clarksville and Shippingport. It would have been the major means of crossing the river in that immediate area, and probably was a profitable business. It most likely was the means by which Clark crossed to Louisville from Clarksville and back. This may be the ferry he mentions buying from Floyd (see letter dated 5 October 1808, note 8).

4. Lot No. 138 is just upstream from the mouth of Mill Creek. Clark's out lots were just to the east and also to the north of the in lots. The date of purchase is recorded as 11 April 1803, about the time of Clark's move to Clarksville. Lot 138 may be the lot on which he actually lived. The farm itself may have consisted of out lots 4, 5, 6, 35, 36, 37, 42, 43, and 44, which adjoined each other. Clark apparently owned the property not only as an investment but possibly because of George's financial difficulties. It was at their farm at the Point that Clark, Lewis and the rest of the nucleus of the Corps of Discovery are believed to have stayed after the boats had been piloted through the Falls from Louisville, before setting off down the Ohio on 26 October 1803. The lots listed reflect Clark's large holdings in Clarksville and make his interest in town and land affairs there understandable. A map of the area dated around 1836 is in Clark's papers at the Missouri Historical Society. It shows his extensive holdings in the area. (Clark Family Papers; Yater (1), 48–49; WCP-VMC.)

5. William Clark (d. 1791) was Clark's first cousin.

6. Those speeches were in the 28 November and 12 December 1810 editions of the *Louisiana Gazette*. The speech that appeared in Charless's paper on 28 November was delivered to Clark by the Sauk chief Quas quam ma. It professed peace and brotherhood and asked for presents, including a little "milk" (whiskey). The 12 December edition carried

Chouteau's speech preceded by a letter written by Bates stating what an excellent Indian speech it was. Thus Clark's comment. Jean Pierre "Peter" Chouteau was agent for the Osage Indians and something of a rival of Clark's for authority in Indian affairs. Although Chouteau, Bates, and Clark were all part of the St. Louis elite, there obviously were differences and difficulties between them. At this time the former two basically were allied, and Bates owed Chouteau a number of favors (according to Clark). See letter dated 22, 24 November 1808, note 19. (*American State Papers: Indian Affairs*, 4:763–67; *Louisiana Gazette*, 28 November 1810, 12 December 1810; Loos, 849–55.)

7. The outer right-hand portion of this page has been torn away, resulting in loss of some text and Clark's signature. Clark's 31 January 1811 letter states that it was Julia who was having difficulty with her eyes. Julia's apparent remark to the effect that Clark's spelling should not be used to learn by is a wonderful comment and shows his shortcomings in that area were recognized and apparently cause for teasing among his family.

∾

      –   St. Louis 31st. Jany 1811

Dear Brother

               We have not had the pleaser of hereing from you for a long time, indeed I fear our friends are begining to forget us as they do not write _ we are Striving to get along as well as we can, and as Clear of desputes or Brocks[1] as possible, which is a dificuelt matter I believe I told you a Duell took place in which I acted as Second _ in this affair [∧]3 fires[∧] the man whome I was actng for wounded his advosary every Shot, which was Close Shooting for a young hand _ a report got into Circulation that I had gave private Signals which I gave to enable the Gentleman to get the first Shot. This report has vexed me a little, and [I] Caled [on] the opposit Sides for a certificate which is in the paper inclosed, and Shall brng forward the man whome ~~gave~~ [∧]made[∧] the report.[2] This business originated with Liet. Campbell[3] ~~whom~~ has been in the oppinion of maney about this place much injured. he is now arrested and all must come out. his friends in Town I beleve are powerfull, those in Camp I am told Confined to his Capt. Owens'[4] _ Such proceedings has not been common. Campbell is full of fight but cant get a fight _ he Says he wished you were convenent that he might take your advice[5] _ I have paid $1000 to wards the Bond given Manuel Liza, Settld my public accounts and balancd them all up to the first of January what I owe now is $1501 to manul[6] _ for the goods I purchased and a Balance to E. & J.H. Clark which I Shall pay as Soon as I can __ I fear they are uneasy about it _ Julias Eyes have been Sore for Several weeks but are better, She joins me in love to you Sister nany and all you[r] familey about you

prey write to us as often as you can.

acupt my wormest wisshes

yo. frend & Bro
Wm Clark

one news paper inclosed [note written on address leaf]

1. A "brock" is a contemptible fellow. If this is what Clark meant, it certainly would fit given that they are trying to stay clear of disputes and that he recently had been involved in a duel in which charges of improper conduct had been made against him.
2. The duel was between Dr. Bernard G. Farrar and James A. Graham (d. 1811) and occurred in the closing days of December 1810 on either the east side of the Mississippi or an island in the river. Frederic Billon states that it was the first duel fought in St. Louis (at least in the American period). Graham was a native of Cumberland County, Pennsylvania. He was an attorney who settled in St. Louis in April 1810. Lt. John Campbell took offense at something Graham said about him, and sent him a challenge by Dr. Farrar. Graham refused, saying Campbell's behavior was such that he did not deserve an affair of honor. Dr. Farrar consequently believed his own honor had been insulted by Graham's refusal and sent him a challenge by William Clark. Lt. Col. Daniel Bissell of the First U.S. Infantry acted as Graham's second. The standard distance of ten paces (approximately sixty feet) with pistols was observed, but the matter was deadly serious because multiple fires were exchanged. Three fires took place, as Clark reported, and Graham was indeed hit with each one: in the side, with the ball passing along his ribs and lodging in his back; through both legs; and in the right hand. Farrar was wounded in the second fire in the buttocks. Graham lost so much blood that Clark and Bissell agreed to stop the proceedings until Graham was ready to take the field again if Farrar should request it. It initially was believed that Graham would recover, but he died of his wounds. The 2 January 1811 edition of the *Louisiana Gazette* mentioned the duel but refused to report the particulars of the "barbarous custom, hooted at by civilized society." The 31 January edition that Clark refers to carried a

statement by Graham declaring that the entire duel was conducted in a fair and honorable manner, and any charges directed toward Farrar and Clark to the contrary were malicious and false.

Houck provides additional details about the duel. He reported that while watching a game of cards in which Campbell was a player, Graham observed the lieutenant cheating and proclaimed it to the group present. Campbell claimed his honor had been insulted and demanded satisfaction by a note carried by his second, Dr. Farrar. Houck noted that Farrar was Campbell's brother-in-law and was thus compelled to act on his behalf. (This revisits the confusion over the relationship between Campbell, Farrar, Clark, and the Christys. It seems doubtful that Farrar and Campbell were brothers-in-law. See note 3 of this letter and note 2 of the letter dated 21 January 1809.) Graham refused, saying that Campbell was not a gentleman and did not deserve the opportunity to defend his honor. Farrar claimed that, by refusing Campbell, Graham had insulted his honor, and he demanded satisfaction from Graham, even though they were friends (according to Houck). The duel took place on Bloody Island, an island in the Mississippi off-shore from St. Louis, used for duels. Houck reported that Farrar as well as Graham was wounded on all three fires (which I think can be discounted, since contemporary reports state he was wounded only once) and that a fourth was called off by the seconds because the wound to Graham's hand prevented him from holding his pistol. It was agreed that the duel would resume when Graham recovered sufficiently, but at this point it was discovered that the ball from the first fire had severely injured his spine. It took Graham four months to recover enough to leave his room. He attempted to return to the East by horseback, but the effort proved too much for his wound, and he was found dead one morning some one hundred miles from St. Louis. It is not known whether Clark regretted his role in this unfortunate affair, but it is enlightening as to his apparent adherence to the *code duello*. I found no information that Clark himself actually ever engaged in a duel. Perhaps his actions here as a second were the closest he ever came to becoming a possible victim of this "barbarous custom." (Colter-Frick, 472–75; Houck, 3:75–76; Billon, 81–82, 242–43; *Louisiana Gazette*, 2, 31 January 1811.)

3. John Campbell was a native of Virginia. He was commissioned an ensign in the First U.S. Infantry in June 1808, and rose to the rank of captain in May 1814. He was honorably discharged in June 1815. He was a second lieutenant at this time, apparently stationed at Belle Fontaine. Scharf states that he married Polly Nicholes (or Nicholls) in St. Louis in 1810, but Dennis Northcott of the Missouri Historical Society reported to me that no such marriage is listed in the records. Polly has not posi-

tively been identified, including her relationship to the Christys and Clarks, but there was some kind of family connection. Letters Campbell wrote to Clark in 1811 and 1812 and notes in M. Lewis Clark's family genealogy confirm this. See letter dated 21 January 1809, note 2. Regardless of his possible Christy connection, Campbell still was an associate of Clark's. He was not the Capt. John Campbell of the Second Infantry, from whose company at South West Point, Tennessee, some of the members of the expedition were drawn and who most likely is the John Campbell who served as Benjamin Howard's brigade major during the War of 1812 and was involved in the Prairie du Chien campaign, in which he reportedly was severely wounded. What Lt. John Campbell had done following the duel to result in being jailed is unknown, but it seems to be connected with the duel in some way. (Heitman (2), 278; Scharf, 1:315n.)

4. Most likely Capt. Simon Owens. A native of Virginia, he was serving in the First Infantry at the time. He arrived at Cantonment Belle Fontaine in the spring of 1810 with some 120 soldiers (possibly including Lt. Campbell?). He was dismissed from the army in October 1814. (Heitman (2), 764.)

5. A wonderful testimony to Jonathan Clark's apparent wisdom and good advice. Campbell either knew Jonathan or had heard about his wise counsel through William Clark. His reputation extended from Virginia to St. Louis, the breadth of the then-settled United States!

6. This may be a reference to the same debt that Lisa listed in the 28 June 1810 and several subsequent editions of the *Louisiana Gazette.* While crossing the Des Pres River six miles south of St. Louis, below Carondelet, at 1:00 p.m. on 28 June, Lisa lost his pocketbook containing promissory notes of various people, including William Clark's for $2440.95. If this is the same debt, Clark must have paid off some of it. One can assume that he was not pleased to have this debt listed publicly.

~

[no place - St. Louis] [no date - ca. 1 March 1811][1]

Dear Brother

I intended to writes you a long letter but it is So late at night must make it Short, and refur you to Mr. Luttig[2] for perticulars he has been my Store keeper for Some time and can give you the perticulars of my affairs perhaps more Satisfactorey than I could detail them on paper _ I have Sent on Some orders for goods to be got in Baltimore to

Bro E. & John under an expectatun that they may be going on this Spring for goods, or Some friend who will brng them out for me. a good deel of money can be made here with goods _   I have also Sent fer Some articles which I expect can be got in Kentucky which I am in want of.

I belev I wrote to you that I had purchaise[d] Goods to the amount of $8700, of this Sum I hav discharged $3000, the balanc to be paid July, Octo. next and april 1812. if I can get Supplied [I] Shall be enabled to discharge my Debts to manul which is reducd to $1500 _ prey write to me Julia joins me in best love to you & Sister and may health and hapiness attend you both for many years is the Sincer wissh of yr. Aff.

Wm Clark

[Letter carried by Mr. Luttig.]

1. This letter was written on or about 1 March 1811. The date was determined by using the letter of 1 March 1811 that Clark wrote to Edmund and John H. Clark (printed in the Appendix). It was carried to Louisville by John Luttig, and apparently placed in Jonathan's hands by him.
2. John C. Luttig (d. 1815) apparently was a native of Germany and educated there. He immigrated to America and settled in Baltimore, where he became a successful merchant. By 1809 he was living in St. Louis. He worked for the Missouri Fur Company as a clerk, and for Clark as his clerk, on either government or personal business, perhaps both. He also worked for St. Louis merchant Christian Wilt. He moved ca. 1814 to the White River settlements in present Arkansas and was appointed justice of the peace for that area by Clark as governor. He died ca. 19 July 1815 in Lawrence (present Lawrenceville possibly), Arkansas. It is Luttig's 1812–1813 journal of a fur trading expedition up the Missouri that records the death of Sheheke in either late September or early October 1812 (see letter dated 24 September 1806, note 3) and the death of Sacagawea at Fort Manuel (near present Kenel, South Dakota) on 20 December 1812. (Luttig, 11–14, 68, 82–83, 106, 131–34.)

~

Saint Louis August 17th 1811

Dear Brother

It has been a long time Sence I have had the pleasure of hearing from you, I am afraid that you are unwell, or have too much on your hands to attend to; the other day I heard that Sister Clark was about Russelsville and had been down for a long time,[1] I herd also that Mr. Temple was in philadelphia not long Sence_ John wrote me from Cincinnati, we appear to be much Scattered, I wish we were all to gether Some where _ I Send Ben o Fallon to Louis ville to pay Some Debts I have Contracted at that place for goods, he is also to Collect Some money for me on the way, he will pay $2000 or obtain recepts for that amount,[2] I would not be compelled to Send if I could hear by letter from that place, I have Sent on Several Sums of money or Drafts which I am not certain ever got to hand, indeed I have been duned[3] for money which I Sent on Several months ago. This payment will be about $6800 paid for the goods I have purchased, and Several hundred dollars to manuel Lisa of that large Debt he advotisud.[4]

Some time past an alarm was Stured up on the frontiers of Illinois— a Demand is made of the murderers & property by a party which is now in the Indian Country, I have Suckceded in alarming the Indians in that quarter, and the Settlements is again Tranquel,[5] I hear that there is Some Stur about vencennes – There is also a good deel of Stur about Prarie de Chen[6] and about the British lekes.[7] we are quiet on this Side of the mississippi, about 70 Osage is in Town Some Toways and a Day or too ago a large party of Fox Indians left us and returnd home[8] _ I think the prophets[9] party must be despursed they do much harm. all to yourself _

I have been very unwell fer Some time, Lewis waes also a little Sick but recovered Julia Complains verry much, but her Complaint[10] is not owing to Climate & c.

prey write me and let me know how all Drive on Julia joins me in Love to yourself & Sister

You[r] affty. Brothr
Wm Clark

What Chance is thr to Sell the lands in and about Clarks ville

1. Sarah Hite Clark had gone to Logan County near Russellville to be with daughter Ann "Nancy" Clark Pearce for the birth of her first child, Sarah Pearce, born on 6 August 1811. Following the birth Ann Pearce became ill and Sarah Clark stayed there a bit longer. Jonathan and Sarah's oldest child, Eleanor Temple, also lived near Russellville, an added inducement for Sarah to go there for a visit. Dorman states that Sarah Pearce was born near Louisville, but evidence indicates she was

born in Logan County. (Dorman (1), 117; James Pearce to Jonathan Clark, 6 September 1811, 19 November 1811, Bodley Family Papers.)

2. Benjamin O'Fallon (1793–1842) may have been born at Mulberry Hill in Jefferson County, Kentucky, and not in Lexington as biographical sources for him state. His parents were Dr. James and Frances Clark O'Fallon. As with his older brother John O'Fallon, Uncle William Clark took an active interest in his upbringing and education. Ben O'Fallon's health and academic abilities apparently were not good, and he suffered from a bad temper and other character flaws according to Clark. Perhaps in exasperation and in an effort to help him get set up in business and begin making his way in the world, Clark had O'Fallon come live with him as early as April 1810. Clark put him to work as his business assistant and later helped set him up in business with a mill and helped him obtain a position in the Indian Department. O'Fallon enjoyed a successful career as an Indian agent and retired in 1827. He continued his involvement in the Indian trade, was associated with the Missouri Fur Company, and was active in politics as a Jacksonian Democrat. In 1828 he settled on a farm in Jefferson County, Missouri. His association with William Clark significantly assisted his career. He married Sophia Lee in St. Charles, Missouri, in November 1823. O'Fallon arrived in Louisville on 28 August, and in a letter dated 31 August he informed his Uncle William about his trip from St. Louis and how he was doing in taking care of the business Clark had given him to do. (*DAB*, 13:631–32; Lamar, 857–58; WCP-VMC.)

3. Dun means an urgent or repeated demand for payment.

4. This most likely is the debt that Manuel Lisa advertised in the *Louisiana Gazette* in the 28 June 1810 and several subsequent editions of the newspaper. I saw no other debts that Clark owed Lisa listed in the paper. See letter dated 31 January 1811, note 6, for an explanation as to why it was advertised.

5. Indian hostilities in the Illinois Territory included the murder of a Mr. Price at the mouth of Wood River and the murder of whites by Potawatomie Indians in the Chicago area. A militia expedition pursued one raiding party, and regular army troops established a presence in the area, which succeeded in preventing hostilities from escalating further until November, following the Battle of Tippecanoe (see note 9). (*Louisiana Gazette*, 30 May 1811, 27 June 1811, 18 and 25 July 1811, 1 and 15 August 1811.)

6. Prairie du Chien (Dog Prairie or Prairie of the Dog), located three miles above the confluence of the Wisconsin and Mississippi Rivers, had served as a meeting point for Native and Euro Americans since the seventeenth century. Its situation at the western terminus of the Fox-Wis-

consin water route between the Great Lakes and Mississippi River made it an important meeting and trading site. One source states that its name refers to the Indian chief Alim, whose name meant or referred to a dog. The famous French explorers Marquette and Joliet reached the area in 1673, and only Green Bay predates it as the earliest white settlement in Wisconsin. The first fort was established at Prairie du Chien by the French in 1685 in connection with the fur trade. The British later maintained a post there after acquiring the area following the French and Indian War. At the time Clark wrote this letter, there was no fort at the site, but there was a trading post. The 15 August 1811 edition of the *Louisiana Gazette* reported that the British were trying to stir up the Indians at Prairie du Chien. Its strategic location regarding transportation and area Indian tribes resulted in Clark's leading an expedition there in 1814 to help protect settlers from Indian attack and to counter the British during the War of 1812. He oversaw the beginning of construction of Fort Shelby there before returning to St. Louis. The fort soon fell to the British, who in turn abandoned and destroyed it in 1815. In 1816 the Americans built Fort Crawford but moved to a site just north of the old one the following year because of flooding. In 1825 Clark visited Prairie du Chien as one of the leaders of a U.S. delegation that signed a treaty with the Indians of the area. (Smith, 1: 77–99; Lamar, 961.)

7. The British Lakes are the Great Lakes. Because of British presence and influence in the area and their proximity to Canada, the lakes were often referred to in this period as the British Lakes.

8. The *Louisiana Gazette* during this period is full of reports of Indian affairs and troubles. A particular problem was the illegal sale of whiskey to visiting Indians and the drunken actions that followed. The Toways were the Ottawa Indians, an Algonquian tribe living in eastern Michigan and adjoining areas of Ohio and Ontario at the time of initial European contact. By the early 1800s the Ottawas had drifted westward to northern Indiana and Illinois, and they eventually crossed to the west side of the Mississippi. By the mid-1800s remnants of the tribe had been settled on a reservation in Kansas and later Indian Territory. (*Louisiana Gazette*, 30 May 1811, 27 June 1811, 18 and 25 July 1811, 1 and 15 August 1811, 12 September 1811; Lamar, 948.)

9. A reference to the Prophet or Tenskwatawa (the Open Door, ca. 1775–1836), brother of the famous Shawnee leader Tecumseh (ca. 1768–1813). Tecumseh had met with William Henry Harrison in July 1811 and then went south to recruit among the Five Civilized Tribes for his Indian Confederacy. In his absence the Prophet acted as the leader of the warriors gathered at Prophetstown on Tippecanoe Creek in northwestern Indiana near present Lafayette. The Prophet had a difficult

time controlling the warriors and actually helped incite them toward open hostilities with the Americans. Harrison saw the opportunity to force a military action with the Indians in Tecumseh's absence and possibly defeat them, thereby eliminating a possible military threat and eventually opening up more land to white settlement. Consequently, he marched an army of 1,000 regulars and Kentucky militia north from Vincennes to Prophetstown, and there on the banks of Tippecanoe Creek on 7 November 1811 he defeated the Indians and "despursed" them as William Clark believed they must be. A general Indian war on the frontier followed, an opening act to the War of 1812 in which the tribes of the lakes region allied themselves with the British. Tecumseh was killed in the war, and the Prophet's influence essentially disappeared because of his failure at Tippecanoe. He lived in Ontario, Canada, until 1824 and drifted westward from Ohio in 1826, settling in Kansas and dying there. Clark's concern with the Prophet rather than with Tecumseh, who was the real power among the Indians, was not unusual at the time. The Prophet was used by Tecumseh as something of a front man and mouthpiece. Historians still debate the respective influence and importance of the brothers and their accomplishments. (Sugden, 22–23, 386–89; Lamar, 1162–63.)

10. Julia's complaint was that she was some eight months pregnant. She would give birth to their second child, William Preston Clark, in September.

∼

St. Louis August 30th. 1811

Dear Brother

Mr. Fitzhugh who arrived here about a week ago handed me your favor of the 4th. instant which gave us much pleasure. Mr. F. is about to return to day and will hand you this hasty Scraul. I find you will not be able to Sell the lands received of B. G_ [brother George] for as much as he ows me, Mr. Fitzhugh dos not think the land will Sell for as much as they may be worth and advises me not to Sell, I am not anxious to Sell those lots I purchased myself, The lott below the Silver Creek[1] has been Conveyed I do not know where the Deed is _ I Set down to write you a long letter but must Cut it Short as I am bothered with Indians and Mr. Fitzhugh Sets out after the Council. I am getting a little tired of mercantile business and if I do not get Such a person to join as I wish Shall Sell out.[2] not withstanding money is to be made at it I will mearly mention my Debts to Shew you how I drive on,   I owe for the Goods to Comegys a balanc of $2673 to be paid 11[?] March 1812. a Sum of $800 to be paid at Christmas _ and to Mr. Fitzhugh for artls. Sent by Luttig a balance of about $1000 payable next month _ on Mr. manuels Debt of $2400_ I owe about $900. I owe Some other Debts of Less amt. but Shall get thro them all I beleev pretty well in time _ my Salary as factory agent is raised to $400 which ads a little —

Mr. Fitzhugh tells me that Isaac is living at mulbery hill, and will make a good farmer, and that Brother Edmund is building a valueable mill which is nearly finished Indeed he has told me a great [deal] of the acurrnces of the neighbourhood

Sister is below³ and you must be quit[e] lonesom, I wish I could be with you a fiew days

Julia Sends her best love to you. Lewis is very Sick with worms.

Accupt my Afft. Wishus

y. Bro

Wm Clark

1. Clark owned much property in that Clarksville–Silver Creek area (also see letter dated 22, 24 November 1808, note 8). Some sources state that it was Silver Creek that the expedition pushed off from on 26 October 1803 when it left the Falls of the Ohio area. Better evidence, however, indicates the Mill Creek and Point of Rocks area on the eastern (rather than Silver Creek on the western) side of Clarksville was the departure place. A good harbor, the Clark residence, and the ferry across the river to the lower landing and the road to Louisville were all located there.

2. This statement seems to verify that Clark had indeed entered into the mercantile business, as he had long planned to do. One of the reasons he resigned from the army in 1796 was his desire to go into this potentially lucrative field. He never established himself as a merchant before leaving in 1803 on the expedition, however, and it was not until settling in St. Louis in 1808 that he could again turn his attention to mercantile enterprises. His desire to prosper through trade is recorded in his letters to Jonathan, Edmund, and John H. Clark. A number of sources checked were murky as to whether he ever entered into trade personally. John Loos made a diligent effort to ascertain the nature of Clark's personal mercantile enterprise, but he failed to determine its exact nature and extent. Clark certainly wrote and talked about it, and he did serve as agent for the factory system in that area. His recitation of debts owed various merchants for goods and this blunt statement about growing tired of the

mercantile business and possibly selling out seem to verify his personal involvement. Yet a cautionary note should be added. Given Clark's tendency to refer to personal and official activities together and neglect to distinguish between them, it is possible this mercantile endeavor was associated with the Missouri Fur Company or possibly even the government (regarding goods sold). (Loos, 958–80.)

3. Clark's mention of his sister-in-law Sarah Hite Clark being below refers to her being in the Russellville, Kentucky, area (see note 1 of the 17 August 1811 letter).

~

St. Louis 14th. Sepr. 1811

Dear Brother

Col. William Preston has been with us for nearly two weeks and from this he goes to Louis ville where I believe he intends to divide his land adjoining to you and I believe will ultomitely Settle near you.[1] this Country does not pleas him, this year it has been remarkably Sickly and at present Shews to a very great dis advantage.

I have not heard from my friends Since Mr. Fitzhugh was with us. Ben o Fallon I expect has Set out before this time with Some fiew articles for this place which I expect will Sell in this Country. I Sent money by Ben to pay all the debts I owed except Mr. S. T. Fitzhugh,[2] by Col. Preston I now Send more money than the amount of Fitzhughes a/c, the amount of which he was anxious to recevee.

Our Indian relations is not verry favourable perticularly towards the lakes, influencd by the british to hold them ready at ther Call, or wish to hold them So, and from their Councils with those Indians and the great quantity of presents they recive will keep a part ready to act in the event of War with England. the Indians on this Side are well disposed. The government has extended my Duties to both Sides of the Mississippi and over the agency of Mr. Chouteau and Boilvin,[3] which gives me more duty without ˄more[˄] pay.

I cant Conclude without mentioning to you that I have another Son,[4] a great rough red headed fellow who is now four days old. Julia is tolerably well as [is all] my familey except a little negrow. If

I wish much to See you and if I had time would ride over this fall.

I have Some inclination to purchase a Lot or two of those to be Sold in the tract of preston adjoining Louis ville, and have Some money $110 in Col. Prestons hands for that purpose he will Consult you on the Subject.

Julia joins me in love to you Sister and those of our friends [and] your familey –

yr. Afft. Bro

Wm Clark

1. Sources do not indicate that William Preston ever achieved the rank of colonel, but the title-conscious Clark must have referred to him as such for a reason. The best guess is that he had become a colonel in the Virginia militia. He and his family did eventually settle in Jefferson County as Clark supposed, moving there in November 1814. Preston's land that Clark mentions was extensive and located just east of what was then the limits of Louisville and farther eastward in the county. He had inherited it from his father, Col. William Preston. It was at Preston's Middletown farm that Clark's seven-year-old daughter Mary Margaret (1814–1821) died. She was buried at Mulberry Hill, and reinterred in Cave Hill Cemetery in 1868 (with Jonathan and other Clarks) according to M. Lewis Clark's family genealogy. Clark originally had written that she had been reinterred in Bellefontaine Cemetery, but he crossed that out and wrote Cave Hill. Other family documents indicate she was eventually buried by the grave of her aunt Caroline Hancock Preston. (Dorman (2), 57–60; MLClark, 2–3; Meriwether Lewis Clark Papers, TFHS; Bond, 190; Cave Hill Cemetery Records; Bellefontaine Cemetery Records.)
2. Samuel T. Fitzhugh was the brother of Clark's brother-in-law Dennis Fitzhugh.
3. Nicholas Boilvin (1761–1827) was a French-Canadian trader, interpreter, and Indian subagent. He was stationed up the Mississippi among the Sauk and Fox Indians, many of whom still lived east of the Mississippi in Illinois and southern Wisconsin. (Jackson (1), 1:195n.)
4. William Preston Clark (1811–1840) was William and Julia's second child. He lived in St. Louis, never married, and was buried first at John O'Fallon's estate, Athlone, in the Font Hill vault and then moved in 1860 to Bellefontaine Cemetery. M. Lewis Clark in his genealogy and the George Rogers Hancock Clark (1816–1858) family bible both state that William Preston Clark was born 5 October 1811. Clark's statement here makes it clear that he was born almost a month earlier on 10 September. The incorrect date apparently was mistakenly entered in family records. (MLClark, 2–3; Bond, 190.)

Appendix

"You Shall Hear from Me Often"

Letters to Fanny Clark O'Fallon,

Edmund Clark, and John H. Clark, 1795–1811

William Clark was a faithful correspondent to family and friends. While the letters he wrote to Jonathan are the most revealing about himself and the most informative, he also wrote good newsy letters to other family members. Apparently believing in the theory that writing letters would get you letters, he corresponded with his sister, brother, and nephew in addition to many others. Whether while away in the army in the 1790s or from St. Louis in 1809, Clark strived to maintain ties with his family in Kentucky.

The letters he wrote to Edmund and John H. Clark included here were part of the group of Clark letters found in that Louisville attic in 1988. They supplement the letters to Jonathan. The letters to Fanny O'Fallon written in the 1790s have been in the collection of The Filson Historical Society for many years, but given their revealing nature and relevance in contributing to our understanding of the character and life of William Clark, they also are included.

The three letters written to Fanny all date from 1795 and are written from Fort Greenville in present Ohio. While Clark passes along some news about Indian and military affairs, his main focus is on news of a social and romantic nature. He relays gossip about affairs of the heart—his own and others'—in both the Cincinnati and Louisville areas. Whether it be the particulars in the turbulent romance of Capt. Thomas Lewis and the "cruel" Miss B.C. or his solicitous concern for the "wellfar of the Ladees" of Louisville, William Clark makes clear his interest in the affairs of the heart. "Love was a favourable Subject" with the young Lieutenant Clark in 1795 and he never lost interest in it. In October 1810 Brigadier General Clark offered advice to his nephew John on a "man in that State of mind."

Just like his letters to Jonathan, those to Fanny, Edmund, and John are full of family news and queries, and as in some of his letters to Jonathan, in some of those to Edmund and John he writes that he and Julia worry that family and friends will forget them. He encourages them to come visit and, being a booster for his new home, suggests they invest in area enterprises.

One of these enterprises was trade. Mercantile affairs are a regular feature of his letters to Edmund and John. In the same letter in which he offers his advice for a man in love he confesses that his "head is full of mercantile business." He hoped to form a partnership with his brother and nephew, with them buying in the east and funneling the goods through Louisville to St. Louis. He would manage the St. Louis end, where certain supplies were in great demand and good profits could be made. With him in St. Louis and them in Louisville he believed they could not fail. Clark was thwarted in his hope for such a partnership, but he did engage in mercantile pursuits, and he did business with the firm of Edmund and John H. Clark. On 1 March 1811 he wrote them about his mercantile needs and included a lengthy list of articles he wanted for the Indian trade. That he refers to the goods as being for his own business but then labels the list as goods for the Missouri Fur Company may help explain the confusion over the exact nature of his mercantile pursuits.

The ten letters included here are only a small sampling of the many that Clark wrote to Fanny, Edmund, and John. Others are scattered in other collections at various institutions, and some are perhaps in private hands. Many of them most likely have been destroyed over the years. These letters therefore help to open the window on William Clark and his world a bit further.

~

Greene Ville[1]

HeadQuarters May 9th 1795

Dear Sister

Nothing verey material has hapined Since my last letter to you from <u>Cincunati</u> by Vanoy[2] –ᐱ only [ᐱ] my reception from the General[3] at my arrival was more favourable then I had any reason to expect, from my inatention to his orders in returng at a Stated time – but as he is a reasonable as well as a Galant man, and had Some <u>Idea</u> of my <u>Persute</u>, he treated my inatention as all other good fathers would on the Same acasion (Galentrey is the Pride of a Soldur – and atachment followers in corse) — I am very Solecetious concerning the wellfar of the <u>Ladees</u> of your Nabouring hood perticularly Miss —— My long and painfull absence fron her Conversation is a Source of the greatist affliction to me, — The agreable anticipations that I have frequntly made of Spending a great part of this Spring & Summer in her (and there) Companys has been baffled by the Calls of Duty — Sensibility (like hers) can easly conceive the embarisment & distress that this Combat between Love & duty has produced, previous to my departur from <u>her</u>, She will I hope reflect that the duty of a Soldur is of a nature not to be dispenced with; and even <u>Love</u> must yeald to its calls — "but when ever kind fortune will again give me an opertunity, I will flie with all the ardour of Sincsrity & Seek a Deᐱter[ᐱ]mination of my fate —" I should feel hapy to dwell longer on this Subject but the <u>Drums</u> beats for parade[4] —

I have Some hopes of visiting your Purt of the world after the Indian Treaty, at which time I hope to know my fate, at a certain place, Captain T Lewis[5] tells me in Confidence that If he could flatter himself with the Smallest hopes of Suckcess, he would once more actack Miss <u>B.C.</u>[6] but as he can't — he must Content himself with admroing her amuable qualulties, ~~and~~ he ᐱ likewise [ᐱ] Sai's that if, I obtain permition to vesit Kentucky he will most Certainly accompany me & See Miss <u>BC</u> once more, and Should he be So fortunate as to receive a Smile from the anuiable [amiable or admirable], it will encourage him very much. I fear you are tried [tired] of this Subject and Shall no more—

The news of this place is in the Small way, a number of Indians are daily here, peacably inclined — one of our Captains was <u>Broke</u> & dismissed two days ago for geting <u>Drunk</u> whilst on Court martial[7]— prey write to me and give me the news fully –

Give my compliments to relations & Friends & I remain your obt. Brother

William Clark

[Letter carried by Rose.[8]]

1. Greenville was the military base established in west-central Ohio in October 1793 by Gen. Anthony Wayne during his campaign against the confederacy of Northwestern Indians. Named in honor of Gen. Nathanael Greene, Revolutionary War hero and Wayne's former commander, Fort Greenville was established as part of Wayne's plan to train his men and to move against the Indians in 1794. That campaign culminated in the American victory at the Battle of Fallen Timbers on 20 August 1794. After the victory Wayne used Greenville as the site for treaty negotiations with the Indians. It was there, on 3 August 1795, that the Treaty of Greenville was signed. This treaty established a peace that lasted for over fifteen years and that acquired most of the present state of Ohio from the Indians. The fort was later burned and abandoned. Greenville, Ohio, was established on the site of the fort. (McIntosh and Freeman, 209–12; Hurt, 124–25, 131–40; Wilson, 96–118.)

2. Mr. Vanoy has not been identified. Two possibilities are French author Constantin F. Volney and Cincinnati resident Isaac VanNuys. Volney was traveling in the Ohio Valley at this time and visited Fort Greenville, Cincinnati, and Louisville. It is reasonable to assume that he may have met the Clarks in Louisville. VanNuys's name had variant spellings and, given Clark's flair for creative spelling, it is possible that Vanoy was VanNuys. The nature of Clark's mention of the name infers that Fanny knew "Vanoy" as well. Even if she did not, it was common practice for those traveling to a town or area where mail was going to carry that mail with them. (Volney, v–ix; McIntosh and Freeman, 212; Burress, 72; Smith, 49.)

3. Clark most likely is referring to Gen. Anthony Wayne (rather than James Wilkinson). He had reported to Wayne in the past upon returning from a mission or leave and it is probable that he did so in this instance. Anthony Wayne (1745–1796) was a native of Pennsylvania. He was one of the heroes of the American Revolution and acquired the sobriquet "Mad" for his aggressiveness, daring, and sometimes impetuous actions in battle. He retired from active service in 1783 but returned to duty in 1792 as commander of the army whose object it was to defeat the Northwest Indians. Wayne used his time to build and train his army while ultimately futile peace negotiations were held. The desire for revenge

against the Indians was strong among U.S. Army and Kentucky militia forces because of defeats they had suffered at Indian hands in 1790 and 1791 under Harmar and St. Clair, respectively. Wayne's patience and thoroughness caused dissension among some of the troops who preferred faster action. William Clark and other young officers were among this group. The journals Clark kept during this campaign reflect his unhappiness and lack of confidence in Wayne, and his support for James Wilkinson, second-in-command of the army. Wilkinson's ability to sow the seeds of discord and persuade others to support him has already been discussed (see letter dated 2 September 1792). Clark was one of those who fell under Wilkinson's influence. He and most of the others had a change of heart after the army's victory over the Indians at Fallen Timbers, when Wayne's caution, strategy, and military ability proved him even to his critics to be an excellent commander. His masterful handling of negotiations with the Northwestern tribes at Greenville in 1795 resulted in a treaty extremely favorable to the United States. He died at Presque Isle (present Erie, Pennsylvania) on 15 December 1796 of complications from a severe attack of gout, exposure, and poor medical care. Captain Russell Bissell, who would play a future role in the Lewis and Clark Expedition, commanded the post at Presque Isle and gave what comfort he could to Wayne. Wayne was buried there at his request. In 1809 his son removed the remains to St. David's Episcopal Church near Radmor, Pennsylvania, where other Wayne family members were buried. (*DAB*, 19:563–65; William Clark Journal, 1794, TFHS; Loos, 48; Wilson, 118–19; Hurt, 120–42.)

4. It has never been determined who the woman was that Clark apparently was so smitten with in the spring of 1795. He waxes rather eloquent about his feelings and hopes for the romance, going so far as to quote from literature. Given the prominence and connections of the Clark family, and William Clark's own gregarious personality and abilities, he undoubtedly was popular with the young ladies of the Louisville area and would have been one of its most eligible bachelors.

5. Thomas Lewis (d. 1809) was a native of Virginia. He served as a lieutenant in the 15th Virginia (redesignated the 11th in 1778) during the Revolution. He rejoined the army in 1792 as a captain and served in Wayne's campaign against the Northwestern Indians, resigning from the service in March 1801. He may have been a cousin of Meriwether Lewis, though no definite connection could be established. If they were indeed cousins, it is possible that Thomas Lewis played a role in William Clark and Meriwether Lewis's becoming friends. When the younger Lewis, new to the army, reported to Wayne's Legion his veteran cousin

would have welcomed him and introduced him to his comrades, including his friend William Clark. This is speculation, but an interesting possibility. (Heitman (2), 1:631; Gwathmey, 472–73.)

6. Miss B.C. could not be identified. On a guess that her surname started with "C," a survey of prominent Jefferson County families was made but failed to find an appropriate candidate, especially one whose christian name began with a "B" or an "E."

7. During the winter of 1794–1795 and the spring and summer of 1795 many Indians visited and camped near Fort Greenville. The Americans' defeat of them the previous summer at Fallen Timbers and Wayne's strong diplomatic and military actions in the months following that victory assured treaty negotiations that summer at Greenville. The defeated tribes had suffered severe losses of their food stocks, and many Indians visited the fort for presents of food and other desirable items, as well as to attend the peace negotiations. A rather detailed description of the treaty negotiations is in Frazer Wilson's *Advancing the Ohio Frontier.*

Alcohol abuse in the army was a common problem. Officers as well as enlisted men could suffer dire consequences, like the captain Clark notes here being stripped of his rank and dismissed from the army for drunkenness. This officer compounded his offense by committing it while apparently serving on a court-martial, a duty in which a soldier decided the fate of a fellow soldier and was supposed to be on his best behavior and set an example. Alcohol was a major factor in almost ending Meriwether Lewis's military career by a court-martial six months after Clark wrote this letter. He was brought up on charges stemming from a drunken altercation with Lt. Joseph Elliott, in which Lewis was accused of using "reproachful" and "provoking" language toward Elliott and challenging him to a duel. Elliott served with the artillerists and engineers, and was a veteran of the Revolutionary War. The accusation by a fellow officer who was not only senior to Lewis but a veteran of the Revolution could not be ignored. Lewis, at that time an ensign, was tried and found not guilty. He was well aware that he had been spared from a disgraceful end to his young military career and apparently curbed his drinking and temper. (Wilson, 96–118; Ambrose, 45; Heitman (2), 1: 402.)

8. It is possible that this letter was being carried back to Louisville by Clark family slave Rose. Clark does not include the normal form of address before the name, which is very unusual if he was referring to a white man or a white woman. Either Clark made an etiquette blunder, or the person carrying the letter very possibly was the slave Rose.

~

Camp GreeneVille June 1st 1795

Dear Sister
                      Inexpressable was the pleasure I receved
in hearing from you and my friends with you; by my Boy¹ who arrived
here a fiew days ago, but I fear that my letter to you from <u>Cincinnati</u>, you
have not receved; "or if you have," you have not answered, either that or
the one of a later date from this place – (Say three weeks) which letter I
fear has like wise been neglected by you, or perhaps thought too Trifle-
ing to merit an Answer, as <u>Love</u> was a favourable Subject with me at the
time I wrote – I wished much to receive an Answer on the Subject of my
letter, but how Desapointd. I was at the return of the Soldier, to find only
[∧] a [∧] letter from E Taylor,² and what he informed only Serve'd to
hightnd. my ambition; as he mentioned that he partooke of a Dance in
Louisville, where all the Ladies of the Country were assembled, & Spent
their Times agreably—,
     I am happy to here that the Spirits of the people has once more become
enlivened, & hope they will not let Interested motives Deprive them of
the enjoyments that they may easily partake of __ I Should be glad to
Know the founder's, of the late Assembly. The Ladies & Gentlemen that
was at it, and if thure is a probibility of its being Kept up, I hope you will
inform me the Perticulars __ as well as how the Ladies of your nabeur-
inghood are, and if the Miss Er__ Ms__ Fds__ & c & c are at, or on the
verge of matrimony, and whith whome __ I hope my Cozn. N__ has not
Caused any more Contentious <u>riots</u>, if She has who is the unfortunate
<u>one</u> __ Miss F__ is Cruel, and I Should not be Surprised to hear of her
having a Dozen is <u>Too</u> agreable to an old Custome __ Miss B.C has I am
perswaded been Cruel to a Brother Soldur of mine – I hope her Cruelty
will not Continue, "if it Should," I have to pity the unfortunate one, tho' I
hope will ∧ he [∧] meet his fate like a valuent Soldur, who after a long and
Serious <u>Siege</u> is repulsed and falls a Victim to his <u>Foe</u> God forbid my fate
Should ever be ∧ So [∧] Determond, let my attacks be at what time they
may I hope to be allowed Some terms of Recapitulations³——"—
     At my arrival here from Kentucky, the Camp appeared to me a new
world __ all is gaiety, good humer & Devertion. The eye is constantly
entertained with the Splendour of Dress and equipage, and the year
[ear] with the Sounds of Drums, fifes, Bugles, Trumpets, and other In-
strementeals. we have Daily Parades, & Manuvers, when we are amused

by the roreing of the Connon, and the yells of the Guards that perform those manuvers daily;

The Indians likewise engage Some part of our attention, as the[y are] continuerly here ingreat number and when Drunk (as they are often) Cut a number of antick tricks, Such as are verry amuseing to us,[4]—— The Ladies of Fort Washington[5] are Cuming out to the Treaty, and ∧ it is said they [∧] have actuelly Set out Viz. Mrs. Allison, Ford Hopkins & Miss Mercer & Spencer[6] I am Surprised at their Coming out, but Shall leave the propriaty of their Conduct for you to judge of —

You will please to write me by all Safe oppertunities, & you Shall hear from me often, – Prosent my compts. to all Frunds & I remn. yr. ob. Bro

Wm Clark

[Letter carried by Mr. Irvin.]

1. Clark's mention of "my Boy" may be a reference to York, his long-time body servant. It is reasonable to assume that York may have traveled from Jefferson County to Fort Greenville; it is known that Clark and the Clark family trusted him to make long trips with a high degree of independence. This possibility is even more likely if it was indeed the Clark family slave Rose by whom Clark sent his letter of 9 May. If correct, this may indicate a pattern of Clark slaves periodically visiting William Clark with provisions, news, etc. from home. If this mention does refer to York, it is the earliest known reference to him. The term "boy" was commonly used for male slaves. It is not necessarily a reflection of York's age because he was approximately the same age as Clark, perhaps a bit younger, and old enough and experienced enough to make the trip. I think it does, however, reflect the slaveholder tendency to dehumanize slaves.

2. Edmund Haynes (or Hanes) Taylor (1772–1839) was a member of the large Taylor clan, early settlers in Jefferson County and elsewhere in Kentucky. He joined the army in 1793 as an ensign, rose to the rank of lieutenant, and resigned in April 1795. He and Clark served together in Wayne's army. He reentered the army as a captain in 1799 when war with France threatened, and was honorably discharged in 1800. He married Eloise (or Eloiza) Thruston (b. 1782), the half sister of Clark's brother-in-law Charles Mynn Thruston and neighbor John Thruston, in February 1797. An additional tie to Clark was created when Taylor's sister Martha married his good friend and "brother in arms" William Christy. Taylor eventually settled in Bullitt County and died there. (Trabue, 74, 76.)

3. Clark's continued desire to know about the young ladies of their neighborhood and the romantic activities occurring there indicates his interest in both the ladies, possibly eligible ladies, and the social news. His rather dramatic philosophizing on romance and a man's pitiable state when wooing the object of his affections is an opinion he remained remarkably consistent in, as revealed in a letter to his nephew John Hite Clark dated 27 October 1810 and printed in this Appendix. It is unfortunate that he refers to the ladies only by their initials. The same is true regarding his cousin "N." None of them could be identified.

4. Wayne had sent word to the Indians to gather at Greenville by 15 June to begin treaty talks. Records kept at the time record that by 12 June there were 1,130 Indians at Greenville. Relations between them and the Americans were friendly, but Wayne kept an alert guard posted and the cannons of the fort loaded. Official distribution of alcoholic beverages to the Indians in any quantity generally was prohibited. Clark's observation that many of them were often drunk indicates that this rule had been relaxed or the Indians were being supplied from unapproved sources, and officials either could not rid the area of them or looked the other way. (Hurt, 137–38.)

5. Fort Washington was built in the summer of 1789 opposite the mouth of the Licking River at present Cincinnati. It was a major fortification, capable of housing 1,500 men. The small frontier village of Losantiville already was located there and began to flourish owing to the protection the installation provided. Arthur St. Clair, governor of the Northwest Territory, established his headquarters there the following year, and soon renamed Losantiville Cincinnati in honor of the Society of the Cincinnati, to which he belonged. (Goss, 49–51; Galbreath, 195–96.)

6. Mrs. Allison is Rebecca Strong Allison, the wife of the surgeon general of the army, Richard Allison (d. ca. 1815), and daughter of Capt. Daniel Strong. Allison was from Pennsylvania and had served as a surgeon's mate in the Revolution. They were married in Hamilton County, Ohio, on 12 December 1791. Mrs. Ford is Sophia Spencer Ford (1774–1846), wife of Capt. Mahlon Ford (d. 1820), and daughter of Judge Oliver Spencer (1736–1811) of Columbia, Hamilton County. They were married 31 August 1793 in Hamilton County. Both the Spencers and Ford were from New Jersey. Ford had served as a lieutenant and Judge Spencer as a colonel in New Jersey regiments during the Revolution. Miss Spencer undoubtedly was a sister of Sophia Spencer Ford and could have been Nancy (1768–1842), Sarah (1777–1851), or possibly Dorothea (1779–1841), though she seems a bit young for such an outing. Sarah is a good candidate, being about eighteen years old. She did not marry until 1800. Miss Mercer may have been the daughter of Ham-

ilton County resident Capt. Aaron Mercer of Columbia. Mrs. Hopkins could not be identified, but she may have been the wife of Noah E. Hopkins, who lived in Hamilton County and was at least an acquaintance of Dr. Richard Allison. The trip from Fort Washington to Greenville would have been somewhat rigorous, and the propriety of ladies visiting this frontier outpost, especially in the presence of Indians just recently hostile to Americans, apparently was questioned by Clark and others. It seems questionable that Fanny would have known these women, but it is possible. More likely, however, brother William was just making sure that he passed on all the news he thought would interest Fanny and friends and family back home, especially that of a social gossip kind. (Burress, 1:1, 22, 24; Heitman (2), 1:160, 429; Spencer, 133–34; White, 2:1231; Hamilton County Chapter, 19.)

~

Greene Ville July 1st 1795

Dear Fanny

I wrote to you a fiew days ago by Mr. Hite,[1] but informed you but little, as I was in a horry at that time, I can now inform you but little more ∧ not haveing any thing Intrsgn. [∧] Lieutenant Strother[2] the Bearer of this letter, I make no doubt, but you will See him, as he entends to Spend Some time in your nabouringhood, you will find him an agreable man in conversation, Should you get acquainted with him — The accurrencus of this Cantunement Can't be in the Smalles interesting to you, and Shall Say but little, Mrs. Allison, Ford & Hopkins, are here, and are much Galanted by the officers, we have like wise, a Mrs. Shaylor,[3] wife to a Major, but as She was of <u>low</u> burth & less breading She is not noticed at all.[4] — I heard from Pope[5] yesterday. I find from his letter that as the famas Mariah[6] has turned out to be of bad Canection (and the moon nearly full [paper and text loss] — Capt. T. Lewis tels me that he [paper and text loss] Miss B.C this fall, with me — [paper and text loss] if She Says any thing in [paper and text loss] will give him great encouragement [paper and text loss] write to me every perticelar that [paper and text loss] that part of the world, And write freely. I would be glad to rcvee a letter from my Sister Croghan[7] could I be so favored but I Surpose She cant' Spear the time, — I Should have wrote to my father[8] but have nothing to Say more then my respect, which I hope you will prosent to him & my mother Bro: & Sister Croghan, compliments to all the girls & I rmn. your obt. Brother

Wm Clark

[Letter carried by Lt. Strother.]

1. This is one of the large family of Hites that settled in Jefferson County, Kentucky. Since Clark refers to him as "Mr." to Fanny I assume that he bore no military title (since Clark usually, but not always, used a person's military title), and thus is not Isaac Hite, Jr., previously identified. He may have been Joseph Hite (1757–1831), the third son of Col. Abraham Hite and younger brother of Isaac Hite. (Sallee, 51.)
2. Benjamin Strother, who served with Clark in the Fourth Sub-Legion. He was a native of Virginia and joined the army as a lieutenant in March 1792 just as Clark had. He resigned his commission in September 1797. (Heitman (2), 1:933.)
3. Mary Shaylor was the wife of Maj. Joseph Shaylor (d. 1816). She was the widow of a man named Fowler who was recorded as "killed on hill hunting buffalo," thus indicating that she had been living on the frontier, possibly in Hamilton County. Joseph Shaylor was a native of Massachusetts, had served as an officer in Connecticut regiments during the Revolution, and reentered the army as a captain in 1791. He was a major in the Third Sub-Legion at this time, and resigned from the army in May 1797. They married 17 July 1792 in Hamilton County. (Heitman (2), 1:878; Burress, 63.)
4. This statement is quite informative about Clark and society at that time. Even on the frontier, on the edge of wilderness surrounded by Indians, social distinctions were made and people evaluated on the basis of their social standing and abilities. Clark's evaluation of Mrs. Shaylor as being of "low burth & less breading" seems rather snobbish and judgmental but would not have been unusual. Despite marrying an army officer, an officer superior in rank to Clark, she could not overcome the stigma of her social position prior to her marriage or possibly her lack of the social graces expected of the upper social classes at that time. Clark definitely belonged to that upper social class, and obviously made a distinction between his and many of his peers' position and that of those in a lower position. While perhaps the attitude was tempered over time and with maturity, Clark almost certainly would have retained something of it and made such distinctions throughout his life.
5. Most likely Worden Pope, previously identified.
6. Mariah (or possibly a young lady named Maria) has not been identified.

It is unfortunate that paper loss to the letter has resulted in information about the "famas Mariah" and more gossip about the travails of Captain Thomas Lewis and the "cruel" Miss B.C. being lost.

7. Sister Croghan is of course his sister Lucy Clark Croghan, previously identified.

8. John Clark (1725–1799) was a native of King and Queen County, Virginia. He married Ann Rogers (1728–1798) in 1748 or 1749, and they moved westward to frontier Albemarle County to a plantation he had inherited. In the mid-1750s the family returned eastward to another inherited plantation in Caroline and Spotsylvania Counties, and lived in Caroline County. In 1784 John Clark removed his family to Kentucky, arriving in Jefferson County in March 1785, after wintering at Redstone Landing near Pittsburgh. He lived on his plantation, Mulberry Hill, until his death on 29 July 1799. (William reported the death of their father as occurring on the previous day in a letter to Jonathan dated 30 July 1799. Sister Fanny recorded his death as 30 July on a note identifying a lock of his hair. Since William's record of the death was written at the time, I have used it, although he may have misdated his letter.) Both John and Ann Clark were buried in the family cemetery there and remained there after many of its occupants were transferred to Cave Hill Cemetery in 1868. (Dorman (1), 25–26; Draper Mss., 2L51; Clark family file.)

~

St. Louis December 15th [and 16] 1808.

Dear John

Inclosed you will recive Mr. Saml. Gwathmey['s] Bond on which thre is a ballance remaining of $567.60 cts. after deducting the two Credits on the bond and the five hundred dollars receved by my brother, I Shall request Sam to pay you this money, and inform him that his bond is in your possession. Mr. Evreat Clarks Bond is in possission of your father. I have requested him to put the money Collected on it into your possession, I hope that those Gentlemen will be able to pay you about 1214 Dollars— if Cozen Sam. pays you it will be necessary for you to take in my Order in favor of your father when you delivr the Bond _ I also inclose you the ballance of my Salary fer this year in a Draft of 94 Dols. & 52 cents No. 29 which you will place to my Credit _ I this moment received a Letter frome Mr. William Morrison of Kaskaskia requsting me to make Some arrangements to pay Mr. Fry for Williams Schooling and expencus. he Counts your fathers Letter in which there is Certain arrangements which Suits me verry well. I must request you to pay <u>hundred & fifty</u> Dollars to Mr. Fry for expences which has already encured and Such other Charges as may appear autherised & take receipts Specifying fer what Srvice & Expenditures the money was applied, and Send all Such receipts to me _ ask Mr. Fitzhugh if he has been paid his account fer furnishing Wm. morrison, and if in that account he had Charged £5. advanced by me to Mr. Fry _

16th. ~~Will you tell~~ John Sullivan has just arrived and put into my hands three letters one from your Father, Uncle Edmd. and Mr. Fitzhugh_ I Shall answer all those letters imedeately _ your uncle Edmend has joined you ∧in the mercantile business[∧] and writes to me on the Subject, if it is your wish and his wish ∧which I have reason to beleve it is,[∧] for me to be Connected it is perfectly mine, and I am highly pleased, much pleased with the Connection, I thought Bro: Edmund was averse to the mercantile business or I Should have mentioned him in our first proposition for this business. Dear John It is now the time to Speek candidly to each other, let us Say what we Can do, what we wish to be done & what we will do, for my part I have Said what I Could do, I wish to be Connected with you[r] uncle Edmond & yourself equally in a S[t]ore at Louisville and this placee, and a Small branch from this place to the Camp &c. and I must have goods ~~here~~ here _ I must be doing Something, and I know of nothing which appears So certain as mercantile business, and no time is to be lost _ Say my Dear Sir ~~my Dear Sir~~ if my plan of Trade, my funds, and my Situotion in public business (which will deprive the Compy. of much personal aid from me) if it will be perfectly Consistent with your wishes, Consult with one another, and Consult your father who is equally friendly to us all. let us not do any thing which may not be perfectly agreeably to all _ Not that if we enter into this Trade ~~let~~ our acts [∧]will[∧] be Such when bounded by the fullst Confidence in each other and utechd [attached] by both interest & affection we may prosper in friendship & Love.

If there is any objections or Dificultes prey let us not risque our hapiness and love fer each other. I will Say again that there is no two men I would as Soon resque my all with in trade as you[r] uncle Edmund & your Self (leaving Bro Jo_ out of the question) under the heavins.

Your Aunt joins in best wishes for your health & hapiness

Yr. Friend

Wm Clark

not'd   Send on the Draft fer [in] a few Days
            please to Send Mr. Tompkins letter
                    Tell Mr. Fitzhugh that I Should write him if I had time
                    this mail

Note: Clark's great love and respect for his family is evident in this letter to
his nephew, as well as his forthright and practical manner of addressing
matters. It also is interesting to note that Clark spells his brother Edmund's
name three different ways in this one letter. Three! He normally spells it
correctly. He certainly knew how to spell it. Why he took his scatter-gun
approach to spelling to Edmund's name here is not known. My guess
would be his usual spelling carelessness and creativity were particularly
pronounced that day.

$\sim$

St. Louis January 27th 1809

Dear Brother
                    I wrote to you Some time ago, Since that time I have noth-
ing of consequence to relate, excupt that we anticipate great Satisfaction
in you being with us a great portion of your time.[1] I have purchased a
house and lot in the Center of the Town, Shall purchase another fer the U
S near it on which I expect to build Several houses[2] _ I wish you would
engage & Send potts[3] here if he is not too much of a Drunkard. I would
give a handsom job to a Stone mason if one could be here in time __ all
those macanicks are here but ther prices are higher than I wish to give. _
I wrote to temple Gwathmey[4] about a copy of my rules for the Troop of
horse which I formerly Commanded in Jefferson.[5] Temple has never answered my letter. please to ask im if he ever receved my letter
        The weather has been extreamly cold fer a long time and a great deel
of Skeeting Slaying[6] & fun with the young people of this neighbourhood.
        we have not had the mail from Louis ville for two months, and we are
now oblige[d] to Send oure letters and Despatches by an express as far
as vincennes where we expect the mail is _ this expence bear hard on us
but the merchents at this Town has a notion of under bidding M. Lyons
and have the mail Carred themselves.[7]

I wrote bro Jona. and John verry laterly & have nothing to Say to them of any importance at this time.

my Julia Joins me in best wishes for your health and hapiniss.

yr. afft. Brother

Wm Clark

Prey let me know how all Drive on

1. Clark seems to indicate that Edmund Clark is either coming for a lengthy visit or even relocating to St. Louis. Although he encouraged his brother to move to St. Louis, Edmund apparently never seriously considered it, and by early 1809 he and John Hite Clark had formed a mercantile partnership in Louisville. It is not known whether Edmund was simply planning a visit or if he did visit St. Louis. It is interesting that William Clark does not mention the birth of his son. Perhaps he thought reporting it to Jonathan was sufficient, and he would spread the word among family and friends in Louisville.

2. Clark had previously mentioned this house, and would do so again in succeeding letters. It apparently was the house at the southeast corner of Main and Vine.

3. Probably John B. Potts (1769–1847) of Jefferson County, Kentucky. He was a native of either Pottstown, Pennsylvania, or Washington County, Maryland (probably the latter). He knew William Clark and had witnessed the 10 January 1800 sale of five slaves (Kitt, Lew, Venos, Frankey, and Tanner) to him by George Rogers Clark. No mention was found of Potts being a stonemason, but there were stonemasons in the family. The surname also appears as Botts. This John Potts is not, of course, to be confused with the John Potts of the Lewis and Clark Expedition. (Potts family file, TFHS; JCBPAB, 2:25.)

4. Temple Gwathmey (ca. 1775–1855) was the son of Owen and Ann Clark Gwathmey, and thus another of William Clark's Gwathmey nephews. He was a native of Virginia and had settled in Jefferson County with his parents and siblings by the late 1790s. He married Ann Meriwether Marks (d. 1848), on 14 June 1803. She had come to Louisville from Charlottesville, Virginia. Given her name and place of birth, she undoubtedly was related to Meriwether Lewis. See letter dated 13 August 1801, note 4, for related information. (Gwathmey family file; Rogers Index.)

5. Clark is referring to the troop of cavalry he commanded in the Jefferson County militia, First Regiment, Kentucky Militia. He received his com-

mission as a captain on 28 May 1800. Thus he could rightly be called captain while on the expedition, although he was officially a second and later first lieutenant of artillery in the regular army during that period. He was called captain before the expedition because of his militia rank. In November 2000 President Bill Clinton signed the appropriate documents promoting Clark to the rank of captain in the U. S. Army. A number of the men mentioned in these letters were comrades of Clark's from his years in the militia. (Clift (1), 104.)

6. A wonderful example of William Clark's spelling and the very different meanings his statements could have if taken literally. The young people of St. Louis were not, of course, having fun shooting skeet and slaying each other out on the Mississippi. They were skating and sleighing.

7. The mail service between St. Louis and Vincennes was erratic and delay-ridden at this time. It was a common topic in the *Missouri Gazette.* Post office–related legislation and routes were regularly reported, and wails of frustration about the delayed mail or no mail at all were often expressed. An alternate, more appropriate route through southern Illinois was also proposed as a solution. Clark, Meriwether Lewis, and others were so frustrated by the poor mails that they paid for expresses to carry their mail to Vincennes so that it could be transmitted on to Washington and elsewhere. No M. Lyon or Lyons was found in St. Louis sources relating to the mails. The M. Lyons mentioned might be the colorful Matthew Lyon (ca. 1746–1822), a native of Ireland who came to America in 1765. He was a Revolutionary War veteran and served as a congressman and judge from Vermont before moving to Eddyville in western Kentucky. Lyon later again served as a U.S. congressman. His rough-and-tumble style of politics earned him the nicknames "The Spitting Lyon" (for spitting in an opponent's face), "Roaring Lyon," and the "Scourge of Aristocracy." No mention was found of his serving as a postmaster or having a mail contract, but given his business activities and position it certainly is possible he was the Mr. Lyons to which Clark refers. (*Missouri Gazette,* 10 August 1808, 25 January 1809, 1 February 1809, 15 February 1809, 31 May 1809; *Louisiana Gazette,* 26 July 1810, 14 November 1810, 5 December 1810; Scharf, 2:1430–31; Loos, 865; *DAB,* 11:532–34; *BDAC,* 1487; *KE,* 587–88; *The Courier-Journal,* 28 September 1998; Mayo, 157–58.)

~

St. Louis 15th 1809 April

Dear Brother

Mr. Tompkins arrived here yesterday by whome I had the pleasure of receiving a letter from you by which I am informed that you decline being Concerned in the St. Louis missouri fur Compy. _ Mr. Fitzhugh is at New Orleans & John H. Clark to the Eastward, those falurs in the expectation of the Company has disapointed them a little in the Source of precureing men as well as to vend Some of their furs &c &c. _ The two Sheares which are remaining on my hands I believe Can be Disposed of one whole Share is more than I wished to retain, from my present cercumstancus, the Compy has no aversion to my Continueing as they think my influence will do them no harm, and they want both advice and an agent of a perticular discription here ___ I have not the Smalest doubt of Suckcess, and if I did not think the risque of 2 Shares more than my Slender fortune Could justify Should not hesitate in keeping both. Mr. Wilkinson I [∧]fear[∧] has not explained to you as I expected he would have done, and I have not had time to write you fully on the Subject ___ I am much Concerned about Bro. georges unfortunate Situation, I hope he is will[well] attended to. give him my most fervent preyers for his ease and Safe recovery.¹ _ The Boys² give me Some uneaseness _ The one I have with me is violently hot, of good Sence without the knowledge of any one thing except the latin grammer _ the one in L. _ I Shall keep there a Short time longer, and must in my own Case talk about Clothes &c_ &c. I Send him money, he has not recved it I Suppose as he wants more. You did not inform me that you had recved my letters' and Draft on you in favour of Mr. Elliott³ for $500, which money I had directed Mr. Wilkinson to leave in John's hands Subject to my order. please to inform me on this Subject without loss of time what has been the result? have you recved the money of W. _ or have you payed the Bill on your own account in Conformity to the advice. if you have paid on your own accounts, I will add that Sum to the accounts you have paid for me and Send you a Bill &c. for all.

I wish to employ a Stone mason at 2/6 a purch to build a large house, or I will give him the lowest Kenty. price he finding himself will you See Mr. Bartlet⁴ on this Subject.

will you employ a mill wright for me to Send to the Fort on the Missouri to put up the Osage mill. I will give $40 a month and furnish one ration per day   Mr. Terrel[5] who worked with Mr. Fishback[6] promised me he would Come, please to Send out and know of him, or git any other you please for this Service who Can work, please to write me on these Subjects as Soon as possible.

The Indians on the Illinois River and up the mississippi have thretened to attack the fort up the Mississippi, and make war &c. and the govr. has taken Some measures to repell the attack which if effected will prevent a war with those people[7]

Mr. Capron I am told is comeing on here, and wishes me to rent him a house &c. I offered thro' John H. Clark to Mr. Capron a Certain Salary for which he was to perform Certain duties, he axcepted, and in a Second letter, he Signified that ~~he expected~~ [∧]If I would[∧] pay from the time of John, Spokeing to him on the Subject that it would be Sufficent, or Something to that purpote which inducd me to belevee that he was not contented with the pay, or expected more than I thought proper to give, and wrote to John on the Subject, that I Should not make any Such bargain &c. and as I have not heard from either Since that time, have Concluded that he had declined, and have employed another man who Sutes me verry well, please to make this Known to Mr. Capron if he has not left your Town.[8]

Docr. Dunlap[9] the man who ows the note which you inclosed to Mr. Pope,[10] has run away Several months for murdering young Jones.[11] and it is Said more in Debt than he was worth. I do not think the debt worth one Cent and it is probable that it must have been known — I Shall Send the letter to pope and request him to write you.

I wished you or John had informed me more pertcularly about the Comercial business, if I am to be Conserned or not, I fear we have lost the time, if I could have got a fiew goods here last fall or winter, we Could have with much ease [made] $5000 with a tolerable assortment, I Speak on a Certainty as Mr. Rania[12] Sold out all his goods and Cleared more money. but now Several Stores are here and one verry good assortment, when those Stores are decorted [deserted] then will be again a favourable time perhaps.

Please to present my Compts. to all friends. Julia joins in effectunate love to you. we are all well. I will write to Bro. Jona. & frends in answer to their letters by Mr. Tompkins[13] when I have time at present I have not. exuse this hasty Scraul which I have not red over.[14] Yr. Affly.

Wm Clark

1. See Clark's letter to Jonathan dated 28 May 1809, note 2. Since this letter predates that one, Clark is more specific than in Jonathan's letter. He only recently would have learned of George's accident and possibly of his leg being amputated (three weeks before this letter was written).

2. The "Boys" were his nephews Benjamin O'Fallon, who had moved to St. Louis and was completing his education there and who would soon become involved in Indian affairs and trade, and John O'Fallon, then in school in Lexington, Kentucky.

3. Possibly Dr. Aaron Elliott (ca. 1758–1811) of Ste. Genevieve, Missouri. He and his family had moved from Connecticut to Louisiana Territory ca. 1804. He was a doctor and druggist and often ran an ad for drugs in the *Missouri Gazette*. In 1808 he served as a trustee of the town and as Charless's agent for the *Gazette* in Ste. Genevieve. The *Louisiana Gazette* reported that Elliott died in Ste. Genevieve on 5 August 1811. There was also a druggist named E. A. Elliott in St. Louis (apparently Aaron Elliott's son). (Houck, 3:82; *Missouri Gazette*, 5 July 1809, 13 September 1809; *Louisiana Gazette*, 1 February 1810, 8 August 1811.)

4. Mr. Bartlett could not be positively identified. He may be James Bartlett who owned a farm along Floyds Fork in eastern Jefferson County, Kentucky.

5. Possibly John Terrell, who is listed in the 1810 Jefferson County, Kentucky, census. Since he is listed in the 1810 census, it would seem that he did not go to Missouri. Clark would have known him and other millwrights because of his own experience with owning and operating mills. Getting a mill built at Fort Osage was a priority that year. (Jefferson Co., Ky., 1810 Census, 19A.)

6. Probably Charles Fishback whose wife was Rebecca Vanmeter Hite. He was therefore part of the extended Clark family. In April 1808 Fishback had been paid by the mercantile firm of Fitzhugh and Rose of Louisville for building a horse mill. (JCMB, 1:50; Fitzhugh and Rose Account Books, 1809–1814.)

7. See Clark's letter to Jonathan dated 28 May 1809, note 8. Fears of a general Indian war up the Mississippi and east of there ran high in the spring of 1809, but measures taken by Lewis and Clark helped defuse the situation. (Loos, 865–74.)

8. It is not known what duties Clark expected Capron to perform for him. Capron did indeed soon settle in St. Louis but apparently did not work for Clark (see letter dated 22 August 1808, note 4).

9. Dr. James Dunlap (or Dunlop) was a respected physician in Kaskaskia, Illinois, until 7 December 1808 when he murdered Rice Jones. The two men had been involved on opposite sides in a canceled duel. The matter still festered, and apparently Jones had made some cutting

remarks about Dunlap. Dunlap retaliated with threats and then by approaching Jones on the street and shooting him in the chest at point-blank range. It is not known what happened to Dunlap, but a James Dunlap does appear in the 1818 and 1820 Illinois censuses in White County in southeastern Illinois along the Wabash River. One would think that Dunlap would have been brought to trial for the murder if his whereabouts were known. Clark obviously knows the details of the case, including Dunlap's poor financial situation. (*Kentucky Gazette,* 17 January 1809; *Missouri Gazette,* 14 December 1808; Norton (1), 201; Norton (2), 351.)

10. It is not definitely known who this Mr. Pope is. It may be Worden Pope of Louisville (see letter dated 22 August 1808, note 2), or Nathaniel Pope (1784–1850) of Illinois. Given the context, it probably is the latter. Nathaniel Pope was the son of William and Penelope Edwards Pope and Worden Pope's first cousin. He was born in Louisville, educated in law at Transylvania University, and by 1806 had settled in Ste. Genevieve, Missouri. He soon moved to Kaskaskia to practice law and was appointed secretary of Illinois Territory when it was organized in 1809. He briefly served as acting governor of Illinois Territory following the resignation of John Boyle. He did much to organize the territory's government until the new governor, and his cousin, Ninian Edwards, arrived. In 1816 he was elected a territorial delegate to Congress. Following two years in Congress he was appointed registrar of the land office at Edwardsville, Illinois, and served until March 1819 when he was appointed U.S. district judge for Illinois. He served as district judge until his death. He died in St. Louis and was buried at Font Hill, the John O'Fallon family cemetery (which probably means he was reinterred at Bellefontaine Cemetery). He married Lucretia Backus in 1809, and they had six children, including the Civil War general John Pope. In a letter dated 24 October 1809, before he knew of Meriwether Lewis's death, Frederick Bates requested Pope's assistance in having John Coburn appointed territorial governor in place of the embattled and embarrassed Lewis when James Madison took office. (*DAB,* 15:77–78; *BDAC,* 1693; Johnston, 2:645–46; Loos, 875–77; Marshall, 100–101.)

11. Rice Jones (1781–1808) was a native of Wales who came to America in 1784 with his father John Rice Jones (1759–1824). The elder Jones practiced law in London before immigrating. He first settled in Philadelphia and then in 1785 in Louisville. He was a member of George Rogers Clark's 1786 expedition against the Indians and served as commissary general of the Vincennes garrison. He settled at Vincennes, was active in militia affairs, was the first English-speaking

lawyer in Indiana, and the first practicing lawyer in Illinois. He held various governmental posts, including that of attorney general of Indiana Territory, postmaster at Vincennes, and supreme court judge in Missouri. He settled in Kaskaskia in 1808 and in Missouri in 1810. The younger Jones was trained in both medicine and the law. He was a member of the Indiana territorial legislature from Randolph County (Kaskaskia is in Randolph County), and was considered someone with a bright future at the time he was killed by Dunlap. (*Missouri Gazette*, 14 December 1808; "John Rice Jones," *The Twentieth Century Biographical Dictionary*, vol. 6; Jackson (1), 1:135.)

12. Mr. Rania most likely is Francis Regnier, a St. Louis merchant at this time. He supplied many of the goods the St. Louis Missouri Fur Company bought in the spring of 1809 in preparation for its trip up the Missouri. (Loos, 897.)

13. This could be one of several Tompkins. The definite one was not identified. George Tompkins might have been visiting the area in preparation for moving to St. Louis and opening a school. William Tompkins was in the area in mid-1810 (see letter dated 3 July 1810, note 1).

14. This mention concerning reading over his "Scraul" confirms that Clark usually did proof his letters. Although this is evident from his corrections it is nice to have this statement.

~

Septr. 3rd. 1810 St. Louis

Dear Brother

I recved your letter of the 18th. of august with much pleasure. you Say that you have not recved a letter from me Since I left you, I have wrote two or three times. I wrote you about your debt at Kaskaskia, and also Stated my Situation with the Missouri Company I recved Some return from the M Conpy. not Sufficent to pay the expence of hands, if we get as much as will pay the hands and outfit I Shall be Satisfied, but I fear that we Shall not receive more than Sufficent to pay the expences, and I Shall have to pay $2400, which is not very pleasent for me. it has alarmed me Some. and made me extreemly frugal and a little unhapy, but with a little aid I think I shall get through.[1] Keep my Sitiation to your Selves.

I have Succeded in Stoping the war party of 4 or 500 Indians ₍Sha-wonees Delaweys Cherekees & others[₍] going to war against the

Osage. Some flying reports of Indian dis content on the waubash, Some Horses have been Stole, and Six weeks ago 4 men were killed about 100 mils from this place by Indians near the lakes.[2]

Julia Joins me in best wisshes for the hapiness [of] your self & John And belev me to be affly.

yr. Bro & frend

Wm Clark

[postscript running vertically bottom to top]

I will purchase furs for Mr. Duncan[3] if he will let me know he wants this _ in time to get the best

I have Sent By Wm. Brazel[4] with the public furs Sundery packs of Beaver to be delivered to you at the lower landng for Mr. Smith[5] of Lexington, which I wish you to recve & pay freght for Mr. Smith who will deposit mony for that purpose _ they will probaley get up About 12 or 15 inst.   WC.

[Letter carried by John Sullivan.]

1. John Loos gives a good account of the activities and expenses of the St. Louis Missouri Fur Company at this time. Most of the partners in the enterprise were optimistic regarding their chances for future success, and 1811 indeed proved to be a good year. (Loos, 958–68.)

2. The *Louisiana Gazette* chronicles the various Indian troubles during this period. The activities of Tecumseh and his brother the Prophet, scattered murders, and Clark's success in stopping a large war party of Shawnee and Delaware with recruited allies from attacking the Arkansas Osages are all reported. "The lakes" refers to the Great Lakes, still the area of a large concentration of Indians, many hostile to the United States and friendly, if not actively allied, with the British. (*Louisiana Gazette,* 19 July 1810, 2, 30 August 1810, 20 September 1810, 31 October 1810.)

3. Henry Duncan (d. 1814) was a Louisville hatter in partnership with Daniel S. Howell (see letter dated 2 January 1809, note 4). In addition to the Louisville shop he had a hat manufactory in Shelbyville, Kentucky. He married Nancy Ship in April 1795 in Jefferson County, Kentucky. Whether Clark ended up purchasing furs for him in 1810 is not known, but by April 1811 the two men were engaged in business with each other. Duncan requested specific types and numbers of furs at certain prices and sent Clark a large box containing gunpowder, whiskey,

and tobacco for him to either buy or sell for him (apparently to finance the furs). As noted earlier, Clark was engaged in some type of trading enterprise, but its exact nature and connection (if any) to the fur company, his brother and nephew, or anyone else, has not been definitely determined. (JCWB, 2:15–16; JCMB, 1:21; Duncan to Clark, 6 April 1811, WCP-VMC; Loos, 968–72.)

4. William Brazel (or Beazel) has not been identified. Apparently he was a government employee who oversaw trips carrying government furs eastward. Clark might be referring to a member of the Brazeau family, residents of St. Louis at this time.

5. Mr. Smith has not been positively identified. He may be William Smith (1772–1817), a native of Culpeper County, Virginia, who settled in Lexington, Kentucky, then moved to St. Louis in 1810 and established a store. He may have been the Smith in the Lexington firm of Smith and Von Phul, retail merchants and possibly hatters. The 1811 Fayette County tax list includes a listing for a town lot with a retail store owned by them. It certainly is plausible that Clark would send a shipment of furs to Smith for his business. Edmund and John H. Clark obviously had a business relationship with him. There are no advertisements for the store listed in the index to the *Kentucky Gazette,* but there is a 24 September 1819 notice that a Graff Von Phul, formerly of Lexington and lately of St. Louis, had drowned in the Ohio River. A Henry Von Phul (1784–1874) clerked in Thomas Hunt, Jr.'s store in Lexington from 1800 to 1810 and moved to St. Louis in 1811. I do not recall seeing an advertisement in the *Louisiana Gazette* for a store under the name of Smith or Von Phul up to September 1811, but Billon cites a notice in the 19 September 1812 edition of that newspaper for the dissolution of the partnership of Smith, Von Phul & Co. (continuing business as Smith & Von Phul). This may place their actual arrival in St. Louis between September 1811 and September 1812. (Billon, 126, 246–47, 265–66; Fayette Co., Ky., Tax List, 1811; Green, 293.)

~

Saint Louis 27th Octr. 1810

Dear John

I have not had the Satisfaction of receiving a letter from you for a long time, I Seppose the pressure of your business has has prevented your writing as often as usial. your uncle Edmund has favoured me with Several letters which I have answered. In one of his letters he in-

formed me nancy was to be maried to Mr. pierce,¹ and hinted at your being a little in love &c. I know whin a man is in that way his mind is bent
on the Object of his admoration and he thinks every attention he can pay
to the fair Object, is Scerce Sufficent to Shew the arder of his passion.
man in that State of mind deserves not only pity but the applaus of his
friend[s].² do John, let me know how you Suceed; and if I am consistent
would ask the name of the ladey. we have expected you to visit us ever
Since we were informed of the Sale of your goods, and Still have flattering hopes of Seeing you here with us Soon, Can't you ride over and See
us. I have a great deel to Say to you and your Aunt wishes much to See
you here. my head is full of mercantile business here and I Should be
glad to have a little talk with you on that Subject. we hear of but little of
the acurinces of your neighbourhood. and have only herd thro' the
medein [medium] of a Louis ville paper of nancies being maried.³ you
have Sold your goods and your uncle Edmund writes me fer part whiskey that article Sold in this Town yesterday for <u>one dollar and a quarter</u>
pr. gallon by the Barrel. Mr. Morehead⁴ a merchnt of this place Sent a
young man to Louis ville to purchase a quantity of Whiskey to bring
here. you can Judge if it will be of advantage to Sind that article here or
not.

your aunt Says you must tell nancy that She must have forgotn. her,
but She hopes that She will again think of her. Lewis begins to talk tolerably well walks about & Beats his drum thro' the Streets,

your aunt joins me in the very best wishes for you[r] health and hapiniss rember us to you[r] Fathr mothr Sister uncle Edmd. and acupt of
my

Sincer affects. yr. Sinc_ Uncle
Wm Clark

I Send this by Judge Coburn
who is just about to Set out.
[Letter carried by John Coburn.]

1. James Anderson Pearce (1777–1825) was a native of Cumberland
County, Virginia, the son of Edmund and Mary Anderson Pearce. He
was a farmer and businessman. He married Jonathan and Sarah Clark's
daughter Ann on 30 September 1810. They moved to Logan County,
Kentucky, near Russellville following their wedding and later lived at
Trough Spring (most likely not long before or following Sarah Clark's
death in 1818). They were buried at Mulberry Hill in the Clark ceme-

tery and reinterred with Jonathan and some of the other Clarks at Cave Hill Cemetery in 1868. Although their remains are at Cave Hill (with markers there), they also have memorial tombstones in the Mulberry Hill graveyard. (Rogers Index; Jonathan Clark Diary, 30 September 1810; Dorman (1), 29.)

2. A wonderful insight into William Clark's opinion of love and a man in love. While possibly intentionally written with a bit of humor, his reflection on a man in "that way" not only shows his observation of men in love, including possibly his own experience, but also I think indicates a familiarity with popular literature of the period. It is interesting to compare this passage with those about love and romance that he wrote his sister Fanny in 1795. He still holds similar views fifteen years later, and after being married almost three years.

3. The Louisville paper was probably the *Western Courier,* founded in 1810 by Nicholas Clarke, or the *Louisville Gazette and Western Advertiser,* a weekly that appeared from 1807 to 1812. (Lathem, 48, 81–82.)

4. Forgus or Fargus Moorhead (it sometimes appears as Fergus Morehead) was quite the entrepreneur. He probably had only recently moved to St. Louis from the Pittsburgh area, and he quickly involved himself in business and civic affairs. He first appears in the *Louisiana Gazette* as being associated with the Pittsburgh mercantile firm of Henry M. Shreve & Co., and soon after as operating a store and a slaughterhouse, buying hides, and being a partner in a blacksmith shop. In December 1810 he was serving as a justice of the peace for the district of St. Louis. (*Louisiana Gazette,* 16 August 1810, 5 December 1810, 28 March 1811, 12 September 1811; William Clark Power of Attorney, 10 December 1810, JCP-TBC; Colter-Frick, 199.)

~

Saint Louis March 1st 1811

Dear Sirs [Edmund and John Hite Clark]

The articles mentioned in the anexed List,[1] I am much in want of in my marcantile business,[2] and if you Can precure them on my credit or with the assistance of yours, the remittances Shall be made to you or them as may be agreed on as Soon as possible. if you Can't precure all those articles, please to Send me Such as you Can precure— Mr Lettig the Bearer of this is will acquainted with the quality and prices of Such articles and may be of Service to you [in?] [word and paper loss] the choice if they Can be had.

I wish very much to have a Correspond[ent] [last three letters of word missing due to paper loss] in your place who will agree to furnish me with Such articles the produc of Kentucky &c. or Ohio as will Sell here— if it would be quit[e] agreeable to you, or Mr. Fitzhugh to do So please to inform me— it will probably at Some times be in my power to Send the Cash, but it may not at all times and in that Case a Credit will be necessary.

with high respect & esteem
You[r] Ob H[umble]. Sret [Servant]
Wm Clark

List of Indian Goods for <u>M F C</u>

300 lbs. of powder
1 piece of Scarlet Cloth to cost about 5/–
1 " Spoted Swans Down
1 " figured flannel
20 par 3 pt. Blankets
20 " 2½ " do [ditto]
6 " 2 " "
6 " 1½ " "
6 " 1 " "
10 Doz. red handle knives [Clark illustrates the style he wants]
1000 Flints
200 Fire Steels [Clark illustrates the type he wants] - - - - - 9d.
1 Gross Mockerson awls
1 Doz Sail needles
2 " fine horn Combs
2 " common Ivorey Do.
2 " large Black Silk Hdkfs [handkerchiefs]
1 " Small do. - - - - - do
12 Gross Hawks Bells
6 Rifles — 6 Smoth borus [smooth bores]
20 Tin kettles with Covers asst [assorted sizes]
20 Copper do — lined with pewter if possible
    Wampom (Beeds)
2 ps. Non so pretty — assorted
2 lbs. white Beeds (Corse)
12 masses Garnet
2 Doz paper looking Glasses

2 "   ovel _ Do. __ do Small & guilt

1 Gross Brass rings

1 or 2 Doz Beaver Traps

   Tomahawks a fiew if good

   Paint red of the best kind

                      double the different descripations
                      of the abov articles if they can be
                      prcured on Credit at a low price
                      and the Credit Sufficently long to
                      meet the payments
                                  Wm Clark

1. The list is with the letter and is included following it. MFC no doubt stands for the Missouri Fur Company. It contains all the kinds of trade goods, in various quantities, that were desirable for the Indian trade. Clark even illustrated the type of knife and fire steel he wanted.

2. The nature of Clark's mercantile enterprise is the source of some confusion, but this letter with the list headed goods for the Missouri Fur Company perhaps helps clear the matter up. He clearly is ordering these goods for the St. Louis Missouri Fur Company, and John Luttig is known to have been the clerk for the company. Clark rather habitually tended to refer to possessions or enterprises of a plural nature in a singular possessive manner which sometimes causes confusion. Thus when he writes "my" mercantile business, or clerk, or even brother or sister, he often does not mean solely his, but rather his in partnership or as one of the Clark siblings, or even just as one of the group. That may be what he is doing here and in other letters when he refers to his mercantile pursuits in the singular possessive form. However, there is evidence, as some of the other letters indicate, that he was engaged in some sort of personal mercantile enterprise during this period. Loos attempted to ascertain the nature of these activities but could not. (Loos, 958–80.)

Sources Cited

MANUSCRIPT COLLECTIONS

Bellefontaine Cemetery, St. Louis

Bellefontaine Cemetery Records

Cave Hill Cemetery, Louisville

Cave Hill Cemetery Records

The Filson Historical Society, Louisville
Special Collections Department

Arthur Campbell Papers
Bodley Family Papers
Charles W. Thruston Papers—Charles W. Thruston Collection
Clark Family Papers
Dennis Fitzhugh Papers
Edmund Clark Papers
Edmund and John H. Clark Papers

Edmund Rogers Miscellaneous Papers
Fenley Family Miscellaneous Papers
Fenley-Williams Family Papers
Fitzhugh and Rose Account Books—Charles W. Thruston Collection
Isaac Clark Papers
John Hardin Miscellaneous Papers
John Hite Clark Papers
John O'Fallon Papers
Jonathan Clark Diary—Jonathan Clark Papers—Clark-Hite Collection
Jonathan Clark Papers—Clark-Hite Collection
Jonathan Clark Papers—Temple Bodley Collection
Meriwether Lewis Clark Family Record
Meriwether Lewis Clark Papers
Michael Lacassagne Miscellaneous Papers
Preston Family Papers—Joyes Collection
Preston Family Papers—Preston Davie Genealogical Collection
Robert E. McDowell Collection
Sullivan-Gates Family Papers
William Clark Journal
William J. Clark Diary
William Preston Miscellaneous Papers

Library

Booth Family File
Bullitt Family File
Clark Family File
Farrar Family File
Fitzhugh Family File
Floyd Family File
Gwathmey Family File
Hinkle Family File
Hite Family File
Hopewell L. Rogers Genealogical Index
Jefferson County (Ky.) Houses—Trough Spring Historical File
Map Collection
Oldham Family File
Potts Family File
Rogers Family File
Short Family File
Sullivan Family File
Thruston Family File

Historical Society of Pennsylvania, Philadelphia

Croghan Papers (Typescript copy of original cited. Copy in George Rogers Clark Collection, Locust Grove Historic Home, Louisville, Ky.)

Indiana Historical Society, Indianapolis

John Armstrong Papers
Northwest Territory Collection

Missouri Historical Society, St. Louis

John O'Fallon Collection
William Clark Papers—Voorhis Memorial Collection

State Historical Society of Missouri, Columbia

William Clark Memorandum Book, 1798–1801—Breckenridge Collection
William Clark Memorandum Book, 1809—Breckenridge Collection

State Historical Society of Wisconsin, Madison

Draper Manuscripts (Microfilm edition at The Filson Historical Society): George Rogers Clark, Jonathan Clark. and Kentucky Papers and Draper's Historical Miscellanies collections

University of Virginia

Carr-Terrell Papers

INDIANA PUBLIC RECORDS

Clark County Deed Books

KENTUCKY PUBLIC RECORDS

These records were consulted either in the original form at the Kentucky Department for Libraries and Archives in Frankfort or the Jefferson County Office for Historic Preservation and Archives in Louisville, or in various transcript and microfilm forms at the Filson.

Fayette County Tax List, 1811
Hardin County Circuit Court Records
Henderson County Tax List, 1808
Jefferson County 1810 Census
Jefferson County Bond and Power of Attorney Books

Jefferson County Chancery Court Records
Jefferson County Circuit Court Records
Jefferson County Court Minute Books
Jefferson County Deed Books
Jefferson County Inventory and Settlement Books
Jefferson County Marriage Books
Jefferson County Marriage Records
Jefferson County Marriages
Jefferson County Minute Order Books
Jefferson County Order Books
Jefferson County Tax Lists
Jefferson County Will Books
Shelby County Tax List, 1807–1809

NEWSPAPERS

The Courier-Journal, Louisville
The Democratic Clarion, Nashville
The Farmer's Library, Louisville
Herald-Post, Louisville
The Kentucky Gazette, Lexington
Louisville Correspondent, Louisville
Louisville Gazette, Louisville
Louisville Gazette and Western Advertiser, Louisville
The Missouri Gazette/Louisiana Gazette, St. Louis
The Palladium, Frankfort
West End Word, St. Louis
The Western Christian Advocate, Cincinnati
The Western Courier, Louisville
The Western Spy, Cincinnati
The Western World, Frankfort

PUBLISHED PRIMARY AND SECONDARY SOURCES

Abel   Abel, Annie Heloise, ed. *Chardon's Journal at Fort Clark, 1834–1839.* Pierre: Department of History, State of South Dakota, 1932.

Allen   Allen, John Logan. *Passage through the Garden: Lewis and Clark and the Image of the American Northwest.* Urbana: University of Illinois Press, 1975.

Ambrose   Ambrose, Stephen E. *Undaunted Courage: Meriwether*

Lewis, Thomas Jefferson, and the Opening of the American West. New York: Simon and Schuster, 1996.

Anderson   Anderson, E. L. *Soldier and Pioneer: A Biographical Sketch of Lt.-Col. Richard C. Anderson of the Continental Army.* New York: G. P. Putnam's Sons, 1879.

Anderson (1)   Anderson, Sarah Travers (Scott). *Lewises, Meriwethers and Their Kin.* Richmond: Dietz Press, 1938.

Appleman (1)   Appleman, Roy E. *Lewis and Clark: Historic Places Associated with Their Transcontinental Exploration (1804–1806).* Washington, D.C.: United States Department of the Interior, National Park Service, 1975. Second printing, St. Louis: Lewis and Clark Trail Heritage Foundation and Jefferson National Expansion Historical Association, 1993.

Appleman (2)   ———. "Joseph and Reubin Field, Kentucky Frontiersmen of the Lewis and Clark Expedition and Their Father, Abraham." *The Filson Club History Quarterly* 49 (January 1975): 5–36.

A.S.P.   *American State Papers: Indian Affairs.* Volumes 5 and 6 of 21 volumes. Washington, D.C.: Gales and Seaton, 1832.

Atwater   Atwater, Caleb. *A History of the State of Ohio, Natural and Civil.* Cincinnati: Glezen and Shepard, 1838.

Bagnall   Bagnall, Norma Hays. *On Shaky Ground: The New Madrid Earthquakes of 1811–1812.* Columbia: University of Missouri Press, 1996.

Baird   Baird, Lewis C. *Baird's History of Clark County, Indiana.* Indianapolis: B. F. Bowen, 1909.

Bakeless (1)   Bakeless, John. *Background to Glory: The Life of George Rogers Clark.* Philadelphia: J. B. Lippincott, 1957.

Bakeless (2)   ———. *Lewis & Clark: Partners in Discovery.* New York: William Morrow, 1947.

Banta   Banta, R. E. *The Ohio* in the *Rivers of America* series, Hervey Allen and Carl Carmer, eds. New York: Rinehart, 1949.

Barlow and Powell   Barlow, William, and David O. Powell. "Heroic Medicine in Kentucky in 1825: Dr. John F. Henry's Care of Peyton Short." *The Filson Club History Quarterly* 63 (April 1989): 243–56.

Basye   Basye, Otto, comp. *The Basye Family in the United States.* Kansas City: Privately printed, 1950.

BDAC   *Biographical Directory of the American Congress, 1774–*

1949. Washington, D.C.: United States Government
Printing Office, 1950.

BDIGA   *Biographical Directory of the Indiana General Assembly.*
Compiled and edited by Rebecca A. Shepherd et al.
2 vols. Indianapolis: The Select Committee on the Cen-
tennial History of the Indiana General Assembly, 1980.

BEK   *The Biographical Encyclopedia of Kentucky.* Cincinnati:
J.M. Armstrong, 1878.

Betts   Betts, Robert B. *In Search of York: The Slave Who Went to
the Pacific with Lewis and Clark.* Rev. ed. with a new epilogue by James J. Holmberg, Boulder: University
Press of Colorado and Lewis and Clark Trail Heritage
Foundation, 2000.

Bigham   Bigham, Darrel E. *Towns and Villages of the Lower Ohio.*
Lexington: University Press of Kentucky, 1998.

Billon   Billon, Frederic L. *Annals of St. Louis in its Territorial
Days from 1804 to 1821.* St. Louis: Privately printed,
1888.

Bodley (1)   Bodley, Temple. *History of Kentucky.* Vol. 1 of 4.
Chicago: S. J. Clarke, 1928.

Bodley (2)   ———. *George Rogers Clark: His Life and Public Services.*
Boston: Houghton Mifflin, 1926.

Bond   Bond, Christy Hawes. *Gateway Families.* Edited by Ali-
cia Crane Williams. Privately printed, 1994.

Brigham   Brigham, Clarence S. *History and Bibliography of American Newspapers: 1690–1820.* 2 vols. Worcester, Mass.:
American Antiquarian Society, 1947.

Bullitt   Bullitt, Emily Montague. "Genealogies of Emily Montague Bullitt." Unpublished manuscript. The Filson
Club, 1960.

Bullitt (1)   Bullitt, Thomas. *My Life at Oxmoor: Life on a Farm in
Kentucky before the War.* Louisville: Privately printed,
1911. Updated edition, 1995.

Burress   Burress, Marjorie Byrnside, ed. *A Collection of Pioneer
Marriage Records: Hamilton County, Ohio, 1789–1817.*
Vol. 1. Cincinnati: Privately printed, 1978.

Burt   Burt, Jesse C. *Nashville: Its Life and Times.* Nashville:
Tennessee Book Company, 1959.

Campbell   Campbell, Mrs. John W., comp. *Biographical Sketches;
with other Literary Remains of the Late John W. Campbell.*
Columbus: Scott and Gallagher, 1838.

Capps   Capps, Randall. "Some Historic Kentucky Orators."

The Register of the Kentucky Historical Society 73 (October 1975): 356–89.

Carstens   Carstens, Kenneth C. "George Rogers Clark's Fort Jefferson, 1780–1781." *The Filson Club History Quarterly* 71 (July 1997): 259–84.

Casseday   Casseday, Ben. *The History of Louisville from its Earliest Settlement Till the Year 1852.* Louisville: Hull and Brother, 1852. Reprint edition, Louisville: G. R. Clark Press, 1970.

Cauthorn   Cauthorn, Henry S. *A History of the City of Vincennes, Indiana from 1702 to 1901.* Privately printed, 1901.

Chappelear and Hatch   Chappelear, Nancy, and Kate Binford Hatch. *Abstracts of Early Louisa County, Virginia, Will Books, 1743–1819.* Washington, D.C.: Privately printed, 1964.

Chittenden   Chittenden, Hiram Martin. *The American Fur Trade of the Far West.* 2 vols. New York: The Press of the Pioneers, 1935.

Chuinard   Chuinard, Eldon G. "Lewis and Clark, Master Masons." *We Proceeded On* 15 (February 1989): 12–15.

Cincinnati   *Cincinnati Miscellany.* Cincinnati, November 1844.

Clayton   Clayton, W. W. *History of Davidson County, Tennessee.* Philadelphia: J. W. Lewis, 1880.

Clift (1)   Clift, G. Glenn, comp. *The "Corn Stalk" Militia of Kentucky, 1792–1811.* Frankfort: Kentucky Historical Society, 1957.

Clift (2)   ———. *"Second Census" of Kentucky 1800.* Baltimore: Genealogical Publishing, 1970. Reprint.

Coke   Coke, Ben H. *John May, Jr. of Virginia: His Descendants and Their Land.* Baltimore: Gateway Press, 1975.

Collier   *Collier's Encyclopedia.* 24 vols. New York: P. F. Collier, 1993.

Collins   Collins, Richard H. *History of Kentucky.* 2 vols. Covington, Ky.: Collins and Company, 1882. Reprint, Easley, S.C.: Southern Historical Press, 1979.

Collot   Collot, Victor. *A Journey in North America.* Florence: O. Lange, 1924. Reprints of Rare Americana, No. 4 with *Atlas*, 3 vols.

Colter-Frick   Colter-Frick, L. R. *Courageous Colter and Companions.* Washington, Mo.: Privately printed, 1997.

Comstock   Comstock, Jim, ed. *The West Virginia Heritage Encyclopedia.* 25 vols. Richwood, W. Va.: Privately printed, 1976.

Cook and Cook   Cook, Michael L., and Bettie A. Cummings Cook, comps. *Jefferson County Records.* Vol. 2 (vol. 20 in the Kentucky Records series). Evansville, Ind.: Cook Publications, 1987.

Craik   Craik, James. *Historical Sketches of Christ Church, Louisville, Diocese of Kentucky.* Louisville: John P. Morton, 1862.

Crutchfield   Crutchfield, James A. *Early Times in the Cumberland Valley: From Its Beginning to 1800.* Nashville: First American National Bank, 1976.

Cutright   Cutright, Paul Russell. *Lewis and Clark: Pioneering Naturalists.* Urbana: University of Illinois Press, 1969. Reprint, Lincoln: University of Nebraska Press, 1989.

DAB   *Dictionary of American Biography.* 20 vols. Edited by Allen Johnson and Dumas Malone. New York: Charles Scribner's Sons, 1928–1936.

Denton   Denton, Carolyn S. "George Shannon of the Lewis and Clark Expedition: His Kentucky Years." In George H. Yater and Carolyn S. Denton, *Nine Young Men from Kentucky* supplement to *We Proceeded On,* WPO publication no. 11. Great Falls, Mont.: Lewis and Clark Trail Heritage Foundation, 1992.

Dorman (1)   Dorman, John Frederick. "Descendants of General Jonathan Clark, Jefferson County, Kentucky, 1750–1811." *The Filson Club History Quarterly* 23, nos. 1, 2, and 4 (January, April, October 1949): 25–33, 117–39, 278–305.

Dorman (2)   ———. *The Prestons of Smithfield and Greenfield in Virginia.* Louisville: The Filson Club, 1982.

Eberlein and Hubbard   Eberlein, Harold Donaldson, and Cortlandt Van Dyke Hubbard. "Music in the Early Federal Era." *The Pennsylvania Magazine of History and Biography* 69 (1945): 103–27.

Eddlemon   Eddlemon, Sherida K., comp. *Genealogical Abstracts from Tennessee Newspapers, 1791–1808.* Bowie, Md.: Heritage Books, 1998.

EL   Kleber, John E., ed. *The Encyclopedia of Louisville.* Lexington: University Press of Kentucky, 2000.

Ellison   Ellison, Ernest M. *Mulberry Hill Plantation: The Clark Family Home in Louisville, Kentucky.* Privately printed, 1991.

English   English, William Hayden. *Conquest of the Country*

Northwest of the River Ohio 1778–1783 and the Life of Gen. George Rogers Clark. 2 vols. Indianapolis: Bowen-Merrill, 1896.

Esarey   Esarey, Logan. *A History of Indiana: From Its Exploration to 1850.* Indianapolis: W. K. Stewart, 1915.

Ewers   Ewers, John C. *Artists of the Old West.* New York: Promontory Press, 1982.

Fischer   Fischer, Marjorie Hood, comp. *Tennesseans before 1800: Davidson County.* Galveston, Tex.: Frontier Press, 1997.

Flint   Flint, Margaret A., comp. *Chronology of Illinois History, 1673–1954.* Springfield: Illinois State Historical Library, 1955.

Folmsbee (1)   Folmsbee, Stanley J., Robert E. Corlew, and Enock L. Mitchell. *Tennessee: A Short History.* Knoxville: University of Tennessee Press, 1969.

Folmsbee (2)   ———. *History of Tennessee.* 4 vols. New York: Lewis Historical Publishing, 1960.

Fortier   Fortier, Alice. "The French and Spanish Dominations." In *Standard History of New Orleans,* ed. Henry Rightor. Chicago: Lewis, 1900.

Fowler   Fowler, Ila Earle. "The Tradewater River Country in Western Kentucky." *Register of the Kentucky State Historical Society* 32 (October 1934): 277–300.

Franklin   Franklin, Ann York, comp. *Clues for Revolutionary War Soldiers with Connections to Louisville and Jefferson County, Kentucky.* N.p.: Ancestors, Inc., n.d.

Frye   Frye, George W. *Colonel Joshua Fry of Virginia and Some of His Descendants and Allied Families.* Cincinnati: Privately printed, 1966.

Galbreath   Galbreath, Charles B. *History of Ohio.* 5 vols. Chicago: American Historical Society, 1925.

Goolrick   Goolrick, John T. *Historic Fredericksburg: The Story of an Old Town.* Richmond: Privately printed, 1922.

Goss   Goss, Rev. Charles Frederic. *Cincinnati: The Queen City, 1788–1912.* 4 vols. Chicago: S. J. Clarke, 1912.

Green   Green, Karen Mauer. *The Kentucky Gazette, 1801–1820: Genealogical and Historical Abstracts.* Baltimore: Gateway Press, 1985.

Gregg   Gregg, Kate L., ed. *Westward with Dragoons: The Journal of William Clark on His Expedition to Establish Fort Osage, August 25 to September 22, 1808.* Fulton, Mo.: Ovid Bell Press, 1937.

Gwathmey   Gwathmey, John H., comp. *Historical Register of Virginians in the Revolution.* Richmond: Dietz Press, 1938.

Hasskarl   Hasskarl, Eula Richardson. *Shelby County, Kentucky, Marriages, 1792–1833.* Ada, Okla.: Privately printed, 1983.

Hall   Hall, Clayton Coleman, ed. *Baltimore: Its History and Its People.* 3 vols. New York: Lewis Historical Publishing, 1912.

Hamilton County   Hamilton County Chapter, Ohio Genealogical Society. *Abstract of Book 1 & Book A Probate Record 1791–1826, Hamilton County, Ohio.* Cincinnati: Privately printed, 1977.

Hammon   Hammon, Neal O. "The Fincastle Surveyors at the Falls of the Ohio, 1774." *The Filson Club History Quarterly* 47 (January 1973): 14–28.

Harris   Harris, Malcolm H. *History of Louisa County, Virginia.* Richmond: Dietz Press, 1936.

Heffington   Heffington, Ruth, comp. *Abstracts from Will Books A–G, 1811–1914,* Union County, Kentucky. Morganfield, Ky.: Union County Historical Society, 1995.

Heitman (1)   Heitman, Francis B., comp. *Historical Register of Officers of the Continental Army during the War of theRevolution.* Baltimore: Genealogical Publishing Company, 1967; reprint of 1914 edition.

Heitman (2)   ———. *Historical Register and Dictionary of the United States Army from Its Organization, September 29, 1789, to March 2, 1903.* 2 vols. Washington, D.C.: Government Printing Office, 1903. Reprint, Urbana: University of Illinois Press, 1965.

Hening   Hening, William Waller, ed. *The Statutes at Large; Being a Collection of all the Laws of Virginia.* Vol. 11, 1782–1784. Richmond: Privately printed, 1823.

Heywood   Heywood, John H. *Judge John Speed and His Family.* Louisville: John P. Morton, 1894.

HOFC   *History of the Ohio Falls Cities and Their Counties.* 2 vols. Cleveland: L. A. Williams, 1882.

Holmberg (1)   Holmberg, James J. "Monument to a 'Young Man of Much Merit.'" *We Proceeded On* 22 (August 1996): 4–13.

Holmberg (2)   ———. "'I wish you to See and know all': The Recently Discovered Letters of William Clark to Jonathan Clark." *We Proceeded On* 18 (November 1992): 4–12.

Houck   Houck, Louis. *A History of Missouri from the Earliest Ex-*

plorations and Settlements until the Admission of the State into the Union. 3 vols. Chicago: R. R. Donnelley, 1908.

Hurt   Hurt, R. Douglas. *The Ohio Frontier: Crucible of the Old Northwest, 1720–1830.* Bloomington: Indiana University Press, 1996.

Illinois   Illinois Department of Natural Resources. *Fort Massac State Park.* Springfield: Illinois Department of Natural Resources, 1998.

Jackson (1)   Jackson, Donald, ed. *Letters of the Lewis and Clark Expedition with Related Documents, 1783–1854.* Second edition. 2 vols. Urbana: University of Illinois Press, 1978.

Jackson (2)   ———. *Thomas Jefferson and the Stony Mountains: Exploring the West from Monticello.* Urbana: University of Illinois Press, 1981.

Jackson (3)   ———. "A Footnote to the Lewis and Clark Expedition." *Manuscripts* 24 (Winter 1972): 3–21.

Jackson (4)   ———. *The Journals of Zebulon Montgomery Pike with Letters and Related Documents.* 2 vols. Norman: University of Oklahoma Press, 1966.

Jacob   Jacob, J. G. *The Life and Times of Patrick Gass.* Wellsburg, Va. [W. Va.]: Jacob & Smith, 1859.

James   James, James Alton. *The Life of George Rogers Clark.* Chicago: University of Chicago Press, 1928.

Joblin   M. Joblin and Company. *Louisville Past and Present: Its Industrial History.* Louisville: John P. Morton, 1875.

Johnston   Johnston, J. Stoddard, ed. *Memorial History of Louisville from Its First Settlement to the Year 1896.* 2 vols. Chicago: American Biographical Publishing, 1896.

Kentucky Census   *Kentucky Census for 1810, 1820, 1830.* 3 vols. Edited by Ronald Vern Jackson, Gary Ronald Teeples, and David Schaefermeyer. Bountiful, Utah: Accelerated Indexing Systems, 1976–1978.

KE   Kleber, John E., ed. *The Kentucky Encyclopedia.* Lexington: University Press of Kentucky, 1992.

Lamar   Lamar, Howard R., ed. *The Reader's Encyclopedia of the American West.* New York: Harper and Row, 1977.

Large (1)   Large, Arlen J. "'Additions to the Party': How an Expedition Grew and Grew." *We Proceeded On* 16 (February 1990): 4–11.

Large (2)   ———. "Lewis and Clark Meet the 'American Incognitum.'" *We Proceeded On* 21 (August 1995): 12–18.

Lathem   Lathem, Edward Connery, comp. *Chronological Tables of American Newspapers, 1690–1820.* Barre, Mass.: American Antiquarian Society and Barre Publishers, 1972.

Leonard   Leonard, Lewis A., ed. *Greater Cincinnati and Its People: A History.* 4 vols. New York: Lewis Historical Publishing, 1927.

Lewis   Lewis, Mary Newton. "A Postscript to *In Search of York.*" *We Proceeded On* 16 (May 1990): 21.

Lipscomb   Lipscomb, Andrew A., ed. *The Writings of Thomas Jefferson.* 20 vols. Washington, D.C.: The Thomas Jefferson Memorial Association, 1905.

Loos   Loos, John. "A Biography of William Clark, 1770–1813." Ph. D. dissertation, Washington University, 1953.

Ludlow   Ludlow, N. M. *Dramatic Life As I Found It.* St. Louis: G. I. Jones, 1880.

Luttig   Luttig, John C. *Journal of a Fur-Trading Expedition on the Upper Missouri, 1812–1813.* Edited by Stella M. Drumm. Rev. ed. with new preface by A. P. Nasatir, 1920. Reprint, New York: Argosy Antiquarian Press, 1964.

McDermott   McDermott, John Francis, ed. *Old Cahokia: A Narrative and the Documents Illustrating the First Century of Its History.* St. Louis: St. Louis Historical Documents Foundation, 1949.

McIntosh and Freeman   McIntosh, W. H., and H. Freeman, comps. *The History of Darke County, Ohio.* Chicago: W. H. Beers, 1880. Reprint, Evansville, Ind.: Unigraphic, 1970.

Majors   Majors, Harry M. "John McClellan in the Montana Rockies, 1807: The First Americans after Lewis and Clark." *Northwest Discovery* 2 (November–December 1981): 554–630.

Marshall   Marshall, Thomas Maitland, ed. *The Life and Papers of Frederick Bates.* 2 vols. St. Louis: Missouri Historical Society, 1926.

Mayo   Mayo, Bernard. *Henry Clay, Spokesman of the New West.* Cambridge, Mass.: Riverside Press, 1937.

Meriwether   Meriwether, Nelson Heath. *The Meriwethers and Their Connections.* Baltimore: Gateway Press, 1991. Reprint.

Metcalf   Metcalf, Bryce, comp. *Original Members and Other Officers Eligible to the Society of the Cincinnati, 1783–1938.* Strasburg, Va.: Shenandoah, 1938. Reprint, Beverly

	Hills, Calif.: The Historic Trust—Eastwood Publishing, 1995.
Moulton	Moulton, Gary E., ed. *The Journals of the Lewis and Clark Expedition.* 13 vols. Lincoln: University of Nebraska Press, 1983–2001.
Moulton and Holmberg	Moulton, Gary E., and James J. Holmberg. "'What we are about': Recently Discovered Letters of William Clark Shed New Light on the Lewis and Clark Expedition." *The Filson Club History Quarterly* 65 (July 1991): 387–403.
Munson and Parrish	Munson, Dabney Garrett, and Margaret Ware Parrish, eds. *Woodford County, Kentucky: The First Two Hundred Years, 1789–1989.* Lexington, Ky.: Privately printed, 1989.
Norton (1)	Norton, Margaret Cross, ed. *Illinois Census Returns: 1810 and 1818.* Baltimore: Genealogical Publishing, 1969.
Norton (2)	———. *Illinois Census Returns: 1820.* Baltimore: Genealogical Publishing, 1969.
Oglesby	Oglesby, Richard Edward. *Manuel Lisa and the Opening of the Missouri Fur Trade.* Norman: University of Oklahoma Press, 1963.
Osgood	Osgood, Ernest Staples, ed. *The Field Notes of Captain William Clark, 1803–1805.* With an introduction and notes by same. New Haven: Yale University Press, 1964.
Pennsylvania Magazine (1)	"Notes and Queries." *The Pennsylvania Magazine of History and Biography* 23 (1899): 126.
Pennsylvania Magazine (2)	"Washington's Household Account Book, 1793–1797." *The Pennsylvania Magazine of History and Biography* 31 (1907): 53–82, 176–94, 320–50.
Pierce	Pierce, Albert E., comp. "Ormsby Families of Louisville, Kentucky." Unpublished manuscript, 1968. Available in the library of The Filson Historical Society.
Portage	Portage Route Chapter of the Lewis and Clark Trail Heritage Foundation. *Lewis and Clark at the Great Falls of the Missouri River.* Great Falls, Mont.: Portage Route Chapter, 1988.
Quinn	Quinn, S. J. *The History of the City of Fredericksburg, Virginia.* Richmond: Hermitage Press, 1908.
Ravenholt	Ravenholt, Reimert T. "Triumph Then Despair: The

Tragic Death of Meriwether Lewis." *Epidemiology* 5 (May 1994): 366–79.

Rennick   Rennick, Robert M. *Kentucky Place Names.* Lexington: University Press of Kentucky, 1984.

Rice   Rice, Howard C. Jr., ed. "News from the Ohio Valley as Reported by Barthélemi Tardiveau in 1783." *Bulletin of the Historical and Philosophical Society of Ohio* 16 (October 1958): 267–73.

Ronda (1)   Ronda, James P. *Lewis and Clark among the Indians.* Lincoln: University of Nebraska Press, 1984.

Ronda (2)   ———. "A Moment in Time: The West—September 1806." *Montana: The Magazine of Western History* 44 (Autumn 1994): 2–15.

Sallee   Sallee, Helen Hite. "Col. Abraham Hite and His Three Sons, Isaac, Abraham Jr., and Joseph." Unpublished manuscript prepared for the Fincastle Chapter NSDAR, 1970. Copy available in the library of The Filson Historical Society.

Scharf   Scharf, J. Thomas. *History of Saint Louis City and County.* 2 vols. Philadelphia: Louis H. Everts, 1883.

Short   Short, Charles Wilkins, and Mary Churchill Richardson. "A Chronological Record of the Families of Charles Wilkins Short and Mary Henry Churchill." Unpublished manuscript, 1879. Available in the library of The Filson Historical Society.

Simmons   Simmons, Clayton C., comp. *Historical Trip Through East Barren County, Kentucky and the Hamilton-Sanderson Murder Trial.* Glasgow, Ky.: Privately published, n.d.

Sistler   Sistler, Byron, and Barbara Sistler, comps. *Index to Tennessee Wills & Administrations 1779–1861.* Nashville: Byron Sistler & Associates, 1990.

Smith   Smith, Alice E. *From Exploration to Statehood.* Vol. 1 of the 6 volume *The History of Wisconsin.* Edited by William Fletcher Thompson. Madison: State Historical Society of Wisconsin, 1973.

Smith (1)   Smith, Alma Aicholtz, comp. *Ohio Lands: Hamilton County Deed Book A, 1787–1797, Territory Northwest of the River Ohio.* Cincinnati: Privately printed, 1992.

Smith and Swick   Smith, Dwight L., and Ray Swick, eds. *A Journey through the West: Thomas Rodney's 1803 Journal from*

Delaware to the Mississippi Territory. Athens: Ohio University Press, 1997.

Sparks   Sparks, Everett L. "Where the Trail Begins: The Illinois Legacy to the Lewis and Clark Expedition." *We Proceeded On* 14 (February 1988): 4–9.

Speed   Speed, Thomas. *Records and Memorials of the Speed Family.* Louisville: Courier-Journal Job Printing, 1892.

Spencer   Spencer, Harold L. Jr., comp. *A Spencer Genealogy: The Descent from Gerard of Haddam, Conn.* Privately printed, 1977.

Staples   Staples, Charles R. *The History of Pioneer Lexington, 1779–1806.* Lexington: Transylvania Press, 1939. Reprint, Lexington: University Press of Kentucky, 1996.

Steffen   Steffen, Jerome O. *William Clark: Jeffersonian Man on the Frontier.* Norman: University of Oklahoma Press, 1977.

Stein   Stein, Susan R. "Jefferson's Museum at Monticello." *Antiques* (July 1993): 80–82.

Stubbs   Stubbs, Dr., and Mrs. William Carter. *Descendants of Mordecai Cooke, of "Mordecai's Mount," Gloucester Co., Va., 1650, and Thomas Booth, of Ware Neck, Gloucester Co., Va., 1685.* New Orleans: Privately printed, 1923.

Sugden   Sugden, John. *Tecumseh: A Life.* New York: Henry Holt, 1997.

Tannehill   Tannehill, James B. *Genealogical History of the Tannahills, Tannehills, and Taneyhills.* Privately printed, n.p.

Tennessee   *Tennessee: The Volunteer State, 1769–1923.* 4 vols. Chicago: S. J. Clarke, 1923.

Thomas (1)   Thomas, Samuel W. "William Croghan, Sr. [1752–1822] A Pioneer Kentucky Gentleman." *The Filson Club History Quarterly* 43 (January 1969): 30–61.

Thomas (2)   ———. "William Clark's 1795 and 1797 Journals and Their Significance." *Bulletin of the Missouri Historical Society* 25 (July 1969): 277–96.

Thompson   Thompson, Evelyn Belle, comp. "Family and Ancestors of Frances Young Nicholas." Unpublished manuscript, 1949. Copy available in the library of The Filson Historical Society.

Thruston   Thruston, Rogers Clark Ballard. "Some Recent Findings Regarding the Ancestry of General George

Rogers Clark." *The Filson Club History Quarterly* 9 (January 1935): 1–34.

Thruston and Healy — Thruston, Rogers Clark Ballard, and Katharine Healy, comps. *Jefferson County, Virginia–Kentucky, Early Marriages. Book 1: 1781–July 1826.* Louisville: The Filson Club, 1941. Reprint, Owensboro, Ky.: Cook and McDowell, 1980.

Thwaites (1) — Thwaites, Reuben Gold, ed. *Original Journals of the Lewis and Clark Expedition, 1804–1806.* 8 vols. New York: Dodd, Mead, 1904–1905.

Thwaites (2) — ———. *Cuming's Sketches of a Tour to the Western Country, 1807–1809.* Vol. 4 of the 26-volume *Early Western Travels.* Cleveland: Arthur H. Clark, 1904.

Tischendorf and Parks — Tischendorf, Alfred, and E. Taylor Parks, eds. *The Diary and Journal of Richard Clough Anderson, Jr., 1814–1826.* Durham: Duke University Press, 1964.

Todhunter — Todhunter, Charles Timothy. *The Churchill Family Genealogy.* 2 vols. Privately printed, 1988–1992.

Trabue — Trabue, Alice, comp. "Taylor Genealogy". Unpublished manuscript available in the library of The Filson Historical Society, n.d.

Trail — Trail, Robert. "Livingston County, Kentucky—Steppingstone to Illinois." *The Register of the Kentucky Historical Society* 69 (July 1971): 239–77.

Twentieth Century — *The Twentieth Century Biographical Dictionary of Notable Americans.* Edited by Rossiter Johnson and John Howard Brown. 10 vols. Boston: The Biographical Society, 1904.

Verhoeff — Verhoeff, Mary. *The Kentucky River Navigation.* Louisville: The Filson Club, 1917. Filson Club publication number 28.

Volney — Volney, Constantin F. *A View of the Soil and Climate of the United States of America.* Translated by C. B. Brown. Philadelphia: J. Conrad, 1804.

Wayland — Wayland, John W. *The Bowmans: A Pioneering Family in Virginia, Kentucky, and the Northwest Territory.* Staunton, Va.: McClure, 1943.

Wheeler-Voegelin — Wheeler-Voegelin, Erminie, Emily J. Blasingham, and Dorothy R. Libby. *Miami, Wea, and Eel-River Indians of Southern Indiana.* New York: Garland, 1974.

White — White, Virgil D., comp. *Genealogical Abstracts of Revolu-*

	tionary War Pension Files. 3 vols. Waynesboro, Tenn.: National Historical Publishing, 1992.
Whitley	Whitley, Edna Talbott. *Kentucky Antebellum Portraiture.* N.p.: The National Society of the Colonial Dames of America in the Commonwealth of Kentucky, 1956.
William and Mary	*William and Mary College Quarterly Historical Magazine* 22 (July 1913): 70.
Wilson	Wilson, Frazer Ells. *Advancing the Ohio Frontier: A Saga of the Old Northwest.* Blanchester, Ohio: Brown Publishing, 1937.
Wooley	Wooley, Carolyn Murray. *The Founding of Lexington, 1775–1776.* Lexington, Ky.: Lexington-Fayette County Historic Commission, 1975.
WPA	Work Projects Administration of the State of Pennsylvania, comp. *Pennsylvania: A Guide to the Keystone State.* New York: Oxford University Press, 1940.
Wright	Wright, F. Edward, comp. *Western Maryland Newspaper Abstracts, 1786–1810.* 3 vols. Silver Spring, Md.: Family Line Publications, 1985–1987.
Wulfeck	Wulfeck, Dorothy Ford, comp. *Marriages of Some Virginia Residents, 1607–1800.* 2 vols. Baltimore: Genealogical Publishing, 1986.
Yater (1)	Yater, George H. *Two Hundred Years at the Falls of the Ohio.* Louisville: The Filson Club, 1987.
Yater (2)	———. "Nine Young Men from Kentucky." In George H. Yater and Carolyn S. Denton, *Nine Young Men from Kentucky* supplement to *We Proceeded On*, WPO Publication no. 11. Great Falls, Mont.: Lewis and Clark Trail Heritage Foundation, 1992.

Index